CRIMINAL LAW

THIRD EDITION

Other books in the *Essentials of Canadian Law* Series

ESSENTIALS OF
CANADIAN LAW

CRIMINAL LAW

THIRD EDITION

KENT ROACH

Faculty of Law and Centre of Criminology

University of Toronto

IRWIN LAW

Criminal Law, Third Edition
© Irwin Law Inc., 2004

Published in 2004 by

Irwin Law
14 Duncan Street
Suite 206
Toronto, Ontario
M5H 3G8
www.irwinlaw.com

ISBN: 1-55221-091-X

Library and Archives Canada Cataloguing in Publication

Roach, Kent, 1961–
    Criminal law / Kent Roach. — 3rd ed.

(Essentials of Canadian law)
Includes bibliographical references and index.
ISBN 1-55221-091-X

    1. Criminal law--Canada. I. Title. II. Series.

KE8809.R62 2004   345.71   C2004-904385-4
KF9220.ZA2R59 2004

The publisher acknowledges the financial support of the Government of Canada through the Book Publishing Industry Development Program (BPIDP) for its publishing activities. The publisher also acknowledges the Government of Ontario through the Ontario Media Development Corporation's Ontario Book Initiative.

Printed and bound in Canada.

2 3 4 5   08 07 06

SUMMARY
TABLE OF CONTENTS

DETAILED
TABLE OF CONTENTS

FOREWORD

It is a great pleasure to write this foreword to the third edition of my colleague Kent Roach's book, *Criminal Law*. There is no Canadian book like it and all those studying criminal law will be indebted to Professor Roach for his very readable and careful analysis of Canadian criminal law. This book will be an excellent companion for students in criminal law courses both in the law schools and criminology and criminal justice departments. As is demonstrated by its citation by the Supreme Court and other courts, even judges and seasoned criminal lawyers will benefit from reading the thoughtful views on the basic principles of criminal law articulated in this book. In addition, it deals with many new developments in criminal law, such as new provisions relating to corporate liability and new terrorism offences. The fact that Professor Roach has acted as counsel in a number of important *Charter* and sentencing cases discussed in the book provides an added dimension to this work. This thoroughly revised third edition, like the first and second, is destined to be widely used and praised. I look forward to many future editions of this valuable book.

Martin L. Friedland, C.C., Q.C.
Professor of Law and University Professor Emeritus
University of Toronto

PREFACE

to the Third Edition

This book is designed to provide a concise and current discussion of the basic principles of Canadian criminal law. To this end, the heart of this book examines the principles of the general part of the criminal law: the elements of offences and the relevant defences. It follows the traditional conceptualization of the general part, but it examines unfulfilled crimes and participation in crimes earlier than other works because of their great practical importance and their effective expansion of the prohibited act. Regulatory offences and corporate criminal liability are examined together because of their functional and contextual similarities. Provocation is examined with self-defence, necessity, and duress because of the common use of the modified objective standard. An overview is provided to introduce readers to the basic conceptual structure of the criminal law.

A few chapters attempt to place the general principles of the criminal law in the context of the entire criminal process by examining the constitutional principles that affect the investigation of crime, the criminal trial process, and the substantive criminal law (chapter 1); by examining the principles of sentencing (chapter 9); and by examining models of the criminal process, trends in the criminal law, and perspectives that can be brought to the study of the law (chapter 10). These chapters are not intended to be comprehensive, and each deserves a book in its own right, but it is hoped they will provide readers with a fuller sense of the criminal law than would be provided if the book were restricted to the general part of the criminal law.

I have avoided the temptation to engage in extended criticisms of decided cases in order to focus on how each case fits into the overall structure of the criminal law. Unfortunately, the fit is not always natural and my impression after fifteen years of teaching is that Canadian criminal law is becoming ever more complex, challenging, and at times incoherent, even for the brightest of students. It is hoped that both Parliament and the Courts will attempt to simplify the criminal law in the years to come so that it is easier for all to understand.

This third edition comes at an opportune time. Parliament has just enacted new provisions affecting corporate criminal liability. The Supreme Court has also issued a number of important decisions concerning limits on the criminal law, air of reality tests, and the defences of necessity and duress. I am grateful to many colleagues and students who have read the book and made encouraging comments or helpful suggestions for improvement. Don Stuart deserves particular credit for his generous yet challenging and helpful review of the first edition. I have benefited greatly from discussions with Marty Friedland, Patrick Healy, Ken Jull, Martha Shaffer, Hamish Stewart, and Gary Trotter about many of the issues discussed in this book.

K.R.
June 2004

OVERVIEW

Criminal law is enacted and applied in Canada in an increasingly complex constitutional framework that is examined in chapter 1. The basic elements of criminal and regulatory offences are the prohibited act and the required fault element, which are examined in chapters 2 and 4, respectively. Chapter 3 examines how criminal offences are expanded by various provisions prohibiting attempted and unfulfilled crimes and participation as an accomplice in crimes. Special provisions governing regulatory offences and corporate crime are examined in chapter 5. Various defences to crimes are examined in subsequent chapters, including intoxication (chapter 6), mental disorder and automatism (chapter 7), and provocation, self-defence, necessity, and duress (chapter 8). Punishment depends on the exercise of sentencing discretion, which is examined in chapter 9. A final chapter examines models of the criminal justice system, trends in the criminal law, and perspectives on the basic principles and jurisprudence examined in the book.

1) CRIME IN CANADA

In any year, approximately one-quarter of all Canadians report having been victimized by crime. Most who suffer crimes do not report them to the police. About 90 percent of sexual assaults, 68 percent of assaults, 53 percent of robberies, 54 percent of vandalism, 48 percent of motor vehicle thefts, and 32 percent of break and enters are not reported to the police. The reasons vary but often relate to a perception that reporting would not be useful for the crime victim. The perpetrator of most violent crime is often someone known to the victim and the site of most violence is the home.

In 2002, there were just over 2.4 million crimes reported to the police. The majority (52 percent) of these crimes are property crimes and only 13 percent of reported crimes are crimes of violence. The majority of crimes reported to the police do not result in charges. The majority of cases in which charges are laid are resolved without a trial, and end in a finding of guilt. In a process commonly known as plea bargaining, the prosecutor may withdraw some charges or take certain positions on sentence if the accused agrees to plea guilty. The accused may receive a more lenient sentence because he or she has pled guilty. Only a minority of cases go to trial and of these only a very small minority are ever appealed. Nevertheless, appeal cases are crucial to the development of the criminal law. Appeal courts, most notably the Supreme Court of Canada, interpret the *Criminal Code*. They also develop judge-made common law, so long as this law is not inconsistent with the *Code* and does not create new offences. Appeal courts also apply the *Canadian Charter of Rights and Freedoms* (the *Charter*) to the activities of police and prosecutors, as well as to laws enacted by legislatures.

In 2002–03, adult criminal courts processed 467,500 cases involving over a million charges. The accused were found guilty in 60 percent of cases heard and acquitted in 3 percent. The remaining cases were generally stayed or withdrawn by the prosecutor. The most frequently occurring offences were impaired driving (12 percent), common assault (11 percent), and theft (9 percent), with homicide and attempted murder only accounting for 0.2 percent and sexual offences amounting to 2 percent. Although it is much lower than in the United States, Canada has one of the highest rates of incarceration of the developed democracies. Males represent the majority of prisoners. Prisoners have significantly less education and employment than other Canadians. Aboriginal people represent from 15 to 17 percent of prison admissions, but only 2 percent of the population. The following chart illustrates how the criminal law only affects a small percentage of crime committed.

2) THE CRIMINAL PROCESS

The criminal law assumes concrete meaning when it is administered through the criminal justice system or the criminal process. The process starts with a decision of a legislature to make certain conduct illegal. The criminal law is then enforced by the police who respond to

the decisions of crime victims to report crime and sometimes, especially in drug and prostitution cases, proactively investigate the crime
themselves. As examined in chapter 1, the investigative activities of the
police are restricted by various rights under the *Charter*, such as the
right to counsel and the right against unreasonable search and seizure.
If the accused is charged, then the trial process begins. A prosecutor
(sometimes called the Crown) will decide what of any charges are warranted and can make a decision to divert the charges out of court to
alternative-measure programs. If charges proceed, the accused will
have to make a decision whether to hire a lawyer or, if a lawyer cannot
be afforded, to apply for legal aid to have a lawyer paid by the state. The
trial process may include pre-trial detention by the denial of bail and
in the most serious cases may include the holding of a preliminary
inquiry and trial by jury. As noted above, most cases do not result in
full trials, and the judge only has to engage in sentencing after the
accused has pled guilty to some offence. The trial process is affected by
various *Charter* rights, such as the right not to be denied reasonable
bail without just cause and the right to be tried in a reasonable time. If
the accused is convicted, the judge must then sentence the accused and
the accused may appeal. Jails and penitentiaries are the end of the criminal process, and parole boards have powers to determine if a prisoner
will be released from custody before the expiry of his or her sentence.

Each year, governments spend about $10 billion on the criminal process with 60 percent of this money going to the police, 25 percent to corrections, 9 percent to courts, and 6 percent to legal aid for those who cannot afford a defence lawyer. The following chart outlines the major steps in the criminal process.

The Major Steps in the Criminal Process

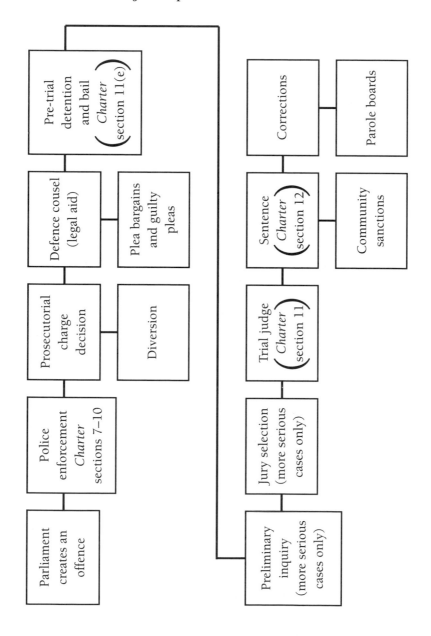

3) SOURCES OF CRIMINAL LAW

There are three main sources of criminal law in Canada: 1) the Constitution, including both the division of powers and the *Canadian Charter of Rights and Freedoms*; 2) statutes enacted by legislatures, including the *Criminal Code of Canada* and other statutes creating offences; and 3) judge-made "common law" in the form of defences that have not been codified in the *Criminal Code*. Although it is not technically common law, judicial decisions interpreting both the Constitution and statutes play an important role in determining the precise ambit of the criminal law.

Not all sources of the criminal law are equal. The Constitution is the supreme law and prevails over both statutes and common law. Statutes prevail over judge-made common law. Thus, Parliament could abolish a common law defence to a crime through clear legislation. At the same time, however, the result must accord with the Constitution and statutory abolition of some defences might be held to be unconstitutional because it would result in convictions that violate the *Charter*. In such a case, the courts would develop and apply a common law defence that would satisfy the standards of the Constitution. Judge-made common law should reflect constitutional standards.

An emerging source of criminal law may be international law. Parliament has created statutory offences such as crimes of terrorism, war crimes, hate propaganda, and torture in order to fulfill its obligations under international law. The courts also make increasing reference to various forms of international law to guide their interpretation of the *Charter*, statutes, and the common law.

4) CRIMINAL OFFENCES

Criminal law in Canada is enacted by the federal Parliament. The *Criminal Code* contains many offences, ranging from traditional crimes such as murder, assault, robbery, and theft to newer crimes such as driving with a blood alcohol level "over 80." Some offences such as assault or sexual assault protect bodily integrity, while others such as theft protect property. Crimes such as firearms and drunk-driving offences attempt to prevent conduct that presents a significant risk of harm to others. Crimes against the possession and sale of illegal drugs or obscene material may prevent harm, but they also proclaim standards of socially acceptable behaviour. Criminal laws are primarily designed to denounce and to punish inherently wrongful behaviour, and to deter people from committing crimes or engaging in behaviour that presents a serious risk of harm. Courts consider these purposes when sentencing offenders, but they are also concerned with the incapacitation and rehabilitation of the particular offender and with providing reparation to the victim and the community for the crime committed.

5) REGULATORY OFFENCES

The *Criminal Code* contains many crimes, but they constitute only a small number of all the offences in Canada. Most offences are regulatory offences that can be defined in legislation enacted by the federal Parliament, provinces, or municipalities. Regulatory offences include traffic offences such as speeding, environmental offences, offences for engaging in a regulated activity without a licence or proper records, and offences relating to harmful commercial practices such as misleading advertising or not complying with health and safety regulations. The punishment for regulatory offences is usually a fine, but may include imprisonment. In any event, the accused is frequently a corporation that cannot be imprisoned. The primary purpose of regulatory offences is to deter risky behaviour and prevent harm before it happens, rather than to punish intrinsically wrongful and harmful behaviour. The standards used to govern the investigation of regulatory offences and to impose convictions for such offences are more favourable to the state than the standards used for criminal offences.

6) THE CRIMINAL LAW AND THE CONSTITUTION

Criminal offences must be consistent with the supreme law of the Constitution. In Canada, this means that only the federal Parliament can enact criminal laws. The provinces (and their delegates, the municipalities) can, however, enact regulatory offences. In addition, a criminal law may be unconstitutional if it infringes a right or a freedom protected under the *Canadian Charter of Rights and Freedoms*, and if it cannot be justified under section 1 as a reasonable and demonstrably justified limit on a right.

Sections 7 and 11(d) of the *Charter* are particularly important to the criminal law. Section 7 provides that people cannot be deprived of life, liberty, and security of the person except in accordance with the principles of fundamental justice. Imprisonment most definitely affects the liberty or security of the person. Thus, it is necessary that the criminal law be in accord with the principles of fundamental justice. These principles have been defined as the fundamental tenets of the legal system. They address the substantive fairness of criminal laws to ensure that the morally innocent are not convicted and punished and that people who could not have reasonably been expected to obey the law are not punished for conduct committed in a morally involuntary fashion. As well, the principles of fundamental justice support the procedural fairness of the criminal law to ensure that the accused is treated fairly. Section 11(d) protects the accused's most important procedural right to be presumed innocent and to receive a fair and public hearing by an independent and impartial court.

7) SUBSTANTIVE FAIRNESS

A criminal law or a regulatory offence can be declared invalid by the courts if it results in an unjustified violation of a *Charter* right such as freedom of expression. Expression has been interpreted broadly to include non-violent attempts to convey meaning. Thus, offences prohibiting hate literature, communication for the purposes of prostitution, defamatory libel, or pornography must be justified by the government under section 1 of the *Charter* as a reasonable limit on the *Charter* right.

The principles of fundamental justice in section 7 of the *Charter* have been interpreted as prohibiting the punishment of the morally innocent. The question of what constitutes moral innocence is quite complex and depends very much on the particular context. What is required under section 7 of the *Charter* to sustain a conviction for murder or war crimes is quite different from what is required to sustain a manslaughter conviction. It is also quite different from what is required for a conviction of a regulatory offence, such as misleading advertising. A denial or a restriction on a defence, such as the defences of intoxication, mental disorder, or duress, may also violate section 7 of the *Charter* if it results in a deprivation of liberty in a manner that is not in accordance with the principles of fundamental justice. For example, it would be fundamentally unjust to convict a person for involuntary conduct or for committing a crime where threats or dire circumstances meant that there was no other realistic choice but to commit the crime. Section 7 jurisprudence, as it affects criminal and regulatory offences, will be examined at various junctures of this book.

8) PROCEDURAL FAIRNESS

Both the police and the prosecutor must comply with the accused's *Charter* rights, or risk having the trial process diverted from the issue of guilt or innocence by the accused seeking a *Charter* remedy for the violation of his or her legal rights. Sections 8 and 9 of the *Charter* provide individuals with the rights to be free from unreasonable searches and seizures and from arbitrary detentions during the investigative process. Section 10 ensures that people will know why they have been arrested or detained, and that they can obtain legal advice from a lawyer. Sections 7 and 11 of the *Charter* protect an accused's right to a fair trial. These rights include the right to a trial in a reasonable time, and the right to a trial by jury when the accused faces five years' imprisonment or more. The prosecutor, often known as the Crown, has special obligations of fairness and must disclose relevant evidence in its possession to the accused.

An important procedural protection is the presumption of innocence protected under section 11(d) of the *Charter*. The Crown must bear the burden of proving that the accused is guilty beyond a reasonable doubt. A reasonable doubt is not imaginary or frivolous, but is based on reason and common sense derived from the evidence or absence of evidence. The Crown must go well beyond demonstrating that it is probable or likely that the accused is guilty, but does not have to establish guilt as an absolute certainty. The accused is entitled to the benefit of any reasonable doubt about any matter essential to conviction. The matters essential to conviction include the elements of the offence, as well as the existence of any defence that would excuse or justify the commission of the offence. The presumption of innocence is offended if an accused is required to prove that he or she did not have one of the elements of the offence or even if he or she did not have a defence to the crime. The presumption of innocence is designed to ensure that the accused always receives the benefit of any reasonable doubt as to guilt and that the judge and jury are never forced by the law to convict the accused even though there might be a reasonable doubt. At the same time, violations of the presumption of innocence may be justified under section 1 of the *Charter* on the basis that they are necessary to protect social interests.

9) THE ELEMENTS OF CRIMINAL OFFENCES

The basic elements of a criminal offence are the act or omission that is prohibited by the legislation, or the *actus reus*, and the fault element, or *mens rea*, with which the accused must commit the prohibited act or omission. The Crown must prove beyond a reasonable doubt that the accused committed the prohibited act, and did so with the required fault element. For murder, the Crown would have to prove that the accused committed the prohibited act of causing another person's death, and had the fault element of knowing that the victim's death was likely to occur. It is possible that the accused could commit a criminal act without the required fault, and in such a case, the accused would not be convicted.

The Crown must, subject to exceptions justified under section 1 of the *Charter*, also prove beyond a reasonable doubt that the accused did not have a relevant defence. An accused will, for example, be acquitted of murder if there is a reasonable doubt that he or she acted in self-defence as defined by the *Criminal Code*, or if there is a reasonable doubt that intoxication prevented him or her from knowing that the victim was likely to die. A few defences, most notably mental disorder and automatism, must be established by the accused on a balance of probabilities even though this violates the presumption of innocence by allowing a conviction even if there is a reasonable doubt about the existence of a defence. If the Crown proves the prohibited act and fault element beyond a reasonable doubt, and there is no defence, then the accused will be convicted. Maximum sentences are set out for each offence, and a few, including murder, have mandatory minimum sentences.

10) THE PROHIBITED ACT, OR *ACTUS REUS*

Every criminal or regulatory offence will have a prohibited act or omission, or *actus reus*. The prohibited act depends on how the legislature has worded the offence. For example, the prohibited act of theft is defined by Parliament in section 322(1) of the *Criminal Code* as the taking and conversion of anything. The prohibited act also depends on how the courts interpret the words of an offence. Sometimes the courts interpret these words restrictively to benefit the accused, but they may not do so if a restrictive interpretation defeats the clear purpose of the offence. The Supreme Court has interpreted the word "anything" in the offence of theft not to include the taking of confidential information from a computer screen, even though taking a piece of paper with confidential information on it would be theft. Parliament could always amend the criminal law to state clearly that confidential information constitutes a "thing" that can be stolen, or it could create a new offence of stealing confidential information from a computer. The definition of the prohibited act is perhaps the most important policy component of the criminal law. The trend is towards expansive legislative definitions of the prohibited act, with the most obvious example being the replacement of the offence of rape with sexual assault.

The *actus reus* is usually defined as an overt act, such as the taking of another person's property. The legislature can, however, define the prohibited conduct as an omission or a failure to take action. For example, a parent can be guilty of the criminal offence of failing to provide the necessities of life to his or her child. Regulatory offences may often prohibit the failure to take action, such as keeping proper business records or taking health and safety precautions. The definition of the criminal act must not be so vague or broad that it fails to give fair notice to the accused or to limit law enforcement discretion. Although each offence must have an *actus reus* that is not excessively vague or overbroad, it is generally no excuse that the accused did not know that his or her conduct was illegal.

Whether the accused has committed the prohibited act is usually a distinct issue from whether the accused had the required fault element. For example, a person commits the prohibited act of theft if he or she mistakenly takes another person's jacket at a party. If the person honestly believes that it is his or her jacket, however, then the person may not have committed the crime with the fault element required for theft. The person would have taken another's property, but not with the required moral fault, or *mens rea*. There is some blurring of the concepts of *actus reus* and *mens rea* when a person acts in an involuntary manner because, for example, he or she is sleepwalking or having a seizure. In such cases, it may not be fair to say even that the accused has committed the criminal act.

11) ATTEMPTS AND OTHER UNFULFILLED CRIMES

The criminal law intervenes even before the accused has committed the criminal act required for a complete crime. Thus, a person who attempts to steal an object but fails can be charged with attempted theft. Section 24 of the *Criminal Code* states that anyone, having an intent to commit an offence, who does or omits to do anything beyond mere preparation to commit a criminal offence is guilty of attempting to commit the offence regardless of whether or not it was possible to commit an offence. A person who had just entered a backyard to steal a barbecue, but had not started to remove it, could be guilty of attempted theft. The Crown would have to prove beyond a reasonable doubt that the accused had gone beyond mere preparation to commit the offence and had the intent to steal the barbecue. A person punished for an attempted crime is punished more for his or her intent to commit the crime than for the harm caused.

In addition to attempts, a person could be guilty of conspiracy to commit a theft if he or she had agreed with others to commit the theft. This offence would apply even though they had done nothing more but agree to commit a crime. A person could also be guilty of counselling a crime if he or she had procured, solicited, or incited another person to commit an offence, even though that second person never committed the offence. For example, Jane could be guilty of counselling theft if she attempted to persuade Sam to steal a barbecue, even though Sam never stole the item, and never intended to do so. If Sam did go on to steal the barbecue, Jane could, as will be examined below, be guilty of theft as a party to the offence. Finally, a person who knowingly assists another person to escape after a crime can be guilty of the separate crime of being an accessory after the fact.

As can be seen, the criminal law prohibits and punishes not only complete crimes such as theft or murder, but attempts to commit crimes, conspiracies to commit crimes, counselling other people to commit crimes, and assisting known criminals to escape. All of these offences, with the exception of conspiracies, are not subject to as severe punishment as the commission of the complete crime, but they are crimes nevertheless.

12) PARTICIPATION IN CRIMES

Often a crime is committed by more than one person. A person who assists in the commission of an offence can be convicted of the same offence as the person who actually commits the offence. Section 21 of the *Criminal Code* provides that people are parties to an offence and guilty of that offence not only if they commit the offence, but also if they aid or abet the commission of the offence. A person would aid a theft if he or she acted as a lookout or caused a distraction for the purpose of allowing another person time to take the property without being caught. A person would abet a crime if he or she encouraged or procured the commission of a crime. A store clerk might, for example, encourage and knowingly allow a customer to shoplift.

Section 21(2) provides that once two or more people have formed a common intent to carry out an unlawful purpose, they are guilty of every offence that each of them commits provided they knew or ought to have known that the commission of the crime would be a probable consequence of carrying out the unlawful purpose. If Jane and Sam agreed to assault a person and, in carrying out that assault, Jane also steals the victim's wristwatch, then Sam would be guilty of theft if he knew or ought to have known that it was probable that Jane would also steal when assaulting the victim. If Jane murdered the victim during the assault, Sam would not, because of the special stigma and penalty that accompany a murder conviction, be guilty of murder, unless he subjectively knew that it was probable that Jane would also murder the victim they had planned to assault.

The parties' provisions in section 21 mean that people who had different levels of involvement in a crime may be found guilty of the same offence. Because section 21 makes those who actually commit an offence, as well as those who aid or abet the offence, a party to the offence, a jury can convict a person of the crime without necessarily agreeing on whether the person actually committed the crime or aided or abetted the crime. Both the person who performs the actual theft and a person who assists in the theft can be convicted of theft. The extent of an offender's participation in a crime will be considered by the judge when determining the appropriate sentence.

Expansive definitions of the criminal act are found in the above criminal prohibitions that apply to those who have attempted or planned to commit a crime, and to those who have assisted others in committing a crime. In order to convict a person of an attempted crime or for being a party to an offence, however, the Crown must also prove that the person had the fault or mental element of intending to commit the full offence or intending to assist the other person in the commission of the crime. In other words, the commission of a broadly worded prohibited act, or *actus reus*, is not enough; the accused must also have acted with the required fault element, or *mens rea*.

13) THE FAULT ELEMENT, OR *MENS REA*

A great variety of fault elements are used in criminal and regulatory offences. Sometimes the fault element is specified in the wording of an offence by words such as "intentionally," "knowingly," "recklessly," or "negligently." Frequently, however, the courts will have to infer what type of fault element is required. Often a distinction between "subjective" and "objective" fault elements is drawn. A subjective fault or mental element depends on what was in the particular accused's mind at the time that the criminal act was committed. In determining this condition, the judge or jury must consider all the evidence presented, even if it reveals factors, such as the accused's diminished intelligence, which are peculiar to the accused. On the other hand, an objective fault element does not depend on the accused's own state of mind, but on what a reasonable person in the circumstances would have known or done.

Some argue that in order to be fair to the accused, the reasonable person used to administer an objective fault element in criminal cases should have those characteristics of the accused that might affect the accused's ability to perceive the prohibited circumstances and consequences of his or her actions. For example, a nineteen-year-old accused would not be expected to act like a reasonable person, but rather like a reasonable nineteen year old. The Supreme Court, however, has decided that such an approach would erode the distinction between subjective and objective fault elements and has held that the characteristics of the particular accused are only relevant if they make the accused incapable of perceiving the prohibited circumstances or consequences. Thus, an accused's illiteracy might be considered if it made that person incapable of reading a written warning on a dangerous product. In the majority of cases, however, the age or education of the accused would not matter. This ensures that objective standards of fault are distinct from subjective standards, but can produce some harsh results. All but the most serious criminal offences may require an objective fault element, but it is often necessary to demonstrate gross negligence in the form of a significant or marked departure from what a reasonable person would have done. A person carelessly taking a coat belonging to another would probably not demonstrate such conduct, but a person who withheld treatment from his or her child might. Such a parent might demonstrate a marked departure from what a reasonable person would have done, even though for some reason peculiar to the accused (for example, a sincere belief in faith healing) he or she may not have subjectively recognized the dangers of such highly risky conduct.

Courts will often presume that a criminal offence requires proof of a subjective fault element unless the offence clearly or by implication only requires proof of objective fault. There are significant gradations among subjective mental elements. To be convicted of theft, for example, an accused must act with a fraudulent purpose or intent. A person who mistakenly takes another's coat at a party does not act with the fraudulent purpose of taking and keeping that person's coat. Other forms of subjective *mens rea* require less elaborate thought processes. As will be seen, it is enough in a murder case to prove that the accused knew that death was likely to occur, even though he or she may not have had the purpose or intent to kill. In many other cases, some subjective awareness of the prohibited conduct or consequence will be enough. In Canada, this is called recklessness. It is distinct from negligence because it requires some awareness of the prohibited risk by the accused, and it is not sufficient to conclude that a reasonable person would have been aware of the risk that the coat belonged to someone else. Sam would recklessly commit theft if the thought crossed his mind that the coat he took might not belong to him. He would negligently commit theft if a reasonable person in his situation would have taken the necessary care to determine the proper ownership of the coat.

The actual offence of theft, however, requires more than negligence or even recklessness.

The Supreme Court has found that sometimes the principles of fundamental justice under section 7 of the *Charter* require that the Crown prove that the accused subjectively knew that the prohibited act was likely to occur. This principle has only been applied with respect to a few serious crimes — murder, attempted murder, and war crimes — that because of their stigma and penalty have a constitutionally required form of subjective *mens rea*. Thus, in order to obtain a conviction for murder, the Crown must prove that the particular accused knew that the victim was likely to die, not simply that a reasonable person in the accused's position would have recognized the likelihood of death. Note, however, that knowledge is not the highest form of subjective *mens rea* and it is not necessary under section 7 of the *Charter* to prove that an accused's intent or purpose was to kill the victim. The *Charter* only provides minimum standards and Parliament could require such higher forms of *mens rea*. The courts have only constitutionalized subjective *mens rea* for a few serious crimes and their conclusions that the stigma of certain crimes either require subjective fault or do not require subjective fault have been criticized by many as circular and tautological.

Another important consideration is the relation between the fault element and the prohibited act. In the case of murder, the fault element of knowledge must relate to the prohibited act of causing death. In other cases, however, such a matching or symmetry between the *actus reus* and the *mens rea* is not required. Thus, the fault element for unlawful act manslaughter is the objective risk of causing non-trivial bodily harm, whereas the prohibited act requires that the accused have caused the victim's death. A number of other crimes, such as dangerous or impaired driving causing death or bodily harm, recognize the consequences of the accused's actions, but do not require proof of fault with respect to these consequences. In other words, the *mens rea* or fault element does not always relate to every aspect of the *actus reus* or prohibited act.

14) REGULATORY OFFENCES AND CORPORATE CRIME

Regulatory offences are an important feature of penal law in Canada and may be enacted by Parliament, the provincial legislatures, or municipalities. Traditionally, courts were in a dilemma of interpreting a regulatory offence to require either absolute liability, for which a conviction follows from the commission of the prohibited act, or subjective fault, as is presumed for criminal offences. As will be seen, both of these options were problematic.

An absolute liability offence could punish a person who was morally innocent or without fault. The Supreme Court invalidated an absolute liability offence under section 7 of the *Charter* on the basis that it could send a person to jail for driving with a suspended licence when that person did not have subjective fault (that is, she did not know or was not aware of the risk that her licence was suspended) and did not have objective fault (that is, a reasonable person in her circumstances would not have known that the licence was suspended). Although absolute liability offences offend the principles of fundamental justice by punishing the morally innocent, they will not violate section 7 of the *Charter* unless they threaten the accused's right to life, liberty, and security of the person. The courts have upheld absolute liability that could not result in imprisonment.

Requiring proof of subjective fault for a regulatory offence would mean that the Crown would have to prove some form of subjective fault beyond a reasonable doubt even if the conduct was risky and harmful and could have been avoided by reasonable precautions. A compromise between absolute liability and subjective fault has now been adopted for most regulatory offences. In Canada, this halfway house is called a strict liability offence. Because it is based on the fault element of negligence, strict liability offences, unlike absolute liability offences, cannot be criticized for punishing without fault and they would generally not violate section 7 of the *Charter* even if they imposed imprisonment. Unlike criminal offences, however, the prosecutor does not have to prove the existence of the fault element beyond a reasonable doubt. The fault of negligence is presumed to exist once the commission of the prohibited act has been proven beyond a reasonable doubt. The accused must demonstrate that it was not negligent by establishing a defence of due diligence on a balance of probabilities. A corporation, for example, would have to establish that it took reasonable precautions to prevent pollution. Requiring the accused to prove a defence or lack of fault to escape a conviction violates the presumption of innocence, which requires the state to prove all aspects of guilt beyond a reasonable doubt. It would, however, generally be justified under section 1 of the *Charter* because of the difficulty that the Crown might have in establishing beyond a reasonable doubt that a person or corporation accused of a regulatory offence was negligent. Placing the onus on the accused to establish the due diligence defence to a regulatory offence also creates incentives on those individuals and corporations who enter a regulated field to take reasonable precautions to prevent harms.

Corporations may be charged not only with regulatory offences, but also with more serious criminal offences that require some form of *mens rea*. Until recently, only a "directing mind" of a corporation — a senior official with responsibility for creating corporate policy — could have his or her fault or *mens rea* attributed to the corporation for the purpose of determining the corporation's liability for criminal offences. Parliament has recently amended the *Criminal Code* to make it somewhat easier to convict corporations and other organizations of criminal offences. The fault of "senior officers" in the corporation is now attributed to the corporation and senior officers are defined in the *Criminal Code* to include not only those who play an important role in the establishment of the organization's policies, but also those who are responsible for managing an important aspect of the organization's activities. A corporation can be held liable for a subjective fault crime if the responsible senior officer commits the offence or intentionally directs the work of any representative of the corporation (including contractors and agents of the corporation) so that they commit the offence. In addition, the corporation may be liable if the senior officer knows that any representative is committing or is about to commit an offence, but fails to take all reasonable measures to stop the representative from committing the offence. A corporation can be liable for a negligence-based crime if the responsible senior officer(s) depart markedly from the standard of care that, in the circumstances, could reasonably be expected to prevent representatives from committing the offence.

15) DEFENCES

Even if the Crown proves that the accused committed the prohibited act and had the required fault element, the accused may still avoid conviction by raising a relevant defence. Some common defences, such as mistake of fact and intoxication, are not really defences but conditions that prevent the Crown from proving the required mental or fault element. A person accused of murder could be so intoxicated that he or she did not know that the victim was likely to die. Likewise, a hunter accused of murder could commit the prohibited act of causing another hunter's death but have had the mistaken impression that he or she was shooting a deer. In such instances, the Crown can prove the commission of the prohibited act, but will be unable to prove that the accused had the mental element required for murder. The defences of intoxication and mistake of fact are derived from the fault element of the particular crime. For example, an offence requiring objective negligence will allow a defence of mistake of fact only if the mistake was a reasonable one. It will also generally not allow any intoxication defence because the reasonable person is sober.

Other defences may excuse or justify conduct, even though the accused committed the offence with the required fault element. Those who defend themselves may have a defence of self-defence, even if they intentionally kill or harm the attacker. Self-defence is usually considered a defence that justifies conduct, and it leads to a full acquittal. Those who commit a crime in reasonable response to serious threats of harm by third parties may have a defence of duress, even if they commit the crime with the required fault element. An example would be the person who goes along with a robbery with a gun at his or her head. Similarly, a person who commits a crime in response to circumstances of dire peril may have a defence of necessity. This would apply to a lost hiker who intentionally breaks into a cabin because he or she desperately needs food and water. Those who have valid defences of duress and necessity act in a morally involuntary manner because in the circumstances it was impossible for them to comply with the law and there was no safe and lawful avenue of escape. The defences of necessity and duress are usually thought to excuse conduct, but they also lead to a full acquittal.

Defences are related to the appropriate disposition of the accused. Provocation is a controversial defence available when an accused kills in a rage produced by a sudden and wrongful act or insult that would have caused an ordinary person to lose self-control. This defence does not lead to a complete acquittal, but reduces murder to manslaughter. This avoids the mandatory penalty of life imprisonment that follows a murder conviction. The defence of intoxication has traditionally been available only as a defence to some offences, known as specific intent offences, but not to others, known as general intent offences. Thus, an accused so intoxicated as to be unable to have the subjective foresight of death would be acquitted of murder, a specific intent offence, but almost always convicted of manslaughter, a general intent offence. Manslaughter is a less serious offence than murder, and it allows for the exercise of sentencing discretion. The new defence of extreme intoxication to a general intent offence is controversial in no small part because it may lead to the complete acquittal of an accused who commits a crime after voluntarily becoming intoxicated.

Defences related to mental disorders are also influenced by concerns about the appropriate disposition of the accused. The insanity or mental disorder defence applies to those who, because of a mental disorder, cannot appreciate the physical consequences of the prohibited act they commit or know that it is legally or morally wrong. Such a person, although not convicted, would be detained and examined to determine if further detention was required to protect the public from a significant threat of danger. Automatism refers to involuntary behaviour that may prevent the Crown from proving the fault element or even the prohibited act of a crime. An accused found to be in such a state will not be convicted. If the automatism is caused by a mental disorder, however, the accused can be subject to detention as a person held not criminally responsible by reason of mental disorder. If the automatism is caused by a factor that is not a mental disorder, such as a blow on the head, the accused is simply acquitted. The accused now has the burden of establishing both the mental disorder and non-insane automatism defences on a balance of probabilities.

Many defences require that the accused act in a reasonable fashion. For example, an act or insult must be sufficient to deprive an ordinary person of self-control before it can be provocation. To be able to claim self-defence, the accused must not only subjectively believe that he or she is being threatened and that the actions taken in self-defence are necessary, but there must be a reasonable basis for such beliefs. The criminal law generally excuses crimes committed in response to threats and dire circumstances only if a reasonable person in the accused's circumstances would have committed the crime. The use of objective standards in defences raises the question of who is the reasonable person. Unlike in the case of objective fault elements, the trend in Canada is to consider the particular accused's own experiences and characteristics when applying objective standards relating to defences such as provocation, self-defence, duress, and necessity. In the self-defence context, the Supreme Court has indicated that what is reasonable to expect of a man in a bar-room brawl may not be reasonable to expect of a woman who has been previously battered by the person she kills. In judging whether an ordinary person would have lost self-control when provoked, the courts consider the accused's characteristics and experiences, as they affect the gravity or meaning of the insult. This provides a more generous defence that is sensitive to the particular experiences and frailties of the accused, but it also blurs the conceptual distinction between objective and subjective standards.

Restrictions on a defence may violate the principles of fundamental justice protected under section 7 of the *Charter*. The Supreme Court has held that the complete denial of an intoxication defence when a person is charged with a general intent offence, such as an assault, or sexual assault, violates the principles of the fundamental justice. It could result in the conviction of a person who acted in an involuntary manner because of extreme intoxication. Statutory restrictions on the defence of duress also offend the principles of fundamental justice because they allow a person to be convicted even though he or she acted in a morally involuntary manner in response to threats. A person acts in a morally involuntary manner if any reasonable person in the same circumstances with the same characteristics would have committed the offence. A conviction of a person who acts in a morally involuntary manner because of external pressures offends section 7 of the *Charter* because it would deprive a person of liberty in a manner that is not in accordance with the principles of fundamental justice.

16) SENTENCING

Most accused plead guilty to some charge and proceed directly to sentencing without a criminal trial. A significant number of those who do go to trial are convicted of some offence and are subject to sentencing. In Canada, judges have significant sentencing discretion because they are guided only by general principles in the *Criminal Code* and high maximum penalties. Robbery, for example, is subject only to a maximum punishment of life imprisonment, with no minimum sentence. Committing a robbery with a firearm, however, does have a mandatory minimum sentence of four years' imprisonment. Mandatory penalties can be challenged as violating the right against cruel and unusual punishment, but most mandatory penalties have been upheld from such challenges.

The fundamental principle of sentencing is that a sentence must be proportionate to the gravity of the offence and the degree of responsibility of the offender. This is an important principle, given the various types of conduct that can be caught under broad legislative definitions of the prohibited act, and the provisions that make parties to an offence guilty of the same offence as those who actually "pull the trigger." This principle also suggests that the punishment should fit the crime and that an offender should not be treated more harshly than the crime warrants in order to deter others or to incapacitate or even rehabilitate the offender.

Despite the fundamental principle that a sentence must fit the crime, there are other legitimate purposes of sentencing, including deterring others from committing crimes; deterring the particular offender from reoffending; incapacitating the particular offender from committing more crimes; rehabilitating the particular offender; and providing reparation for harm done to victims or the community. In fulfilling these multiple purposes, judges can impose punishments other than actual imprisonment, including community service orders, discharges with conditions in the form of probation orders, fines, and restitution orders.

Conditional sentences allow offenders to serve sentences of imprisonment in the community so long as they satisfy prescribed conditions. If a person is imprisoned, he or she can usually apply to a parole board before the end of the sentence for various forms of supervised release into the community. There are also provisions that allow repeat offenders to be declared dangerous and subject to indeterminate detention.

17) CONCLUSION

The criminal law is the result of a complex process that starts with the decision of a legislature to define something as a prohibited act. The next steps are usually the investigation by the police and the prosecution by the Crown. These phases of the criminal process must be procedurally fair, or the accused will be able to seek a remedy for the violation of his or her rights under the *Charter*. The offence and the available defences must ensure that the morally innocent are not punished. The Crown must also prove beyond a reasonable doubt to the judge or jury that the accused committed the prohibited act with the required fault element. The accused has available various defences, most of which will apply if there is a reasonable doubt as to their existence. Some defences such as self-defence lead to a complete acquittal, while others such as intoxication and provocation may result in the accused being acquitted of a serious offence such as murder, but still convicted of a less serious offence such as manslaughter. The mental disorder defence leads to a special disposition in which the accused, although not convicted, may be subject to further detention or treatment if he or she presents a significant threat to public safety. The judge at sentencing has wide discretion to tailor punishment to the offender's degree of responsibility, but also to consider what punishment will best deter, rehabilitate, or incapacitate the particular offender, deter others from committing the same crime, and provide reparation to the victims and the community for the crime.

FURTHER READINGS

GARTNER, R., & A.N. DOOB, "Trends in Criminal Victimization: 1988–1993" (1994) 14:13 Juristat 1

"Adult criminal court statistics, 2002/03" (2003) 23:10 Juristat 1

"Crime Statistics in Canada, 2002" (2003) 23:5 Juristat 1

THE CRIMINAL LAW AND THE CONSTITUTION

In order to understand criminal law in Canada, it is increasingly necessary to understand constitutional law. The Constitution, which is the supreme law of the land, has always played a role in the criminal law. The constitutional division of powers between the federal and provincial governments, created in 1867, allows only the federal Parliament to enact laws concerning criminal law and procedure. The provinces can, however, enact regulatory offences to help them govern matters within their jurisdiction, such as liquor licensing. The federal government can also enact regulatory offences to help it govern matters such as navigation and shipping that are within federal jurisdiction. In deciding whether an offence is within federal or provincial jurisdiction, the courts are concerned with the law's primary purpose.

In 1982 the *Canadian Charter of Rights and Freedoms* was added to the Constitution, and it places new restraints on the state's ability to enact and apply criminal laws. It does so by recognizing various rights, such as the right to be free of unreasonable searches and seizures, the right to counsel, and the right to a fair trial. In most cases, people will only have the incentive to invoke their *Charter* rights when they are charged with an offence. Hence, the majority of *Charter* litigation arises in criminal cases. Many of the rights in the *Charter* require procedural fairness or due process in the investigation and prosecution of crime. Other rights are concerned that the substance of the law is fair, and does not punish a person who is morally innocent or only exercising constitutional rights such as freedom of expression. A law or practice can infringe a *Charter* right because it has the effect of violating an individual's right, even if it was enacted for a valid and legitimate purpose.

If a criminal or regulatory offence or procedural provision violates a right protected under the *Charter*, the government will have an opportunity to justify the law under section 1 of the *Charter* as a reasonable limit that is demonstrably justifiable in a free and democratic society. The government must demonstrate not only that the law has been enacted for an important purpose, but that there is no other reasonable manner to fulfil that purpose except by violating the accused's rights and the good that the law achieves in advancing its objective outweighs the harm to the *Charter* right. If the accused's rights have been violated and the violation not justified under section 1, the courts can order a range of constitutional remedies. For example, they can strike down an unconstitutional offence, terminate a prosecution through a stay of proceedings, or exclude relevant evidence because it was obtained through a *Charter* violation such as an unconstitutional search or interrogation.

The new emphasis on the accused's rights in Canadian criminal law has diverted some trials away from their traditional focus on whether the accused was factually guilty. The *Charter* protects the rights of the accused to due process or fair treatment, but section 1 allows the government to justify some restrictions on the accused's rights as necessary for crime control or some other important objective. Other people affected by a criminal law, including victims, witnesses, or the media, may also have *Charter* rights such as the rights to privacy and the equal protection and benefit of the law. The *Charter* does not eliminate the need to balance competing interests in criminal laws and prosecutions, but it provides a new framework for reconciling these interests.

A. CRIMINAL JUSTICE AND THE DIVISION OF POWERS

1) Federal Jurisdiction over Criminal Law

Under section 91(27) of the *Constitution Act, 1867*, only the federal Parliament can enact laws concerning criminal law and procedure. Most criminal law is contained in the *Criminal Code of Canada*[1] although the *Controlled Drugs and Substances Act*[2] and the *Youth Criminal Justice*

---

1   R.S.C. 1985, c. C-46 [*Code*].
2   S.C. 1996, c. 19.

Act[3] are often considered criminal law. Not all laws enacted by the federal government fall under its power to enact criminal law and procedure. For example, a federal law prohibiting the sale of margarine or establishing the alcohol content of light beer would not be a valid criminal law.[4] Courts have, however, been quite generous in allowing the federal government to enact laws that facilitate the administration of the criminal law. For example, federal laws regulating the detention of the criminally insane[5] and enabling judges to order the accused to make restitution to the victims of crime[6] have been upheld as valid criminal law. Parliament's criminal law power has also been interpreted broadly to allow laws restricting the advertising of tobacco,[7] prohibiting pollution,[8] and prohibiting the possession of marijuana.[9] When the federal government relies on its criminal law power, it must emphasize the use of prohibitions and punishments, as opposed to other forms of regulation such as licensing and inspections.

Unlike in the United States and Australia, the provinces (or states) cannot make laws that are classified by the courts as having the dominant purpose of prohibiting acts by the criminal sanction. Provincial and municipal attempts to prohibit the propagation of ideas,[10] the use of streets for prostitution,[11] or abortions,[12] have all been struck down as infringing the federal government's exclusive jurisdiction over criminal law. A provincial offence or a municipal by-law will be unconstitutional if its prime purpose is to punish behaviour as criminal. Before the enactment of the *Charter*, these restrictions acted as an indirect but important protection of civil liberties.

2) Provincial Jurisdiction to Enact Regulatory Offences

Under section 92(15) of the *Constitution Act, 1867*, the provinces (and their delegates, the municipalities) can create offences punishable by

---

3   S.C. 2002, c. 1.
4   *Canadian Federation of Agriculture v. Quebec (A.G.)*, [1951] A.C. 179 (P.C.);
    Labatt Breweries of Canada Ltd. v. Canada (A.G.), [1980] 1 S.C.R. 914.
5   *R. v. Swain* (1991), 63 C.C.C. (3d) 481 (S.C.C.).
6   *R. v. Zelensky* (1978), 41 C.C.C. (2d) 97 (S.C.C.).
7   *RJR-Mcdonald Inc. v. Canada (A.G.)* (1995), 100 C.C.C (3d) 449 (S.C.C.). The
    advertising restrictions were, however, struck down under the *Charter* as an
    unjustified restriction on freedom of expression.
8   *R. v. Hydro–Quebec* (1997), 118 C.C.C. (3d) 97 (S.C.C.).
9   *R. v. Malmo-Levine* (2003), 179 C.C.C. (3d) 417 (S.C.C.) [*Malmo-Levine*].
10 *Switzman v. Elbling* (1957), 117 C.C.C. 129 (S.C.C.).
11 *R. v. Westendorp* (1983), 2 C.C.C. (3d) 330 (S.C.C.).
12 *R. v. Morgentaler* (1993), 85 C.C.C. (3d) 118 (S.C.C.) [*Morgentaler*].

fine, penalty, or imprisonment for matters within their jurisdiction. The provinces have been allowed to enact highway traffic offences,[13] and to make provisions for the classification and censorship of films[14] and even the compulsory treatment of heroin addicts.[15] Provincial offences will be constitutional provided that their dominant purpose is to regulate some matter within areas of provincial jurisdiction, such as property and civil rights and matters of a local and private nature.

Provincial offences are often classified as regulatory or public welfare offences. They can be tried in the same courts as criminal offences and can even result in imprisonment. The standards for investigation and conviction of regulatory offences are generally less protective of the accused than those for criminal offences.[16] The federal government can also enact regulatory offences under other areas of its jurisdiction, such as its power over fisheries. In terms of offences and prosecutions, regulatory offences far outnumber criminal offences. Individuals are more likely to be charged with speeding or performing an act without a licence than with crimes such as murder, theft, or break and enter.

3) Prosecutors, Police, and Prisons

The Attorney General of a province will generally prosecute offences under the *Criminal Code*,[17] but the federal Attorney General may prosecute drug offences.[18] The same division of labour is true of policing, with the provinces being able to establish police forces to enforce the *Criminal Code* (this power in turn often being delegated to a municipality or a region) and the federal government being able to create police to investigate other offences under federal law. Many provinces, however, purchase policing services from the Royal Canadian Mounted Police, the federal police force. Peace officers (including the public police, customs officials, and jail guards, but not usually private police or security guards) have special powers, duties, and protections under the *Criminal Code*.[19] A fundamental feature of the rule of law is that

---

13   *O'Grady v. Sparling* (1960), 128 C.C.C. 1 (S.C.C.).

14   *McNeil v. Nova Scotia (Board of Censors)* (1978), 44 C.C.C. (2d) 128 (S.C.C.).

15   *R. v. Schneider* (1982), 68 C.C.C. (2d) 449 (S.C.C.).

16   See ch. 5, "Regulatory Offences and Corporate Crime."

17   *Code*, above note 1, s. 2. The attorney general of Canada is the prosecutor for the Northwest and Yukon Territories and Nunavut and can prosecute *Criminal Code* crimes with extraterritorial effect and crimes involving terrorism or United Nations personnel.

18   *R. v. Hauser* (1979), 46 C.C.C. (2d) 481 (S.C.C.).

19   *Code*, above note 1, ss. 25, 129, 270, 495, and 503. Peace officers are defined in s. 2.

peace officers are bound by the law including the *Criminal Code* and the *Charter*. Ordinary individuals have legal powers to arrest a person fleeing from the commission of a serious offence[20] and to go before a judicial official to establish reasonable and probable grounds that a criminal offence has been committed.[21]

The provinces have jurisdiction over those sentenced to less than two years imprisonment, while the federal government administers penitentiaries for those sentenced to longer periods.[22] The provinces generally administer probation orders, while provincial and federal parole boards administer gradual release or parole from imprisonment before an offender's sentence has expired.

4) Trials and Trial Courts

The vast majority of criminal cases are resolved in provincial courts formally known as magistrates' courts. Provincial court judges are appointed by the provinces and they cannot sit with a jury. They can, however, hear most serious indictable offences,[23] provided that the accused decides or elects to be tried in provincial court without a jury or a preliminary inquiry to determine whether there is enough evidence to put the accused on trial. The least serious indictable offences can only be tried in provincial court,[24] and provincial courts or justices of the peace also hear the least serious criminal offences, known as summary conviction offences, as well as provincial regulatory offences enacted under section 92(15) of the *Constitution Act, 1867*. Both summary conviction and provincial offences can generally only be punished by up to six months' imprisonment and $2000 in fines.[25] Some offences, such as sexual assault, if prosecuted by way of summary conviction can be punished by up to 18 months imprisonment. In "hybrid" offences, the Crown has the discretion to prosecute the offence by indictment or as a less serious summary conviction offence. If the prosecutor elects to prosecute the offence as a summary conviction offence, the accused is not entitled to a preliminary inquiry or a trial by jury but the maximum punishment is limited. Those under 18 years of age are

---

20 *Ibid.*, s. 494.
21 *Ibid.*, ss. 504 and 507.
22 *Constitution Act, 1867* (U.K.), 30 & 31 Vict., c. 3, ss. 91(28) and 92(6) [*CA 1867*]; *Code*, above note 1, s. 743.1.
23 But not those, such as murder, listed in the *Code*, above note 1, s. 469.
24 Including theft and other offences listed in the *Code*, above note 1, s. 553.
25 *Ibid.*, s. 787.

generally tried in youth court, which in most provinces is the provincial court. Youth sentences are lower from those available upon conviction of the same offence in adult court. In some cases, however, adult sentences can be imposed on young offenders.

Only federally appointed superior court judges can sit with a jury in what is known in different provinces as the Superior Court, Supreme Court, or Queen's Bench.[26] Murder charges must be tried by a superior court judge, usually with a jury.[27] Superior court judges may also try most other indictable offences, provided the accused elects to be tried in this higher level of trial court. The accused can elect to be tried in the superior court with a preliminary inquiry (heard by a provincial court judge or justice of the peace) and with or without a jury. The appearance of a superior court trial can be impressive (for example, the lawyers are gowned), but it should be remembered that most criminal cases are resolved in the less formal and more hectic atmosphere of the provincial courts.

5) Appeals and Appellate Courts

Canada has a generous appellate structure that allows both the accused and the Crown wide rights of appeal. Appeals in summary conviction offences can be made by either the accused or the prosecutor and are heard by a superior court judge with further appeals on questions of law to the Court of Appeal.[28] Appeals for indictable offences go directly to the provincial Court of Appeal, which has federally appointed judges and hears appeals in panels of three and sometimes five judges. The accused has broad rights of appeal and can appeal matters of fact or law, as well as the fitness of his or her sentence.[29] The accused's appeal can be allowed on three grounds: 1) that the conviction is unreasonable or cannot be supported by the evidence; 2) that the conviction entails a miscarriage of justice; or 3) that the trial judge made an error of law. In the last case, the appeal can be denied if the appeal court concludes that notwithstanding the legal error, "no substantial wrong or miscarriage of justice has occurred."[30] If the accused's appeal is successful, a new trial will usually be ordered, but in some cases an acquittal may be entered. In addition, the Minister of Justice can order

---

26   *CA 1867*, above note 22, s. 96.
27   *Code*, above note 1, s. 469.
28   *Ibid.*, ss. 813, 830, and 839.
29   *Ibid.*, s. 675.
30   *Ibid.*, s. 686(1)(b)(iii).

a new trial, or direct an appeal to a provincial Court of Appeal when he or she is "satisfied that there is a reasonable basis to conclude that a miscarriage of justice likely occurred" after having inquired into an application by a person convicted of an offence whose appeal rights have been exhausted.[31] A similar power was used to order new appeals in cases involving miscarriages of justice, such as the wrongful convictions of Donald Marshall, Jr., and David Milgaard.

The prosecutor may appeal questions of law and the fitness of sentence to the Court of Appeal.[32] If the appeal is allowed and the prosecutor can show that the outcome would not have been the same without the legal error, a new trial will be ordered. In rare cases, the appeal court might enter a conviction instead of ordering a new trial, but this cannot be done if the accused was acquitted at trial by a jury. The right of the prosecutor to appeal acquittals and to have new trials ordered is much broader in Canada than in either the United States or the United Kingdom.

Either the accused or the prosecutor can appeal to the highest court, the Supreme Court of Canada, with nine federally appointed judges. Appeals to that Court are of right on any question of law from which a judge in the provincial Court of Appeal dissents, and by leave on any matter of law of national importance.[33]

B. CRIMINAL LAW AND THE *CHARTER OF RIGHTS*

In 1982 the *Canadian Charter of Rights and Freedoms* was added to the Canadian Constitution. The *Charter's* greatest impact has been on the criminal justice system, and it provides constitutional standards that affect the criminal process from the investigation of crime to the punishment of offenders. A violation of the *Charter* may occur if police, prosecutorial, or correctional practices or some law has the effect of violating the accused's rights. Under section 24 of the *Charter*, courts can provide a range of remedies if police, prosecutors, or prison officials violate the *Charter* rights of the accused. These remedies can include the termination of a prosecution through a stay of proceedings,

---

31 *Ibid.*, s. 696.3(3). Pardons may also be granted under s. 748 of the *Code* and pursuant to the royal prerogative of mercy.
32 *Ibid.*, s. 676.
33 *Ibid.*, ss. 691 and 693; *Supreme Court Act*, R.S.C. 1985, c. S-26, s. 40.

the release of a person, and the exclusion of unconstitutionally obtained evidence. Criminal laws passed by Parliament can also be struck down by the courts under section 52 of the *Constitution Act, 1982*, if they are found to violate one of the rights in the *Charter* and the government cannot justify the violation under section 1 of the *Charter* as a proportionate means to fulfil an important purpose. Parliament and the provincial legislatures retain the final, but very rarely exercised, option to declare that a law will operate notwithstanding the fundamental freedoms, legal rights, or equality rights otherwise guaranteed under the *Charter*.[34]

1) Division of Powers and the *Charter* Compared

The division of powers in the *Constitution Act, 1867* and the *Charter* provide a complex constitutional framework that governs the enactment of criminal and regulatory offences in Canada. The history of legislation requiring Sunday observance provides a good illustration. At the turn of the century, provincial legislation requiring Sunday observance was struck down on the grounds that it was criminal law that only Parliament could enact.[35] The federal *Lord's Day Act*[36] was subsequently upheld as valid criminal law because it was designed with the religious purpose of requiring the observance of the Christian sabbath.[37] By that time, however, the *Charter* had been enacted, and the Supreme Court decided that a law enacted with the religious purpose of compelling observance of a common sabbath was a direct violation of freedom of conscience and religion as protected under section 2(a) of the *Charter*.[38] Since the law was based on a purpose contrary to *Charter* values, it could not be justified by the government under section 1 and was declared to be invalid.

A year later, the Supreme Court had to decide the constitutionality of a provincial law requiring Sunday closing. The Court found that the law had been enacted for the secular purpose of establishing a common rest day, a matter of civil and property rights within provincial jurisdic-

---

34 *Canadian Charter of Rights and Freedoms*, Part I of the *Constitution Act, 1982*, being Schedule B to the *Canada Act 1982* (U.K.), 1982, c. 11, s. 33 [*Charter*].

35 *Ontario (A.G.) v. Hamilton Street Railway Co.*, [1903] A.C. 524 (P.C.). Subsequent provincial attempts to compel observance of religious holidays were struck down as invasions of federal jurisdiction over criminal law. *Henry Birks & Sons v. (Montreal) Ltd. (City)*, (1955), 113 C.C.C. 135 (S.C.C.).

36 R.S.C. 1970, c. L-13.

37 *R. v. Big M Drug Mart Ltd.* (1985), 18 C.C.C. (3d) 385 (S.C.C.).

38 *Ibid.*

tion. At the same time, however, the Court found that the law violated the right to freedom of religion and conscience because it had the effect (but not the purpose) of placing burdens on those who, because of their religious beliefs, could not open their stores on either Sunday or their own religious sabbath.[39] That conclusion did not end the constitutional analysis, however, because the Court held that the government had justified the law under section 1 of the *Charter* as a reasonable limit that was necessary to ensure a common rest day. The legislatures in many Canadian jurisdictions had the last word when they repealed Sunday closing laws in response to public opinion.

2) The *Charter* and the Investigation of Crime

Before the enactment of the *Charter*, courts conducting a criminal trial were generally not concerned with the manner in which the police investigated crime. The failure of the police to warn suspects that their statements might be used against them did not affect the admissibility of their statements[40] and evidence could not be excluded because it was unfairly obtained.[41] The only real restraint was that confessions had to be proven to be voluntary in the sense that they were not obtained through fear or hope of advantage. This was done to ensure the reliability of confessions more than their fairness. The *Charter* has changed this exclusive emphasis on crime control by recognizing rights to be secure against unreasonable search and seizures (section 8); rights not to be arbitrarily detained or imprisoned (section 9); and rights to be informed of the reason for arrest or detention and to retain and instruct counsel without delay (section 10(a)(b)). A violation of any of these rights can result in the exclusion of relevant evidence from the criminal trial if its admission will bring the administration into disrepute (section 24(2)).

a) Search and Seizure

Section 8 of the *Charter* provides that everyone has a right to be secure against unreasonable search and seizure. This provision protects all reasonable expectations of privacy, and such expectations are not sacrificed simply because an accused was committing a criminal offence or risked that the state would discover his or her illegal activities.[42]

---

39 R. v. *Edwards Books & Art Ltd.* (1986), 30 C.C.C. (3d) 385 (S.C.C.).
40 R. v. *Boudreau* (1949), 94 C.C.C. 1 (S.C.C.).
41 R. v. *Wray*, [1970] 4 C.C.C. 1 (S.C.C.).
42 R. v. *Duarte* (1990), 53 C.C.C. (3d) 1 (S.C.C.) [*Duarte*]; R. v. *Wong* (1990), 60 C.C.C. (3d) 460 (S.C.C.) [*Wong*].

What constitutes a reasonable expectation of privacy, however, depends on the context. Individuals and businesses who operate in a regulated field have diminished expectation of privacy over their business records.[43] Regulatory inspections, like regulatory offences, are thought to carry with them less stigma and for this reason the state is given greater scope in its activities. Similarly, a demand by government investigators for the production of documents is seen as less intrusive than an actual search.[44] The Supreme Court has made clear, however, that warrant requirements apply when regulators "cross the Rubicon" from regulation to prosecution. This occurs when the predominant purpose of their inquiries is the determination of penal liability.[45]

It is not only those who operate in a regulatory context that have diminished or no expectations of privacy. An individual who occasionally stays at an intimate friend's home may have no reasonable expectation of privacy when that friend's home is searched,[46] and passengers may not have a reasonable expectation of privacy when the car they are driving in is searched.[47] Students in schools also have diminished expectations of privacy from searches,[48] as do prisoners,[49] drivers asked to produce their licences,[50] individuals who pass customs,[51] and those whose power consumption can be determined by access to commercial records.[52]

If there is a reasonable expectation of privacy, the state must generally obtain prior judicial authorization to authorize a search and seizure, except if there are exigent circumstances that make it impossible to obtain a warrant.[53] The police need not wait to obtain a warrant if there is imminent danger that evidence of a crime will be destroyed or that someone will be harmed. They also do not need to obtain a warrant if the person consents to a search or if they are conducting a rea-

---

43   R. v. Potash (1994), 91 C.C.C. (3d) 315 (S.C.C.).
44   Thomson Newspapers Ltd. v. Canada (Director of Investigation & Research) (1990), 54 C.C.C. (3d) 417 (S.C.C.); R. v. McKinlay Transport Ltd. (1990), 55 C.C.C. (3d) 530 (S.C.C.).
45   R. v. Jarvis (2002), 169 C.C.C. (3d) 1 (S.C.C.) [Jarvis].
46   R. v. Edwards (1996), 104 C.C.C. (3d) 136 (S.C.C.).
47   R. v. Belnavis (1997), 118 C.C.C. (3d) 405 (S.C.C.).
48   R. v. M.(M.R.) (1998), 129 C.C.C. (3d) 361 (S.C.C.).
49   Weatherall v. Canada (A.G.) (1993), 83 C.C.C. (3d) 1 (S.C.C.).
50   R. v. Hufsky (1988), 40 C.C.C. (3d) 398 (S.C.C.) [Hufsky].
51   R. v. Simmons (1988), 45 C.C.C. (3d) 296 (S.C.C.); R. v. Jacques (1996), 110 C.C.C. (3d) 1 (S.C.C.).
52   R. v. Plant (1993), 84 C.C.C. (3d) 203 (S.C.C.).
53   R. v. Grant (1993), 84 C.C.C. (3d) 173 (S.C.C.).

sonable search incident to arrest.[54] Searches incident to arrest must not be conducted in an abusive fashion and do not include the power to seize bodily samples for dna testing[55] or to take body impressions.[56] The power to conduct a strip search does not follow automatically from the power to conduct a less instrusive search incident to arrest. There must be reasonable and probable grounds for concluding that a strip search is necessary in the particular circumstances of the arrest in order to discover weapons or evidence.[57]

When prior judicial authorization for a search and seizure is sought, it should generally be granted only if there are reasonable and probable grounds established on oath to believe that an offence has been committed and that the search will reveal evidence of the offence.[58] Searches must also be authorized by law, and the law must be reasonable.[59] In response to numerous decisions holding warrantless and illegal searches to be unreasonable, Parliament has enacted new laws to grant warrants and authorizing warrantless searches in exigent circumstances. For example, the Court's decision that wearing a wire without a warrant violated section 8 of the *Charter* was followed by the enactment of new provisions allowing judges to issue such warrants and also authorizing the use of wires without warrants in urgent circumstances and to prevent bodily harm.[60] The Court's decision declaring the warrantless use of videotaping to be a violation of section 8 of the *Charter* led to the enactment of a new general warrant provision that allows a judge to grant a warrant authorizing any investigative technique that, if not authorized, would constitute an unreasonable search and seizure.[61] When the Supreme Court declared the common

---

54 *Cloutier v. Langlois* (1990), 53 C.C.C. (3d) 257 (S.C.C.); *R. v. Caslake* (1998), 121 C.C.C. (3d) 97 (S.C.C.).

55 *R. v. Stillman* (1997), 113 C.C.C. (3d) 321 (S.C.C.) [*Stillman*]. Warrants can be issued for obtaining DNA samples. See *Code*, above note 1, ss. 487.04–487.091. These warrant provisions have been upheld under the *Charter*. *R. v. S.A.B.*, [2003] 2 S.C.R. 678.

56 *Stillman*. But see *Code*, above note 1, s. 487.092 for warrants to obtain body impressions.

57 *R. v. Golden*, [2001] 3 S.C.R. 679 at 733.

58 *Canada (Director of Investigation & Research, Combines Investigation Branch) v. Southam Inc.*, (1984), 14 C.C.C. (3d) 97 (S.C.C.).

59 *R. v. Collins* (1987), 33 C.C.C. (3d) 1 (S.C.C.).

60 *Duarte*, above note 42. See *Code*, above note 1, ss. 184.1–184.4.

61 *Wong*, above note 42. See now *Code*, above note 1, ss. 184.1–184.4 and 487.01.This general warrant provision does not authorize interference with bodily integrity. Parliament, however, has enacted other provisions which allow war-

law rule that allowed a warrantless search of a dwelling house in order to make an arrest violated section 8 of the *Charter*, Parliament enacted new provisions that allowed such warrants to be granted and also authorized warrantless entries into dwelling houses to make arrests in exigent circumstances.[62]

Evidence obtained in violation of section 8 of the *Charter* will be excluded under section 24(2) of the *Charter* if it required the accused's participation.[63] The evidence would also be excluded if it brought greater harm to the administration of justice to admit it rather than to exclude it. Body samples that have been unconstitutionally seized are usually excluded, unless the state can establish that they would have been discovered without a *Charter* violation. Otherwise, the courts have been reluctant to exclude evidence that was unreasonably seized if the police have acted in good faith and have not committed flagrant improprieties. They will balance the seriousness of the *Charter* violation against the harm to the repute of the administration of justice caused by the exclusion of evidence.

b)   Arbitrary Detention and Imprisonment

Section 9 of the *Charter* provides that everyone has the right not to be arbitrarily detained or imprisoned. Detention has been defined broadly. People are detained when pulled over to the side of the road by the police, and laws authorizing random vehicle stops violate section 9 because they provide no objective criteria to govern who is detained. Nevertheless, these laws have been upheld under section 1 as reasonable limits necessary to prevent drunk driving and to ensure traffic safety[64] despite a strong dissent that argued that the Court was allowing "any individual officer to stop any vehicle, at any time, at any place. The decision may be based on any whim. Individual officers will have different reasons."[65] Random stops are permissible when undertaken for reasons of traffic safety.

When the police do not act for traffic safety reasons, the courts are more prepared to intervene. They excluded incriminating evidence

---

rants to be obtained to seize DNA samples and take body impressions. See *Code*, above note 1, ss. 487.04–487.09 and 487.091.

62   *R. v. Feeney* (1997), 115 C.C.C. (3d) 129 (S.C.C.). See *Code*, above note 1, ss. 487.04–487.09, 487.091 and 529. Exigent circumstances are defined to include the need to prevent imminent bodily harm or death and the imminent loss or destruction of evidence. *Code*, above note 1, s. 529.3.

63   *R. v. Mellenthin* (1992), 76 C.C.C. (3d) 481 (S.C.C.); *Stillman*, above note 55.

64   *Hufsky*, above note 50; *R. v. Ladouceur* (1990), 56 C.C.C. (3d) 22 (S.C.C.).

65   *Ladouceur*, *ibid.* at 29.

obtained after an investigative detention because the police were only relying on a hunch that the teenagers had been involved in a break-in as opposed to reasonable grounds to believe that a crime was committed.[66] The Ontario Court of Appeal has held that section 9 was violated and drugs should be excluded in a case where the police stopped and frisked a person without articulable cause or a reasonable suspicion of a crime. This requires less than reasonable and probable grounds to believe a crime was committed, but more than a subjective hunch based on the officer's experience or intuition. The Court of Appeal indicated that "such subjectively based assessments can too easily mask discriminatory conduct based on such irrelevant factors as the detainee's sex, colour, age, ethnic origin or sexual orientation."[67] In another case, a description of a suspect as "male, black, 5'8 to 5'11," with a short Afro, wearing a dark jacket, armed with a knife and a gun" was found to be too general and produced an arbitrary detention and arrest.[68] There is some evidence in Canada that unpopular minorities are disproportionately targeted for investigative stops by the police.[69]

A detained person has the right under section 10(c) of the *Charter* to seek *habeas corpus* and to be released if the detention is not lawful. Under section 11(e) of the *Charter*, a detainee has a right not to be denied reasonable bail without just cause. A person can be detained for valid reasons such as ensuring their appearance in court or preventing the continuation of a crime. Despite recognizing the difficulty of predicting future danger, the Supreme Court has upheld denial of bail to prevent the substantial likelihood of future crime or interference with the administration of justice on the basis that "the bail system . . . does not function properly if individuals commit crimes while on bail."[70] The Court also upheld a reverse onus which required those charged with drug trafficking to establish why they should not be detained.[71] The Court did strike down pre-trial detention in the public interest as excessively vague on the basis that "a standardless sweep does not become acceptable simply because it results from the whims of judges

---

66 R. v. *Duguay* (1989), 46 C.C.C. (3d) 1 (S.C.C.).

67 R. v. *Simpson* (1993), 79 C.C.C. (3d) 482 at 502 (Ont. C.A.).

68 R. v. *Charley* (1993), 22 C.R. (4th) 297 (Ont. C.A.).

69 *Report of the Manitoba Aboriginal Justice Inquiry* (Winnipeg: Queen's Printer, 1991); *Report of the Commission on Systemic Racism in the Ontario Criminal Justice System* (Toronto: Queen's Printer, 1995); Ontario Human Rights Commission, *Paying the Price: The Human Cost of Racial Profiling* (Toronto: Ontario Human Rights Commission, 2004).

70 R. v. *Morales* (1992), 77 C.C.C. (3d) 91 at 107 (S.C.C.) [*Morales*].

71 R. v. *Pearson* (1992), 77 C.C.C. (3d) 124 (S.C.C.).

and justices of the peace rather than the whims of law enforcement officials. Cloaking whims in judicial robes is not sufficient to satisfy the principles of fundamental justice."[72] In 1997, Parliament responded by authorizing the denial of bail for "any other just cause . . . and, without limiting the generality of the foregoing, where detention is necessary in order to maintain confidence in the administration of justice, having regard to all the circumstances, including the apparent strength of the prosecution's case, the gravity of the nature of the offence, the circumstances surrounding its commission and the potential for a lengthy term of imprisonment."[73] The Supreme Court held that this provision, with the exception of the vague phrase "any other just cause" did not violate section 11(e) of the *Charter* because the maintenance of confidence in the administration of justice was a legitimate object of the bail system. Four judges dissented and argued that the new section was not fundamentally different from the prior and vague public interest ground and that it could allow an accused's liberty to be deprived on the basis of subjective and irrational fears by the public.[74]

If the accused has been arbitrarily detained, there is a limit to what the criminal court can do. If evidence was obtained, it can be excluded under section 24(2). A criminal court cannot award damages, but some courts might reduce the accused's sentence if convicted. Halting the prosecution by a stay of proceedings may be an option if the violation is very serious.

c) Right to Counsel

Section 10(b) of the *Charter* provides those who are subject to arrest or detention with both a right to retain and instruct counsel without delay and a right to be informed of that right. Detention has been interpreted broadly to include not only deprivation of liberty by physical constraint, but also the assumption of control over a person by a demand with significant legal consequences that would otherwise impede access to counsel and psychological compulsion in the form of a reasonable perception of a lack of freedom of choice. Even a brief five-minute detention in the back of a police car may require a right to counsel warning, if the police ask questions.[75] A person is detained when required to provide a breath sample, either at the roadside or at a police station. However, the denial of the right for counsel for a per-

---

72   *Morales*, above note 70 at 101.
73   *Code*, above note 1, s. 515(10) as am. by S.C. 1997, c. 18, s. 59.
74   *R. v. Hall* (2002), 167 C.C.C. (3d) 449 (S.C.C.).
75   *R. v. Elshaw* (1991), 67 C.C.C. (3d) 97 (S.C.C.).

son who must give a breath sample into a roadside screening device has been held to be justified under section 1 of the *Charter* as a reasonable limit required to combat drunk driving.[76] Nevertheless, a person facing a demand for a breath sample at the police station must be informed of his or her right to retain and instruct counsel without delay.[77]

Upon arrest or detention, the police must inform detainees not only that they can consult a lawyer, but also about the availability of publicly funded legal aid for those who cannot afford a lawyer and duty counsel who can provide temporary legal advice regardless of the suspect's financial status.[78] Most provinces have established toll-free telephone numbers that allow detainees to contact duty counsel on a twenty-four-hour basis. The police must generally inform detainees of available services, including the toll-free telephone number, but the Supreme Court has refused to require governments to establish such services despite evidence that they are efficient and practical.[79] The courts have also not required the police to videotape or audiotape interrogations.[80]

Once a detainee asks to speak to a lawyer, the police must facilitate access to counsel by offering the use of a telephone[81] and they cannot elicit evidence from the detainee. The police must hold off eliciting evidence until the suspect has had a reasonable opportunity to contact counsel. The detainee should be allowed, within reason, to consult a lawyer of his or her own choice and to consult with that lawyer in privacy. The detainee must, however, exercise the right to contact counsel with reasonable diligence.[82] Once an accused has been given a reasonable opportunity to consult counsel, questioning may resume without again informing the accused of the right to counsel or providing another reasonable opportunity to consult counsel.[83] This seems to apply even in cases where the accused and/or counsel have indicated a desire not to talk. The right to counsel may, however, be violated by prolonged questioning without counsel being present, police denigration of counsel, or the offer of a plea bargain without counsel being present.[84]

The accused's right to counsel can be subject to informed and voluntary waiver. A murder suspect who was too drunk to be aware of the

---

76 R. v. *Thomsen* (1988), 40 C.C.C. (3d) 411 (S.C.C.).

77 R. v. *Therens* (1985) 18 C.C.C. (3d) 481 (S.C.C.).

78 R. v. *Brydges* (1990), 53 C.C.C., (3d) 330 (S.C.C.) [*Brydges*].

79 R. v. *Prosper* (1994), 92 C.C.C. (3d) 353 (S.C.C.) [*Prosper*].

80 R. v. *Barrett* (1995), 96 C.C.C. (3d) 319 (S.C.C.).

81 R. v. *Manninen* (1987), 34 C.C.C. (3d) 385 (S.C.C.) [*Manninen*].

82 R. v. *Smith* (1989), 50 C.C.C. (3d) 308 (S.C.C.).

83 R. v. *Hebert* (1990), 57 C.C.C. (3d) 1 (S.C.C.) [*Hebert*].

84 R. v. *Burlingham* (1995), 97 C.C.C. (3d) 385 (S.C.C.) [*Burlingham*].

consequences cannot waive her rights to counsel.[85] Accused persons who answered baiting questions or participated in an line-up before being given a reasonable opportunity to consult counsel have not waived their right to counsel.[86] An accused who asked about legal aid, but was not informed about its availability, did not waive the right to counsel when he subsequently answered questions.[87] An accused who confessed after the police had insulted his counsel of choice also did not waive the right to counsel.[88] Evidence taken in violation of the right to counsel will generally be excluded as unconstitutionally obtained conscriptive evidence under section 24(2). The rationale is that the admission of such conscriptive evidence would render the trial unfair.[89]

Section 10(a) of the *Charter* also requires a person to be informed promptly of the reason for detention or arrest. This does not require an explicit warning if the matter being investigated was obvious.[90] The right was violated, however, when an accused was not aware that he was also held for a second more serious sexual assault[91] or when he believed he was being held for drug offences, not murder.[92] If an attempted murder becomes a murder after the victim dies, the accused should be so informed and have another opportunity to consult counsel.[93] There is no constitutional obligation to inform detainees of their right to silence, but such a warning is customary.

An independent right to silence under section 7 of the *Charter* may also be violated where the state tricks an accused under detention into making a statement by having an undercover officer or informant elicit a statement from him or her. Listening to an incriminating statement that was volunteered would not violate the right to silence.[94] The division between regulatory and criminal contexts is also relevant to the right to silence. A person who enters into a regulated environment may have to answer questions from state regulators, but such co-operation cannot be required when the Rubicon from regulation to prosecution

---

85   *R. v. Clarkson* (1986), 25 C.C.C. (3d) 207 (S.C.C.).
86   *Manninen*, above note 81; *R. v. Ross* (1989), 46 C.C.C. (3d) 129 (S.C.C.).
87   *Brydges*, above note 78.
88   *Burlingham*, above note 84.
89   *Prosper*, above note 79; *R. v. Bartle* (1994) 92 C.C.C. (3d) 289 (S.C.C.).
90   *R. v. Evans* (1991) 63 C.C.C. (3d) 289 (S.C.C.) [*Evans*].
91   *R. v. Borden* (1994) 92 C.C.C. (3d) 404 (S.C.C.).
92   *Evans*, above note 90.
93   *R. v. Black* (1989) 50 C.C.C. (3d) 1 (S.C.C.).
94   *Hebert*, above note 83; *R. v. Broyles* (1991), 68 C.C.C.(3d) 308 (S.C.C.); *R. v. Liew* (1999), 137 C.C.C. (3d) 353 (S.C.C.).

has been crossed and the dominant purpose of the inquiry is the determination of criminal liability.[95]

d) Entrapment

Before the advent of the *Charter*, Canadian courts were reluctant to recognize a defence of entrapment. In the 1982 case of *R. v. Amato*,[96] the Supreme Court affirmed a conviction for trafficking in narcotics even though an undercover police officer had persistently solicited the accused to sell him cocaine and made implied threats of violence. In a strong dissent, Estey J. concluded that entrapment should be recognized as a common law defence designed to ensure that the administration of justice is not brought into disrepute. He would have stayed proceedings because of the police conduct in the case. Six years later in *R. v. Mack*,[97] the Supreme Court recognized the defence of entrapment. The Court stressed that the defence could be available even though the accused committed the *actus reus* with the requisite degree of fault. A finding of entrapment results in a permanent stay of proceedings rather than an acquittal. Because it is a matter independent of guilt or innocence, entrapment must be established by the accused on a balance of probabilities, and the determination of entrapment can be left until after the accused's guilt has been established. The judge, rather than the jury, decides whether entrapment has been made out because the judge is the best person to determine whether the state's activities would bring the administration of justice into disrepute.

Entrapment occurs if the state offers a person an opportunity to commit a crime without reasonable suspicion that the person was engaged in criminal activity *or* while not engaged in a *bona fide* inquiry into crime in a high crime area. Even if there is a reasonable suspicion or a *bona fide* inquiry, entrapment will also occur if the state goes beyond providing the accused with an opportunity to commit a crime and actually induce its commission.

A reasonable suspicion is less than reasonable and probable grounds to believe a person has committed a specific crime. In *Mack*, the Court determined that the police acted with reasonable suspicion in conducting a six-month drug sting because the accused was a former drug user with several drug convictions and even though the accused told the police informer he was only interested in real estate. On the other hand, the police officer in *Barnes* who had a (correct)

---

95   *Jarvis*, above note 45 at para. 88.
96   (1982), 69 C.C.C. (2d) 31 (S.C.C.).
97   *R. v. Mack* (1988), 44 C.C.C. (3d) 513 (S.C.C.) [*Mack*].

hunch that a scruffily dressed male who looked around a lot was selling marijuana did not have a reasonable suspicion because her impressions of the suspect were too general and subjective.[98]

Even though the police did not have a reasonable suspicion and
engaged in random virtue testing in *Barnes*, the Supreme Court held
there was no entrapment because the police were acting pursuant to a
bona fide inquiry into criminal activity by offering a person an opportunity to commit the crime because he was present in a place (the
Granville Street Mall in Vancouver) associated with the particular criminal activity. McLachlin J. dissented on the basis that the high-crime
area was described very broadly and that insufficient attention had
been paid to the likelihood of the crime at the location targeted, its seriousness, the number of innocent people affected, and the availability of
less intrusive investigative techniques. In any event, the majority's
approach would allow random virtue testing of those found in areas
associated with drugs or prostitution. In other words, the police can
offer someone an opportunity to sell drugs or solicit prostitution simply because that person is in an area associated with that crime and
even if they do not have a reasonable suspicion that the person is
engaged in the particular crime.

Even if they have reasonable suspicion or are acting on a *bona fide*
inquiry, the police should never go beyond providing the suspect an
opportunity to commit a crime and actually induce the commission of
a crime. The police will go over this line if their conduct is so objectionable that it brings the administration of justice into disrepute and
would have induced an average person to have committed the crime. A
few phone calls to an old friend to set up a drug buy do not go over the
line, but persistent solicitation accompanied with veiled threats does.[99]
The courts will also examine the proportionality between the conduct
of the state and the accused and whether the state had instigated the
crime and exploited the accused. The fact that the police may have
acted illegally in selling the accused narcotics does not automatically
merit a stay unless the activity would shock the conscience of the community and be so detrimental to the proper administration of justice
that it warrants judicial intervention.[100] When determining whether the
state has gone beyond providing an opportunity, the focus is on the
propriety of the conduct of police and their agents. There may still be
entrapment even though the accused was predisposed to commit the

---

98 *R. v. Barnes* (1991), 63 C.C.C. (3d) 1 (S.C.C.).
99 *Mack*, above note 97; *R. v. Showman* (1988), 45 C.C.C. (3d) 289 (S.C.C.).
100 *R. v. Campbell* (1999), 133 C.C.C. (3d) 257 (S.C.C.).

crime and had the intent to commit the crime.[101] At the same time, the fact that the police or a state informant violated the law does not automatically result in entrapment and a stay of proceedings.[102] There will not be an entrapment defence, when the accused is entrapped into committing a crime by private individuals not acting for the state. Depending on the threats used, such an accused may nevertheless have a defence of duress. That defence is examined in chapter 8.

3) The *Charter* and the Criminal Trial Process

The *Charter* also plays an important role in the criminal trial process by ensuring that the trial is conducted in a fair manner. Section 7 of the *Charter* provides the basic guarantee that everyone has the right to life, liberty, and security of the person and that these rights can only be taken away "in accordance with the principles of fundamental justice." This broad guarantee affects all aspects of the criminal process, with section 11 of the *Charter* articulating specific rights possessed by any person charged with an offence. Section 11 includes the right to be tried within a reasonable time (11(b)); not to be compelled to be a witness in proceedings against that person in respect of the offence (11(c)); to be presumed innocent until proven guilty according to law in a fair and public hearing by an independent and impartial tribunal (11(d)); to trial by jury where the maximum punishment for the offence is imprisonment for five years or more (11(f)); and protection from double jeopardy (11(h)).

a) Disclosure
One of the most important rights in the criminal trial process is the Crown's obligation to disclose to the accused all relevant evidence in its possession. Disclosure is considered necessary to protect the accused's right to make full answer and defence under section 7 of the *Charter*. The Crown has a special obligation within an adversarial system of criminal justice to treat the accused fairly. The Supreme Court has explained:

> [T]he fruits of the investigation which are in the possession of counsel for the Crown are not the property of the Crown for use in securing a conviction but the property of the public to be used to ensure that justice is done. In contrast, the defence has no obligation to

---

101 *R. v. S.(J.)* (2001), 152 C.C.C. (3d) 317 (Ont. C.A.).
102 *R. v. Campbell* (1999), 133 C.C.C. (3d) 257 (S.C.C.) See now s. 25.1 of the *Criminal Code* authorizing the police to do acts that would otherwise constitute an offence.

assist the prosecution and is entitled to assume a purely adversarial role toward the prosecution.[103]

In general, all relevant evidence in the Crown's possession should be disclosed to the accused and there is no distinction between inculpatory and exculpatory evidence. Evidence disclosed to the defence will usually include statements that witnesses made to the police and physical evidence seized at the crime scene. The Crown can decide what evidence is relevant and can delay disclosure for legitimate reasons, such as protecting informers. In controversial decisions, the Supreme Court has ruled that the Crown must disclose to the accused all medical and therapeutic records in its possession without regard to the privacy and equality interests of complainants in sexual assault trials[104] and stayed proceedings because a rape crisis centre had shredded its records of an interview with a complainant.[105] Parliament has responded to these decisions with new legislation restricting the accused's access to the personal records of complainants in sexual assault cases including material in the Crown's possession. The legislation has been upheld as a reasonable balance of the accused's and complainant's rights.[106] Criminal courts may also award costs and order new trials as remedies for disclosure violations.[107]

b) Right to Full Answer and Defence

Section 7 of the *Charter* also has been interpreted to provide the accused with a right to make a full answer and defence in response to criminal charges. In general, the prejudice of evidence must substantially outweigh its probative value before the accused is prevented from calling evidence. In *R. v. Seaboyer*,[108] the Supreme Court held that section 277, which bans evidence about sexual reputation to challenge or support the credibility of the complainant in a sexual assault trial, did not violate section 7 because there was no logical link between one's sexual reputation and one's truthfulness. The Court did, however, find that a "rape shield" provision that restricted the admissibility of the complainant's prior sexual conduct with people other than the accused

---

103 R. v. *Stinchcombe* (1991), 68 C.C.C. (3d) 1 at 7 (S.C.C.).
104 R. v. *O'Connor* (1995), 103 C.C.C. (3d) 1 (S.C.C.).
105 R. v. *Carosella* (1997), 112 C.C.C. (3d) 289 (S.C.C.).
106 *Code*, above note 1, ss. 278.1–278.89. Upheld in R. v. *Mills*, [1999] 3 S.C.R. 668.
107 R. v. *974649 Ontario Inc.* (2001), 159 C.C.C. (3d) 321 (S.C.C.); R. v. *Taillefer*, [2003] 3 S.C.R. 307.
108 (1991), 66 C.C.C. (3d) 321 (S.C.C.).

did violate the accused's right to make full answer and defence in part because such conduct might be relevant to the controversial defence that the accused honestly but perhaps not reasonably had a mistaken belief that the complainant consented. Parliament responded to this ruling by modifying the mistaken belief in consent defence and by establishing a new procedure that requires judges to balance the accused's right to make full answer and defence against other factors, including society's interest in encouraging the reporting of sexual assaults, the need to remove discriminatory bias from fact-finding and potential prejudice to the complainant's rights of privacy, personal security, and the full protection and benefit of the law.[109] This new provision has been held to be consistent with the accused's rights.[110]

c)   Trial in a Reasonable Time

An important right in the pre-trial process is the Crown's obligation under section 11(b) of the *Charter* to provide a trial in a reasonable time. If the accused's section 11(b) right is violated, the accused is entitled to a stay of proceedings.[111] This right does not usually apply to delay before a charge is laid, and there is no statute of limitations that prevents the prosecution of indictable offences committed long ago.[112] Courts have allowed charges to proceed even though the allegations relate to matters that occurred decades ago.[113] A stay of proceedings might be entered if the passage of time has made it impossible for the accused to exercise the right to full answer and defence because of the unavailability of crucial evidence.[114]

Whether the accused's right to a trial in a reasonable time has been violated depends on the length of the delay (delays of more than eight to ten months can be suspect) and the explanation for the delay (some delays may be attributable to the accused, but systemic delay caused by a backlog of cases and unavailability of judges is charged to the Crown). It also depends on whether the accused has waived his or her rights by consenting to the delay, and whether the accused has suffered preju-

---

109   *Code*, above note 1, s. 276.

110   *R. v. Darrach* (2000), 148 C.C.C. (3d) 97 (S.C.C.) [*Darrach*].

111   *R. v. Askov* (1990), 59 C.C.C. (3d) 449 (S.C.C.).

112   There is a six-month statute of limitations on less serious summary conviction offences but this can be waived with the agreement of the prosecutor and the accused. The accused might agree to waive the limitation in cases in which the prosecutor has the discretion to lay the charge as a more serious indictable offence. *Code*, above note 1, s. 786(2).

113   *R. v. L.(W.K.)* (1991), 64 C.C.C. (3d) 321 (S.C.C.).

114   *R. v. MacDonnell* (1997), 114 C.C.C. (3d) 145 (S.C.C.).

dice. This latter factor has been stressed more in cases after the 1990 *Askov* decision indicating that delays beyond six to eight months were unreasonable led to the stay of more than 50,000 charges.[115]

d) Pre-trial Publicity

Courts can order that evidence heard at bail hearings or at preliminary inquiries, or when a jury is not in the courtroom, not be published until after a trial in order to protect the accused's right to fair trial.[116] Courts should attempt to harmonize the public's right to freedom of expression with the accused's right to a fair trial by devising, where possible, alternatives short of publication bans.[117] Alternatives include adjournments of trials; changing the location or venue of the trial to where there has been less publicity; allowing the accused to question prospective jurors more closely; sequestering juries and instructing them to disregard matters that they heard outside the courtroom. Even if a publication ban is the only way to protect the accused's right to a fair trial, it must be as limited in scope and time as possible, and the Court must determine that the good achieved by the ban in protecting a fair trial outweighs the harm the ban causes to freedom of expression.

e) Right to a Jury Trial

An accused who faces five years of imprisonment or more has a right to trial by jury under section 11(f). If the accused fails to appear for trial, however, he or she can subsequently be denied trial by jury.[118] If the accused is charged with an indictable offence that is not listed in section 553 of the *Criminal Code*, he or she may elect or select a trial by jury. A jury is composed of twelve citizens who should represent a fair cross-sample of the public in the place where the case is tried. It is possible, however, to have a jury trial moved to another location within the province.[119] In selecting the jury, the Crown and the accused can challenge prospective jurors for cause, with the most important ground being that the person is not indifferent between the Crown and the accused. They can ask prospective jurors questions provided a judge has decided that the questions respond to a realistic potential for partiality.[120] The last two jurors called, as opposed to the judge, determine

---

115 *R. v. Morin* (1992), 71 C.C.C. (3d) 1 (S.C.C.).
116 *Code*, above note 1, ss. 517, 539, and 648.
117 *Dagenais v. Canadian Broadcasting Corp.* (1994), 94 C.C.C. (3d) 289 (S.C.C.).
118 *R. v. Lee* (1989) 52 C.C.C. (3d) 289 (S.C.C.).
119 *Code*, above note 1, s. 599.
120 *R. v. Williams* (1998), 124 C.C.C. (3d) 481 (S.C.C.).

whether the next juror is impartial. The accused and the Crown each
have the same limited number of peremptory challenges they can use to
remove prospective jurors without giving any reasons.[121] The jury delib-
erates in secret and they must agree unanimously to a verdict of guilt or
innocence. If they cannot agree, they are a "hung jury" and a new trial
may be held. Except in limited circumstances, it is a criminal offence for
a juror to disclose information about the jury's deliberations.[122]

Section 11(d) protects the right to a fair and public hearing by an
independent and impartial tribunal. Judges must have security of
tenure, and can only be removed for cause related to their capacity to
perform judicial functions. They must also have financial security and
independence over their administration as it bears directly upon the
exercise of their judicial function. Provincial court judges and even
part-time judges have been held to be sufficiently independent, but
military officers acting as court martial judges have not.

The accused's right to a fair trial will in more complex cases include
a right to have a lawyer if the accused cannot afford one. In such cases,
courts can stay proceedings until a lawyer is appointed or order that
counsel be provided. The accused also has a right to effective assistance
of counsel. To violate that right, however, it is necessary that the accused
establish both that the performance by the lawyer was unreasonable and
that it caused prejudice in the form of a miscarriage of justice.[123]

g) Right to Be Presumed Innocent

Section 11(d) also provides that the accused has the right "to be presumed innocent until proven guilty according to law in a fair and public hearing by an independent and impartial tribunal." The first part of
the right embraces the presumption of innocence, which has been
referred to as the "one golden thread" running "throughout the web of
the English common law."[124] The presumption of innocence refers to
the burden placed on the Crown to prove the accused's guilt. It also
includes the requirement that the Crown prove guilt by a high degree
or quantum of proof. Chief Justice Dickson has stated that "[t]he presumption of innocence confirms our faith in humankind; it reflects our

---

121 *Code*, above note 1, s. 634. The accused's right to a fair trial was violated by previous provisions that effectively gave the Crown over four times as many
peremptory challenges as the accused. *R. v. Bain* (1992), 69 C.C.C. (3d) 481
(S.C.C.).
122 *Code*, above note 1, s. 649.
123 *R. v. B.(G.D.)* (2000), 143 C.C.C. (3d) 289 (S.C.C.).
124 *Woolmington v. D.P.P.*, [1935] A.C. 462 at 481 (H.L.).

belief that individuals are decent and law-abiding members of the community until proven otherwise."[125]

i)   Quantum of Proof

Proof beyond a reasonable doubt is not easily defined, but it requires the Crown to go beyond the burden used in private law cases of proving that something is more probable than not. If proof on a balance of probabilities as required in civil cases (and when an accused in a criminal trial bears a reverse onus) represents something like a "51 percent rule," then proof beyond a reasonable doubt requires the Crown to establish a significantly higher likelihood that the crime was committed. This mathematical analogy is quite rough and ready and should not be used by judges in their directions to juries.

In R. v. Lifchus,[126] the Supreme Court held that the meaning of reasonable doubt must be explained to a jury and undertook that difficult task. The Court indicated that the jury should be told that the reasonable doubt standard is related to the presumption of innocence. It requires more than proof that the accused is probably guilty, but does not require proof to an absolute certainty. A reasonable doubt is not a frivolous or imaginary doubt, but rather a doubt based on reason and common sense that must logically be derived from evidence or absence of evidence. It is not an imaginary or frivolous doubt nor one based on sympathy or prejudice. The Supreme Court approved of the following suggested charge to the jury which explains the meaning of a reasonable doubt and relates it to the presumption of innocence.

> The accused enters these proceedings presumed to be innocent. That presumption of innocence remains throughout the case until such time as the Crown has on the evidence put before you satisfied you beyond a reasonable doubt that the accused is guilty.
>
> What does the expression "beyond a reasonable doubt" mean?
>
> The term "beyond a reasonable doubt" has been used for a very long time and is a part of our history and traditions of justice. It is so engrained in our criminal law that some think it needs no explanation, yet something must be said regarding its meaning.
>
> A reasonable doubt is not an imaginary or frivolous doubt. It must not be based upon sympathy or prejudice. Rather, it is based on reason and common sense. It is logically derived from the evidence or absence of evidence.

---

125 R. v. Oakes (1986), 24 C.C.C. (3d) 321 at 333–34 (S.C.C.) [Oakes].
126 (1997), 118 C.C.C. (3d) 1 (S.C.C.).

Even if you believe the accused is probably guilty or likely guilty, that is not sufficient. In those circumstances you must give the benefit of the doubt to the accused and acquit because the Crown has failed to satisfy you of the guilt of the accused beyond a reasonable doubt.

On the other hand you must remember that it is virtually impossible to prove anything to an absolute certainty and the Crown is not required to do so. Such a standard of proof is impossibly high.

In short if, based upon the evidence before the Court, you are sure that the accused committed the offence you should convict since this demonstrates that you are satisfied of his guilt beyond a reasonable doubt.[127]

In *R. v. Starr*,[128] a majority of the Supreme Court held that trial judges would err if they did not make clear to the jury that the reasonable doubt standard was much closer to absolute certainty than the balance of probabilities standard used in civil trials and everyday life.

ii) *Persuasive Burdens*

The presumption of innocence is infringed whenever the accused is liable to be convicted despite the existence of a reasonable doubt about a factor essential for conviction. In *Oakes*, section 11(d) was violated by a statutory provision that required, once the Crown had proven beyond a reasonable doubt the possession of narcotics, that the accused establish on a balance of probabilities that he or she did not have the intent to traffic in order to escape a conviction for the offence of possession of narcotics with the intent to traffic. Dickson C.J. explained how the provision could allow a conviction despite a reasonable doubt:

> If an accused bears the burden of disproving on a balance of probabilities an essential element of an offence, it would be possible for a conviction to occur despite the existence of a reasonable doubt. This would arise if the accused adduced sufficient evidence to raise a reasonable doubt as to his or her innocence but did not convince the jury on a balance of probabilities that the presumed fact was untrue.[129]

Another approach is to examine the relationship between the element that the Crown proves (in this case, possession of narcotics) and the element that is presumed (in this case, the intent to traffic in the narcotics) unless the accused satisfies the burden placed upon him or

---

127 *Ibid.* at 14.
128 (2000), 147 C.C.C.(3d) 449 (S.C.C.).
129 *Oakes*, above note 125 at 343.

her. The substitution of one element for an essential element of an offence violates section 11(d) unless "if upon proof beyond reasonable doubt of the substituted element it would be unreasonable for the trier of fact not to be satisfied beyond a reasonable doubt of the essential element."[130] In *Oakes*, there was not this extremely close or inexorable link between what was proved (possession of narcotics) and what was presumed (intent to traffic), and the provision violated section 11(d). In many cases, the jury may have been satisfied beyond a reasonable doubt that the accused had the intent to traffic upon proof of possession of a large quantity of narcotics. The problem was that the provision stated that the jury must draw such a conclusion in all cases. This would include those where the accused failed to provide enough evidence to prove on a balance of probabilities that there was no intent to traffic, but the jury still had a reasonable doubt about the intent to traffic. An important purpose of the presumption of innocence is to ensure that the jury always has the ability to find a reasonable doubt on the basis of any evidence in the case.

iii) Presumption Applies to Elements of Offences, Collateral Factors, and Defences

The presumption of innocence applies not only to essential elements of an offence but to defences and collateral factors. This makes sense once it is recognized that whether something is an element of an offence, a defence, or a collateral matter is a simple matter of legislative drafting. For example, murder could be redrafted to include all killings, with the accused then having the ability to establish on a balance of probabilities a defence of a lack of intent to kill. Similarly, Parliament could provide that the intent to kill be presumed unless the accused established a collateral factor such as the victim's death was unavoidable. If the presumption of innocence was not applied to these defences and factors, the accused could still be convicted despite a reasonable doubt as to his or her guilt. As Dickson C.J. has explained:

> The exact characterization of a factor as an essential element, a collateral factor, an excuse, or a defence should not affect the analysis of the presumption of innocence. It is the final effect of a provision on the verdict that is decisive. If an accused is required to prove some fact on the balance of probabilities to avoid conviction, the provision violates the presumption of innocence because it permits a convic-

---

130 *R. v. Vaillancourt* (1987), 39 C.C.C. (3d) 118 at 136 (S.C.C.) [*Vaillancourt*].

tion in spite of a reasonable doubt in the mind of the trier of fact as to the guilt of the accused.[131]

In *Whyte*, the Court examined a provision that required an accused found in the driver's seat while intoxicated to prove an absence of intent to put the vehicle in motion in order to escape a presumption that the accused was in care and control of the vehicle. This provision violated section 11(d) because it required the accused to be convicted even if he or she was able to raise a reasonable doubt about the intent to put the vehicle in motion, but was unable to prove on a balance of probabilities that there was no such intent. This, in turn, triggered a mandatory presumption that the accused was in care and control of the vehicle, which was an essential element of the offence of care and control of a vehicle while impaired. Looked at another way, proof of the substituted fact (being in the driver's seat), plus the accused's inability to prove on a balance of probabilities that there was no intent to drive the car, did not lead inexorably to the conclusion that the presumed fact (care and control) exists. The accused could be convicted even though there was a reasonable doubt about whether he was guilty.

Subsequent to *Whyte*, the Court has held that requiring an accused to prove a defence on a balance of probabilities violates section 11(d) because it allows a conviction despite a reasonable doubt about a factor essential for a conviction. For example, section 319(3) of the *Criminal Code* violates section 11(d) because it requires the accused to prove on a balance of probabilities the defence of truth when charged with a hate propaganda offence. The accused could be convicted even though there was a reasonable doubt that his or her statements were true.[132] Requirements that an accused prove a defence of due diligence when charged with a regulatory offence violates section 11(d), because the accused could be convicted even though there was a reasonable doubt that he or she was negligent.[133] Similarly, a requirement that the accused establish the mental disorder defence on a balance of probabilities also violates section 11(d), because the accused could be convicted despite a reasonable doubt about his or her sanity.[134] In all these cases, however, the Court found that the legislation was justified under section 1 of the *Charter* as a reasonable limit on section 11(d), because

---

131 *R. v. Whyte* (1988), 42 C.C.C. (3d) 97 at 109 (S.C.C.).
132 *R. v. Keegstra* (1990), 61 C.C.C. (3d) 1 (S.C.C.) [*Keegstra*].
133 *R. v. Wholesale Travel Group Inc.* (1991), 67 C.C.C. (3d) 193 (S.C.C.) [*Wholesale Travel Group*].
134 *R. v. Chaulk* (1990), 62 C.C.C. (3d) 193 (S.C.C.).

of the difficulties of requiring the Crown to prove beyond a reasonable doubt that the accused did not have the respective defences.

To justify an infringement of section 11(d) or any *Charter* right under section 1 of the *Charter*, the Crown must demonstrate that the objective of the limit is a compelling objective. Moreover, the Crown must then show that there is a rational connection between the violation and the objective. In *R. v. Laba*,[135] the Supreme Court held that it is not necessary for there to be a rational connection between the proven and the presumed factors for a reverse onus to be justified under section 1 of the *Charter*. The Court did note, however, that the lack of a rational connection between the proven and presumed factors would increase the danger of convicting the innocent.[136] Even if the section 11(d) violation is rationally connected with a compelling objective, it must also be the least restrictive means of advancing the objective, and there must be proportionality between the objective and the rights violation. In *Laba*, the Court held that a reverse onus requiring a seller of precious metals to prove legal ownership was not a proportionate limitation on the presumption of innocence because the objective of deterring the theft of such metals could be as effectively advanced by the less restrictive alternative of requiring the accused to meet an evidential burden as to the presence of legal authorization. Once the accused pointed to some evidence of legal authorization, the Crown would still have to prove beyond a reasonable doubt that the accused did not have such authorization. An evidential burden is a less restrictive alternative to a persuasive burden, even though, as will be seen, it also violates section 11(d) if accompanied by a mandatory presumption.

The courts have on their own initiative imposed persuasive burdens on the accused. In the pre-*Charter* case of *R. v. Sault Ste. Marie (City)*,[137] the Supreme Court imposed a persuasive burden on the accused to establish a new defence of due diligence to strict liability offences. If the accused did not establish this defence, it would be presumed to have been negligent in allowing the *actus reus* to have

---

135 *R. v. Laba* (1994), 94 C.C.C. (3d) 385 at 417 (S.C.C.) [*Laba*].

136 A rational connection between the proven and the presumed fact would not be sufficient under section 11(d) of the *Charter*, above note 33, because it means only that upon proof of the proven fact, it is probable that the presumed fact was present. Section 11(d) contemplates that the Crown prove its case beyond a reasonable doubt, not on a simple balance of probabilities. In other words, s. 11(d) requires an inexorable connection between the proven element and the presumed element, a condition that would make it unreasonable for the jury to have even a reasonable doubt about the presumed factor.

137 (1978), 40 C.C.C. (3d) 353 (S.C.C.).

occurred. The Court also reasoned that the accused was in a good position to prove due diligence. Even after the *Charter* entrenched the presumption of innocence, courts have imposed burdens on the accused. In *R. v. Daviault*,[138] the Supreme Court imposed a persuasive burden on the accused to prove a defence of extreme intoxication to a general intent offence such as manslaughter or assault, even though the traditional defence of intoxication applies whenever there was a reasonable doubt that the accused had the intent for a specific intent offence such as murder or robbery. In *R. v. Stone*,[139] the Court again on its own initiative held that the accused must establish the defence of non-mental disorder automatism on a balance of probabilities. Thus, an accused no longer will have the benefit of a reasonable doubt that he or she acted in an involuntary manner because of a condition such as sleepwalking or a severe physical or emotional blow. The Court was concerned about consistency in the law and noted that the accused already had to establish the mental disorder and extreme intoxication defences on a balance of probabilities.

In many recent cases, the presumption of innocence seems to be honoured more in its breach. This makes it easier for the Crown to obtain a conviction, but it also opens the possibility for a conviction even though there may be a reasonable doubt that the accused was not guilty.

iv) Evidential Burdens and Mandatory Presumptions

The Supreme Court has held that section 11(d) is violated not only by persuasive burdens that require an accused to prove some factor on a balance of probabilities, but also by evidential burdens that only require the accused to point to evidence to raise a reasonable doubt about a mandatory presumption. In *R. v. Downey*,[140] the Court held that a provision violated section 11(d) when it required the trier of fact to conclude "in the absence of evidence to the contrary" that an accused was guilty of the offence of living off the avails of prostitution once the prosecution had proven that the accused was habitually in the company of prostitutes. Cory J. stressed: "the fact that someone lives with a prostitute does not lead inexorably to the conclusion that the person is living off the avails."[141] This mandatory presumption violated section 11(d), even though it could be displaced by an accused pointing to

---

138 *R. v. Daviault* (1994), 93 C.C.C. (3d) 21 (S.C.C.) [*Daviault*].
139 *R. v. Stone* (1999), 134 C.C.C. (3d) 353 (S.C.C.) [*Stone*].
140 (1992), 72 C.C.C. (3d) 1 (S.C.C.).
141 *Ibid.* at 14.

some evidence in either the Crown's or the accused's case to raise a reasonable doubt as to the presumed fact and did not require the accused to establish on a balance of probabilities that he did not live off the avails of prostitution. The Court, however, held that the mandatory presumption that could be displaced by satisfying an evidential burden was justified under section 1 of the *Charter* because of the difficulties of requiring prostitutes to testify against their pimps and the ease that a person in a lawful relationship with a prostitute would have in pointing to some evidence that could raise a reasonable doubt about the presumption.[142]

v) Threshold "Air of Reality" Tests

The above combination of an evidential burden with a mandatory presumption should be distinguished from the requirement that there be an air of reality to justify the judge in instructing the jury about a particular issue or defence. These sorts of evidential burdens are quite common. They do not require the accused to prove anything and they make no mandatory presumptions about the commission of the crime. They have generally been seen as a matter of efficient and orderly trial administration and not as raising any presumption of innocence problems.

At the same time, air of reality tests can be quite important and determine the practical meaning of a particular defence. For example, the administration of the defence of mistaken belief in the complainant's consent in sexual assault cases often depends on whether there is an air of reality to justify instructing the jury about the controversial defence.[143]

The air of reality test may also be influenced by whether the accused bears a persuasive burden on the issue. In both *Daviault*[144] and *Stone*,[145] the Court indicated that in order to establish an air of reality about the extreme intoxication and automatism defences respectively, the accused must point to evidence upon which a properly instructed jury will find that the defence has been established on a balance of probabilities. The holding in *Stone* has been qualified in the subsequent case of *Fontaine*[146] in which the Court stressed that the judge should

---

142 Three judges dissented on the basis that there was not only no inexorable but also no rational connection between the proven fact (living with a prostitute) and the presumed fact (living off the avails). The requirement of such a connection under s. 1 has now been rejected in *Laba*, above note 135.

143 See ch. 4, "Mistake of Fact and Sexual Assault."

144 *Daviault*, above note 138.

145 *Stone*, above note 139 at 430.

146 2004 SCC 27.

not determine whether evidence is credible or will support proof by the accused on a balance of probabilities of a defence such as extreme intoxication or automatism. Fish J. stated that the threshold air of reality test is not "intended to assess whether the defence is likely, unlikely, somewhat unlikely or very likely to succeed at the end of the day. The question for the trial judge is whether the evidence discloses a real issue to be decided by the jury and not how the jury should ultimately decide the issue. The 'air of reality' test . . . should not be used to. . . . introduce a persuasive requirement."[147] The Court also noted that "the cost of risking a wrongful conviction and possibly violating the accused's constitutionally protected rights by inadvisably withdrawing a defence from the jury is a high one."[148]

In *R. v. Cinous*,[149] a majority of the Supreme Court indicated that a consistent air of reality test should be applied throughout the criminal law and it justified not instructing the jury about a particular defence if there was no evidence that a properly instructed jury acting reasonably could acquit on the basis of the evidence. In *Fontaine*,[150] a unanimous Court similarly stated: "In determining whether the evidential burden has been discharged on any defence, trial judges, as a matter of judicial policy, should therefore always ask the very same question: Is there in the record any evidence upon which a reasonable trier of fact, properly instructed and acting judicially, could conclude that the defence succeeds?" Although the Court in both cases stressed that the accused did not have a persuasive burden to overcome the air of reality test and that the credibility of evidence should be left to the jury, decisions about whether there is an air of reality about a particular defence can be very important in a criminal trial. The air of reality test for each defence depends on the necessary elements of the particular defence and will be discussed in relation to various defences in chapters 6 through 8.

vi) Summary
Section 11(d) of the *Charter* has been interpreted broadly, so that it is violated any time a statutory provision allows an accused to be convicted in the face of a reasonable doubt as to any factor essential to conviction, including any applicable defences. It also has been interpreted to apply to evidential burdens that only require the accused to point to

---

147 *Ibid.* at paras. 68 and 70.
148 *Ibid.* at para. 61 quoting Arbour J. in dissent in *R. v. Cinous* (2002) 162 C.C.C. (3d) 129 at para. 200 (S.C.C.).
149 (2002), 162 C.C.C. (3d) 129 (S.C.C.).
150 2004 SCC 27 at para. 57.

some evidence to raise a reasonable doubt about a mandatory presumption. At the same time, however, the courts frequently uphold violations of section 11(d) under section 1 of the *Charter* and have on their own initiative imposed a persuasive burden on the accused to establish the defences of extreme intoxication and automatism. Statutory requirements that the accused prove the defence of due diligence in regulatory offences or the defences of mental disorder have also been upheld on the basis that it would be too difficult for the Crown to prove beyond a reasonable doubt that the defence did not apply. There need not be a rational connection between the proven and presumed factors for a presumption to be upheld under section 1 of the *Charter*. Even though an evidential burden with a mandatory presumption itself violates section 11(d), it can be a less drastic alternative to a persuasive burden.

h) Other Trial Rights

Accused have the right in section 14 of the *Charter* to continuous, competent, and contemporaneous interpretation at trial if they are deaf or do not understand or speak the language in which the proceedings are conducted.[151] Under section 11(c), accused cannot be compelled to testify in their own trials. This protection does not extend to corporations and an officer of a corporation can be compelled to testify against his or her corporation.[152] It also generally does not require judges to instruct juries that they should not draw adverse inferences from the accused's failure to testify.[153] It is not violated by requirements that the accused apply and provide detailed particulars when he wishes to introduce evidence of a complainant's prior sexual conduct in a sexual offence trial.[154]

Under section 13, evidence that an accused gave as a witness in a prior proceeding cannot be used to incriminate him or her "except in a prosecution for perjury or for the giving of contradictory evidence." A person can generally be forced to testify in other proceedings such as the trial of another person or at a public inquiry, but evidence derived from such testimony cannot be admitted in a subsequent trial against that person unless the Crown can demonstrate that it could have been discovered without forcing the accused to participate in his or her own self-incrimination.

---

151 R. v. *Tran* (1994), 92 C.C.C. (3d) 218 (S.C.C.).
152 R. v. *Amway Corp.*, [1989] 1 S.C.R. 21.
153 R. v. *Boss* (1988) 46 C.C.C. (3d) 523 (S.C.C.).
154 *Darrach*, above note 110.

Other *Charter* rights are designed to protect the principle of legality by requiring that a person charged with an offence has the right "to be informed without unreasonable delay of the specific offence" (section 11(a)). Section 11(i) protects the accused against the burden of retroactive criminal laws, as does section 11(g), which provides that the accused has the right not to be found guilty unless the act or omission at the time it was committed was an offence under Canadian law or international law, or was criminal according to the general principles of law recognized by the community of nations. The latter phrase was included to allow for the prosecution of war crimes committed in other nations, and such legislation has been upheld under the *Charter*.[155] At the same time, the Court indicated that because of the special stigma of such crimes, the Crown must prove the accused knew or was wilfully blind to facts and circumstances that would bring his acts within the definition of war crimes or crimes against humanity.[156]

4) The *Charter* and Substantive Criminal Offences and Defences

Although they have been primarily concerned with the procedural fairness of investigations and prosecutions, courts under the *Charter* have also evaluated the substance of offences. An accused cannot be convicted if the criminal offence itself results in an unjustified violation of one of the rights guaranteed by the *Charter*. Criminal offences have generally been challenged on the grounds that they violated fundamental freedoms, such as freedom of expression, or the principles of fundamental justice.

a) Fundamental Freedoms
Section 2(b) of the *Charter* has been interpreted broadly to include protection for all forms of expression short of violence. At the same time, however, the courts have recognized that criminal prohibitions on some types of expression can be justified as a reasonable limit under section 1 of the *Charter*.

A criminal offence prohibiting solicitation in a public place for the purpose of prostitution has been held to violate freedom of expression, but to be justified as a reasonable response to "the social nuisance of

---

155 *R. v. Finta* (1994), 88 C.C.C. (3d) 417 (S.C.C.) [*Finta*].
156 *Ibid.* at 503.

street solicitation."[157] The restriction in section 163 of the *Criminal Code* on the making and distribution of obscene materials also has been found to violate freedom of expression. This restriction, however, is a reasonable limit on freedom of expression provided it is interpreted not to "proscribe sexually explicit erotica without violence that is not degrading or dehumanizing."[158] The Supreme Court has indicated that the criminal law cannot be used to enforce morality per se, but that it can act to respond to Parliament's "reasoned apprehension of harm" even if the causal links between the expression and the harm of violence against women and children are not conclusive. The Court also approved of the use of the criminal law "to enhance respect for all members of society, and non-violence and equality in their relations with each other," especially as this relates to the enforcement of "*Charter* values" such as equality.[159] The Court has subsequently held that a peep show in which patrons in a private room could masturbate but not touch nude dancers[160] was not indecent, whereas lap dancing in a public room which involved touching was indecent because it was degrading and dehumanizing.[161] The crime of possession of child pornography that depicts a person under eighteen years of age in explicit sexual activity or which encourages unlawful sexual activity with those under eighteen years of age has been held to be a reasonable limit on freedom of expression. The Supreme Court, however, indicated that defences of artistic merit, educational, scientific, or medical purpose or the public good should be liberally interpreted to protect freedom of expression. In addition, exceptions for expressive material created and held privately and for consensual visual recordings of lawful sexual activity that are held privately and not distributed publicly were read into the offence by the Court in order to protect freedom of expression and privacy.[162]

A provision prohibiting the wilful promotion of hatred against an identifiable group has been held to be a reasonable limit on freedom of expression. Dickson C.J. stressed that the requirements that the accused have the intent of wilfully promoting hatred and that the Attorney General approve any prosecution restrict the reach of the provision. He also argued that Parliament can act to prevent the serious harms

---

157 *Reference re ss. 193 & 195.1(1)(c) of the Criminal Code (Canada)* (1990), 56 C.C.C. (3d) 65 at 77 (S.C.C.).

158 *R. v. Butler* (1992), 70 C.C.C. (3d) 129 at 165 (S.C.C.).

159 *Ibid.* at 168.

160 *R. v. Tremblay* (1993), 84 C.C.C. (3d) 97 (S.C.C.).

161 *R. v. Mara* (1997), 115 C.C.C. (3d) 539 (S.C.C.).

162 *R. v. Sharpe*, [2001] 1 S.C.R. 45.

caused by racial and religious hatred and to respond to "the severe psychological trauma suffered by members of those identifiable groups targeted by hate propaganda."[163] Two years later, the Supreme Court struck down a provision prohibiting wilfully spreading false news that is likely to injure the public interest. McLachlin J. argued that although the provision could be used to prohibit statements, such as the accused's denial of the Holocaust, which denigrate vulnerable groups:

> Its danger, however, lies in the fact that by its broad reach it criminalizes a vast penumbra of other statements merely because they might be thought to constitute a mischief to some public interest, however successive prosecutors and courts may wish to define these terms. The danger is magnified because the prohibition affects not only those caught and prosecuted, but those who may refrain from saying what they would like to because of the fear that they will be caught.[164]

This provision was struck down because it was broader and less narrowly tailored than the hate propaganda provision examined above. The crime of defamatory libel was also upheld as a justified restriction on freedom of expression, given the need to protect reputations and to establish that the accused intended to make defamatory statements.[165]

In summary, an offence that prohibits any form of expression short of violence will likely violate freedom of expression. Depending on the objective and reach of the offence, however, the courts may find it to be a reasonable limit on expression that can be justified under section 1 of the *Charter*.

b) Principles of Fundamental Justice

Section 7 of the *Charter* provides that "everyone has the right to life, liberty, and security of the person and the right not to be deprived thereof except in accordance with the principles of fundamental justice." Corporations are not entities that enjoy rights to life, liberty, and security of the person.[166] Nevertheless, courts have allowed corporations to challenge offences that they are charged with on the basis that the offence can also apply to natural persons who enjoy rights under section 7 of the *Charter*.[167] A corporation should be precluded from bringing a section 7 challenge to provisions that only apply to corpora-

---

163 *Keegstra*, above note 132 at 58.
164 *R. v. Zundel* (1992), 75 C.C.C. (3d) 449 at 521 (S.C.C.).
165 *R. v. Lucas* (1998), 123 C.C.C. (3d) 97 (S.C.C.).
166 *Irwin Toy Ltd. v. Quebec (Attorney General)*, [1989] 1 S.C.R. 927.
167 *Wholesale Travel Group*, above note 133.

tions,[168] because section 7 of the *Charter* does not protect the principles of fundamental justice in the abstract, but only in cases where a human being is deprived of the right to life, liberty, and security of the person.

Criminal offences have been struck down under section 7 of the *Charter* as deprivations of liberty and security of the person that are not in accordance with the principles of fundamental justice. The most famous case is *R. v. Morgentaler (No. 2)*,[169] in which the Supreme Court found that a law that made it a criminal offence to obtain or provide an abortion without the approval of a hospital committee violated section 7 of the *Charter* and could not be justified under section 1 of the *Charter*. The majority stressed that the law was procedurally unfair to women because of geographic variations in the availability of committees and delays in the process of committee approval. This unfairness was especially significant because committee approval was necessary if a person was to avoid conviction of a criminal offence for either performing or having an abortion. Dickson C.J. stressed the vagueness of the requirement that the committee conclude that the continuation of the pregnancy would likely endanger the woman's life or health. Beetz J. did not think this was too vague, but believed that the provision violated section 7 of the *Charter* because it required delays that were not rationally connected to either the protection of the fetus or the life and health of the pregnant woman. Wilson J. took a more substantive approach and argued that it was a matter of a woman's conscience whether or not to have an abortion and that the state could regulate this decision only in the later stages of the pregnancy. Two judges dissented on the grounds that the law did not violate constitutional rights and the availability of abortions was a matter of policy for the elected legislature.

In *Rodriguez v. British Columbia (A.G.)*,[170] a 5 to 4 majority of the Supreme Court upheld section 241(b) of the *Criminal Code*, which prohibits a person from assisting a suicide. The majority concluded that the provision affected the applicant's security of the person because it prevented her from receiving assistance in taking her life. However, it did not violate the principles of fundamental justice because of a consensus about the value of protecting human life. In dissent, two judges argued that, following the principles of *Morgentaler*, Sue Rodriguez should be able to make the decision to terminate her own life, while

---

168 See, e.g., *Code*, above note 1, ss. 22.1–22.2 on organizational liability, which is discussed in ch. 5, "Regulatory Offences and Corporate Crime."
169 *R. v. Morgentaler (No. 2)* (1988), 37 C.C.C. (3d) 449 (S.C.C.) [*Morgentaler (No. 2)*].
170 (1993), 85 C.C.C. (3d) 15 (S.C.C.).

two others argued that the law discriminated against her because of a physical disability that would eventually prevent her from committing suicide without assistance from another person. The Supreme Court has held that smoking marijuana does not engage either protected liberty[171] or privacy[172] interests under section 7 of the *Charter*.

c) Vagueness

The principles of fundamental justice in section 7 of the *Charter* are offended by offences that are so vague or overbroad that they fail to give fair notice to citizens and provide no limit for law enforcement discretion. As this doctrine relates to the manner in which the courts have defined the criminal act, it will be discussed in chapter 2, which examines the definition and interpretation of the criminal act. It should be noted, however, that courts are very reluctant to hold that criminal offences or defences are unconstitutionally vague and they make allowances for the ability of courts to add an interpretative gloss on vague words such as "undue" or "reasonable."

A law's vagueness may also be a consideration in determining if the law violates a *Charter* right or can be justified under section 1 of the *Charter*. A limitation on a *Charter* right under section 1 must be "prescribed by law" and provide an intelligible standard to determine the manner in which the legislature has limited a *Charter* right.

d) Gross Disproportionality

In *R. v. Malmo-Levine*,[173] the Supreme Court considered whether section 7 of the *Charter* restricted Parliament to criminalizing conduct that harmed others. The accused challenged the criminal offence that prohibited the possession of marijuana. The majority of the Court rejected the idea that the harm principle was a principle of fundamental justice or that Parliament could only criminalize conduct that harmed others. It held that there was little agreement about what constituted harm and that Parliament could be justified in criminalizing conduct that was not harmful or only harmful to the accused. The Court's subsequent finding that there was a reasonable apprehension of harm for criminalizing marijuana suggests that even the constitutionalization of the harm principle would not have been a robust tool for demanding Parliamentary restraint in the use of the criminal sanction. The courts below, which unlike the Supreme Court had applied the harm princi-

---

171 *Malmo-Levine*, above note 9.
172 *R. v. Clay* (2003), 179 C.C.C. (3d) 540 (S.C.C.).
173 (2003), 179 C.C.C.(3d) 417 (S.C.C.).

ple as a principle of fundamental justice, also found that there was sufficient harm to justify criminalizing the possession of marijuana.[174]

The Supreme Court indicated that a criminal law that was arbitrary, irrational, and grossly disproportionate to the state interest being protected would violate section 7 of the *Charter*. In this case, a majority of the Court upheld the marijuana possession offence, concluding that criminalization was not grossly disproportionate to the state interest. The new section 7 standard that criminal laws not be arbitrary, irrational, and grossly disproportionate seems no more certain than the harm principle that the Court criticized and rejected under section 7 of the *Charter*. The Court held that the availability of imprisonment for the offence of marijuana possession did not violate section 7 of the *Charter* even though it also indicated that imprisonment would ordinarily not be a fit sentence for possession of small amounts of marijuana. The Court seemed to have relied on the availability of sentencing appeals to uphold the criminalization of marijuana under section 7 of the *Charter*. Two judges dissented on the basis that the criminalization of marijuana possession was disproportionate to the harms of marijuana consumption. A third judge dissented on the basis that Parliament could only use the criminal sanction to prevent harm or a risk of harm to others and there was not sufficient harm to others to justify criminalizing the possession of marijuana. It remains to be seen how often judges will invalidate laws on the basis of gross disproportionality under section 7 of the *Charter*, but it seems likely as in the case of vagueness challenges, that courts will be quite deferential to Parliament and recognize that the criminal justice system itself can mitigate laws that may on their face may appear to be vague or arbitrary or disproportionate.

e) Fault Requirements

Fault requirements will be discussed in greater detail in chapters 4 and 5. Nevertheless, at this juncture it will be helpful to provide a somewhat less detailed overview of how section 7 of the *Charter* requires certain minimal fault requirements.

i) *Moral Innocence and Absolute Liability*

In the *B.C. Motor Vehicle Reference*,[175] the Supreme Court indicated that a "law enacting an absolute liability offence will violate section 7 of the

---

174 See also *R. v. Murdoch* (2003), 11 C.R. (6th) 43 (Ont. C.A.).

175 *Reference re s. 94(2), of the Motor Vehicle Act (British Columbia)* (1985), 23 C.C.C. (3d) 289 at 311 (S.C.C.). See ch. 5, "Absolute Liability Offences," for further discussion.

Charter only if and to the extent that it has the potential of depriving of life, liberty, and security of the person." In that case, there was no doubt that the regulatory offence would deprive an accused of liberty, because it set a minimum penalty of seven days' imprisonment. The law specifically stated that the offence was one of absolute liability so that an accused would be convicted of driving with a suspended licence regardless of whether the accused knew that his or her licence was suspended or was negligent in respect to whether it was suspended. The Supreme Court concluded that the offence could allow the morally innocent to be punished, and suggested that a better alternative would have been to allow the accused a defence of due diligence or lack of negligence once the Crown proved the prohibited act of driving with a suspended licence. A strict liability offence, as opposed to one of absolute liability, would do "nothing more than let those few who did nothing wrong remain free."[176]

In *R. v. Pontes*,[177] the Supreme Court subsequently upheld an absolute liability offence but only on the basis that an accused could not be imprisoned for violating it. The rationale would seem to be that while absolute liability offends the principles of fundamental justice by allowing the morally innocent to be punished, it does not violate section 7 of the *Charter* because a sentence other than imprisonment does not affect the accused's rights to life, liberty, or security of the person. At the same time, the Court has not yet decided whether a fine that may result in imprisonment if the accused defaults on payment also affects the accused's right to liberty and security of the person.

The Supreme Court has also held that absolute liability criminal offences also violate section 7 of the *Charter*. In *R. v. Hess*,[178] the Court held that a "statutory rape" offence that made sex with a girl under fourteen years of age a crime regardless of whether the accused had an honest belief that she was older constituted an absolute liability offence. The Court held that "a person who is mentally innocent of the offence — who has no *mens rea* with respect to an essential element of the offence — may be convicted and sent to prison."[179] The majority also held that the violation of the accused's section 7 rights could not be justified under section 1 of the *Charter* because a person who honestly believed a girl was over fourteen could not be deterred from com-

---

176 *Ibid.* at 316.
177 (1995), 100 C.C.C. (3d) 353 (S.C.C.).
178 (1990), 59 C.C.C. (3d) 161 (S.C.C.).
179 *Ibid.* at 168.

mitting the crime and, in any event, it would be unjust to punish a morally innocent person in order to deter others. The Court also noted that Parliament had already replaced the unconstitutional offence with one that allowed the accused a defence that he had taken "all reasonable steps to ascertain the age of the complainant."[180] This new provision violated the accused's rights less because it allowed an honest and reasonable mistake that the child was older than fourteen years of age to be a defence. In other words, the new offence imposed fault on the basis of negligence and not simply on the basis that the accused committed the criminal act.

ii) Negligence as a Sufficient Fault Element under the Charter for Most Offences

The above cases indicate that absolute liability offences, where a conviction follows from proof of the prohibited act, will violate section 7 of the *Charter* whenever the offence has the potential to deprive the accused of life, liberty, or security of the person.[181] In these circumstances, section 7 of the *Charter* requires a fault element of at least negligence.[182]

The courts have been more cautious about striking down offences because they do not have fault elements higher than negligence. Criminal offences prohibiting unlawfully causing bodily harm,[183] dangerous driving,[184] careless use of a firearm,[185] and failing to provide the necessities of life[186] have all been upheld on the basis that they require proof of a marked departure from the standard of care that a reasonable person would take in the circumstances. In addition, subjective fault or subjective knowledge of the prohibited consequences is not required to convict an accused of "unlawful act manslaughter"[187] or of misleading

---

180 *Code*, above note 1, s. 150.1(4).

181 Corporations do not enjoy life, liberty, or security of the person. Section 7 of the *Charter*, above note 34, would not apply if the offence was drafted to apply only to corporations, but corporations are allowed to argue that an offence is unconstitutional because of its effects on natural persons. *Wholesale Travel*, above note 133.

182 Negligence can be defined in various ways. See ch. 4, "The Fault Element, or *Mens Rea*."

183 *R. v. DeSousa* (1992), 76 C.C.C. (3d) 124 (S.C.C.).

184 *R. v. Hundal* (1993), 79 C.C.C. (3d) 97 (S.C.C.) [*Hundal*].

185 *R. v. Gosset* (1993), 83 C.C.C. (3d) 494 (S.C.C.); *R. v. Finlay* (1993), 83 C.C.C. (3d) 513 (S.C.C.) [*Finlay*].

186 *R. v. Naglik* (1993), 83 C.C.C. (3d) 526 (S.C.C.).

187 *R. v. Creighton* (1993), 83 C.C.C. (3d) 346 (S.C.C.) [*Creighton*].

advertising.[188] In other words, "an objective fault requirement is consti-tutionally sufficient for a broad range of offences other than those falling within the relatively small group of offences"[189] so far including only murder, attempted murder, and war crimes.

Objective fault is sufficient even for serious crime such as manslaugh-ter that may be punished by up to life imprisonment. An objective fault element of reasonable foresight of non-trivial bodily harm was held in *Creighton* not to violate section 7 of the *Charter* because:

> by the very act of calling the killing *manslaughter* the law indicates that the killing is less blameworthy than murder. It may arise from negligence, or it may arise as the unintended result of a lesser unlaw-ful act. The conduct is blameworthy and must be punished, but its stigma does not approach that of murder.[190]

Section 7 of the *Charter* will not be violated so long as 1) the *mens rea* and the available penalties reflect the particular nature of the crime and its stigma; 2) the punishment is proportionate to the moral blamewor-thiness of the offender; and 3) those who cause harm intentionally are punished more severely than those who cause harm unintentionally. As will be seen, the courts have held that murder, attempted murder, and war crimes have a special stigma that requires subjective fault in rela-tion to the prohibited act. Although the last standard could affect that ability of Parliament to combine objective and subjective forms of lia-bility, the above three principles has so far made a minimal impact on the substantive criminal law.

iii) Negligence Standards: Marked Departure From the Standards of a Non-Individuated Reasonable Person

There remains some uncertainty about how section 7 of the *Charter* requires an objective standard of liability to be applied. There is a grow-ing consensus that there must be more than simple negligence, but rather "a marked departure from the standards of a reasonable per-son,"[191] in order to convict a person of a criminal offence based on objective fault. This applies even if the offence seems to contemplate a

---

188 *Wholesale Travel Group*, above note 133.
189 *Creighton*, above note 187 at 354–55, Lamer C.J. in dissent, but not on this issue.
190 *Ibid.* at 374.
191 *Ibid.* at 371–72, quoting *Hundal*, above note 184. See ch. 4, "The Degrees of Objective *Mens Rea*," for further discussion.

lower standard of negligence such as carelessness, because "the law does not lightly brand a person as a criminal."[192]

A majority of the Court in *Creighton* also held that when applying an objective standard, personal characteristics of the accused are only relevant if they establish incapacity to appreciate the nature and quality of one's conduct or incapacity to appreciate the risk involved in one's conduct.[193] Four judges dissented and argued that the accused's personal characteristics should be factored into the objective standard to the extent that they indicate either enhanced or reduced foresight from that of a reasonable person.[194] Section 7 is thus not offended by applying objective standards without consideration of the accused's own characteristics, at least when those characteristics do not render the accused incapable of appreciating the relevant risk.

iv) *No Requirement of Correspondence or Symmetry Between Prohibited Act and Fault Element*

A majority of the Court in *Creighton* held that section 7 of the *Charter* does not require that objective fault relate to all the prohibited consequences in the offence, so that proof of objective foresight of bodily harm (as opposed to death) is sufficient to convict a person of manslaughter.[195] Four judges dissented and argued that the fault element of objective foresight should be related to the prohibited consequences of the offence. Section 7 is thus not offended by offences that punish a person for causing certain harm even though the accused may not have subjectively or objectively been at fault for causing the harm that forms part of the *actus reus*.

v) *Subjective Fault Required in Relation to the Prohibited Act for a Few Offences with Special Stigma*

The Supreme Court has held that section 7 of the *Charter* requires proof of subjective fault for only a limited number of offences. *R. v.*

---

192 *Finlay*, above note 185 at 521.

193 *Ibid.* at 384–85, McLachlin J. For further discussion, see ch. 4, "The Fault Element, or *Mens Rea*."

194 *Ibid.*, Lamer C.J.

195 McLachlin J. stated: "It is important to distinguish between criminal law theory, which seeks the ideal of absolute symmetry between *actus reus* [the prohibited act] and *mens rea* [the required fault requirement], and the constitutional requirements of the *Charter*. Provided an element of mental fault or moral culpability is present, and provided that it is proportionate to the seriousness and consequences of the offence charged, the principles of fundamental justice are satisfied." *Creighton*, above note 187 at 378–79. For further discussion, see ch. 4, "Conceptual Considerations."

Vaillancourt[196] and *R. v. Martineau*[197] established that because of its stigma and mandatory life imprisonment, the offence of murder requires proof that the accused either intended to cause death or knew that death was likely to occur. In those cases, the Court struck down "felony" or constructive murder provisions that allowed an accused committing some other serious offence such as robbery or sexual assault to be convicted of murder "whether or not the person means to cause death to any human being and whether or not he knows that death is likely to be caused."[198] In *Vaillancourt*, the section provided that a person committing a serious offence such as robbery was guilty of murder if death resulted from the use or possession of a weapon. In *Martineau*, the section provided that a person was guilty of murder if he or she meant to cause bodily harm for the purpose of facilitating a serious offence. The Court also suggested that it was unconstitutional to convict a person of murder under section 229(c) of the *Criminal Code* on the basis that while pursuing an unlawful object, he or she ought to have known that death was likely to result. Under section 7 of the *Charter*, the Crown must at least prove that an accused has subjective knowledge that death is likely to result before that person can be convicted of murder.[199]

The Supreme Court has also stated that section 7 is violated by provisions that allowed an accused to be convicted as a party to attempted murder on the basis that he or she ought to have known death was likely to result.[200] Even though the penalty was more flexible, the Court stressed that a person convicted of attempted murder would suffer the same stigma as a murderer. Hence, the Crown must establish as a constitutional minimum that the accused subjectively knew that death was likely to occur. In *Finta*,[201] the Court indicated that the "stigma and opprobrium" that would accompany conviction of crimes against humanity or war crimes required the Crown to prove that the accused knew, was aware of, or was wilfully blind to the aggravating facts and circumstances that would make crimes such as robbery or manslaughter a war crime or a crime against humanity.

---

196 *Vaillancourt*, above note 130.
197 *R. v. Martineau* (1990), 58 C.C.C. (3d) 353 (S.C.C.) [*Martineau*].
198 *Code*, above note 1, s. 230.
199 At the same time, the Court has defined manslaughter quite broadly to apply to an accused who causes death when a reasonable person would have foreseen the likelihood of bodily harm, provided that the accused had the capacity to see such a risk. *Creighton*, above note 187.
200 *R. v. Logan* (1990), 58 C.C.C. (3d) 391 (S.C.C.).
201 *Finta*, above note 155 at 499–503.

Beyond the limited context of murder, attempted murder, and war crimes, the Supreme Court has refused to require subjective fault under section 7 of the *Charter*. The Court has held that the stigma attached to offences such as unlawfully causing bodily harm, dangerous driving, misleading advertising, careless use of a firearm, failure to provide the necessities of life, and unlawful act manslaughter is not sufficient to require proof of subjective as opposed to objective fault. It could, however, be argued that new crimes based on the commission of terrorist activities should require subjective fault in relation to the prohibited act and the circumstances that elevate a crime to an act of terrorism because of the stigma and enhanced penalties attached to crimes of terrorism. An analogy could be drawn to war crimes. If terrorism is seen as a stigma offence, some of the new crimes enacted by Parliament after the terrorists attacks of 11 September 2001 may be found not to satisfy constitutional requirements of subjective fault.[202] The stigma concept has often been criticized as circular and tautological, but there is no consensus that the Court should constitutionalize subjective fault beyond the offence of murder and attempted murder.

Even if subjective fault is required as an essential element of an offence under section 7 of the *Charter*, it is theoretically possible that another fault element could be substituted for that essential element. Following the section 11(d) jurisprudence outlined above, Parliament can substitute proof of another element for an essential element if proof of the substituted element leads inexorably to proof of the essential element, so that the trier of fact could not have a reasonable doubt about the essential element. In *Martineau*, the majority held that proof of the *mens rea* for the underlying offence and the intent to cause bodily harm did not lead inexorably to the conclusion that the accused had the essential element of subjective foresight of death.[203] Proving under section 230(c) of the *Criminal Code* that the accused "wilfully stops, by any means, the breath of a human being" also does not lead inexorably

---

202 In general the new terrorism offences in ss. 83.01–83.23 appropriately require proof of subjective fault in the form of knowledge or purpose. Section 83.19 prohibits the knowing facilitation of a terrorist activity but may be vulnerable because it states that it is not necessary that "any particular terrorist activity was foreseen or planned at the time it was facilitated."

203 In dissent, L'Heureux-Dubé J. argued that proof of the substituted element would lead to the "inexorable conclusion" that there was objective foreseeability of death which, in her view, should be the constitutionally required minimal mental element for murder. *Martineau*, above note 197 at 375.

to proof that the accused had subjective foresight of death.[204] In cases of suffocation, it is now necessary to charge the accused with murder under section 229 of the *Criminal Code* and prove that he or she had subjective foresight that death was likely to result. The jury could infer from the attempt at suffocation that the accused knew that death was likely, but it cannot be required by the wording of the offence to draw this inference. Following the presumption of innocence, it would be obliged to acquit the accused of murder if it had a reasonable doubt about his or her subjective foresight of death for any reason, including intoxication or diminished intelligence.

In both *Vaillancourt* and *Martineau*, the Supreme Court considered whether the violation of sections 7 and 11(d) of the *Charter* could be justified under section 1 of the *Charter*. The Court stated that the goals of the "felony murder" provisions — namely, deterring the carrying of weapons and the use of force when committing serious crimes such as robbery — were important enough to justify overriding a constitutional right. The Court also conceded that there was a rational connection between the objective of deterrence and convicting those who caused death but did not have subjective knowledge that death would result. However, in both cases the Court concluded that the restrictions on sections 7 and 11(d) were not reasonable because there were other ways Parliament could achieve its objectives. Parliament could punish the possession of a weapon while committing an offence as a separate offence.[205] In cases where death results from the possession of a weapon or the infliction of harm, "very stiff" sentences for manslaughter would be available. The Court concluded that:

> To label and punish a person as a murderer who did not intend or foresee death unnecessarily stigmatizes and punishes those whose moral blameworthiness is not that of a murderer, and thereby unnecessarily impairs the rights guaranteed by ss. 7 and 11(d) of the *Charter*.[206]

---

204 *R. v. Sit* (1991), 66 C.C.C. (3d) 449 at 453 (S.C.C.). Similar reasoning would apply to *Code*, above note 1, s. 230(b), providing that a person who "administers a stupefying or overpowering thing" in order to facilitate an offence was guilty of murder if death ensues.

205 The use of a firearm while committing an offence is punishable as a separate offence with a mandatory minimum sentence of one year imprisonment. *Code*, above note 1, s. 85. The commission of certain offences with a firearm such as robbery now has a mandatory minimum sentence of four years. *Code*, above note 1, s. 344.

206 *Martineau*, above note 197 at 362.

In other words, departures from constitutional requirements of subjective fault could not be justified under section 1 of the *Charter* because of the availability of other means more respectful of *Charter* rights to pursue the state's legitimate objective of deterring the use of weapons and violence in the commission of crimes.

f)   Criminal Defences

As will be examined in greater depth in chapters 6 through 8, statutory or common law restrictions on defences may also violate the *Charter*. One exception is if a defence would be inconsistent with the very purpose of a offence. For example, intoxication is not recognized as a defence for impaired driving.[207] At the same time, however, the courts have been most active with respect to the defence of intoxication and have held that various common law restrictions on that defence violate section 7 of the *Charter*. They have expressed concern that not considering evidence of extreme intoxication when an accused is charged with a general intent offence such as assault or sexual assault could result in the conviction of the morally innocent, at least in cases where the accused is so extremely intoxicated that he or she is in a state akin to automatism and acts in an involuntary manner.[208] The Court has also held that traditional common law rules which focus on whether evidence of intoxication raises a reasonable doubt about the accused's capacity to commit a specific intent crime such as murder could allow the conviction of an accused who may have been capable of having the required intent, but did not actually have the intent.[209]

The Supreme Court has held that section 43 of the *Criminal Code*, which authorizes parents and teachers to use reasonable force to correct a child or pupil, does not violate sections 7, 12, or 15 of the *Charter*. The Court acknowledged that the defence affected the security of the person of children, but held that it was not so vague or overbroad as to violate section 7 of the *Charter*. The Court also indicated that the "best interests of the child" was not a principle of fundamental justice; that the application of reasonable force was not cruel and unusual; and that the offence did not demean the equal dignity of children. The later holding was related to the adverse effects that striking down section 43 would have on families and ultimately on children because it would criminalize all applications of force without the child's consent. The

207   *R. v. Penno* (1990), 59 C.C.C. (3d) 344 (S.C.C.).

208   *Daviault*, above note 138. But see now *Code*, above note 1, s. 33.1, both discussed in ch. 6, "The Legislative Response to *Daviault*."

209   *R. v. Robinson* (1996), 105 C.C.C. (3d) 97 (S.C.C.).

Court also indicated that restrictions or denials of defences could violate the *Charter* with the exception of cases in which the defence would be inconsistent with the nature of the offence. For example, the purpose of the offence of intoxicated driving would be defeated if the *Charter* was interpreted to allow an accused to raise the defence of intoxication.[210]

g)   Moral Involuntariness

As discussed above, cases such as *B.C. Motor Vehicle Reference* and *R. v. Hess* indicated that the principles of fundamental justice will be violated if a morally innocent person who is not at fault will be imprisoned as a result of a criminal offence. In the context of defences, the Supreme Court in *R. v. Ruzic* indicated that the appropriate focus under section 7 of the *Charter* is not on whether restrictions or denial of a defence will result in the conviction of the morally innocent, but rather whether they will result in the conviction of a person who has acted in a "morally involuntary" manner. A person acts in a morally involuntary manner if he or she did not have "any realistic choice" in the circumstances but to commit the crime. "In the case of morally involuntary conduct, criminal attribution points not to the accused but to exigent circumstances facing him, or to threats of someone else. . . . Depriving a person of liberty and branding her with the stigma of criminal liability would infringe the principles of fundamental justice if the accused did not have any realistic choice."[211] A person who commits a crime in such exigent circumstances acts in a morally involuntary manner even though he or she committed the crime with a physically voluntary act and with the required fault element and even if they cannot be said to be morally innocent.

Applying the principle of fundamental justice that a person should not be punished for morally involuntary actions, the Supreme Court has held that severe statutory restrictions under section 17 of the *Criminal Code* on the defence of duress violate section 7 of the *Charter* because they would allow the conviction of a person who had no realistic choice but to commit the crime in response to threats. The Court struck down the requirement under section 17 of the *Criminal Code* that threats must be of immediate death or bodily harm from a person who is present when the offence is committed.[212] It left open the ques-

---

210 *Canadian Foundation for Children v. Canada (Attorney General)* 2004 SCC 4.
211 *R. v. Ruzic* (2001), 153 C.C.C. (3d) 1 (S.C.C.) at paras. 47 and 46.
212 *Ibid.*

tion of whether the categorical restrictions in section 17 on the commission of a long list of offences in response to threats would also violate section 7 of the *Charter*. The decision in *Ruzic* points in the direction of striking such down offence-based exclusion on the defence of duress if the accused committed such offences when he or she had no realistic choice but to do so. If the accused acted in a morally involuntary manner than a conviction should violate section 7 of the *Charter*. Moreover, the Court in *Ruzic* indicated that violations of section 7 of the *Charter* can only be justified in "exceptional circumstances, such as the outbreak of war or a national emergency."[213]

5) The *Charter* and Punishment

The *Charter* places restrictions on the state's ability to punish people for criminal offences. Section 12 provides that everyone has the right not to be subjected to cruel and unusual treatment or punishment and the Court's jurisprudence on this issue will be examined in chapter 9. In general, however, section 12 of the *Charter* prohibits grossly disproportionate punishments.[214]

In a landmark case, the Supreme Court has interpreted section 7 of the *Charter* generally to preclude the extradition of a fugitive to face trial in another country unless assurances are received that the death penalty will not be applied. The Court stressed both an emerging international consensus on this issue and the risk of wrongful convictions.[215] This decision reviews a number of wrongful convictions that have occurred in Canada, the United Kingdom, and the United States and stands as an important reminder of the inherent falliability of the criminal process.

Section 11(h) provides protection against double jeopardy, which is being tried or punished twice for the same offence. This does not preclude criminal trials after a person has been tried on disciplinary charges at work or in prison.[216] In Canada, protection against double jeopardy applies only if a person has been "finally acquitted of the offence." This right accommodates the generous rights of appeal that

---

213 *Ibid.* at para. 92.
214 R. v. *Smith* (1987), 34 C.C.C. (3d) 97 (S.C.C.); R. v. *Latimer* (2001), 150 C.C.C. (3d) 129 (S.C.C.).
215 *United States of America v. Burns and Rafay* (2001), 151 C.C.C. (3d) 97 (S.C.C.) effectively reversing *Kindler v. Canada (Minister of Justice)* (1991), 67 C.C.C. (3d) 1 (S.C.C.).
216 R. v. *Wigglesworth* (1987), 37 C.C.C. (3d) 385 (S.C.C.); R. v. *Shubley* (1990), 52 C.C.C. (3d) 481 (S.C.C.).

the prosecutor enjoys in Canada which allow an appeal even after a jury has acquitted the accused.[217] The section is violated, however, if the accused is retried for the same offence after an acquittal, as opposed to having the Crown take a more limited appeal on specific grounds that the trial court had made errors of law.[218] The principle of double jeopardy also prohibits conviction for multiple offences if there are no additional or distinguishing elements among the offences.[219] Thus, an accused could not be convicted of using a firearm while committing an indictable offence and of pointing a firearm, because there is no distinguishing element between these two offences.[220]

CONCLUSION

Constitutional law has a pervasive and foundational influence on criminal law and it is relevant at all stages of the criminal process. The division of powers limits the enactment of criminal law to Parliament but allows provinces and municipalities to enact regulatory offences. Sections 7 to 10 of the *Charter* restrain the investigative activities of the police. These rights are enforced primarily by the decisions of courts under section 24(2) of the *Charter* to exclude unconstitutionally obtained evidence if its admission would bring the administration of justice into disrepute. In the *Charter* era, Canadian courts are also prepared to stay proceedings if the accused has been entrapped into committing a crime. At the same time, the entrapment defence allows police to offer people an opportunity to commit a crime so long as they have a reasonable suspicion that the suspect is engaged in criminal activity or the suspect is present in a high crime area. Even if they have a reasonable suspicion or are acting on a *bona fide* inquiry into crime, the police cannot actually induce the commission of a crime by shocking activity that would bring the administration of justice into disrepute.

The *Charter* affects the trial process by giving the accused various rights including the right to make full answer and defence and the right to be presumed innocent. The presumption of innocence is violated whenever the accused has to establish an element of an offence or a

---

217 *Morgentaler (No. 2)*, above note 169.
218 *Corp. professionelles des médecins (Québec) v. Thibault* (1988), 42 C.C.C. (3d) 1 (S.C.C.).
219 See also *Code*, above note 1, s. 12.
220 *R. v. Krug* (1985), 21 C.C.C. (3d) 193 (S.C.C.). See also *R. v. Kienapple* (1974), 15 C.C.C. (2d) 524 (S.C.C.).

defence on a balance of probabilities because this allows a conviction to occur despite a reasonable doubt. Even mandatory presumptions that can be displaced by satisfying an evidential burden violate the presumption of innocence. At the same time, the courts have frequently accepted limitations on the presumption of innocence as reasonable limits and have, on their own initiative, required the accused to establish the defences of extreme intoxication and automatism on a balance of probabilities.

The *Charter* also affects substantive criminal offences that infringe freedom of expression, are excessively vague, overbroad, grossly disproportionate, or allow the punishment of the morally innocent. These matters will be discussed in greater depth in subsequent chapters, but it should be noted that section 7 of the *Charter* is offended by imprisonment of the morally innocent who have committed a prohibited act but through no fault of their own. The courts have found that because of their penalty and stigma, a few crimes — murder, attempted murder, and war crimes — require proof of subjective fault in relation to their *actus reus*. The Court has not, however, extended such requirements to the vast majority of crimes. For crimes such as manslaughter, objective fault is constitutionally sufficient and does not have to extend to all aspects of the *actus reus* or require that the reasonable person be endowed with the same characteristics as the accused.

Section 7 of the *Charter* may also be violated by restrictions on defences. As examined in greater depth in chapters 6 and 8, restrictions on the intoxication and duress defences have been struck down under section 7 of the *Charter*. The Court has recognized a general principle under section 7 of the *Charter* that people should not be punished for crimes that are committed in a morally involuntary manner in the sense that they have no realistic choice but to commit the crime. Although many of these matters will be revisited in subsequent chapters, it is important to have a sense of how the *Charter* affects the entire criminal process and how constitutional law has become fundamental to the criminal law in Canada.

FURTHER READINGS

HOGG, P.W., *Constitutional Law of Canada*, 4th ed. (Toronto: Carswell, 1997), chs. 18–19, 33–41, and 44–52

LASKIN, J., ET AL., eds., *The Canadian Charter of Rights and Freedoms Annotated* (Aurora, ON: Canada Law Book, 2004)

QUIGLEY, T., *Procedure in Canadian Criminal Law* (Toronto: Carswell, 1997)

ROACH, K., *Constitutional Remedies in Canada* (Aurora, ON: Canada Law Book, 1994)

ROACH, K., *Due Process and Victims' Rights: The New Law and Politics of Criminal Justice* (Toronto: University of Toronto Press, 1999), chs. 2, 3, 4, and 5

SHARPE, R.J., K. SWINTON, & K. ROACH, *The Charter of Rights and Freedoms*, 2d ed. (Toronto: Irwin Law, 2002)

STUART, D., *Charter Justice in Canadian Criminal Law*, 3d ed. (Toronto: Carswell, 2001)

THE PROHIBITED ACT, OR *ACTUS REUS*

The *actus reus* or prohibited act of any offence has important policy elements. For example, in 1983 the offence of rape, which was defined as non-consensual sexual intercourse by a man with a woman who was not his wife, was replaced with the broader, gender neutral offence of sexual assault which applied to all persons. In 1992 the law of sexual assault was again changed, with Parliament defining consent and stating specific instances in which consent did not exist. The Supreme Court subsequently decided that for purposes of determining the *actus reus*, consent should be based on the subjective views of the complainant. Although much of the controversy over sexual assault has concerned the appropriate fault or mental element,[1] the expansion of the prohibited act in this and other crimes plays an important role in determining the extent of criminal liability. The broad nature of many of the prohibited acts in the *Criminal Code*[2] requires the judge to distinguish at sentencing among the relative culpability of various levels of participation in crimes.

Almost all crimes in Canada are defined in the *Criminal Code*. In order to ensure that there is fixed predetermined law, the courts cannot create crimes on their own except in the case of contempt of court. At

---

1   See the discussion of mistake of fact in ch. 4, "The Fault Element, or *Mens Rea*."
2   Including the provisions governing liability as a party or accomplice to an offence, and prohibiting attempts to commit crimes. See ch. 3, "Unfulfilled Crimes and Participation in Crimes."

the same time, however, courts play an important role in interpreting the words used to define crimes. Sometimes, courts interpret words in an offence restrictively in order to benefit the accused, but not in all cases. Laws may be struck down under section 7 of the *Charter* if they are so vague or overbroad that they do not provide fair notice of what is prohibited, or any limitation on law enforcement discretion. The ideal of a fixed, predetermined law should in theory allow citizens to determine beforehand whether conduct is illegal. If citizens do not determine what is illegal, or if they mistakenly think something is legal when it is not, ignorance of the law is not an excuse.

In order to obtain a conviction for a criminal or a regulatory offence, the Crown must always prove beyond a reasonable doubt that the accused committed the prohibited act (*actus reus*). The *actus reus* is only one element of a criminal offence, and it must in theory coincide with the fault element, or *mens rea*, that is required for the crime. It will be seen in this chapter that the courts have sometimes finessed this requirement, often by defining the criminal act in a broad fashion so that it overlaps with a time in which the accused had the required fault element. Sometimes when determining whether the accused has committed the *actus reus*, it is necessary to determine if he or she caused some prohibited result. As will be seen, causation is defined broadly in homicide cases so that an accused may be held to have caused another's death even though other factors, such as lack of medical treatment or the victim's "thin skull," contributed to the death. This approach fits into the trend towards expansive definitions of the criminal act.

The criminal law has traditionally been reluctant to punish an omission or a failure to act, but this attitude seems to be changing as criminal and regulatory offences punish people for failing to act or to fulfil specific legal duties. Although the criminal law generally keeps the physical and mental elements of crimes distinct, an emerging line of authority suggests that an accused who acts involuntarily may not have committed an *actus reus*. This interpretation effectively builds a minimal fault or mental element into the *actus reus*. As a practical matter, it could prevent the Crown from convicting an accused who acted in an involuntary and unconscious manner even though the offence may have no fault element or one based on negligence.

A. CODIFICATION OF THE CRIMINAL ACT

The prohibited act, or *actus reus*, of an offence is a matter of statutory interpretation. Since 1953, section 9 of the *Criminal Code* has provided that no person shall be convicted of an offence at common law (judge-made law) except contempt of court. To be convicted of a criminal or regulatory offence in Canada, a person must do something that is prohibited by a valid statute or regulation. This requirement accords with the ideal that one should not be punished except in accordance with fixed, predetermined law.

The value of certainty and having a predefined criminal law is now supported by some *Charter* rights. As discussed in chapter 1, section 11(a) gives an accused the right to be informed without unreasonable delay of the specific offence charged; section 11(i) protects the accused against the burden of retroactive laws; and section 11(g) provides that the act or omission must, at the time it was committed, have been illegal under Canadian or international law. As will be discussed below, section 7 of the *Charter* has also been interpreted to prohibit criminal sanctions that are so vague or overbroad that they do not provide fair notice to the citizen or limit law enforcement discretion.

Even before the enactment of section 9 of the *Criminal Code* and the *Charter*, Canadian courts were reluctant to create common law or judge-made crimes on the basis that they:

> would introduce great uncertainty into the administration of the criminal law, leaving it to the judicial officer trying any particular charge to decide that the acts proved constituted a crime or otherwise, not by reference to any defined standard to be found in the Code or in reported decisions, but according to his individual view as to whether such acts were a disturbance of the tranquillity of people tending to provoke physical reprisal.[3]

The Court thus held that a common law charge of acting in a manner likely to cause a breach of the peace by being a "peeping tom" was not sustainable.[4] In contrast, courts in England continue to exercise "a residual power, where no statute has yet intervened to supersede the common law, to superintend those offenses which are prejudicial to the public welfare."[5] Crimes such as conspiracy to corrupt public morals or to outrage public decency have been created under this common law

---

3   *Frey v. Fedoruk* (1950), 97 C.C.C. 1 at 14 (S.C.C.). The Supreme Court interpreted a previous offence against conspiring to effect an unlawful purpose to require a purpose contrary to federal and provincial legislation as opposed to the common law. *R. v. Gralewicz* (1980), 54 C.C.C. (3d) 289 (S.C.C.).

4   Parliament subsequently enacted a new crime of loitering and prowling at night on the property of another person near a dwelling house. See *Criminal Code of Canada*, R.S.C. 1985, c. C-46, s. 177 [*Code*].

5   *Shaw v. D.P.P.*, [1962] A.C. 220 at 268 (H.L.).

power. In Canada, a person can only be convicted for conspiring to commit an offence created by a legislature and defined in law.

The only remaining judge-made crime in Canada, contempt of court, has been upheld under the *Charter* on the basis that codification is not required as a principle of fundamental justice and that uncodified crimes can still be consistent with the principle of fixed, predetermined law. The Court stressed that an accused could predict in advance if conduct constituted contempt of court and that a prohibited act and fault must be proven beyond a reasonable doubt to result in a conviction for contempt of court.[6] Thus, there is no constitutional requirement under section 7 of the *Charter* that all crimes be codified by legislation. This does not, however, mean that the *Charter* cannot be applied to the exercise of the contempt power. Some attempts by judges to punish people for contempt of court have been found to violate *Charter* rights, such as the right to an impartial tribunal and to freedom of expression.[7] At the same time, the very concept of a judge-made or common law offence does not offend the principles of fundamental justice.

1) Strict and Purposive Construction of the Criminal Law

Another means of ensuring that the criminal law is fixed and predetermined is to apply the doctrine that it should be interpreted or construed strictly to the benefit of the accused. This doctrine has been defined by the Supreme Court as follows:

> It is unnecessary to emphasize the importance of clarity and certainty when freedom is at stake. . . . [I]f real ambiguities are found, or doubts of substance arise, in the construction and application of a statute affecting the liberty of a subject, then that statute should be applied in such a manner as to favour the person against whom it is sought to be enforced. If one is to be incarcerated, one should at least know that some Act of Parliament requires it in express terms, and not, at most, by implication.[8]

---

6   *U.N.A. v. Alberta (A.G.)* (1992), 71 C.C.C. (3d) 225 at 253–54 (S.C.C.).
7   *R. v. Martin* (1985), 19 C.C.C. (3d) 248 (Ont. C.A.); *R. v. Kopyto* (1987), 39 C.C.C. (3d) 1 (Ont. C.A.). Before determining whether a person is guilty of contempt of court, judges should give the person notice and an opportunity to be represented by counsel and to make representations. The judge should avoid making determinations that will taint the fairness of the trial. *R. v. K.(B.)* (1995) 102 C.C.C. (3d) 18 (S.C.C.); *R. v. Arradi*, [2003] 1 S.C.R 280.
8   *Marcotte v. Canada (Deputy A.G.)* (1976), 19 C.C.C. (2d) 257 at 262 (S.C.C.).

This doctrine was used most extensively three hundred years ago when even comparatively minor criminal offences, such as theft, were subject to capital punishment. The Supreme Court has stated that "while the original justification for the doctrine has been substantially eroded, the seriousness of imposing criminal penalties of any sort demands that reasonable doubts be resolved in favour of the accused."[9] For example, the word "conceals" in the criminal offence of removing, concealing, or disposing of property with the intent to defraud creditors has been interpreted as requiring "a positive act done for the purpose of secreting the debtor's property."[10] The accused would have concealed property if he had hidden it in a remote warehouse, but he did not conceal it simply because he failed to tell bankruptcy officials about its existence. Similarly, people would only be guilty of causing a public disturbance if their shouting, swearing, or singing caused a foreseeable interference with the use of a public place, not mere mental annoyance.[11]

Strict construction in favour of the liberty of the accused suggests that offences, but not defences, should be given a restrictive reading. In *R. v. McIntosh*,[12] the Court invoked strict construction as a rationale for giving the statutory defence of self-defence a reading that favoured the liberty of the accused, as opposed to one that expanded the scope of criminal liability. Defences can also be expanded to favour the accused by giving them a broad and purposive reading.[13]

Strict construction of offences in the criminal law is in some tension with modern purposive approaches to statutory interpretation. Purposive approaches acknowledge the limits of grammatical or dictionary-based interpretation of words and instruct courts to look at the broader purposes of a particular statute. For example, section 12 of the *Interpretation Act*,[14] which applies to all federal law including the *Criminal Code*,[15] states:

---

9   *R. v. Paré* (1987), 38 C.C.C. (3d) 97 at 106 (S.C.C.) [*Paré*].
10   *R. v. Goulis* (1981), 60 C.C.C. (2d) 347 (Ont. C.A.). The accused was acquitted of the criminal offence, but at the same time convicted of regulatory offences under the *Bankruptcy Act*, R.S.C. 1985, c. B-3, which required him to divulge such information.
11   *R. v. Lohnes* (1992), 69 C.C.C. (3d) 289 (S.C.C.).
12   (1995), 95 C.C.C. (3d) 481 at 493 (S.C.C.).
13   *R. v. Cooper* (1979), 51 C.C.C. (2d) 129 (S.C.C.) [*Cooper*].
14   R.S.C. 1985, c. I-21.
15   *R. v. Robinson* (1951), 100 C.C.C. 1 (S.C.C.); *R. v. Hasselwander* (1993), 81 C.C.C. (3d) 471 (S.C.C.) [*Hasselwander*]; *R. v. Gladue* (1999), 133 C.C.C. (3d) 385 (S.C.C.). The *Canadian Charter of Rights and Freedoms*, Part I of the *Constitution Act, 1982*, being Schedule B to the *Canada Act 1982* (U.K.), 1982, c. 11

Every enactment is deemed remedial, and shall be given such fair, large and liberal construction and interpretation as best ensures the attainment of its objects.

The purposive approach to statutory interpretation has been reconciled with the doctrine of strict construction by holding that the preference for the interpretation that most favours the accused applies only if, after consulting the purposes of a statute, reasonable ambiguities remain in its meaning. Thus, a criminal law should first be given a purposive reading and the doctrine of strict construction only applied if there are still reasonable ambiguities after such a broad interpretation.

There are several recent examples of courts interpreting criminal laws in a purposive manner, even though more restrictive interpretations were grammatically possible. For example, in *Paré*,[16] the Supreme Court recognized that while "it is clearly grammatically possible to construe the words 'while committing' . . . as requiring murder to be classified as first degree only if it is exactly coincidental" with the offences listed in section 231(5) of the *Criminal Code*, it was not reasonable to attribute such a restrictive meaning to the provision. The Court held that the purpose of section 231(5) is to punish, as more severe, murders that were committed while the victim was being unlawfully dominated by the commission of an underlying offence. In the result, the Court held that a murder committed two minutes after the accused had indecently assaulted the victim was indeed committed while the indecent assault took place. The murder was part of the same transaction and the same continuous sequence of events involving the illegal domination of the young victim. There was no resort to the doctrine of strict construction because, considering the purpose of the provision, there was no reasonable ambiguity in the provision. Similar purposive reasoning has been applied to hold that an accused murders a person "while committing" a sexual assault, even if the sexual assault takes place after the victim has died;[17] that a police officer is murdered "acting in the course of his duties" when on duty, but not actually enforcing the law;[18] and that a firearm is a prohibited weapon "capable of firing bullets in rapid succession" if it can readily be converted to do so.[19]

[Charter] is also accorded a broad and purposive interpretation by courts. See *Canada (Director of Investigation & Research Combines Investigation Branch) v. Southam Inc.* (1984), 14 C.C.C. (3d) 97 (S.C.C.).

16   Above note 9.

17   *R. v. Richer* (1993), 82 C.C.C. (3d) 385 (Alta. C.A.).

18   *R. v. Prevost* (1988), 42 C.C.C. (3d) 314 (Ont. C.A.).

19   *Hasselwander*, above note 15.

In *R. v. Russell*,[20] the Supreme Court went beyond *Paré* to hold that first-degree murder can be committed even if the underlying offence was committed against a third party and not the person murdered. The Court stressed that strict construction was not relevant because the ordinary words of section 231(5) of the *Criminal Code* did not require that the underlying offence be committed against the victim. It dismissed the idea in *Paré* that first-degree murders were united by the unlawful domination of the murder victim as too narrow and restrictive given the wording of the statute. All that was necessary under section 231(5) was that the killing was "closely connected, temporally and causally, with an enumerated offence. As long as the connection exists, however, it is immaterial that the victim of the killing and the victim of the enumerated offence are not the same."[21] This case underlines that courts will not lightly resort to the doctrine of strict construction and will often give even the most serious criminal offences a generous reading if supported by the language of the enactment.

Resort is only made to the doctrine of strict construction if there are reasonable ambiguities in a law after it has been interpreted in a purposive manner consistent with its intent.[22] As the *Criminal Code* is federal legislation enacted in both French and English, both officially authoritative versions of the *Code* should be consulted to see if one of them resolves an ambiguity that may be present in the other version. This should be done before resorting to the doctrine of strict construction of the criminal law.[23] If, however, the English and French versions of the *Criminal Code* are not consistent, the Court should select the more restrictive provision,[24] something that is consistent with the doctrine of the strict construction of the criminal law.

2) Unconstitutionally Vague and Overbroad Laws

A law that is excessively vague or overbroad because it does not give fair notice to citizens of what is prohibited, or place any limits on law enforcement discretion, violates section 7 of the *Charter*. This is some-

---

20 [2001] 2 S.C.R. 804.
21 *Ibid.* at para. 43.
22 *CanadianOxy Chemical v. Canada*, [1999] 1 S.C.R. 743 at para. 14; *Bell Express Vu v. Canada* (2002) 212 D.L.R. (4th) 1 at para. 21.
23 *R. v. Mac* (2002), 163 C.C.C. (3d) 1 (S.C.C.) (ambiguity in English version resolved by French version); *R. v. Lamy* (2002), 162 C.C.C. (3d) 353 (S.C.C.) (ambiguity in French version resolved by English version).
24 *R. v. Daoust* (2004), 180 C.C.C. (3d) 449 (S.C.C.).

times known as the void for vagueness doctrine. Although the words used in statutes to define criminal acts cannot provide certainty, they should provide some boundaries of permissible and non-permissible conduct. When determining whether an offence is excessively vague, the courts examine not only the words used by Parliament, but the cases in which courts have interpreted those words. In many cases, these interpretations add more certainty about what is prohibited, and limit the extent of the criminal prohibition. For example, the Supreme Court has held that statutory prohibitions against "bawdy houses," or commercial behaviour which "lessens, unduly, competition," are not vague, in large part because courts have been able to give these statutory phrases ascertainable meanings.[25] As McLachlin J. has stated: "Laws must of necessity cover a variety of situations. Given the infinite variability of conduct, it is impossible to draft laws that precisely foresee each case that might arise. It is the task of judges, aided by precedent and considerations like the text and purpose of a statute, to interpret laws of general application and decide whether they apply to the facts before the court in a particular case. This process is not in breach of the principles of fundamental justice; rather, it is in the best tradition of our system of justice."[26]

Most challenges to criminal laws as excessively vague have failed. The Supreme Court has upheld a regulatory offence against impairing the quality of the natural environment for any use that can be made of it, on the basis that the legislature should be able to use broadly worded offences to protect the environment.[27] Statutes that allow people to be detained in order to protect public safety have also been found not to be excessively vague.[28] Section 43 of the *Criminal Code* was held by a majority of the Court not to be unduly vague or overbroad in authorizing the use of force to correct children that is "reasonable under the circumstances." McLachlin C.J. noted that "the criminal law often uses the concept of reasonableness to accommodate evolving mores and avoid successive 'fine-tuning' amendments. It is implicit in this technique that current social consensus on what is reasonable may be considered." The fact that the defence had been subject to varying interpretations in the

---

25 *Reference re ss. 193 & 195(1)(c) of the Criminal Code (Canada)* (1990), 56 C.C.C. (3d) 65 (S.C.C.); *R. v. Nova Scotia Pharmaceutical Society* (1992), 74 C.C.C. (3d) 289 (S.C.C.).

26 *Winko v. British Columbia (Forensic Psychiatric Institute)* (1999), 135 C.C.C. (3d) 129 at 166–67 (S.C.C.) [*Winko*].

27 *R. v. Canadian Pacific Ltd.* (1995), 99 C.C.C. (3d) 97 (S.C.C.).

28 *R. v. Morales* (1992), 77 C.C.C. (3d) 91 (S.C.C.); *Winko*, above note 26.

past was not fatal because it could still be given "a core meaning in tune with contemporary standards" and because it "sets real boundaries and a risk zone for criminal sanction."[29] In this case, the Court placed several new restrictions on the ambit of the defence that clarified its availability. For example, the Court indicated that it would not be reasonable to use force on children under two or over twelve years of age or to use objects or blows to the head. This case affirms that the key question in "void for vagueness" challenges is not the vagueness of the language used by Parliament or even the variety of interpretations placed on the law in the past but rather the Court's ability to interpret the law in an intelligible manner that establishes a "risk zone" for the use of the criminal law. One consequence of the Court's approach is that the public and law enforcement officials can be misled by simplifying reading the terms Parliament has employed in the *Criminal Code* and that they will have to consult the Court's jurisprudence to understand the full extent of the criminal law.

One exception to the Supreme Court's unwillingness to strike down criminal laws as excessively vague or overbroad is its 5 to 4 decision in *R. v. Heywood*[30] to strike down a vagrancy provision that made it illegal for a person convicted of a sexual offence to be "found loitering in or near a school ground, playground, public park or bathing area."[31] The Court held that the provision was too broad in defining the prohibited conduct, and that it did not give the accused fair notice of what was prohibited. Overbreadth, like vagueness, was related to "a lack of sufficient precision by a legislature in the means used to accomplish an objective. In the case of vagueness, the means are not clearly defined. In the case of overbreadth the means are too sweeping in relation to the objective."[32] The law was struck down by the Court. Parliament, however, enacted a new law that allowed those convicted of sexual offences involving children to be prohibited from attending public parks or public swimming areas where children under fourteen years of age could reasonably be expected to attend. This included daycare centres, school grounds, playgrounds, or community centres. This less broad and more carefully tailored law was held not to violate sec-

29   *Canadian Foundation for Children, Youth and the Law v. Canada (Attorney General)* 2004 SCC 4 at paras. 36, 39, and 42.

30   (1994), 94 C.C.C. (3d) 481 (S.C.C.) [*Heywood*].

31   *Code*, above note 4, s. 179(1)(b). See now s. 161.

32   *Heywood*, above note 30 at 516. The dissenters would have saved the legislation on the basis that it should be interpreted only to apply to those who loitered in the named areas for malevolent purposes related to the predicate sexual offences.

tion 7 of the *Charter* except to the extent that it prohibited attendance at community centres in which children might not be present.[33] The Supreme Court has subsequently re-interpreted *Heywood* as a case based on gross disproportionality between the state interest and the rights infringed upon.[34] The problem with such an interpretation of *Heywood* is that the state's interests in protecting children from sexual abuse were particularly compelling compared to the restrictions that the vagrancy offence struck down in *Heywood* placed on the liberties of those convicted of sexual offences. The best rationale for the decision in *Heywood* is not gross disproportionality but rather the original rationales for the void for vagueness doctrine: the lack of fair notice to the offender and the unfettered discretion that the old vagrancy offence gave to the police.

3) Ignorance of the Law

Codification, and the doctrines of strict construction of the criminal law and void for vagueness, help promote the principle that people should only be punished by fixed, predetermined laws. These doctrines are especially important because the criminal law has historically not allowed ignorance of the law to be an excuse to a criminal offence. Early cases held that people were guilty even if they committed an act they could not have known had recently been made illegal or was not illegal in their home country.[35] Since the *Criminal Code* was enacted in 1892, it has provided that "ignorance of the law by a person who commits an offence is not an excuse for committing that offence."[36] This provision is uncontroversial when applied to offences that a person should know are crimes. It can, however, have harsh results when applied to matters that one may reasonably believe to be legal, especially if competent authorities have contributed to that belief.

In *R. v. Molis*,[37] the Supreme Court held that the principle that ignorance of the law is no excuse precluded an accused from arguing that he had a defence of reasonable mistake in believing that drugs he manufactured were not prohibited under the *Food and Drug Act*. The accused had tried to determine if the drugs were legal, and the drugs in question had only recently been added to the prohibited list. Given his efforts,

---

33   *R. v. Budreo* (1996), 104 C.C.C. (3d) 245 (Ont. Gen. Div.).

34   *R. v. Clay* (2003), 179 C.C.C. (3d) 540 at para. 38 (S.C.C.).

35   *R. v. Bailey* (1800), 168 E.R. 651 (C.C.R.); *R. v. Esop* (1836), 173 E.R. 203.

36   *Code*, above note 4, s. 19.

37   (1980), 55 C.C.C. (2d) 558 (S.C.C.).

the accused would have most likely had a valid defence of due diligence if he had made a factual mistake about the nature of the drugs,[38] as opposed to a legal mistake as to whether the drugs had been prohibited under the relevant law. Courts have also rejected as an excuse the accused's reliance on a lower court judgment which wrongly held that the activity in question was legal.[39] People rely on their own knowledge of the law, or even a lawyer's advice, at their peril. The ignorance of the law is no excuse principle can have harsh effects on a person who has made genuine and reasonable attempts to ascertain what the law is and to comply with it.

Nevertheless, the Supreme Court has affirmed that ignorance of the law is no excuse in the post-*Charter* era by stating that "it is a principle of our criminal law that an honest but mistaken belief in respect of the legal consequences of one's deliberate actions does not furnish a defence to a criminal charge, even when the mistake cannot be attributed to the negligence of the accused."[40] An accused who makes reasonable mistakes about the law will generally not have a defence, even though reasonable mistakes about the facts will provide a defence to most criminal and regulatory offences.[41]

a) Distinguishing Mistakes of Law and Fact

The refusal to recognize a mistake of law as a defence means that an accused could be convicted of selling obscene material even though the accused relied reasonably on a newspaper report, a case, or a lawyer's advice that the material was not obscene. On the other hand, if the accused made a mistake about the facts, as opposed to the law, then he or she would have a defence.[42] This would apply, for example, to a vendor who believed a magazine contained pictures of consenting adults, not children, engaged in sexual activity. Thus, the Supreme Court has acquitted a vendor on the basis that he had no knowledge of the fea-

---

38 In *R. v. Beaver* (1957), 118 C.C.C. 129 (S.C.C.), the Supreme Court held that those in possession of a prohibited drug had a defence because they believed it was a harmless substance. See ch. 4, "The Fault Element, or *Mens Rea*" for discussion of the mistake of fact defence.

39 *R. v. Campbell* (1972), 10 C.C.C. (2d) 26 (Alta. Dist. Ct.); *R. v. MacIntyre* (1983), 24 M.V.R. 67 (Ont. C.A.).

40 *R. v. Forster* (1992), 70 C.C.C. (3d) 59 at 64 (S.C.C.).

41 A person accused of a strict liability offence would have a defence if he or she "reasonably believed in a mistaken set of facts which, if true, would render the act or omission innocent." *R. v. Sault Ste. Marie (City)* (1978), 40 C.C.C. (2d) 353 at 374 (S.C.C.). See ch. 5, "Regulatory Offences and Corporate Crime."

42 *R. v. Metro News Ltd.* (1986), 29 C.C.C. (3d) 35 (Ont. C.A.).

tures of videotapes that made them obscene while at the same time indicating that the vendor's belief that the videotapes were not legally obscene was not relevant. Even the fact that the videos had been approved by a provincial film board was not a defence because it only supported the accused's claim to have made a mistake about the law of obscenity.[43]

In *R. v. Jones*,[44] the Supreme Court held that the accused did not have a defence because they believed they were not legally required to have a provincial licence to operate a bingo on an Aboriginal reserve. The Court stressed that the mistake was not a defence because it related not "to those facts here . . . [but] in believing that the law does not apply because it is inoperative on the reserves."[45] The accused might have had a defence if they, for example, had mistakenly believed that the Band had obtained a provincial licence for the bingo. The ignorance of the law is no excuse principle seems to punish those who have formed a mistaken belief about the legality of their actions more than a person who has made a mistake about the facts.

The distinction between a mistake of law, which is no excuse, and a mistake of fact, which may be an excuse, can be slippery and difficult. In 1979, a majority of the Supreme Court stated that a driver's knowledge of whether his licence was suspended was a matter of fact. As such, a driver who believed his licence was not suspended could have a defence of a lack of *mens rea* to a *Criminal Code* offence of driving while disqualified.[46] Three years later, the Court distinguished this finding and stated that while knowledge of a licence suspension was still a matter of fact when the accused was charged with a *Criminal Code* offence, it was a matter of law when the accused was charged with a provincial offence.[47] The Supreme Court has subsequently recognized in *R. v. Pontes*[48] that such arbitrary distinctions cannot be maintained. Unfortunately, the Court was divided on what precedent should be maintained. A majority cast doubt on the later precedent on the basis

---

43   *R. v. Jorgensen* (1995), 102 C.C.C. (3d) 97 (S.C.C.) [*Jorgensen*]. But see the decision discussed below of Chief Justice Lamer, who would have held that the board's approval of the films provided a defence of officially induced error.

44   (1991), 66 C.C.C. (3d) 512 (S.C.C.).

45   *Ibid.* at 517. The Court did note that the accused had not formally challenged the validity of the law as inconsistent with Aboriginal or treaty rights protected under s. 35 of the *Constitution Act, 1982*, being Schedule B to the *Canada Act 1982* (U.K.), 1982, c. 11.

46   *R. v. Prue* (1979), 46 C.C.C. (2d) 257 (S.C.C.).

47   *R. v. MacDougall* (1982), 1 C.C.C. (3d) 65 (S.C.C.).

48   *R. v. Pontes* (1995), 100 C.C.C. (3d) 353 (S.C.C.) [*Pontes*].

that it was decided prior to the *Charter*, while a minority cast doubt on the earlier 1979 precedent. The majority's decision may suggest that in close cases, courts will be more inclined to characterize mistakes as mistakes of fact and in this way shelter the accused from the harshness of the ignorance of the law is no excuse principle.

b) Preclusion of Mistake of Law as the Only Defence Making an Offence One of Absolute Liability

In *Pontes*, Cory J. suggested for the majority that where section 19 operates to deny the accused his only possible defence, then the offence should be classified as one of absolute liability for which imprisonment cannot be imposed.[49] In the case, he held that the accused's lack of knowledge that his licence was suspended was the only possible defence to the offence of driving without a valid licence. Because the licence was automatically and without notice suspended upon the accumulation of a certain amount of demerit points, the defence that the accused did not know that his licence was suspended must amount to a mistake of law and as such be prohibited. This preclusion of the only available defence led the majority of the Court to characterize the offence as one of absolute liability. *Pontes* preserves the ignorance of the law is no excuse principle, but somewhat mitigates its harshness by, in this one limited context, taking imprisonment away as a sentencing option.

c) Non-Publication

There are some exceptions to the principle that ignorance of the law is not an excuse. A person may not be convicted of violating a law or regulation that has not been officially promulgated or published.[50] The rationale would be that it would be impossible for a person to ascertain and comply with a law that was not available to the public.

d) *Mens Rea* and Mistake of Law

Sometimes the *mens rea* or fault element of specific offences will be defined in a manner that can make the accused's mistake of law a matter that will negate proof of *mens rea*. In other words, a person may not be convicted if the fault element required for a particular offence includes some knowledge of the relevant law. Thus, an accused has been acquitted of wilfully breaching his probation order because he

---

49   *Ibid.* at 368.

50   *R. v. Ross* (1944), 84 C.C.C. 107 (B.C. Co. Ct.); *Lim Chin Aik v. R.*, [1963] A.C. 160 (P.C.); *R. v. Catholique* (1980), 49 C.C.C. (2d) 65 (N.W.T. S.C.). See also *Statutory Instruments Act*, R.S.C. 1985, c. S-22, s. 11(2).

wrongly believed that he had not committed the offence of care and control of a vehicle while impaired because the car was not moving.[51] If the accused thought he was doing something perfectly legal, it could not be said that he was wilfully breaching his parole. This was tied to the complex or high fault element implicit in the offence of wilfully breaching parole.[52] A legal error about who owns property may afford a defence to theft because the fault element of the crime itself contemplates that an accused act "without colour of right."[53] Theft has a particularly complex and high fault element and this makes some mistakes of law relevant to proof of *mens rea*. These exceptions to the ignorance of the law principle depend on the particular fault element of the particular offence. They are limited exceptions that would not exonerate an accused who simply argued that he or she did not think that theft or care and control of a vehicle while impaired was illegal.

e) Officially Induced Error

Some courts have recognized a defence of officially induced error for those who reasonably rely on an erroneous legal opinion or advice from an official responsible for the enforcement of a particular law.[54] Without support from other members of the Court, Chief Justice Lamer has argued that a defence of officially induced error should be available to those accused of criminal or regulatory offences who establish on a balance of probabilities that they relied on reasonable legal advice from an appropriate official charged with administering the law.[55] This novel

---

51   *R. v. Docherty* (1989), 51 C.C.C. (3d) 1 (S.C.C.) [*Docherty*].

52   Parliament subsequently amended the offence to provide that an accused was guilty when a probation order was breached "without reasonable excuse." *Code*, above note 4, s. 733.1. It is possible that a court might find that the accused's genuine belief that he was not acting illegally and in breach of a probation order constituted a reasonable excuse, but the Supreme Court's decision in *Docherty* was based on the high level of *mens rea* employed in the previous offence.

53   The fault element of theft requires that the accused act "fraudulently and without colour of right." *Code*, *ibid.*, s. 322(1). A person "who is honestly asserting what he believes to be an honest claim cannot be said to act 'without colour of right,' even though it may be unfounded in law or in fact." *R. v. DeMarco* (1973), 13 C.C.C. (2d) 369 at 372 (Ont. C.A.). See also *R. v. Shymkowich* (1954), 110 C.C.C. 97 (S.C.C.); *R. v. Howson*, [1966] 3 C.C.C. 348 (Ont. C.A); *R. v. Spot Supermarket Inc.* (1979), 50 C.C.C. (2d) 239 (Que. C.A.); *R. v. Lilly* (1983), 5 C.C.C. (3d) 1 (S.C.C.).

54   *R. v. Maclean* (1974), 17 C.C.C. (2d) 84 (N.S. Co. Ct.); *R. v. Cancoil Thermal Corp.* (1986), 27 C.C.C. (3d) 295 (Ont. C.A.).

55   *Jorgensen*, above note 43. Lamer C.J. would have stayed charges of knowingly selling obscene material because the accused had obtained and relied on approval of obscene videos by a provincial review board. The majority of the

defence would apply to all offences and respond to the injustice of the state with one hand approving of conduct that it prosecuted as illegal with the other hand. Even if eventually accepted by the full Court, officially induced error would be a fairly limited defence that would leave the general principle that ignorance of the law is no excuse intact. For example, it would not assimilate the manner in which the law treats mistakes of law and mistakes of fact. Such a more comprehensive reform would only occur should courts conclude that section 19 of the *Criminal Code* itself violates the principles of fundamental justice.

4) Application of the *Criminal Code*: Territorial and Age-based Restrictions

The basic rule in section 6(2) of the *Criminal Code* is that no person can be convicted for offences committed outside Canada.[56] This rule is subject to exceptions for war crimes, crimes committed on aircrafts, crimes in relation to dangerous nuclear materials, sexual offences committed against children by Canadians while abroad, and crimes of terrorism.[57] The conspiracy provisions in section 465 are also worded broadly to apply to those who conspire outside Canada to commit a crime within Canada, and to those who conspire inside Canada to commit a crime outside Canada.

Section 13 of the *Criminal Code* provides that no person shall be convicted of an offence committed while that person was under twelve years of age.[58] Before 1983, only those under seven were deemed incapable of committing a crime, and those between seven and fourteen years of age could only be convicted if they "were competent to know the nature and consequence of their conduct and to appreciate that it was wrong."[59]

Court did not consider this defence because they held the accused had a *mens rea* defence because he had no knowledge of those characteristics of the tapes which made them obscene.

56   A person in Canada who has committed a crime elsewhere can, subject to *Charter*, above note 15, standards, be sent back or extradited to that country. *Extradition Act*, R.S.C. 1985, c. E-23.

57   *Code*, above note 4, s. 7. See also s. 46(3) (treason); s. 57 (forging a passport); s. 58 (fraudulent use of citizenship certificate); s. 74 (piracy); s. 290 (bigamy); s. 462.3 (entreprise crime).

58   Those who are twelve years of age but under eighteen may be convicted of *Criminal Code* offences, but they are tried and punished under the provisions of the *Youth Criminal Justice Act*, S.C. 2002 c. 1.

59   *Criminal Code of Canada*, R.S.C. 1970, c. C-34, s. 13.

5) Policy Elements in the Definition of the *Actus Reus*: The Case of Consent

The definition of the prohibited act is an important policy component of the criminal law. The legislative definition of the *actus reus* indicates what conduct will be prohibited and criminalized in our society. Sexual offences provide an important example. Rape used to be defined in the *Criminal Code* as sexual intercourse with a female person who is not the accused's wife.[60] In 1983, the offence of rape was replaced with offences of sexual assault, sexual assault with a weapon or threats, and aggravated sexual assault. In an attempt to emphasize the violence in sexual offences, Parliament broadened the prohibited act to include all intentional applications of force without consent in circumstances that were objectively sexual.[61] The marital rape exception was also repealed.

In a further attempt to protect the sexual integrity of women and spell out that "no means no," Parliament in 1992 further defined consent for the purpose of sexual assault as "the voluntary agreement of the complainant to engage in the sexual activity in question." Moreover, it provided that no consent is obtained where:

(a) the agreement is expressed by the words or conduct of a person other than the complainant;

(b) the complainant is incapable of consenting to the activity;

(c) the accused induces the complainant to engage in the activity by abusing a position of trust, power or authority;

(d) the complainant expresses, by words or conduct, a lack of agreement to engage in the activity; or

(e) the complainant, having consented to engage in sexual activity, expresses, by words or conduct, a lack of agreement to engage in the activity.[62]

This provision defines certain examples where the accused will be precluded from arguing that the prohibited act of sexual assault did not occur because the complainant consented. It establishes as an objective statement of law that consent is a voluntary agreement to engage in the particular sexual activity and that there cannot be consent if (a) agreement is given by a third party, (b) the complainant is incapable of consenting, (c) the complainant is induced to participate by abuse of a position of trust, power, and authority, or the complainant, expresses a

---

60　*Ibid.*, s. 135.

61　*R. v. Chase* (1987), 37 C.C.C. (3d) 97 (S.C.C.).

62　*Code*, above note 4, s. 273.1, introduced in *An Act to Amend the Criminal Code (Sexual Assault)*, S.C. 1992, c. 38, s. 1.

lack of agreement, by either words or comments, to engage or continue to engage in sexual activity (d, e). The accused can still argue that
although there was no consent in these situations and the *actus reus*
was committed, he still did not have the *mens rea* to commit sexual
assault. This topic will be discussed in chapter 4.

The Supreme Court has rejected the defence of implied consent to
sexual assault.[63] In other words, it has rejected the idea that although
the complainant did not actually consent, her conduct failed to meet
an objective standard of consent. Thus, as a matter of determining the
actus reus of consent "[t]he absence of consent . . . is subjective and
determined by reference to the complainant's subjective internal state
of mind toward the touching, at the time it occurred."[64] The trier of fact
"may only come to one of two conclusions: the complainant either
consented or not. There is no third option. If the trier of fact accepts
the complainant's testimony that she did not consent, no matter how
strongly her conduct may contradict that claim, the absence of consent
is established."[65] The existence of consent for the purpose of defining
the *actus reus* of sexual assault thus depends on the subjective perceptions of the victims as opposed to external and objective standards of
law. Similarly, consent will be negated by the complainant's fear of the
application of force regardless of the reasonableness of the fear or
whether it was communicated to the accused. A statement by the victim that she did not consent or did so because of fear will be determinative unless it is found not to be a credible statement of her state of
mind at the time the offence occurred. The Court is understandably
concerned about maximizing the physical and sexual integrity of
women and rejecting the rape myths that women implicitly consent to
sexual activity unless they protest or resist or clearly expressly fear. The
Court's vehicle for rejecting these myths is to make the issue of consent
for the purpose of defining *actus reus* dependent on the subjective perceptions of the complainant even if they are uncommunicated and
unreasonable.

The Court took a different approach in *R. v. Cuerrier*,[66] which dealt
with the issue of whether a person's non-disclosure of his positive HIV

---

63   *R. v. Ewanchuk* (1999), 131 C.C.C. (3d) 481 (S.C.C.) [*Ewanchuk*].

64   *Ibid.* at 494.

65   *Ibid.* at 495.

66   (1998), 127 C.C.C.(3d) 1 (S.C.C.) [*Cuerrier*]. In *R. v. Esau* (1997), 116 C.C.C.
     (3d) 289 at 312 (S.C.C.) McLachlin J. also stated that "[a]t issue, as elsewhere
     in dealing with consent, is the social act of communicating consent, not the
     internal state of mind of the complainant. The accused is not expected to look
     into the complainant's mind and make judgements about her uncommunicated

status constituted fraud vitiating his partner's consent to unprotected sexual intercourse. Cory J. stated that in determining whether consent was obtained fraudulently "[t]he actions of the accused must be assessed objectively to determine whether a reasonable person would find them to be dishonest."[67] A person only had a duty to disclose if the failure to disclose presented a significant risk of serious bodily harm. Thus, a person must disclose HIV-positive status, but not the existence of a common cold. Finally, it must be proven that the complainant would have refused to have unprotected sex if the accused's HIV status was disclosed. The rest of the Court rejected Justice L'Heureux-Dubé's view that any fraud designed to induce the complainant to consent would nullify the consent. There was a concern that her view would trivialize the criminal process by allowing consent to be nullified because, for example, the accused lied about his age or his job. Although requiring objective dishonesty, Justice L'Heureux Dubé's approach seems more consistent with the approach in *Ewanchuk*, which ties consent not to objective and external legal standards of what society will accept as consent but to the complainant's subjective and perhaps idiosyncratic perceptions.

Parliament has defined what is meant by consent for policy reasons in other sections of the *Criminal Code*. For example, section 14 provides that people cannot consent to their death, and section 286 provides that consent is no defence to the abduction of a child. Section 150.1(1) provides that the complainant's consent is no defence to various sexual offences involving those under the age of fourteen.[68] This provision defines consent for the purpose of determining the *actus reus*. Section 150.1(4) addresses the accused's fault or mental element by providing that a subjective belief that the complainant was fourteen or older is not a defence "unless the accused took all reasonable steps to ascertain the age of the complainant."[69]

In *R. v. Jobidon*,[70] the Supreme Court held that a person could not consent to an assault that intentionally causes "serious hurt or non-

---

thoughts. But neither is he entitled to presume consent in the absence of communicative ability." It is possible, however, that both the above statements might be characterized as relating to the *mens rea* as opposed to the *actus reus* of the offence.

67   *Cuerrier, ibid.* at 49.

68   Some exceptions are made if the accused is under sixteen years of age, less than two years older than the complainant, and not in a position of trust, authority, or dependency with the complainant. *Code*, above note 4, s. 151.1(2).

69   See ch. 4, "The Fault Element, or *Mens Rea*."

70   (1991), 66 C.C.C. (3d) 454 at 494 (S.C.C.) [*Jobidon*].

trivial bodily harm . . . in the course of a fist fight or brawl," and that a minor could not consent to an adult's intentional application of force in a fight. Gonthier J. recognized that "some may see limiting the freedom of an adult to consent to applications of force in a fist fight as unduly paternalistic and a violation of self-rule," but he argued:

> All criminal law is "paternalistic" to some degree — top-down guidance is inherent in any prohibitive rule. That the common law has developed a strong resistance to recognizing the validity of consent to intentional applications of force in fist fights and brawls is merely one instance of the criminal law's concern that Canadian citizens treat each other humanely and with respect.[71]

The Court did indicate that consent would not be negated if the bodily harm was trivial or an accepted part of socially valued activity such as sports. In dissent, Sopinka J. argued that the above rule interfered with Parliament's decision to make lack of consent a requirement for an assault and allowed judges to use the common law to expand the breadth of the offence of assault. On the facts of the case, however, even Sopinka J. found no consent, because what had started as a consensual fist fight had become a severe beating resulting in death. Subsequent cases have found that minors cannot consent to fights where serious harm is intended and caused, but they can consent to schoolyard scuffles where serious harm is not intended or caused.[72] Whether by statutory words or judicial interpretation, the definition of the prohibited act is an important policy element of the criminal law.

Other terms in the criminal law are defined broadly. Assault is defined in section 265 to include not only the non-consensual and intentional application of direct or indirect force on another person, but also attempts or threats "by an act or a gesture, to apply force to another person" if the accused causes the complainant to believe on reasonable grounds that he or she has the present ability to effect his purpose. In addition, section 264.1 creates the separate offence of uttering threats.

---

71   *Ibid.*
72   *R. v. W.(G.)* (1994), 90 C.C.C. (3d) 139 (Ont. C.A.); *R. v. M.(S.)* (1995), 97 C.C.C. (3d) 281 (Ont. C.A.). Some courts suggest that consent will not be vitiated so long as non-trivial bodily harm is not intended even though it may be caused. *R. v. B.(T.B.)* (1994), 93 C.C.C. (3d) 191 (P.E.I.C.A.); *R. v. McIlwaine* (1996), 111 C.C.C. (3d) 426 (Que. C.A.). The Supreme Court's approach in *Jobidon*, above note 70, however, suggests that consent can be vitiated more by the harm caused than the harm intended.

Section 4(3) defines possession broadly to include not only personal possession, but knowingly having something in the actual possession or custody of another person or in another place. Joint possession is deemed where "one of two or more persons, with the knowledge and consent of the rest, has anything in his custody or possession." Courts have interpreted a person's knowledge and consent to require that the person deemed to be in possession must have a measure of control over the matter.[73]

Section 322 defines theft as the taking or conversion of anything. Despite this apparently broad definition of the *actus reus* of theft, the Supreme Court has excluded the taking of confidential information from the offence of theft on the basis that information alone does not constitute property as protected under the criminal law, and its theft does not deprive the possessor of the use or possession of the confidential information.[74] The Court's interpretation of the *actus reus* of theft means that taking confidential information alone is not presently theft, but taking a piece of paper that contains confidential information may be theft. This definition seems anachronistic in the computer age. Parliament can, of course, always amend the crime of theft to make clear that taking confidential information does indeed constitute theft, or it can enact a new offence.[75]

B. THE ROLE OF THE *ACTUS REUS* IN CRIMINAL LIABILITY

1) The Coincidence of the *Actus Reus* and *Mens Rea*

A traditional principle of criminal law has been that the accused must commit the criminal act at the same time that he or she has the fault element required for the particular crime.[76] This requirement, sometimes called the simultaneous principle, has frequently been finessed. In *Fagan v. Metropolitan Police Commissioner*,[77] the accused accidentally

---

73   *R. v. Terrence* (1983), 4 C.C.C. (3d) 193 (S.C.C.).

74   *R. v. Stewart* (1988), 41 C.C.C. (3d) 481 at 494–95 (S.C.C.).

75   For example, see *Code*, above note 4, ss. 326 and 342.1, prohibiting the taking of electricity, gas, or telecommunication services and unauthorized use of a computer.

76   The Latin phrase is *actus non facit reum, nisi mens sit rea* or "the intent and the act must both concur to constitute the crime." *Fowler v. Padget* (1798), 101 E.R. 1103 at 1106 (K.B.).

77   (1968), [1969] 1 Q.B. 439.

drove his car on a police officer's foot. After being informed of this fact, the accused switched off the ignition and swore at the officer, before eventually moving the car. The accused was convicted of assaulting a police officer and the conviction upheld on appeal. In his dissent, Bridge J. noted the theoretical dilemma that when the accused committed the initial act of assault, he did not know what he was doing, while when the accused did know that he was assaulting the officer, he did not act. The majority, however, took a more practical approach and held that the *actus reus* was not complete when the accused first drove onto the officer's foot, but continued while the force of the car was applied and the accused became aware of his actions. Thus, the mental element of knowledge coincided with this expanded definition of the act of assault. An alternative to the continuous act approach would be to hold that the accused, having created a danger by driving onto the officer's foot, was under a duty to take reasonable steps to rectify the situation.[78] This would make the failure to act a sufficient criminal act even though it might not technically fit the definition of the crime of assaulting a police officer.

In murder cases, courts have also been prepared to hold the accused guilty if the mental element was present at any point of time during the transaction that culminated in death. In *R. v. Meli*,[79] the accused struck the victim with the intent to kill, and then threw him over a cliff. The victim survived those events, but died some time later of exposure. The Privy Council upheld the murder conviction, stating that the accused had formed the intent to kill and it was impossible to divide the transaction which resulted in the victim's death. In *R. v. Cooper*,[80] the Supreme Court of Canada adopted *Meli* and upheld a murder conviction, on the basis that at some point during two minutes of strangulation the accused formed the intent to kill. The accused need not have had the intent throughout the entire transaction and the possibility that he may have "blacked out" because of intoxication did not excuse so long as the accused had the fault at some time during the strangulation. Cory J. concluded: "It was sufficient that the intent and the act of strangulation coincided at some point. It was not necessary that the requisite intent continue throughout the entire two minutes required to cause the death of the victim."[81]

---

78   *R. v. Miller*, [1983] 2 A.C. 161 (H.L.) [*Miller*].
79   [1954] 1 W.L.R. 228 (P.C.).
80   (1993), 78 C.C.C. (3d) 289 (S.C.C.).
81   *Ibid.* at 298.

Another departure from the requirement that the fault element and the prohibited act occur at the same time has been the traditional rule with respect to intoxication for general intent offences such as assault or sexual assault. If the accused was so intoxicated at the time the assault was committed that he did not have the minimal mental element required, then the fault in becoming so intoxicated would be sufficient to convict the person of the general intent offence.[82] The fault in becoming extremely intoxicated would be formed long before the prohibited act was committed, but would be sufficient. This departure from the simultaneous principle has been held by the Supreme Court to violate sections 7 and 11(d) of the *Charter* by substituting the fault of becoming drunk for the mental element of a general intent offence, when the former does not lead inexorably to the latter.[83] Parliament has, however, responded by deeming the fault of becoming extremely intoxicated to be sufficient for a conviction of violent offences.[84]

Criminal and regulatory offences based on negligence may also constitute a departure from the principle that fault occurs at the same time as the prohibited act. An accused can be found to be negligent for failing to take precautionary measures long before the prohibited act was committed. For example, an oil tanker may spill its content and the shipping company be negligent because the tanker was not inspected and repaired the last time it was in harbour. The purpose of regulatory and negligence-based offences, of course, is to prevent harm before it occurs, and some departure from the simultaneous principle may be necessary to achieve this end.

2) Causing Prohibited Consequences

When the criminal act prohibits a consequence or a result, it is necessary to determine if the accused's actions have actually caused the prohibited consequence or result. Canadian criminal law does not take an overly strict approach to causation and allows a person to be held liable for causing consequences even if the consequences are caused in part by the victim's peculiar and perhaps unforeseeable vulnerabilities. This is often called the "thin skull" rule, or the principle that accused take their victims as they find them. In addition, it is not necessary that the accused's acts be the sole operative cause of the prohibited conse-

---

82   *R. v. Majewski* (1976), 62 Cr. App. Rep. 262 (H.L.); *R. v. Leary* (1977), 33 C.C.C. (2d) 473 (S.C.C.). See ch. 6, "Intoxication."

83   *R. v. Daviault* (1994), 93 C.C.C. (3d) 21 (S.C.C.) [*Daviault*].

84   *Code*, above note 4, s. 33.1.

quences. This fits into the general trend towards expansive definitions of the criminal act, but may have some harsh results in particular cases. The unanticipated harm caused by actions may be a mitigating factor in sentencing, particularly in manslaughter, which has no minimum penalty.

a) Statutory Provisions in Homicide Cases

Causation issues often arise in homicide cases, and they are in part governed by specific provisions in the *Criminal Code*. Section 222(1) provides that a person commits homicide when, directly or indirectly, by any means, he or she causes the death of a human being. Section 224 provides that a person is responsible for a death even though it might have been prevented by resorting to proper means. This section would apply where victims die as a result of a wound, but could have been saved if they had accepted or received proper medical treatment.[85] A person who stabs another in a remote location will be held responsible for causing that person's death even though the very same wound may not have been life-threatening if inflicted in a place with medical facilities. Section 225 provides that a person who causes a dangerous injury is responsible for death notwithstanding that the immediate cause of death is proper or improper treatment rendered in good faith. A person who stabs another will be responsible even though the immediate cause of death might be negligent treatment of the wound by a doctor. Section 225 might be less favourable to the accused than the common law, which has held that very bad treatment which overtakes the initial wound can break the chain of causation, so that it is unfair to conclude that the accused caused the death.[86] Under section 226 a person is deemed to have caused death even though the bodily injury that results in death accelerates a pre-existing disease. This provision suggests that an accused must assume responsibility if the victim's "thin skull" takes the form of a pre-existing disease. Sections 222(5)(c) provides that a person commits homicide when they cause a person by threats, fear of violence or by deception to do anything that causes the person's death. The Supreme Court has observed that "these statutory provisions and others like them preempt any speculation as to whether the triggering

---

85   In *R. v. Blaue*, [1975] 1 W.L.R. 1411 (C.A.), a manslaughter conviction was upheld when the victim refused a blood transfusion because of her religious beliefs. In *R. v. Smith* (1959), 43 Cr. App. Rep. 121 (C.A.), the accused was held to have caused death even though proper medical treatment would have probably saved the victim's life.

86   *R. v. Jordan* (1956), 40 Cr. App. Rep. 152 (C.C.A.).

of a chain of events was then interupted by an intervening cause which serves to distance and exonerate the accused from any responsibility for the consequences."[87]

b) General Principles of Causation in Homicide Cases

The *Criminal Code* does not comprehensively codify all causation issues that may arise in a homicide case. As the Supreme Court has stated: "[w]here the factual situation does not fall within one of the statutory rules of causation in the *Code*, the common law general principles of criminal law apply to resolve any causation issues that may arise."[88] In *R. v. Smithers*,[89] the Supreme Court upheld a manslaughter conviction on the basis that the accused's action of kicking the deceased in the stomach "was at least a contributing cause of death, outside the *de minimis* range," even though the death was in part caused by the victim's malfunctioning epiglottis, which caused him to choke to death on his own vomit. Dickson J. upheld the applicability of the thin skull principle in the criminal law of homicide by stating:

> Death may have been unexpected, and the physical reactions of the victim unforeseen, but that does not relieve the [accused]. . . .
>
>   It is a well-recognized principle that one who assaults another must take his victim as he finds him.[90]

One Court of Appeal has stated that the contributing cause and thin skull principles set out in *Smithers* establish "a test of sweeping accountability" for causing death that might be vulnerable to challenge under section 7 of the *Charter* as infringing the principles of fundamental justice.[91]

Nevertheless, the *Smithers* approach to causation in homicide cases has survived under the *Charter*. In *R. v. Creighton*,[92] the Supreme Court cited the need to maintain the thin skull principle as a reason for requiring only objective foreseeability of bodily harm as opposed to death as the fault element for unlawful act manslaughter. This suggests that the thin skull principle is relevant to both the *mens rea* and the

---

87   *R. v. Nette*, [2001] 3 S.C.R. 488 at para. 48 [*Nette*].
88   *Ibid.*
89   (1977), 34 C.C.C. (2d) 427 (S.C.C.) [*Smithers*].
90   *Ibid.* at 437.
91   *R. v. F.(D.L.)* (1989), 52 C.C.C. (3d) 357 at 365 (Alta. C.A.).
92   (1993), 83 C.C.C. (3d) 346 (S.C.C.). See ch. 4, "The Fault Element, or *Mens Rea*." Similarly in *Smithers*, above note 89 at 436, Dickson J. stated: "It is no defence to a manslaughter charge that the fatality was not anticipated or that death ordinarily would not result from the unlawful act."

actus reus despite strong arguments that it should be confined to considerations of what happened and not influence the determination of whether the accused was at fault for what happened.

In *R. v. Cribbin*,[93] the Ontario Court of Appeal concluded that the de minimis causation test and thin skull principles approved in *Smithers* and *Creighton* are consistent with the principles of fundamental justice that forbid the punishment of the morally innocent. Arbour J.A. stated:

> As the law of manslaughter stands, if a person commits an unlawful dangerous act, in circumstances where a reasonable person would have foreseen the risk of bodily harm which is neither trivial nor transitory, and the unlawful act is at least a contributing cause of the victim's death, outside the *de minimis* range, then the person is guilty of manslaughter. Both causation and the fault element must be proved beyond a reasonable doubt before the prosecution can succeed. Combined in that fashion, both requirements satisfy the principles of fundamental justice in that any risk that the *de minimis* test could engage the criminal responsibility of the morally innocent is removed by the additional requirement of objective foresight.[94]

The result is that a person could be convicted of manslaughter on the basis that his or her unlawful acts played more than a minimal role in the death, even though death was not reasonably foreseeable. A manslaughter conviction was upheld in *Cribbin* because the accused's assault had contributed to the victim's death, even though the victim had been subject to more serious assaults by another person and had died because he drowned in his own blood.

In *R. v. Nette*,[95] the Supreme Court revisited *Smithers*. Although the Court did not overrule *Smithers*, it reformulated and arguably elevated the test for causation in homicide cases. Arbour J. for a majority of the Court concluded that "the causation standard expressed in *Smithers* is still valid and applicable to all forms of homicide" (that is, murder, manslaughter, and infanticide). Nevertheless, she added:

> In order to explain the standard as clearly as possible to the jury, it may be preferable to phrase the standard of causation in positive terms using a phrase such as "significant contributing cause" rather than using expressions phrased in the negative such as "not a trivial

---

93   (1994), 89 C.C.C. (3d) 67 (Ont. C.A.).
94   *Ibid.* at 88.
95   [2001] 3 S.C.R. 488.

cause" or "not insignificant." Latin terms such as *de minimis* are rarely helpful.[96]

L'Heureux-Dubé J. with three other judges dissented and would have maintained the negative formulation contemplated under *Smithers*. She argued that "[t]here is a meaningful difference between expressing the standard as 'a contributing cause that is not trivial or insignificant' and expressing it as a 'significant contributing cause.'"[97] All the judges were agreed, however, that the accused had caused the death of a ninety-five-year-old widow he had left hog-tied and alone after robbing her home. The victim died of asphyxiation some twenty-four to forty-eight hours later. Medical evidence showed that a number of factors contributed to the death, including the hog-tied position, a moderately tight ligature that the accused had left around the victim's neck, as well as the victim's age, asthma, and congestive heart failure. Arbour J. concluded that "the fact that the appellant's actions might not have caused death in a different person, or that death might have taken longer to occur in the case of a younger victim, does not transform this case into one involving multiple causes."[98] It remains to be seen whether in other cases, there would be a difference between the new significant contributing cause test advocated by the majority in *Nette* as opposed to the non-trivial cause test in *Smithers* and defended by the minority in *Nette*.

c) Substantial Cause and First-Degree Murder

Although the Court stressed in *Nette* that there is one causation test for all homicide cases, it also recognized that section 231(5), contemplates an additional and more stringent causation test for that particular form of first-degree murder. Section 231(5) requires that the death be caused while the accused is committing or attempting to commit a list of enumerated offences, including sexual assault, kidnapping, and hostage-taking. In *Harbottle*, the Supreme Court concluded that an accused may only be convicted of first-degree murder under section 231(5) if his or her actions "form an essential, substantial and integral part of the killing of the victim." Cory J. elaborated:

> The substantial causation test requires that the accused play a very active role — usually a physical role — in the killing. . . . Obviously, this requirement is much higher than that described in *R. v. Smithers* . . . which dealt with the offence of manslaughter. There it was held

---

96   *Ibid.* at para. 71.
97   *Ibid.* at para. 6.
98   *Ibid.* at para. 81. See also *R. v. Knight*, [2003] 1 S.C.R. 156.

. . . that sufficient causation existed where the actions of the accused were "a contributing cause of death, outside the *de minimis* range." That case demonstrates the distinctions in the degree of causation required for the different homicide offences.[99]

The Court found that there was substantial causation in *Harbottle* because the accused had held the victim's legs to stop her from struggling while his co-accused strangled her to death. The Court rejected an even stricter causation test that would have required the Crown to prove that the accused's acts were a physical cause of death, because it would lead to impractical and non-purposive distinctions. On the facts of the case, it was impossible "to distinguish between the blameworthiness of an accused who holds the victim's legs, thus allowing his co-accused to strangle her, and the accused who performs the act of strangulation."[100] At the same time, section 231(5) will in most cases require the accused to play a physical role in the killing.

In *Nette*,[101] the Supreme Court rejected the idea that the substantial causation standard articulated in *Harbottle* should apply in all homicide cases. Rather it was restricted to sections 231(5) and 231(6), which both have the wording "when death is caused by that person." In cases under those sections, the jury must be given two different causation tests. The first that applies to the causing of death is "that the acts of the accused have to have made a 'significant' contribution to the victim's death to trigger culpability for the homicide." The second causation test under sections 231(5) or (6) is that "the accused's actions must have been an essential, substantial and integral part of the killing of the victim."[102] Multiple causation tests, especially those that hinge on the fine distinction between "significant" and "substantial" causation, may be difficult for the jury to understand.

To further complicate matters, the *Harbottle* substantial cause test does not apply to all forms of first-degree murder. There is no substantial cause requirement in section 231(2) that provides for planned and deliberate murders, section 231(3) that applies to contract murders and section 231(4) that applies to murders of police officers and prison guards. Even more striking is the fact that sections 231(6.01), 6.1 and 6.2 all avoid the *Harbottle* substantial cause test by only requiring that death be caused while committing or attempting to commit certain

---

99 *R. v. Harbottle* (1993), 84 C.C.C. (3d) 1 at 13–14 (S.C.C.) [*Harbottle*].
100 *Ibid.* at 12.
101 [2001] 3 S.C.R. 488.
102 *Ibid.* at paras. 73 and 82.

crimes as opposed to death "being caused by that person" during the crimes.[103] Parliament could amend sections 231(5) and (6) to reject the requirement in *Harbottle* that each accused play a substantial role in the killing of the victim. Although this would expand the ambit of liability for first-degree murder, it would end the need for the jury to be instructed about two causation tests in some cases where first-degree murder is charged.

d)   Concurrent Causes of Death

Courts have concluded that an accused caused death when he or she set off a chain of events that ended in a person's death, even though the immediate cause of death had not been at the accused's hands. In *R. v. Kitching*,[104] an accused who had assaulted the victim, causing his "brain death," was held responsible, even though the immediate cause of death was the medical withdrawal of life support. The accused's conduct "need not be shown to be the sole or 'effective' cause of a crime . . . there may be two or more independent operative causes of death." An accused who shot a person who then cut his own throat was still held to have caused the person's death.[105] Similarly, an accused who shot a person who had already been grievously shot by another person was still held to have caused the victim's death.[106] In a manslaughter case, the accused was responsible for causing the death of a victim he had used as a shield even even though the victim had been shot by the police returning the accused's fire.[107] Reasonable acts performed by a victim trying to escape[108] or police officers enforcing the law are not intervening acts breaking the chain of causation, because they are compelled by the accused's actions.

Although an accused may still be held to responsible for causing death when there are concurrent causes of the death, it will be necessary in some cases for the jury to be instructed about whether an intervening event has "severed the chain of causation" in such a manner that the accused's actions are no longer a significant contributing cause of the victim's death. A person engaged in illegal drag racing may be held responsible for causing the death of a fellow racer, a passenger, other vehicles and pedestrians, but only so far as the accused's actions

---

103 *Ibid.* at para. 63.
104 (1976), 32 C.C.C. (2d) 159 at 175 (Man. C.A.).
105 *People v. Lewis*, 57 P. 470 (S.C.Cal. 1899).
106 *R. v. Green* (1988), 43 C.C.C. (3d) 413 (B.C.S.C.).
107 *R. v. Pagett* (1983), 76 Cr. App. Rep. 279 (C.A.).
108 See also *Code*, above note 4, s. 222(5)(c).

constitute a significant cause of the death.[109] A racer has been held not responsible for a fatal crash of a fellow racer because of a reasonable doubt that the deceased would have recognized that the accused "was backing away and had given up the race before the fatal crash."[110] In other words, the Crown failed to proove beyond a reasonable doubt that the accused's actions in racing constituted a significant contributing cause of the death. A new trial was ordered in another case in which the accused caused the victim to become unconscious because of a headlock, but the victim died when his friends' attempts at resuscitation had the unfortunate effect of causing the victim to choke to death on his own vomit. The Nova Scotia Court of Appeal concluded that the jury should be asked whether they were "satisfied beyond a reasonable doubt that the actions [of the accused] are so connected to the death . . . that they can be said to have had a significant causal effect which continued up to the time of his death, without having been interrupted" by the intervening act of the botched resuscitation. The Court of Appeal added that the jury must not be convinced that the accused's actions were "the sole cause" of the death but rather, consistent with *Nette*, that they were "a significant contributing cause."[111] At the same time, however, the Court of Appeal indicated that it was not sufficient to instruct the jury on the *Nette* test of causation; the jury must also be instructed about the intervening event and asked to determine if the accused's actions remained a significant contributing cause of death. These cases indicate that while the accused's actions do not have to be the sole cause of death, there may be situations where the chain of causation will be broken so that the accused's actions are no longer the significant cause of death. For example, the accused would not be responsible for causing a person's death if he assaulted a victim, leaving the victim unconscious, but the victim was then killed by a subsequent and independent fire or building collapse.

e)   Causation in Non-Homicide Cases

Causation issues sometimes arise in non-homicide cases. In *R. v. Winning*,[112] a conviction of obtaining credit by false pretences was overturned because even though the accused made false statements in her application for a credit card, the company did not rely on these statements when issuing the credit card. If the accused had the necessary

---

109 *R. v. Menzies* (2002), 50 C.R.(5th) 343 at para. 105 (Ont. Sup. Ct. J.).
110 *Ibid.* at para. 125.
111 *R. v. Reid and Stratton* (2003), 180 C.C.C. (3d) 151 at para. 89 (N.S.C.A.).
112 (1973), 12 C.C.C. (3d) 449 (Ont. C.A.).

intent, however, it might be possible to convict him or her of attempting to obtain credit by false pretences because the *actus reus* for attempts only requires some step beyond mere preparation to commit the offence. When a person is charged with impaired driving causing bodily harm or death, the Crown must show that the accused's impairment was a contributing cause outside the *de minimis* range to the bodily harm or death. It cannot simply rely on the fact that the driver was impaired with alcohol.[113]

A distinction is sometimes drawn between legal and factual causation. In *R. v. Williams*[114] a man was charged with aggravated assault on the basis that he had sex with a woman, knowing he was HIV-positive. The man learned he was HIV-positive in November and failed to inform the victim, but the sexual relationship had begun in June.The woman became HIV-positive, but there was no certainty about exactly when she became so infected. The Supreme Court held that the man should be acquitted of aggravated assault because it was possible that the woman was already infected at the point in time at which the accused had sex with her knowing he was HIV-positive. This case suggests that the accused will have the benefit of any reasonable doubt about factual cauasation. It also illustrates the continued need for a coincidence between the *actus reus* and *mens rea*. When the accused had the required fault of knowingly risking HIV transmission, he could not commit the *actus reus* because the woman was already infected. When the accused may have committed the act of infecting the victim, he did not have the guilty knowledge. As will be examined in the next chapter, however, the accused in *Williams* was convicted of attempted aggravated sexual assault because at the time he had the necessary fault of knowing he was HIV-positive and not telling the woman, the accused had committed an act that was sufficient to constitute the very broadly defined *actus reus* of attempt. A person can be guilty of an attempted crime even though the commission of the completed offence may be impossible.

3) Omissions

One possible exception to the trend to wide definitions of the criminal act is the traditional reluctance to use a failure to act as an *actus reus*.

---

113 *R. v. Ewart* (1989), 53 C.C.C. (3d) 153 (Alta. C.A.); *R. v. Powell* (1989), 52 C.C.C. (3d) 403 (Sask. C.A.); *R. v. Stephens* (1991), 27 M.V.R. (2d) 24 (Ont. C.A.); *R. v. Fisher* (1992), 13 C.R. (4th) 222 (B.C.C.A.); *R. v. Laprise* (1996) 113 C.C.C. (3d) 87 (Que. C.A.).

114 *R. v. Williams* 2003 SCC 41 [*Williams*].

Traditionally, the criminal law has prohibited harmful conduct; it has not required socially desirable conduct. An omission or failure to act will generally only form the *actus reus* of a criminal offence when an individual has a specific legal duty to act.

Legal duties to act can be found throughout the *Criminal Code* and other statutes. Section 215 of the *Criminal Code* provides that a parent, spouse, or guardian has a legal duty to provide the necessaries of life for their child, spouse, or charge, and makes it an offence to fail to do so without lawful excuse. If a person commits this offence,[115] or is criminally negligent in omitting to perform another duty imposed by law,[116] he or she can be convicted of manslaughter by means of an unlawful act, or criminal negligence.[117] Those who undertake to do an act have a legal duty to perform the act, if an omission to do the act is or may be dangerous to life.[118] This duty could apply to a person who agreed to be a lifeguard, but who did not make reasonable efforts to save a drowning person. On the other hand, a person who had not agreed to be a lifeguard would be under no such duty. He or she legally could walk away from a drowning person. The Ontario Court of Appeal has stressed that only binding and intentional commitments will suffice to expose an accused to criminal liability for failing to act. A mere expression of words will not normally be enough to create a duty under section 217.[119]

There is a duty to use reasonable care when providing medical treatment or other lawful acts that may endanger the life of others.[120] This duty was breached by a person who donated blood that he knew was infected with HIV.[121] It is also an offence not to use reasonable care in handling explosives;[122] to disobey a court order;[123] to fail to assist a peace officer when requested;[124] to abandon a child;[125] not to obtain assistance in child-birth;[126] to fail to stop when your vehicle is involved

---

115 *R. v. Naglik* (1993), 83 C.C.C. (3d) 526 (S.C.C.).

116 *Code*, above note 4, s. 219.

117 *Code*, above note 4, s. 222(5)(a)(b).

118 *Code*, above note 4, s. 217.

119 *R. v. Browne* (1997) 116 C.C.C. (3d) 183 (Ont. C.A.), leave to appeal denied S.C.C.

120 *Ibid.*, s. 216.

121 *R. v. Thornton* (1993), 82 C.C.C. (3d) 530 (S.C.C.) [*Thornton*].

122 *Code*, above note 4, ss. 79–80.

123 *Ibid.*, s. 127.

124 *Ibid.*, s. 129(b).

125 *Ibid.*, s. 218.

126 *Ibid.*, s. 242.

in an accident;[127] to neglect animals;[128] and to fail to take steps to protect holes in ice or open excavations.[129] A new duty provides that those who direct others to perform tasks or how to work have "a legal duty to take reasonable steps to prevent bodily harm to that person, or any other person, arising from that work or task."[130] Regulatory offences even more frequently penalize the failure to act, by, for example, mandating safety measures or keeping proper records. As criminal and regulatory offences are used to regulate conduct, there seems to be a trend away from the traditional reluctance to penalize omissions.

Duties may also be implicit in particular crimes. In *R. v. Colucci*,[131] the accused was convicted of publishing a false statement with intent to deceive shareholders when he failed to inform them about an engineer's report which stated that there were no prospects for development of a particular mine. A refusal to identify yourself to a police officer who saw you commit a crime has been held to be an obstruction of a police officer under section 129 of the *Criminal Code*.[132] In that case, however, Dickson J. wrote a strong dissent warning that "the criminal law is no place within which to introduce implied duties, unknown to statute and common law, breach of which subjects a person to arrest and punishment."[133] There is also the possibility of courts creating common law duties on their own. In *Miller*,[134] the House of Lords held that a person who accidentally set a house on fire had a duty to take reasonable steps to extinguish the fire or to call the fire department. In the Canadian context, however, such common law duties come precariously close to creating common law crimes contrary to section 9 of the *Criminal Code*. Common law duties challenge the principle of legality because they are created and applied retroactively by courts. In Canada, the preferred approach to *Miller* is found in the Court of Appeal's decision which did not create a free-standing common law duty, but instead found that the accused had adopted the act of setting the fire when he awoke and did not take steps to put out the fire.[135] The controlling principle is not that society is not justified in imposing duties

---

127 *Ibid.*, s. 252.
128 *Ibid.*, s. 446.
129 *Ibid.*, s. 263.
130 *Ibid.*, s. 217.1.
131 [1965] 4 C.C.C. 56 (Ont. C.A.).
132 *R. v. Moore* (1978), 43 C.C.C. (2d) 83 (S.C.C.).
133 *Ibid.* at 96.
134 Above note 78.
135 *R. v. Miller*, [1982] 2 All E.R. 386 (C.A.).

on people to take reasonable steps to respond to dangers, but that this should be done by the democratic enactment of general, accessible, and prospective duties in the *Criminal Code* and not by judges imposing retroactive common law duties on a case-by-case basis.

4) Voluntariness of the Act

The criminal law has traditionally kept distinct the issue of whether the accused has committed the *actus reus* from whether he or she had the required fault element. In many cases, this does not create a practical problem because a person who commits a prohibited act while asleep or having an involuntary seizure will not have the required fault element. Problems emerge in those cases in which the Crown is not required to prove some fault element or perhaps fault based on objective negligence. For example, a person brought into the country under custody has been convicted of the regulatory offence of being an illegal alien even though the jury believed she was guilty through circumstances beyond her control.[136]

The Supreme Court of Canada has been a pioneer in building a voluntariness requirement into the *actus reus*.[137] In the 1962 case of *King*, the Supreme Court refused to convict a person of impaired driving when the impairment was caused by involuntarily consuming a drug at the dentist's office. One judge argued that "there can be no *actus reus* unless it is the result of a willing mind at liberty to make a definite choice or decision."[138] This approach builds a minimal mental or fault element into the *actus reus* and suggests that an accused who acts involuntarily may not have committed the *actus reus* of an offence.

In *Theroux*,[139] McLachlin J. stated that the *mens rea* of an offence "does not encompass all of the mental elements of a crime" because "the *actus reus* has its own mental element" — namely, that "the act must be the voluntary act of the accused for the *actus reus* to exist." McLachlin J. and Lamer C.J. have also stated that the involuntary conduct that would accompany a heart attack, an epileptic seizure, a detached retina, or a bee sting would prevent the Crown from proving

---

136 *R. v. Larsonneur* (1933), 24 Cr. App. Rep. 74 (C.C.A.).

137 See also the statement of New Zealand judges that the commission of the *actus reus* cannot be involuntary or unconscious. *Kilbride v. Lake*, [1962] N.Z.L.R. 590 (S.C.).

138 *R. v. King* (1962), 133 C.C.C. 1 at 3 (S.C.C.). In England, however, an accused was convicted despite the involuntary consumption of drugs. *R. v. Kingston*, [1994] 3 W.L.R. 519 (H.L.).

139 (1993), 79 C.C.C. (3d) 449 at 458 (S.C.C.).

the *actus reus* of dangerous driving.[140] LaForest J. has indicated that the unconscious and involuntary behaviour that results in a defence of automatism "is conceptually a subset of the voluntariness requirement which in turn is part of the *actus reus* component of criminal liability."[141] In *Daviault*,[142] Lamer C.J. stated that extreme intoxication that produced involuntary or unconscious behaviour should be seen as negating the *actus reus* of the offence. The majority of the Court held that extreme intoxication would negate the mental element of the assault, but seemed to concede that such a condition could also prevent the voluntary formation of the *actus reus*. In *R. v. Stone*,[143] the Court also acknowledged that, subject to the mental disorder defence, an accused should be acquitted if he or she acted in an involuntary manner. In *R. v. Ruzic*,[144] the Court again referred to the requirement of voluntariness as a fundamental principle of criminal law and a fundamental principle of justice under section 7 of the *Charter*. It related the principle of voluntariness to the requirement that people only be punished if they acted as "autonomous and freely choosing agents." Courts seem increasingly willing to consider a lack of voluntary or conscious conduct as something that prevents the commission of the criminal act, or *actus reus*. This means a lack of voluntariness may be a defence to all criminal and regulatory offences, regardless of the fault element required. In practice, this will be most important in cases with no fault element or one based on negligence because involuntary conduct should usually be inconsistent with subjective forms of fault.

CONCLUSION

Legislative reform could clarify some of the ambiguities in determining the *actus reus* or prohibited act of offences. Although the common law crime of contempt of court survives and codification of all crimes is not required under section 7 of the *Charter*, Parliament could provide that federal laws are the sole source of criminal offences. Even this reform, however, would not truly make the criminal law accessible to most people who understandably do not have the time or inclination to read

---

140 *R. v. Hundal* (1993), 79 C.C.C. (3d) 97 (S.C.C.).
141 *R. v. Parks* (1992), 75 C.C.C. (3d) 287 at 302 (S.C.C.). See ch. 7, "Mental Disorder and Automatism."
142 *Daviault*, above note 83 at 25.
143 *R. v. Stone* (1999), 134 C.C.C. (3d) 353.
144 (2001) 153 C.C.C. (3d) 1 (S.C.C.) at paras. 42 and 46.

thick books of statutes. In order to provide fair notice to the accused and prevent unlimited law enforcement discretion, legislatures should ensure that every criminal act is defined in a manner that is neither excessively vague or overbroad. In reality, however, courts have been very reluctant to strike laws down under section 7 of the *Charter* on the basis that they are excessively vague.[145] They have also added interpretative glosses on offences and defences so that they diverge in significant ways from the words of the statute. The result is that even a conscientious citizen who reads the many pages of the *Criminal Code* will be unable to determine the extent of criminal liability.

The present trend is towards broad legislative definitions of the prohibited act. There will always be a need for judicial interpretation, but controversial policy issues such as whether a person can consent to non-trivial bodily harm[146] and whether consent should be based on the subjective views of the complainant in a sexual assault case[147] should probably be specifically addressed by Parliament. A related issue is whether Parliament should provide new offences to deal with new problems such as those who give blood or have sex without disclosing that they are HIV-positive or whether we should continue to rely on existing offences subject to judicial interpretation.[148]

Parliament could attempt to reconcile the competing approaches to the interpretation of the *Criminal Code* by suggesting that the doctrine of strict construction, which requires judges to give the criminal law a reasonable interpretation that favours the accused, only applies if there are reasonable ambiguities after the law has been given a purposive interpretation designed to achieve its objects. This approach recognizes both the accused's claim to clear and fair notice and society's claim not to have criminal laws trivialized by stunted interpretations that are not designed to achieve Parliament's objectives.

The blunt rule that ignorance of the law is no excuse seems unstable and requires some reform. One issue is whether reasonable mistakes about the law should be an excuse. The present law suggests not, but there is some support for the idea that a reasonable mistake of law that was induced by an official responsible for the administration of the law should prevent a conviction. There is less consensus about whether a mistake of law induced by a lawyer's advice or the accused's own reading of legal materials should be accepted and the present law

---

145 *Heywood*, above note 30.
146 *Jobidon*, above note 70.
147 *Ewanchuk*, above note 63.
148 *Thornton*, above note 121; *Cuerrier*, above note 66; *Williams*, above note 114.

would suggest not. The fault elements of some crimes such as theft allow the accused to argue that a belief that he or she was acting legally raises a reasonable doubt concerning *mens rea*. In any event, courts may continue to be tempted to interpret some matters as mistakes of fact in order to avoid the harshness of holding that they are mistakes of law that offer no excuse.[149] The Supreme Court has also suggested that the operation of section 19 can in some cases turn what might otherwise be a strict liability offence that allows a defence of due diligence into an absolute liability offence.[150] This somewhat mitigates the harshness of the ignorance of the law is no excuse principle because as will be discussed in chapter 5, an accused cannot be imprisoned for an absolute liability offence. At the same time, it does not fundamentally challenge the ignorance of the law is no excuse principle.

Although the present law provides different rules of causation with respect to first-degree murder and other homicide offences, there have been many proposals to have a general test of causation in the *Criminal Code*. Tests based on a substantial contribution with no other unforeseen cause contributing, a significant contribution and more than a negligible contribution have been proposed at various times. The Supreme Court has indicated that the general test is one of a significant contributing cause,[151] but a different substantial causation standard is required for some forms of first degree murder.[152] A single causation test would certainly be easier to explain to juries but there may, however, be a case for continuing to define causation in a contextual manner related to specific crimes. In any event, the accused's actions need not be the sole cause of death, but the possibility that intervening events will break the chain of causation should be considered.

Because they are directed primarily at individuals, it would be helpful if Parliament addressed the issue of criminalizing omissions or failure to act in a principled and comprehensive fashion. Specific duties to act will likely still be imposed on parents and those undertaking dangerous activities, but general duties, such as taking reasonable steps to rescue and taking reasonable steps to rectify a danger that one has created, could be clearly codified. It would be very important that these duties were accessible and well-known to the public. It would also be best if it was specifically recognized that the *mens rea* only need coincide with the

---

149 *Jorgensen*, above note 43.
150 *Pontes*, above note 48.
151 *Nette*, above note 87.
152 *Harbottle*, above note 99.

actus reus at some point during the *actus reus*[153] and that the *actus reus* does not occur if the accused acts in an involuntary manner.

FURTHER READINGS

ASHWORTH, A., "The Scope of Criminal Liability for Omissions" (1989) 105 L.Q. Rev. 424

COLVIN, E., *Principles of Criminal Law*, 2d ed. (Toronto: Carswell, 1991), chs. 3 and 4

GALLOWAY, D., "Causation in Criminal Law: Interventions, Thin Skulls and Lost Chances" (1989) 14 Queen's L.J. 71

GRANT, I., D. CHUNN & C. BOYLE, *The Law of Homicide* (Toronto: Carswell, 1994), ch. 3

HART, H.L.A., & T. HONORE, *Causation in the Law*, 2d ed. (Oxford: Oxford University Press, 1985), chs. 12–14

HOLLAND, W., "HIV/AIDS and the Criminal Law" (1994) 36 Crim. L.Q. 279

MANSON, A., "Rethinking Causation: The Implications of Harbottle" (1994) 24 C.R. (4th) 153

MEWETT, A., & M. MANNING, *Criminal Law*, 3d ed. (Toronto: Butterworths, 1994), ch. 5

STEWART, H. "Mistake of Law Under the *Charter*" (1998) 40 Crim. L.Q. 279

STUART, D., *Canadian Criminal Law: A Treatise*, 4th ed. (Toronto: Carswell, 1995), chs. 2, 4, and 5

WILLIAMS, G., "Criminal Omissions: The Conventional View" (1991) 107 L.Q. Rev. 86

---

153 *Cooper*, above note 80.

CHAPTER 3

UNFULFILLED CRIMES
AND PARTICIPATION
IN CRIMES

The trend towards broad definitions of the criminal act examined in the last chapter can be seen in provisions that make people guilty of crimes even though they have not committed the complete crime. The provisions examined in this chapter cast the net of criminal liability broadly to include those who attempt but fail to complete a crime; those who encourage or plan the commission of a crime; and those who assist others to commit a crime.

A person who goes beyond mere preparation to rob a bank, with the intent to commit the robbery, can be convicted of attempted robbery, even though no robbery took place and it may have been impossible for the complete crime to ever occur. An attempted robbery is, however, subject to less punishment than a robbery. On the other hand, a person who assists in the robbery by driving the getaway car can be convicted of being a party to the robbery by aiding the robbery, even though he or she never took the property with force. Similarly, a bank teller who helped the robber plan the heist might also be guilty of the robbery as a person who abets the crime. The provisions governing attempts and parties to a crime will be considered separately, but they are united in imposing the criminal sanction on those who do not actually commit the complete crime. The relatively high level of *mens rea* required for attempts and parties, however, generally limits these provisions to those who act with guilty intent or knowledge. Sentencing discretion also plays an important role in distinguishing the various degrees of culpability caught by the broad definitions of criminal attempts and parties to a crime.

In section 24 of the *Criminal Code*, Parliament has prohibited attempts at criminal offences. Any act beyond mere preparation may be a sufficient *actus reus* for an attempted crime, even if the act does not amount to a moral wrong or a social mischief. The counterbalance to this broad definition of the *actus reus* is that the Crown must prove beyond a reasonable doubt that the accused acted with the intent to commit the complete offence. In addition to attempts, a person who counsels or solicits the commission of a crime or is part of a conspiracy to commit a crime may also be guilty of the separate crimes of counselling or conspiracy, even though the complete crime was never committed. These unfulfilled crimes are designed to discourage the commission of the complete offence and to recognize that the accused had the intent to commit the complete crime. They are, however, separate offences and, with the exception of conspiracy, subject to less punishment than the complete crime.

The law concerning parties to a crime is in some respects even broader and harsher than the law relating to inchoate crimes such as attempts, counselling, and conspiracy. Parliament has provided in section 21(1)(b) and (c) of the *Criminal Code* that those who assist the person committing the actual criminal offence through aiding or abetting are guilty as parties of the same criminal offence as the person who actually commits the crime. The person who acts as lookout or drives the getaway car can be convicted of robbery just as the person who actually takes the money by force. The *actus reus* is defined to include acts of assistance and acts of encouragement but not mere presence. At the same time, however, the Crown must prove the *mens rea* that the accused intentionally and knowingly aided or abetted the offence. A person who unwittingly delivers a package containing a bomb assists in the bombing, but would not have the intent required to be guilty as an aider or abettor to the bombing.

Section 21(2) makes an accused who has formed an unlawful purpose with an accomplice responsible for crimes that the accused knew or ought to have known would be a probable consequence of carrying out their common purpose. This section requires the formation of an unlawful purpose and either subjective or objective foresight of the additional crimes. The fault element of objective foresight has been found to be unconstitutional when applied to parties charged with murder and attempted murder. Thus, an accused who agreed with an accomplice to assault a person could not be convicted of murder unless he knew that it was likely that the accomplice would actually kill the victim. A requirement for a high level of *mens rea* may counterbalance the broad definition of the prohibited act. At the same time, the courts have indicated that the accused who forms an unlawful purpose does not necessarily have to desire that unlawful purpose. In addition, objective foresight of the further crime is all that is required for most crimes including manslaughter.

The provisions for attempted crimes and participation in crimes examined in this chapter apply to all criminal offences in the *Code* and constitute important extensions of criminal liability. For example, the September 11 terrorists could have been charged with attempted murder or conspiracy to commit murder if they were apprehended before they boarded the planes. Similarly, those who knowingly and intentionally assisted them in carrying out their plots could be charged as parties to their offences. At the same time, however, Parliament may create new crimes that may apply to conduct that might otherwise constitute an attempt to commit to a crime or a form of participation in the commission of the crime.

New crimes can serve as a functional substitute for attempted crimes. For example, charges of attempted sexual assault or attempted sexual interference may not be necessary if a person is guilty of the crime of inviting a person under fourteen years of age to engage in sexual touching.[1] New crimes such as financing, facilitating, or instructing a person to carry out activities for the benefit of a terrorist group may be alternatives to establishing that a person is guilty of attempting or conspiracy to commit the crime intended to be committed by the terrorists.[2] Parliament has also recently created crimes based on participation in the activities of a terrorist group[3] or a criminal organization[4] that can be used instead of charging a person as a party to a crime committed by the group or with an attempt to commit the crime or with a conspiracy to commit the crime.

The multiplication of complete offences to cover what may otherwise be attempts or conspiracies to commit existing crimes or participation in those crimes raises a number of issues. One is simply whether policy-makers and the public understand the extensions of criminal liability examined in this chapter in relation to inchoate offences and participation in offences. Another is whether the new crimes will extend the net of criminal liability by ignoring the general principles studied in this chapter that limit attempts, conspiracies and parties to an offence. If the new crimes do go beyond existing crimes, questions

---

1   *Criminal Code*, R.S.C. 1985, c. C-46, s. 152 [*Code*].
2   *Ibid.*, ss. 83.02, 83.03, 83.04, 83.19, 83.21, and 83.22.
3   *Ibid.*, s. 83.18.
4   *Ibid.*, s. 467.11.

about the appropriate limits of the criminal law can be raised. For example the new crimes could impose criminal liability on the problematic basis of the status of the accused, his or her association with others or for failing to take actions. If on the other hand, the new crimes only make criminal what was already criminal, then they have been enacted mainly to serve symbolic or communicative purposes. Even if the new crimes do not go beyond what would otherwise be an attempt or a party, criminal liability may still be extended because the general principles of attempts, counselling, conspiracies, and parties examined in this chapter can be applied to the new crime even though that crime itself punishes what would otherwise be an attempt or conspiracy to commit a crime or a form of participation in a crime. For example, the many new crimes of terrorism created by Parliament late in 2001 criminalize activities in preparation for terrorism and participation in terrorist groups. At the same time, people can be prosecuted for attempting, conspiring, counselling, or being an accessory after the fact with respect to these new crimes. The result may be to extend the net of criminal liability in unforeseen and complex ways that diminishes the significance of the act requirement and could lead to crimes based on status and guilt by association.

A. ATTEMPTS

Section 24 of the *Criminal Code* provides:

> (1) Every one who, having an intent to commit an offence, does or omits to do anything for the purpose of carrying out his intention is guilty of an attempt to commit the offence whether or not it was possible under the circumstances to commit the offence.
>
> (2) The question whether an act or omission by a person who has an intent to commit an offence is or is not mere preparation to commit the offence, and too remote to constitute an attempt to commit the offence, is a question of law.

Section 463 sets out the punishment for attempted crimes. A person guilty of an attempted crime is generally subject to one-half of the longest term to which a person guilty of the completed offence is liable.[5] A few substantive offences, including bribery and obstructing

---

5   An attempt to commit an offence punishable on summary conviction is itself punishable on summary conviction: *Code*, above note 1, s. 463(c). Attempted murder is subject to life imprisonment: *Code*, above note 1, s. 239.

justice, include attempts as part of the completed offence and, as such, punish them in the same fashion as the completed offence.[6] A broadly defined offence may also be a substitute for charging a person with an attempted crime. For example, many acts that may have been attempted rapes before 1983 could now constitute sexual assaults. Similarly, some unsuccessful thefts could still qualify as thefts if the accused, with the intent to steal, begins to move the object to be stolen.[7] The crime of assault is also defined broadly by Parliament to include not only the striking of another person, but also attempts or threats, by act or gesture, to apply force. Thus, there would be no need to charge a person with attempted assault if he or she threatened a person in a manner that made that person reasonably believe that he or she could be assaulted.[8]

1) *Mens Rea* for Attempts

The *mens rea*, or fault element, is the most important element of attempted crimes because the *actus reus* will, by definition, not include the completed crime. As the Ontario Court of Appeal has observed, "whereas in most crimes it is the *actus reus* which the law endeavours to prevent, and the *mens rea* is only a necessary element of the offence, in a criminal attempt, the *mens rea* is of primary importance and the *actus reus* is the necessary element."[9] Similarly, the Supreme Court has recognized that "the criminal element of the offence of attempt may lie solely in the intent."[10]

After having initially interpreted "the intent to commit an offence" in section 24(1) to include any intent provided in the *Criminal Code* to commit the completed offence,[11] the Supreme Court now interprets the intent to commit an offence as the specific intent to commit the completed offence. In the context of murder, McIntyre J. reasoned as follows:

> The completed offence of murder involves a killing. The intention to commit the complete offence must therefore include an intention to kill. . . . I am then of the view that the *mens rea* for an attempted murder cannot be less than the specific intent to kill. . . .

---

6   *Code*, ss. 119(1)(a)(iii), 123(2) and 139(1).

7   *Ibid.*, s. 322(2).

8   *Ibid.*, s. 265(b)(ii).

9   *R. v. Cline* (1956), 115 C.C.C. 18 at 27 (Ont. C.A.) [*Cline*].

10   *R. v. Ancio* (1984), 10 C.C.C. (3d) 385 at 402 (S.C.C.) [*Ancio*].

11   *R. v. Lajoie* (1973), 10 C.C.C. (2d) 313 (S.C.C.).

. . . Section 24 defines an attempt as "having an intent to commit an offence." Because s. 24 is a general section it is necessary to "read in" the offence in question. The offence of attempted murder then is defined as "having an intent to commit murder." . . .

. . . The fact that certain mental elements, other than an intent to kill, may lead to a conviction for murder where there has been a killing does not mean that anything less than an intent to kill will suffice for an attempt at murder.[12]

The intent that is "read in" for attempted murder is the intent to kill outlined in section 229(a)(i), even though it is constitutionally permissible to convict a person of the completed offence of murder on the basis of a lesser intent.[13] It should be noted that *Ancio* was a decision made without any reference to the *Charter*.

a)   Constitutional Fault Element for Attempted Murder

In *R. v. Logan*,[14] the Supreme Court considered the fault element required under section 7 of the *Charter* for a conviction of attempted murder. Lamer C.J. held that the minimal fault element for attempted murder should be the same as for the commission of murder, on the grounds that the stigma of being convicted of the two offences was the same. He reasoned:

The stigma associated with a conviction for attempted murder is the same as it is for murder. Such a conviction reveals that, although no death ensued from the actions of the accused, the intent to kill was still present in his or her mind. The attempted murderer is no less a killer than a murderer: he may be lucky — the ambulance arrived early, or some other fortuitous circumstance — but he still has the same killer instinct.[15]

In determining whether subjective foresight of death was constitutionally required, "the crucial consideration is whether there is a continuing serious social stigma which will be imposed on the accused upon conviction"[16] and not the existence of sentencing discretion which is

---

12   *Ancio*, above note 10 at 402–3.
13   Namely, subjective foresight of death as required in *R. v. Martineau* (1990), 58 C.C.C. (3d) 353 (S.C.C.) [*Martineau*], discussed in ch. 1, "Fault Requirements."
14   (1990), 58 C.C.C. (3d) 391 (S.C.C.) [*Logan*].
15   *Ibid.* at 399.
16   *Ibid.* at 400.

available for attempted murder but not murder.[17] *Logan* suggests that the minimum fault requirement for attempted murder is the knowledge that death will result and that Parliament could lower the *mens rea* of attempted murder to that point but not below. Nevertheless, it does not overtake the higher standard of an intent to kill that is required by *Ancio*. The *Charter* provides minimum standards of fairness towards the accused, not maximum standards.

b) *Mens Rea* for Other Attempted Offences

The intent required for attempts to commit crimes other than murder is not clear. On the basis of *Ancio*, it could be argued that nothing less than the specific intent to obtain the prohibited result will suffice, even if a conviction for the completed offence could be based on some lesser form of intent. In *R. v. Colburne*,[18] the Quebec Court of Appeal stated that an attempt requires a specific intent to carry out the crime, even if the completed offence requires a lesser intent. On this basis, it could be argued that an attempted sexual assault must be based on the subjective intent to engage in non-consensual sexual activity, even though a person could now be convicted of the completed offence of sexual assault on the basis of recklessness, wilful blindness, or a failure to "take reasonable steps, in the circumstances known to the accused at the time, to ascertain that the complainant was consenting."[19] A discussion of the requirements of the crime of attempted sexual assault may, in many cases, be academic, given the wide definition of the *actus reus* of the completed crime of sexual assault.[20] It is unclear whether courts will accept crimes such as attempted manslaughter or an attempt to commit a strict liability offence as offences because of the difficulties of reconciling such crimes with the idea that attempts require a specific intent to carry out the complete crime.

In *R. v. Williams* ,[21] the Supreme Court recognized the relevance of the high-intent standard contemplated in *Ancio* outside the context of attempted murder. In this case, the Court convicted a man of attempted aggravated assault for having unprotected sex when he knew he was

---

17 Attempted murder is punishable by up to life imprisonment, while murder has a mandatory sentence of life imprisonment.

18 (1991), 66 C.C.C. (3d) 235 at 240, 248–249 (Que. C.A.).

19 *Code*, above note 1, s. 273.2.

20 Section 265(b) of the *Code* defines the *actus reus* of assaults to include attempts or threats to apply force, provided the accused causes the complainant to believe on reasonable grounds that he has the present ability to effect his purpose.

21 2003 SCC 41 [*Williams*].

HIV-positive. As discussed in chapter two, an attempt conviction was entered because there was at least a reasonable doubt that the accused's partner was already infected with HIV when the accused had sex with her, knowing that he was infected. On the *mens rea* issue, Binnie J. stated for the Court:

> The crime of attempt, as with any offence, requires the Crown to establish that the accused *intended* to commit the crime in question: *R. v. Ancio* [1984] 1 S.C.R. 225 at pp. 247–48. The requiste intent is established here. . . . The respondent, knowing . . . he was HIV-positive, engaged in unprotected sex with the complainant intending her thereby to be exposed to the lethal consequences of HIV.[22]

Attempted crimes, by their very nature of not resulting in the prohibited consequences of a completed crime, are characterized by the intent of the accused to carry out the completed crime. Attempts are, in the words of the Supreme Court, crimes where "the *mens rea* of the completed offence is present entirely."[23] Attempts to commit crimes will often require proof of a higher form of *mens rea* than the completed crime because of their very nature as inchoate offences. An intent to commit the complete crime is required for attempt, whereas knowledge or even recklessness will be a sufficient *mens rea* for most complete crimes.

2) The *Actus Reus* of Attempts

Although section 24(2) of the *Criminal Code* states that it is a question of law whether an act or omission "is not mere preparation to commit the offence, and too remote to constitute an attempt to commit the offence," Canadian courts have not been able to provide a universal definition of the prohibited act in criminal attempts. In *Cline*,[24] the Ontario Court of Appeal stated that "a precise and satisfactory definition of the *actus reus* is perhaps impossible," while concluding that "each case must be determined on its own facts, having due regard to the nature of the offence and the particular acts in question." The Court of Appeal added that the *actus reus* for an attempt need not "be a crime or a tort or even a moral wrong or social mischief," nor demonstrate by its nature an unequivocal intent.[25] The *actus reus* must not be

---

22   *Ibid.* at para 62.

23   *Ibid.* at para. 65 quoting *United States of America v. Dynar*, [1997] 2 S.C.R. 462 [*Dynar*] at para. 74.

24   Above note 9 at at 26 and 28.

25   *Ibid.* at 28. See also *R. v. Sorrell* (1978), 41 C.C.C. (2d) 9 (Ont. C.A.) [*Sorrell*].

mere preparation to commit a crime, but it can be the next step done with the intent to commit the crime after preparation is complete. On the facts, the Court of Appeal held that the accused had gone beyond mere preparation when, following his pattern of past indecent assaults, he approached and offered a young boy money to help carry his suitcases. By donning large sunglasses and selecting a secluded alley, the accused had finished preparing to commit the crime, and his approach to the young boy was a sufficient *actus reus*.

In *R. v. Deutsch*,[26] the Supreme Court took a fact and offence specific approach to determining when preparation has ended and the *actus reus* for a criminal attempt has begun. Le Dain J. stated:

> [T]he distinction between preparation and attempt is essentially a qualitative one, involving the relationship between the nature and quality of the act in question and the nature of the complete offence, although consideration must necessarily be given, in making that qualitative distinction, to the relative proximity of the act in question to what would have been the completed offence, in terms of time, location, and acts under the control of the accused remaining to be accomplished.[27]

The Supreme Court went further than *Cline* by holding that the accused had gone beyond mere preparation for the crime of attempted procurement of prostitution when he indicated to job applicants that they could earn up to $100,000 a year and might be required to have sex with clients in order to secure business contracts. By holding out large financial awards in the course of the job interviews, the Court concluded that the accused had gone beyond mere preparation, even though no formal job offer was made and any prostitution would happen "a considerable period of time" in the future.

Determining whether the accused has gone beyond mere preparation and committed an *actus reus* for an attempted crime is difficult to predict. In a subsequent case, the Supreme Court has observed that "the distinction between preparation and attempt is essentially a qualitative one, involving the relationship between the nature and quality of the act in question and the nature of the complete offence." It indicated that "consideration must necessarily be given, in making that qualitative distinction, to the relative proximity of the act in question to what would have been the completed offence, in terms of time, location, and

---

26   (1986), 27 C.C.C. (3d) 385 (S.C.C.) [*Deutsch*].
27   *Ibid.* at 401.

acts under the control of the accused remaining to be accomplished." The Court found that the accused had gone beyond preparation and there was "sufficient proximity" to the completed offence of selling illegally obtained fish when the accused had brought a sample of illegally obtained fish to a store and asked the owner if he was "interested."[28]

In a practical sense, the determination of whether the act has gone beyond mere preparation may depend in part on the strength of the evidence of wrongful intent. Going through the glove compartment of a car has been held to be the *actus reus* for its attempted theft when the accused indicated that he was searching for keys to steal the car.[29] On the other hand, making a plasticine impression of a car key has been held to be only preparation to steal the car.[30] Approaching a store with balaclavas and a gun could be a sufficient *actus reus* for attempted robbery, but retreat when informed that the store was closed may reveal a reasonable doubt about the intent to commit the robbery.[31] In practice, a more remote *actus reus* will be accepted if the intent is clear. Another factor may well be the magnitude of the planned crime. In a case in which the accused intends to commit murder or even mass murder, the approach in *Deutsch* of holding that the accused has gone beyond mere preparation and committed the *actus reus* of an attempt even though the completed crime may still be months aways makes eminent sense.

Something that goes beyond mere preparation may still constitute the *actus reus* of attempt in cases where the complete crime does not and even cannot occur. In *Detering*,[32] the accused had gone well beyond mere preparation in their attempt to commit fraud, but were convicted of attempted fraud as opposed to fraud because the intended victims were not deceived. In *Williams*,[33] unprotected acts of sexual intercourse by an accused who knew he was HIV-positive constituted the *actus reus* of attempted aggravated assault. The accused "took more than preparatory steps. He did everything he could to achieve the infection of the complainant." The fact that it may have been impossible to infect the complainant because she was already infected with HIV did not prevent the conviction of the accused for attempt.

---

28   *R. v. Gladstone* (1996), 109 C.C.C. (3d) 193 at 202 (S.C.C.).
29   *R. v. James* (1971), 2 C.C.C. (2d) 141 (Ont. C.A.).
30   *R. v. Lobreau* (1988), 67 C.R. (3d) 74 (Alta. C.A.).
31   *Sorrell*, above note 25.
32   (1982), 70 C.C.C. (2d) 321 (S.C.C.) [*Detering*].
33   *Williams*, above note 21 at para. 64.

3) Impossibility and Attempts

The theoretical issue of whether an accused should be held liable for attempts when it was impossible to commit the completed offence has been settled by section 24(1) of the *Criminal Code*, which states that a person can be guilty of attempt "whether or not it was possible under the circumstances to commit the offence." This provision precludes either legal or factual impossibility as a possible defence to an attempted crime. Factual impossibility would include a case in which an accused attempted to pick a pocket that contained no money[34] and the case of a person who tried to infect someone with HIV even though she was already infected.[35] Legal impossibility would include attempting to receive goods believed to be stolen, but which were in law not stolen.[36] The distinction between factual and legal impossibility has been rejected on the basis that under section 24 "[t]here is no legally relevant difference between the pickpocket who reaches into the empty pocket [that is, factual impossibility] and the man who takes his own umbrella from a stand believing it to be some other person's umbrella [legal impossibility]."[37] In both cases, the accused had the *mens rea* of a thief, had taken steps beyond preparation to consummate the crime, and was thwarted by circumstances over which he had no control.

On several occasions, the Supreme Court has indicated that impossibility is not a defence to attempted crimes in Canada.[38] In *Dynar*,[39] the Court again affirmed that impossibility was not a defence to an attempt. Thus, an accused who believed he was engaged in laundering drug money could be convicted of attempted money-laundering even though the money was government money provided by the police in a sting operation and not drug money. Similarly, a person who stabs a corpse with the intent to murder a real person would be guilty of attempted murder.[40] A person who accepts a package believing it to

---

34   *R. v. Scott*, [1964] 2 C.C.C. 257 (Alta. C.A.).

35   *Williams*, above note 21.

36   For an acquittal in this scenario, see *Anderton v. Ryan*, [1985] A.C. 560 (H.L.). This case was overruled a year later in *R. v. Shivpuri*, [1986] 2 All E.R. 334 (H.L.).

37   *Dynar*, above note 23 at 504.

38   *Detering*, (1982), above note 32; *R. v. Kundeus* (1975), 24 C.C.C. (2d) 276 (S.C.C.).

39   *Dynar*, above note 23 at 504. In any event, the offence was subsequently amended to criminalize laundering money either knowing or believing that it was the proceeds of crime. *Code*, above note 1, s. 462.31(1).

40   In dissent, Major J. pointed out that this approach could lead to what he saw as the absurdity of convicting someone of attempted murder who placed a voodoo stick in a doll thinking that this would cause the death of a person. *Dynar*, *ibid.* at 36.

contain a large amount of drugs would be guilty of attempting to possess drugs for the purpose of trafficking even if the package did not contain any drugs.[41] A person who comes to a hotel hoping to have sex with an eleven year old is still guilty of attempting to procure the sexual services of a child even though no child was involved in the police sting operation.[42]

The only time impossibility could be a defence would be if a person intended to commit an "imaginary crime." Thus, a person who believed that the possession of $100 bills was illegal would be innocent because that person has "no *mens rea* known to law" and "has not displayed any propensity to commit crimes in the future." It is highly unlikely that a person would ever be charged with the commission of an imaginary crime and it is best simply to conclude that factual or legal impossibility is not a defence to an attempted crime. What matters is whether the accused had the intent to commit the crime and went beyond mere preparation to commit the crime.

B. CONSPIRACY

A conspiracy, like an attempt, is something that occurs before a completed offence is committed. The Supreme Court has indicated that "conspiracy is in fact a more 'preliminary' crime than attempt, since the offence is considered to be complete before any acts are taken that go beyond mere preparation to put the common design into effect. The Crown is simply required to prove a meeting of the minds with regard to a common design to do something unlawful, specifically the commission of an indictable offence."[43] Unlike attempts, however, conspiracies are generally punished as severely as the completed offence.

Section 465(1)(c) establishes the general offence of conspiracy by providing that "every one who conspires with any one to commit an indictable offence . . . is guilty of an indictable offence and liable to the same punishment as that to which an accused who is guilty of that offence would, on conviction, be liable."[44] A general provision for con-

---

41   R. v. *Chan* (2003), 178 C.C.C. (3d)) 269 at paras. 63–64 (Ont. C.A.) (*obiter* ruling).
42   R. v. *Kerster* (2003), 175 C.C.C. (3d) 28 (B.C.C.A.).
43   *Dynar*, above note 23 at para. 87.
44   *Code*, above note 1, s. 465(1)(d), now provides that everyone who conspires to commit a summary conviction offence is guilty of an offence punishable on summary conviction and it is not yet clear whether this includes provincial and regulatory offences that can be prosecuted as summary conviction offences.

spiracies to effect an unlawful purpose was repealed after the Supreme Court indicated a reluctance to recognize conspiracies to commit common law as opposed to statutory crimes.[45] There are specific provisions relating to conspiracy to commit murder;[46] conspiracy to prosecute a person known to be innocent;[47] conspiracy with extraterritorial effects;[48] and conspiracy in restraint of trade.[49] The agreement of more than one person to commit a crime is seen as a particular menace to society that deserves punishment even before the conspirators have taken steps beyond preparation and attempted to commit the crime. In practice, conspiracy charges are most often brought in cases involving organized crime and drug trafficking. Other offences such as participation in the activities in a terrorist organization or a criminal organization may be functional substitutes for conspiracy charges.

1) The *Actus Reus* of Conspiracy

The *actus reus* of conspiracy is an agreement to carry out the completed offence. "The essence of criminal conspiracy is proof of agreement. On a charge of conspiracy the agreement is the gist of the offence. The *actus reus* is the fact of agreement."[50] Once an agreement to commit an offence is reached, however, it is not necessary to do anything else. A criminal plot may be a conspiracy long before it has gone beyond the preparation necessary for a criminal attempt. Thus, "[c]onspiracy is in fact a more 'preliminary' crime than attempt, since the offence is considered to be complete before any acts are taken that go beyond mere preparation to put the common design into effect. The Crown is simply required to prove a meeting of the minds with regard to a common design to do something unlawful, specifically the commission of an indictable offence."[51] An agreement to launder money could be a conspiracy even though the money was not yet transferred between the parties and there would not be a sufficient *actus reus* for an attempt.

Although an agreement must be between two or more people, a person can be convicted of conspiracy even if, for some other reason, the

---

45   R. v. *Gralewicz* (1980), 54 C.C.C. (2d) 289 (S.C.C.).
46   *Code*, above note 1, s. 465(1)(a).
47   *Ibid.*, s. 465(1)(b).
48   *Ibid.*, s. 465(3)(4).
49   *Ibid.*, ss. 466 and 467.
50   R. v. *Cotroni* (1979), 45 C.C.C. (2d) 1 at 17 (S.C.C) [*Cotroni*]. See also R. v. *Douglas* (1991), 63 C.C.C. (3d) 29 (S.C.C.).
51   *Dynar*, above note 23 at 512.

co-conspirators are not convicted.[52] As discussed in the next section, however, the conspirators must not only intend to agree, but also intend to carry out their common design. There must be communication for an agreement to be reached, but an implicit or tacit agreement to commit an offence is enough to prove the act of conspiracy:[53] "So long as there is a continuing overall, dominant plan there may be changes in methods of operation, personnel, or victims, without bringing the conspiracy to an end. The important inquiry is not as to the acts done in pursuance of the agreement, but whether there was, in fact, a common agreement."[54] The *actus reus* of conspiracy is thus an agreement, but the agreement itself need not be etched in stone or carried out.

The courts have refused to recognize an offence of attempted conspiracy when an agreement is not reached between the parties. A person who unsuccessfully attempts to enter a conspiracy may nevertheless be guilty of the independent offence of counselling a crime that is not committed.[55] In addition, a person who abets or encourages any of the conspirators to pursue the object of the conspiracy can be guilty of being a party to the conspiracy even though he or she did not actual agree to the conspiracy.[56]

2) The *Mens Rea* for Conspiracy

The *mens rea* for conspiracy includes both the "intention to agree" and the "intention to put the common design into effect." Taschereau J. explained:

> Although it is not necessary that there should be an overt act in furtherance of the conspiracy to complete the crime, I have no doubt that there must exist an intention to put the common design into effect. . . . The intention cannot be anything else but the will to attain the object of the agreement. I cannot imagine several conspirators agreeing to defraud, to restrain trade, or to commit any indictable offence, without having the intention to reach the common goal.[57]

---

52   *R. v. Murphy* (1981), 60 C.C.C. (2d) 1 (Alta. C.A.); *Cotroni*, above note 50.
53   *Atlantic Sugar Refineries Co. v. Canada (A.G.)* (1980), 54 C.C.C. (2d) 373 at 381 (S.C.C.).
54   *Cotroni*, above note 50 at 17–18.
55   *R. v. Dungey* (1979), 51 C.C.C. (2d) 86 (Ont. C.A.). But see *R. v. Dery* (2002) 7 C.R. (6th) 325 (Que. S.C.) purporting to create an offence of attempted conspiracy.
56   *R. v. McNamara (No. 1)* (1981), 56 C.C.C. (2d) 193 (Ont. C.A.); *R. v. Vucetic* (1998), 129 C.C.C. (3d) 178 (Ont. C.A.).
57   *R. v. O'Brien* (1954), 110 C.C.C. 1 at 3 (S.C.C.).

In that case, no conspiracy was found because only one of the parties to the agreement actually had the intent to carry out the kidnapping. An agreement between one person and an undercover officer could not be a conspiracy because the officer would not intend to carry out the offence.[58] An agreement between two people and an undercover officer could, however, be a conspiracy because in that case two or more people would intend to commit the crime.

In *R. v. Sokoloski*,[59] the Supreme Court convicted two people of conspiracy to traffic in a controlled drug on the basis that the seller of the large quantity of the drugs must have known that the purchaser would in turn sell the drugs. A minority criticized this decision as an unwarranted extension of conspiracy, because the seller and the buyer had not agreed to carry out the trafficking enterprise in common. To support a conspiracy, there should be something more than mere knowledge that drugs will be sold, but rather an agreement on a common design and an intent to implement that agreement.

In *R. v. Nova Scotia Pharmaceutical Society*,[60] the Supreme Court indicated that to be convicted of conspiracy to lessen competition unduly, it was necessary to prove that the accused had a subjective intent to enter into an agreement, and knowledge of its terms. An objective fault element, however, was sufficient in relation to the aims of the agreement, so that the accused would be guilty if reasonable business people in their position would have known that the agreement would unduly lessen competition. An accused who deliberately entered into an agreement could be guilty even if he or she did not intend or know the agreement would unduly lessen competition.

3) Impossibility and Conspiracy

Given the rejection of impossibility as a defence to an attempted crime, it is not surprising that impossibility is also not a defence to the related crime of conspiracy. Thus, two accused[61] could conspire to launder drug money even though it was impossible to launder the money because the money was government money provided in a sting opera-

---

58   As examined in the next section, the suspect might be guilty of the separate
      crime of counselling a crime that was not committed.
59   (1977), 33 C.C.C. (2d) 496 (S.C.C.).
60   (1992), 74 C.C.C. (3d) 289 at 326 (S.C.C.).
61   The two accused would have to both intend to agree and intend to carry out the
      agreement so that an agreement between one person and an undercover officer
      would not be sufficient.

tion. The accused still reached an agreement (the *actus reus*) and their intention to agree and launder drug money (the *mens rea*) remained the same "regardless of the absence of the circumstance that would make the realization of that intention possible. . . . The essential element of conspiracy is the existence of the agreement to put the intention of the conspirators into effect."[62] As with attempts, impossibility would only prevent a conspiracy conviction if two or more people agree to commit what they may think is a crime, but what is actually only an imaginary crime. There is no possible social interest in punishing an agreement to do something that is not a crime.

C. COUNSELLING A CRIME THAT IS NOT COMMITTED

As discussed above, a person could not be convicted of conspiracy for agreeing with an undercover police officer to commit a crime because one party to the agreement would not have the intent to put the common design into effect. In that case, or in any case, where a person attempts to solicit another to commit a crime and the second person is unwilling to do so, the appropriate charge will be counselling a crime that is not committed. This is a separate offence under section 464 of the *Criminal Code* and it is subject to the same reduced punishment as an attempt. It is distinct from counselling an offence that is committed which under section 22 of the *Code* is a method by which a person becomes a party to an offence and is punished as if he or she had committed the complete offence.

1) The *Actus Reus* of Counselling a Crime That Is Not Committed

Section 22(3) provides that for the purposes of the *Criminal Code* "counsel" includes procure, solicit, or incite. It does not matter whether the person counselled either acts on the solicitation or has any intention of doing so.[63] This means that a person can be guilty of counselling an undercover officer to commit a crime, even if the person so solicited would never commit the offence. The Ontario Court of Appeal has stated that a person can be guilty of counselling, even if the

---

62   *Dynar*, above note 23 at 517–18.
63   *R. v. Glubisz (No. 2)* (1979), 47 C.C.C. (2d) 232 (B.C.C.A.).

person solicited immediately rejects the idea of going through with the offence.[64] Of course, if the person counselled does carry out the crime, then the person who counselled the crime is guilty as a party to the offence that is eventually committed.[65]

2) The *Mens Rea* for Counselling a Crime That Is Not Committed

The *mens rea* in section 464 is not spelled out, but given the possible breadth of the *actus reus*, it will be important to require subjective knowledge of the crime counselled and an actual intent by the accused (but not necessarily the person counselled) that the crime be performed. In *R. v. McLeod*,[66] the Georgia Strait Publishing Co. was convicted of counselling the illegal cultivation of marijuana by publishing an article explaining how to grow marijuana. The Court of Appeal concluded that the paper was deliberately counselling readers of the paper to cultivate marijuana, but held that the evidence was insufficient to prove that the editor of the paper had this intent. If this case arose today, the protection of freedom of expression in section 2(b) of the *Charter* would also be a factor.[67] In *R. v. Janeteas*,[68] the Ontario Court of Appeal issued a comprehensive judgment that stressed the importance of *mens rea* in a counselling offence. Moldaver J.A. stated that, as with the other inchoate crimes of attempts and conspiracy, the accused must intend the commission of the offence in order to be guilty of the crime of counselling an offence that is not committed. Recklessness was not a sufficient form of fault because it could result in the conviction of a person who made only casual comments about the possibility of a crime being committed. The Court of Appeal rejected the policy argument that a person should be convicted simply because he may have placed a dangerous thought about the commission of a crime into another's mind. The Alberta Court of Appeal has likewise stressed the requirement of intent as opposed to lesser forms of subjective *mens rea* such as recklessness or wilful blindness for the section 464 offence and has related this high *mens rea* standard to the fact that the offence

---

64   *R. v. Gonzague* (1983), 4 C.C.C. (3d) 505 (Ont. C.A.).
65   *Code*, above note 1, s. 22, discussed below.
66   (1970), 1 C.C.C. (2d) 5 at 8 (B.C.C.A.).
67   *Iorfida v. MacIntyre* (1994), 93 C.C.C. (3d) 395 (Ont. Gen. Div.) (law restricting sale or promotion of drug literature an unjustified violation of freedom of expression).
68   (2003), 172 C.C.C. (3d) 97 (Ont. C.A.).

relates to counselling a crime that is not committed.[69] The decisions are helpful in their recognition that counselling a crime that is not committed is, like an attempt or a conspiracy, a form of inchoate liability and as such one that requires an intent to commit the complete offence.

3) Impossibility and Counselling

Given the willingness to convict an accused for impossible attempts and conspiracies and for counselling crimes that are immediately rejected by the person solicited, it would be expected that impossibility would not be a defence to the crime of counselling a crime that is not committed. In *R. v. Richard*,[70] however, the Manitoba Court of Appeal held that an adult accused could not be convicted of counselling the commission of an indecent assault because the child he attempted to procure was incapable of committing the completed offence because she was under twelve years of age.[71] This strange and impractical result helps to explain Parliament's enactment of a separate offence of inviting a child under fourteen to engage in sexual touching.[72] A broadly worded offence may be a substitute for an inchoate crime such as an attempt or counselling a crime that is not committed.

Parliament has now provided in section 23.1 of the *Criminal Code* that a person could be guilty of being a party to an offence even though the person aided or abetted, counselled or assisted, cannot be convicted of the offence. Strangely, this provision may not change the result in *Richard*, because it applies only to offences that are committed, not to the separate offence in section 464 of counselling a crime that is not committed. Nevertheless, an accused in Richard's position could be charged with the separate crime of inviting a child to engage in sexual touching or attempted sexual interference. For these crimes, as well as for crimes in sections 21–23 of the *Code*, it does not matter that the other person involved could not be convicted of an offence. Thus, adults who counsel young children under twelve years to commit drug offences, can be convicted even though the person they tried to recruit as a runner or seller could not be prosecuted.

---

69 *R. v. Hamilton* (2003) 178 C.C.C. (3d) 434 at paras. 5 and 27 (Alta. C.A.).

70 (1986), 30 C.C.C. (3d) 127 (Man. C.A.). It is also surprising that the Crown did not charge the accused with an attempt to commit indecent assault.

71 As examined in ch. 2 "Application of the *Criminal Code*," s. 13 of the *Code*, above note 1, deems those under twelve years of age incapable of committing any criminal offence.

72 *Code*, above note 1, s. 152.

D. COUNSELLING A CRIME THAT IS COMMITTED

Section 22(1) provides that a person who counsels a crime that is committed becomes a party to that offence and, as such, is subject to the same punishment as if he or she had actually committed the offence. This provision applies "notwithstanding that the offence was committed in a way different from that which was counselled." An accused who counsels a person to kill another with a bomb would still be guilty of murder if the person counselled used a gun instead. In addition, section 22(2) expands liability further by providing that a counsellor becomes a party "to every offence that the other commits in consequence of the counselling that the person who counselled knew or ought to have known was likely to be committed in consequence of the counselling."

1) The *Actus Reus* of Counselling a Crime That Is Committed

The *actus reus* of counselling remains the act of procuring, soliciting, or inciting a crime. In addition, a crime must then be committed by the person counselled. The crime need not be committed in the same way as was counselled or even be the same crime that was counselled. It must, however, be a crime that was reasonably foreseeable from the counselling. Under section 23.1, an accused could be convicted of counselling even though the person who actually committed the offence could not. For example, an adult who involved children under twelve years of age in the drug trade could be convicted even though the children could not. Similarly, a person who procured a reluctant person to commit an offence could be guilty even though the reluctant person might have a valid defence such as duress.

2) The *Mens Rea* for Counselling a Crime That Is Committed

The accused must intentionally counsel a criminal offence under section 22(1). It would not be fair to hold that an accused is a party to an offence for comments that were not intended to solicit or incite a crime, but which had that effect. Under section 22(2), an accused who intentionally counsels an offence is also a party "to every offence that the other commits in consequence of the counselling that the person who counselled knew or ought to have known was likely to be committed in consequence of the counselling." This extends liability not only to the offence intentionally counselled but any other offence that the person knew or ought to have known would be committed as a result of the counselling. The latter fault element of objective foreseeability would violate section 7 of the *Charter* when applied to murder or attempted murder, which has a minimum fault element of subjective foresight of death.[73] Nevertheless, objective foreseeability would be a constitutionally sufficient fault element for most other crimes. For example, an accused who counselled a severe beating could be convicted of manslaughter because he or she ought to have known that manslaughter could result.[74] The accused would, however, only be guilty of murder if he or she actually knew that death was likely to result. Section 22(2) requires less fault than section 464 even though both offences are based on the counselling of a crime. A rationale for the different approaches is that counselling under section 22 constitutes a form of participation in a completed crime whereas counselling under section 464 is a form of inchoate liability that applies when the crime counselled has not been committed.

E. AIDING AND ABETTING

Section 21(1) of the *Criminal Code* provides that every one is a party to an offence who " actually commits it; or does or omits to do anything for the purpose of aiding any person to commit it; or abets any person in committing it." A person who either aids or abets an offence is a party to that offence and guilty of the same offence as the person who actually commits the offence, often known as the principal. It is not necessary for the Crown to specify whether a person is guilty as the principal offender or as an aider or abettor of the offence. In the famous Colin Thatcher case, the Crown was able to argue that the accused was guilty of murder on the alternative theories that he actually killed his ex-wife or he assisted others to do the killing.[75] Similarly, a number of accused could be convicted of murder if they all knowingly assisted in the victim's death even though it was unclear which one of the accused

---

73   *Martineau*, above note 13; *Logan*, above note 14.

74   Because of the fault element required for manslaughter, this conviction requires only objective foreseeability that bodily harm would result. *R. v. Jackson* (1993), 86 C.C.C. (3d) 385 at 391 (S.C.C.) [*Jackson*].

75   *R. v. Thatcher* (1987), 32 C.C.C. (3d) 481 (S.C.C.).

actually killed the victim.[76] Imposing the same liability and maximum penalty on a person who has knowingly assisted an offence as on the person who actually committed the offence may seem harsh in some cases. Limited participation in a crime may, however, be a mitigating factor in sentencing.

1) The *Actus Reus* of Aiding and Abetting

The distinction between aiding and abetting is difficult to define. Aiding refers to giving some assistance in the commission of the crime, while abetting "includes encouraging, instigating, promoting, or procuring the crime to be committed."[77] A person who distracts a security guard so that his or her friend can shoplift may aid a theft, whereas a salesclerk who encourages or allows a customer to shoplift would abet the theft. Both people would be guilty of theft, even though they did not themselves steal the merchandise. The terms *aiding* and *abetting* are generally used together, but they remain distinct forms of liability for being a party to an offence.

In *Dunlop v. R.*,[78] Dickson J. stated that a person is not guilty of aiding or abetting a rape:

> merely because he is present at the scene of a crime and does nothing to prevent it. . . . If there is no evidence of encouragement by him, a man's presence at the scene of the crime will not suffice to render him liable as aider and abettor. A person who, aware of a rape taking place in his presence, looks on and does nothing is not, as a matter of law, an accomplice. The classic case is the hardened urbanite who stands around in a subway station when an individual is murdered.

In the case, the accused were acquitted of rape on the basis that there was no evidence that they "rendered aid, assistance, or encouragement" to the gang rape of a young woman. Dickson J. did indicate, however, that presence at the commission of an offence can be evidence of aiding and abetting if accompanied by other factors such as prior knowledge that the crime was going to be committed. Similarly, presence at a crime which prevents the victim's escape or prevents the

---

76   *R. v. McMaster*, [1996] 1 S.C.R. 740 at para. 33; *R. v. McQuaid*, [1998] 1 S.C.R. 244; *R. v. Biniaris*, [2000] 1 S.C.R. 381; *R. v. Suzack* (2000), 141 C.C.C.(3d) 449 (Ont. C.A.); *R. v. H.(L.I.)* (2004), 17 C.R.(6th) 338 at para 60 (Man. C.A.); *R. v. Portillo* (2003), 17 C.R.(6th) 362 at para 71 (Ont. C.A.).

77   *R. v. Greyeyes* (1997), 116 C.C.C. (3d) 334 at 344 (S.C.C.) [*Greyeyes*].

78   (1979), 47 C.C.C. (2d) 93 at 111 (S.C.C.) [*Dunlop*].

victim receiving assistance is a sufficient *actus reus*.[79] Some members of the Supreme Court have disapproved of a case in which an accused was found not to be a party to a rape, despite having witnessed the crime with his pants down.[80]

The position that mere presence and passive acquiescence in a crime is not sufficient to make a person an aider or abettor mirrors the criminal law's traditional reluctance to penalize omissions. As with omissions, however, courts recognize exceptions to this principle in cases where the person who stands by is under a specific legal duty to act. Owners of cars who do nothing while others engage in dangerous driving have been held to have abetted the dangerous driving because they did not exercise their power to control the use of their vehicle.[81] A senior officer in charge of a police lock-up has also been found to have aided and abetted an assault on a prisoner by failing to exercise his statutory duty to protect a prisoner in his charge.[82] The conclusion in these cases that a failure to act can amount to aiding and abetting is strengthened by the fact that section 21(1)(b) provides that one who *omits* to do anything for the purpose of aiding any person to commit an offence may be charged as a party to that offence. The broad definition of the *actus reus* of aiding and abetting is balanced with a requirement that the act or omission of assistance be committed for the purpose of assisting in the commission of the offence.

2) The *Mens Rea* for Aiding and Abetting

To be convicted as an aider or abettor, the accused must not only assist the principal, but intend to assist the principal.[83] Section 21(1)(b) requires that the accused act or omit to do anything for the purpose of aiding any person to commit an offence. A person who unwittingly delivers a bomb or administers a poison would not be guilty as a party to an offence, even though he or she may have committed the *actus reus* of assisting the commission of the offence.[84] Such a person would not

---

79   *R. v. Black*, [1970] 4 C.C.C. 251 (B.C.C.A.); *R. v. Stevenson* (1984), 11 C.C.C. (3d) 443 (N.S. C.A.).

80   *R. v. Salajko*, [1970] 1 C.C.C. 352 (Ont. C.A.), disapproved of in *R. v. Kirkness* (1990), 60 C.C.C. (3d) 97 at 106 (S.C.C.), Wilson J. (L' Heureux-Dubé J. concurring) [*Kirkness*].

81   *R. v. Halmo* (1941), 76 C.C.C. 116 (Ont. C.A.); *R. v. Kulbacki*, [1966] 1 C.C.C. 167 (Man. C.A.).

82   *R. v. Nixon* (1990), 57 C.C.C. (3d) 97 (B.C.C.A.).

83   *R. v. Morgan* (1993), 80 C.C.C. (3d) 16 at 21 (Ont. C.A.).

84   *R. v. Berryman* (1990), 57 C.C.C. (3d) 375 (B.C.C.A.).

have acted for the purpose of aiding the offence. In *Dunlop*, Dickson J. stated:

> A person cannot properly be convicted of aiding or abetting in the commission of acts which he does not know may be or are intended. . . . One must be able to infer that the accused had prior knowledge that an offence of the type committed was planned.[85]

It is not necessary that the aider or abettor know all the details of the crime committed; it is sufficient that he or she was "aware of the type of crime to be committed"[86] and knew "the circumstances necessary to constitute the offence he is accused of aiding."[87] The Ontario Court of Appeal has concluded with respect to section 21(1)(b) that "purpose is synonymous with intent and does not include recklessness."[88] It has also indicated that the high level of *mens rea* for section 21(1)(b) is justified not only by the specific purpose requirement in the section, but also by the need to ensure that a person who assists in the commission of an offence has a sufficient level of fault to justify convicting that person of the same offence as the person who actually committed the offence.

The requirement that the accused act with the purpose of aiding the offence should not be equated with a requirement that the Crown must establish that the accused's desire or motive was to assist the crime. This means that a person who assists in a robbery by driving the getaway car will have acted with the purpose of aiding the offence, even though he or she participated only because of death threats. Chief Justice Lamer has concluded that "the expression 'for the purpose of aiding' in section 21(1)(b), properly understood, does not require that the accused actively view the commission of the offence he or she is aiding as desirable in and of itself. As a result, the *mens rea* for aiding under section 21(1)(b) is not susceptible of being 'negated' by duress."[89] The issue should be whether the accused intended to commit the crime. The jury should not be confused by being asked to consider duress both in relation to *mens rea* and in relation to the separate defence of duress. A person who arranges a drug buy may intend to aid or abet in trafficking even though his or her motivation may have only

---

85   Above note 78 at 110.
86   *R. v. Yanover* (1985), 20 C.C.C. (3d) 300 at 329 (Ont. C.A.).
87   *R. v. F.W. Woolworth Co.* (1974), 18 C.C.C. (2d) 23 at 32 (Ont. C.A.).
88   *R. v. Roach* (3 June 2004) Docket C38012 (Ont.C.A.) at para. 36.
89   *R. v. Hibbert* (1995), 99 C.C.C. (3d) 193 at 214 (S.C.C.) [*Hibbert*]. Such a person could be acquitted on the basis of the common law defence of duress if there was no safe avenue of escape from the threats. See ch. 8, "Duress."

been to assist the purchaser.[90] This follows the traditional position that motive is not normally relevant to subjective fault.[91]

In *Kirkness*,[92] the Supreme Court stated that an accused aiding or abetting a murder "must intend that death ensue or intend that he or the perpetrator cause bodily harm of a kind likely to result in death and be reckless whether death ensues or not." This suggests that the *mens rea* of aiding an offence requires the same intent necessary for the completed crime and not, as in the case of attempted murder, the intent to kill. At the same time, the above holding ensures that no one will be convicted of murder without proof of at least subjective foresight of death. In the actual case, the Supreme Court affirmed the acquittal of an accused who during a break-in had not participated in suffocating the victim and had told the accused to stop choking the victim. An accused will be acquitted of aiding or abetting a murder if he or she does not have subjective foresight of death, but can be convicted of aiding or abetting manslaughter if "a reasonable person in all the circumstances would have appreciated that bodily harm was the foreseeable consequence of the dangerous act which was being undertaken."[93] This follows from the fault element of manslaughter, which is satisfied by objective foreseeability of bodily harm.[94] Thus, an accused who was aware that his accomplice was beating a victim would likely be found guilty of manslaughter because of the objective foreseeability of bodily harm, but would only be guilty of murder if he knew that the victim was likely to die. In other words, the accused must have the fault element of the particular offence and must also intend to aid and abet the commission of the particular offence. As discussed above, recklessness is not a sufficient form of fault to convict a person as a party to an offence under section 21(1)(b).[95]

The courts are reluctant to find purchasers of drugs guilty of aiding and abetting trafficking on the basis of the purchase alone.[96] They

---

90   *Greyeyes*, above note 77 at 349.

91   See ch. 4, "Intent Distinguished From Motive."

92   Above note 80 at 127.

93   *Jackson*, above note 74 at 391.

94   *R. v. Creighton* (1993), 83 C.C.C. (3d) 346 (S.C.C.).

95   *Hibbert*, above note 89 at para. 26; *R. v. L.* (2003), 172 C.C.C. (3d) 44 at para. 48 (B.C.C.A.).

96   *R. v. Poitras* (1974), 12 C.C.C. (3d) 337 (S.C.C.); *R. v. Meston* (1975), 28 C.C.C. (2d) 497 (Ont. C.A.). As Justice L'Heureux-Dubé has stated: "[D]espite his or her crucial assistance in helping to complete the sale of narcotics, the purchaser cannot *by this action alone* be found guilty of the offence of aiding and abetting the offence of trafficking." *Greyeyes*, above note 77 at 340.

are concerned that such people do not deserve the stigma of a trafficking conviction and are more appropriately convicted of possession of narcotics or possession with the intent to traffic, either as a principal offender or an aider or abettor. Assisting a person to purchase drugs is another matter. In *Greyeyes*, the Supreme Court upheld the trafficking conviction of a person who located a seller for a purchaser, negotiated the purchase price, and accepted $10 for his efforts.[97] The Court reasoned that these were not the acts of a mere purchaser, but rather the acts of one who offered crucial assistance to the trafficking. The accused, who acted as a go-between between the purchaser and the seller and assisted the trafficking transaction, was convicted and sentenced as a drug trafficker. Hopefully, his rather peripheral involvement in the trafficking enterprise would be considered at sentencing.

F. COMMON INTENTION TO COMMIT AN UNLAWFUL PURPOSE AND SECTION 21(2)

Section 21(2) enlarges the scope of who is a party to an offence beyond those who knowingly aid or abet an offence by providing that those who "form an intention in common to carry out an unlawful purpose and to assist each other therein" are parties to any consequential offence committed by one of them provided that the accused "knew or ought to have known that the commission of the offence would be a probable consequence of carrying out the common purpose." Thus, a person who forms a common unlawful intent (for example, to engage in a robbery) is a party to other offences that he or she knew or ought to know would probably occur (such as forcible confinement or manslaughter). In practice, section 21(2) applies when the principal has committed crimes beyond which the parties have intended to aid and abet.[98]

1) The *Actus Reus* of Section 21(2)

Under section 21(2) there must be a formation of a common intent to assist each other in carrying out an unlawful purpose, but not necessarily any act of assistance.[99] It could be argued that this requires an agreement akin to conspiracy, although most cases do not dwell on the

---

97   *Greyeyes, ibid.*
98   *R. v. Simpson* (1988), 38 C.C.C. (3d) 481 (S.C.C.).

issue. In addition, it is assumed that the unlawful purpose means a purpose contrary to the *Criminal Code*. The subsequent offence committed has to be one that the accused either knows or ought to have known would be a probable consequence of carrying out the common purpose. In *Jackson*,[100] the Supreme Court held that the offence is not confined to that which the principal was convicted, but encompasses any included offence. For example, a party to an unlawful purpose could be convicted of manslaughter, even though the principal was convicted of murder. This would happen when the party did not have the subjective foresight of death required for a murder conviction, but did have objective foresight of bodily harm necessary for a manslaughter conviction. Less clear is whether a party with the *mens rea* for murder can be convicted of murder even though the principal offender was only convicted of manslaughter. There is some authority that the party could only be convicted of the same offence as the principal offender,[101] but general principles as well as section 23.1 suggest that a party with the required *mens rea* could be convicted of a more serious offence than a principal offender. For example, a sober or unprovoked accomplice might have the *mens rea* for murder even though the actual killer might only have the *mens rea* for manslaughter.[102]

2) The *Mens Rea* for Section 21(2)

There are two distinct mental or fault elements for section 21(2): the first is the formation of the common unlawful purpose and the second is either subjective knowledge or objective foresight that the actual offence would be a probable consequence of carrying out the unlawful purpose.

a) Common Unlawful Purpose
In *R. v. Paquette*,[103] the Supreme Court held that a person who drove others to a robbery had not formed a common unlawful purpose to assist them in the robbery because he had been forced at gun point to co-operate. Martland J. stated:

---

99 *R. v. Moore* (1984), 15 C.C.C. (3d) 541 at 555 (Ont. C.A.).

100 Above note 74.

101 *R. v. Hébert* (1986), 51 C.R. (3d) 264 (N.B.C.A.).

102 See also *R. v. S.(F.J.)* (1998), 121 C.C.C. (3d) 223 (S.C.C.) discussed below holding that a person could be convicted of being an accessory after the fact even though the principal offender was acquitted.

103 (1976), 30 C.C.C. (2d) 417 (S.C.C.).

A person whose actions have been dictated by fear of death or of grievous bodily injury cannot be said to have formed a genuine common intent to carry out an unlawful purpose with the person who has threatened him with those consequences if he fails to co-operate.[104]

In *Hibbert*, the Supreme Court subsequently rejected this interpretation on the basis that section 21(2) requires only a common intent to commit the offence and not "a mutuality of motives and desires between the party and the principal."[105] On this reasoning, Paquette would have had the required mental element because he intended to commit a robbery even though he did not truly desire to commit the robbery. The fact that he wanted to commit a robbery only because his life was threatened would be a matter of motive that is not relevant to the mental element. It would, however, be relevant to whether Paquette had a common law defence of duress that would prevent his conviction.[106] As with section 21(1)(b), the Court has rejected the idea that intent requires proof of desire even though section 21(2) requires the formation of an intention in common to assist in the commission of an offence. It was concerned that cases such as *Paquette* would complicate the task of the jury by considering duress as both a matter relevant to *mens rea* and as a separate defence and that it would not fulfil Parliament's purpose in widening the net of criminal liability to catch those who assist in the commission of crimes.

b) Knew or Ought to Have Known That the Crime Would Be Committed

In most cases the accused will be liable if he or she either knew or ought to have known that the commission of the offence was a probable consequence of the common unlawful purpose. In *Logan*,[107] however, the Supreme Court declared the phrase "ought to have known" to be an unjustified violation of the *Charter* when the accused is charged with murder or attempted murder. Section 7 of the *Charter* requires subjective as opposed to objective foresight of death for a conviction of murder or attempted murder. As Lamer C.J. explained:

---

104 *Ibid.* at 423.
105 *Hibbert*, above note 89 at 216. See *Dunbar v. R.* (1936), 67 C.C.C. 20 (S.C.C.), also drawing a distinction between intention and motive when an accused was threatened if he did not assist in a robbery.
106 See ch. 8, "Common Law Duress."
107 Above note 14.

When the principles of fundamental justice require subjective foresight in order to convict a principal of attempted murder, that same
minimum degree of *mens rea* is constitutionally required to convict a
party to the offence of attempted murder. Any conviction for attempted murder, whether of the principal directly or of a party pursuant to
s. 21(2), will carry enough stigma to trigger the constitutional
requirement. To the extent that s. 21(2) would allow for the conviction of a party to the offence of attempted murder on the basis of
objective foresight, its operation restricts s. 7 of the *Charter*.[108]

In cases of murder and attempted murder, the objective arm of section
21(2) should not be left to the jury and the jury should only convict if
a party has actual foresight or knowledge that the principal offender
would attempt to kill a person while carrying out their common
unlawful purpose.[109]

Logan is a case of limited application. The Court stated that
"because of the importance of the legislative purpose, the objective
component of section 21(2) can be justified with respect to most offenses."[110] Lamer C.J. concluded that it was not a principle of fundamental
justice that a person convicted as a party to an offence have as high a
mens rea as the principal offender. This means that a party could be convicted under the objective arm of section 21(2) even though subjective
mens rea was required to convict the principal. For example, an accused
who formed an unlawful purpose to rob a bank could be convicted of
assault on the basis that he or she ought to have known an assault
would occur, whereas the person who actually assaulted one of the
guards or tellers would be convicted on the basis of a subjective intent
to apply force. In upholding the objective arm of section 21(2) as constitutional in most cases, the Court emphasized the importance of recognizing different degrees of involvement when exercising sentencing
discretion.[111] A fundamental principle of sentencing is that the punishment be proportionate to the degree of the offender's responsibility.

---

108 *Ibid.* at 401.
109 R. v. *Rodney* (1990) 58 C.C.C. (3d) 408 (S.C.C.); R. v. *LaLiberty* (1997), 117
     C.C.C. (3d) at 108 (Ont. C.A.); R. v. *Portillo* (2004) 17 C.R.(6th) 362 at paras
     72–73 (Ont.C.A.).
110 Above note 14 at 403.
111 Lamer C.J. stated: "It must be remembered that within many offences there are
     varying degrees of guilt and it remains the function of the sentencing process to
     adjust the punishment for each individual offender accordingly. The argument
     that the principles of fundamental justice prohibit the conviction of a party to
     an offence on the basis of a lesser degree of *mens rea* than that required to con-
     vict the principal could only be supported, if at all, in a situation where the sen-

G. ACCESSORY AFTER THE FACT

Section 23 provides a separate offence for receiving, comforting, or assisting a person that one knows has been a party to an offence for the purpose of enabling that person to escape. An accessory after the fact is not a party to an offence, but is punished under section 463 as if he or she had been guilty of an attempt of the crime that the person assisted committed.

1) The *Actus Reus* of Being an Accessory after the Fact

The *actus reus* for this provision requires a person to receive, comfort, or assist a person who has committed a crime. This requires more than the mere failure to inform authorities about the fugitive's whereabouts.[112] At the same time, advising fugitives that the police had their names and licence numbers is enough.[113] This again mirrors the traditional reluctance in the criminal law to punish an omission or failure to act.

Section 23(2) used to provide that a married person cannot be guilty of assisting his or her spouse after the commission of a crime, but it was repealed in 2000. Section 23.1 allows a person to be convicted of being an accessory after the fact even though the person assisted has not been convicted of an offence. The Supreme Court has upheld the conviction of an accused for being an accessory after the fact by assisting her brother by transporting him from a killing and orchestrating a false alibi even though her brother was eventually acquitted of the murder.[114]

2) The *Mens Rea* for Being an Accessory after the Fact

Section 23(2) requires two distinct mental elements: 1) subjective knowledge that the person assisted has been a party to an offence, and 2) assisting the fugitive for the purpose of assisting him or her to escape.

The accused must know or be wilfully blind to the fact that the accused has committed a specific offence such as murder; knowledge that the accused may have committed some general crime is not sufficient.[115] It is not sufficient that the acts of assistance have the effect of

---

tence for a particular offence is fixed. However, currently in Canada, the sentencing scheme is flexible enough to accommodate the varying degrees of culpability resulting from the operation of ss. 21 and 22." *Ibid.* at 398.

112 *R. v. Dumont* (1921), 37 C.C.C. 166 (Ont. C.A.).
113 *Young v. R.* (1950), 98 C.C.C. 195 (Que. C.A.).
114 *R. v. S.(F.J.)* (1997), 115 C.C.C. (3d) 450 (N.S.C.A.) aff'd 121 C.C.C. (3d) 223 (S.C.C.).
115 *R. v. Duong* (1998), 124 C.C.C. (3d) 392 (Ont. C.A.).

helping the person escape[116] or that they be undertaken for the purpose of not being suspected for the crime itself.[117] The requirement that the accused act with the purpose of assisting a known criminal to escape is also a high form of subjective *mens rea* that may be more difficult for the Crown to prove than lower forms of subjective mental elements such as knowledge or recklessness. It should also be noted that some specific crimes such as obstruction of justice or harbouring a terrorist may in some circumstances be functional alternatives to the general crime under section 23 of being an accessory after the fact.

CONCLUSION

The following chart summarizes how various provisions of the *Criminal Code* expand the net of criminal liability to apply to those who did not themselves perform the complete crime. The underlying rationale seems to be that society is justified in intervening and punishing people for their criminal intent or fault and participation in crimes even if they do not commit the complete criminal act.

Conspiracy S.465	Attempts S.24	Conselling a crime that is not committed S.464	Counselling a crime that is committed S.22 Party to the offence	Unlawful purpose and commission of further offence S.21(2) Party to the offence	Aiding or abetting S.21(1)(b) and (c) Party to the offence	Accessory after the fact S.23

An accused could be convicted of counselling murder under section 464 simply for asking an undercover officer to kill someone. The same person could be convicted under section 465 of conspiracy to commit murder if he or she agreed with another person that they would kill someone and both intended to carry out the agreement. If an accused acted alone, he or she could be convicted of attempted murder under section 24 if he or she did anything beyond mere preparation for the purpose of carrying out the intent to kill. The fact that it was impossible to kill the intended victim because he was already dead would not

---

116 *R. v. McVay* (1982), 66 C.C.C. (2d) 512 (Ont. C.A.).
117 *R. v. Morris* (1979), 47 C.C.C. (2d) 257 (S.C.C.).

be a defence. The accused would be punished more for having the intent to kill than the harm that was caused or could have been caused.

An accused could be guilty of murder under section 22 if he or she counselled another person to commit a murder and that person went on to actually commit the murder. The accused would be guilty of murder under section 21(2) if he or she formed an unlawful purpose with another person and he or she knew that it was likely that his accomplice would kill the victim while carrying out the unlawful purpose. For crimes other than murder and attempted murder,[118] all that would have to be proven under section 21(2) would be the formation of the unlawful purpose and that the accused ought to have known that his accomplice would commit the further crime. If the accused aided or abetted the murder with the fault required for murder[119] (the minimum fault is subjective foresight of death), the accused would also be guilty of murder under section 21(1). Finally, knowingly assisting a person to escape after a crime can be punished as a separate offence under section 23.

Although there is a consensus that participation in crime should be criminal, the law could be made clearer and less complex. Any distinctions between counselling, aiding and abetting under sections 21(1) and 22 are quite fine and could be eliminated by a generic provision criminalizing the intentional assistance and encouragement of crime. There is less agreement about whether criminal liability should be extended under section 21(2). The existing law is complex because the objective fault element provided under section 21(2) is unconstitutional as applied to murder and attempted murder but continues to apply to other crimes including manslaughter.[120] One reform option would to eliminate section 21(2) altogether while another would be to require subjective foresight for all crimes that are committed in furtherance to an unlawful objective. A requirement of subjective foresight, however, would blur the practical distinction between section 21(2) and aiding and abetting under section 21(1)(b) and (c). The Supreme Court has simplified the law somewhat by holding that duress cannot negate the *mens rea* requirements under either section 21(1)(b) and 21(2) and that the requirements in those sections that the accused act with the purpose of aiding and form an intention in common to carry out an unlawful purpose should not be equated with either desire or motive.[121]

---

118 *Logan*, above note 14; *Jackson*, above note 74.
119 *Kirkness*, above note 80.
120 *Jackson*, above note 74.
121 *Hibbert*, above note 89.

The law concerning attempts is relatively settled, but there remains uncertainty in determining exactly when an accused's actions will have gone beyond mere preparation[122] and whether an intent to commit the complete offence is required for all crimes.[123] Given that attempts are driven by concerns about intent and not social harm, the intent to commit the complete offence should be established for all attempted crimes, not just murder. There is a case for keeping the *actus reus* flexible and in practice more remote forms of *actus reus* may be accepted if the *mens rea* is clear or if the magnitude of the attempted crime is great. It should now be crystal clear that impossibility will not be a defence to either an attempt or conspiracy. This also makes sense when it is recognized that society is intervening primarily to punish criminal intent, not the complete crime.

FURTHER READINGS

ASHWORTH, A., *Principles of Criminal Law*, 4th ed. (Oxford: Clarendon Press, 2003), chs. 10 and 11

COLVIN, E., *Principles of Criminal Law*, 2d ed. (Toronto: Carswell, 1991), chs. 9 and 10

GRANT, I., D. CHUNN, & C. BOYLE, *The Law of Homicide* (Toronto: Carswell, 1994), ch. 5

MACKINNON, P., "Making Sense of Attempts" (1982) 7 Queen's L.J. 253

MANSON, A., "Re-Codifying Attempts, Parties, and Abandoned Intentions" (1989) 14 Queen's L.J. 85

MEEHAN, E., & J. CURRIE, *The Law of Criminal Attempt*, 2d ed. (Toronto: Carswell, 2000)

MEWETT, A., & M. MANNING, *Criminal Law*, 3d ed. (Toronto: Butterworths, 1994), chs. 8 and 9

ROSE, G., *Parties to an Offence* (Toronto: Carswell, 1982)

STUART, D., *Canadian Criminal Law: A Treatise*, 4th ed. (Toronto: Carswell, 1995), chs. 9 and 10

---

122 *Deutsch*, above note 26.
123 *Ancio*, above note 10, *Williams*, above note 21.

CHAPTER 4

THE FAULT ELEMENT, OR *MENS REA*

Generic references to *mens rea* are confusing because each different crime has a specific fault element which must be related to the *actus reus* of the specific crime. In 1889 Stephen J. indicated that *mens rea* exists only in relation to particular definitions of crime, so that:

> "Mens rea" means in the case of murder, malice aforethought; in the case of theft, an intention to steal; in the case of rape, an intention to have forcible connection with a woman without her consent; and in the case of receiving stolen goods, knowledge that the goods were stolen. In some cases it denotes mere inattention. For instance, in the case of manslaughter by negligence it may mean forgetting to notice a signal. It appears confusing to call so many dissimilar states of mind by one name.[1]

In Canada, confusion about *mens rea* continues because Parliament has not clearly and consistently defined fault elements such as "purposely," "knowingly," "recklessly," or "negligently" or specified what particular fault element applies for each offence.[2] It has also not provided a residual fault element to apply when no particular fault element is specified or provided a general rule that the fault element should relate to all aspects of the *actus reus*. Numerous proposals have called for reforms

---

1   *R. v. Tolson* (1889), 23 Q.B.D. 168 at 185 (C.C.R.) [*Tolson*].
2   But see *Criminal Code of Canada*, R.S.C. 1985, c. C-46, ss. 433 and 436 [*Code*], for clear definitions of separate offences of intentional and negligent arson.

that would bring greater clarity in determining fault elements, but Parliament has not yet comprehensively defined the fault elements required for crimes. As a result, the fault element must still be inferred from the legislative definition of each separate offence.

A. CONCEPTUAL CONSIDERATIONS

In order to explain the fault element of any criminal offence accurately, it is necessary to specify 1) the circumstances and consequences to which the fault element is directed, including its relation to the *actus reus* of the offence, and 2) the precise fault element required. It is not very helpful to say the *mens rea* for murder is subjective. A more precise approach would be to say the *mens rea* for murder requires at least subjective knowledge that the victim would die. Similarly, stating that the *mens rea* of manslaughter is objective tells only part of the story. The fault is objective foreseeability of bodily harm. The degree of negligence should also be explained, as should who is the reasonable person used to apply the objective fault or negligence standard.

It is also important to understand the differences between constitutional requirements and common law presumptions of particular forms of *mens rea* and how the so-called defences of intoxication and mistake of fact are really conditions which prevent the prosecutor from establishing the fault element beyond a reasonable doubt.

1) The Relation of the Fault Element to the Prohibited Act

The fault element does not exist in the air or in the abstract, but must be related to certain consequences or circumstances. As McLachlin J. has stated:

> Typically, *mens rea* is concerned with the consequences of the prohibited *actus reus*. Thus, in the crimes of homicide, we speak of the consequences of the voluntary act — intention to cause death, or reckless and wilfully blind persistence in conduct which one knows is likely to cause death.[3]

---

3   *R. v. Théroux* (1993), 79 C.C.C. (3d) 449 at 458 (S.C.C.) [*Théroux*]. This is not an absolute rule, as seen in her own majority judgment in *R. v. Creighton* (1993), 83 C.C.C. (3d) 346 (S.C.C.) [*Creighton*] and discussed below, note 5.

On this principle, a person is not guilty of assaulting a peace officer in the execution of his or her duties unless the accused has the *mens rea* for assault and subjective knowledge that the person is a peace officer. Similarly, the Court classified the old offence of statutory rape as absolute liability because Parliament had excluded fault in relation to a crucial aspect of the *actus reus*, namely the age of the girl.[4] The fault element should generally extend to all the elements of the prohibited act.

The Supreme Court has recognized that the criminal law "has traditionally aimed at symmetry between the *mens rea* and the prohibited consequence of the offence" as discussed above. Nevertheless, a majority in Creighton concluded:

> It is important to distinguish between criminal law theory, which seeks the ideal of absolute symmetry between the *actus reus* and *mens rea* and the constitutional requirements of the *Charter*. . . .
>
> I know of no authority for the proposition that the *mens rea* of an offence must always attach to the precise consequence which is prohibited as a matter of constitutional necessity.[5]

In the result, McLachlin J. held that objective foresight of the risk of bodily harm was a sufficient fault element for the crime of unlawful act manslaughter, even though the *actus reus* of the crime was causing death as opposed to causing bodily harm. Offences that do not require a fault element in relation to all aspects of the *actus reus* are sometimes called offences of partial intent, constructive crimes, or crimes based on predicate offences.

Constructive murder violates section 7 of the *Charter* because while it required the fault of a predicate offence (such as robbery) and the fault of causing bodily harm, it did not require fault with respect to

---

4   *R. v. Hess* (1990), 59 C.C.C. (3d) 161 (S.C.C.) discussed in chs. 1 and 5.

5   Above note 3 at 378–79. In *R. v. DeSousa* (1992), 76 C.C.C. (3d) 124 at 141 (S.C.C.) [*DeSousa*], the Court noted a number of offences punish a person more severely because of the consequences of his or her actions even though there is no fault requirement with regards to those aggravating consequences. Examples cited included "manslaughter (s. 222(5)), criminal negligence causing bodily harm (s. 221), criminal negligence causing death (s. 220), dangerous operation causing bodily harm (s. 249(3)), dangerous operation causing death (s. 249(4)), impaired driving causing bodily harm (s. 255(2)), impaired driving causing death (s. 255(3)), assault causing bodily harm (s. 267(1)(b)), aggravated assault (s. 268), sexual assault causing bodily harm (s. 272(c)), aggravated sexual assault (s. 273), mischief causing danger to life (s. 430(2)), and arson causing bodily harm (s. 433(b)). As noted by Professor Colvin, '[i]t would, however, be an error to suppose that *actus reus* and *mens rea* always match in this neat way.'"

the prohibited act of killing and did not satisfy the constitutional requirement that a murderer at least have subjective foresight of death.[6] The Supreme Court pulled back, however, from declaring as a general constitutional principle that people could not be punished for the consequences of their actions in the absence of some fault or responsibility for those consequences. Thus, a person can be punished for causing death in a manslaughter case even though his or her fault only related to the objective risk of causing bodily harm.

Other offences require a *mens rea* that extends beyond the commission of the *actus reus*. Any attempted crime is a good example because it requires a *mens rea* that goes farther than the *actus reus* committed by the accused. Similarly, a person who assists a crime does something, such as acting as a lookout, for the further purpose of assisting the commission of the crime. Discharging a firearm with the intent to wound also requires proof of an intent to wound, even though an actual wounding is not part of the *actus reus*. Such offences are sometimes called ulterior intent offences, because they require an intent beyond the *actus reus* that is committed.

2) Subjective and Objective Fault Elements

A broad distinction is often drawn between subjective and objective fault elements. A subjective fault or mental element requires the Crown to establish that the accused subjectively had the required guilty knowledge in relation to the specified circumstances or consequences, whereas an objective fault element requires only that a reasonable person in the accused's position would have had the required guilty knowledge or would have acted differently.

A distinction should be made between the subjective mental elements that the Crown must prove and the means used to establish such guilty knowledge. The judge or jury who must determine what was in an accused's mind must rely on inferences from the evidence presented in the case. In deciding whether to draw these inferences, the trier of fact will almost inevitably consider what a reasonable person in the accused's place would have thought or recognized. As Martin J.A. has explained:

> Since people are usually able to foresee the consequences of their acts,
> if a person does an act likely to produce certain consequences it is, in
> general, reasonable to assume that the accused also foresaw the prob-

---

6   R. v. *Martineau* (1990), 58 C.C.C. (3d) 353 (S.C.C.) [*Martineau*].

able consequences of his act and if he, nevertheless, acted so as to produce those consequences, that he intended them. The greater the likelihood of the relevant consequences ensuing from the accused's act, the easier it is to draw the inference that he intended those consequences. *The purpose of this process, however, is to determine what the particular accused intended, not to fix him with the intention that a reasonable person might be assumed to have in the circumstances, where doubt exists as to the actual intention of the accused.*[7]

In other words, what the reasonable person would have known may provide the basis for the jury to conclude that the accused had a particular subjective mental element, but it never requires the jury to make such a determination.[8] The trier of fact must remain open to all the evidence presented in the case (especially evidence relating to peculiarities about the accused) and acquit the accused if any evidence raises a reasonable doubt as to whether that particular person, with all of his or her frailties and experiences, had the required subjective mental element.

Subjective *mens rea* operates as a doctrine that prevents the conviction of an accused who, for whatever reason, does not have the knowledge and foresight that a reasonable person would have. It operates to protect those who because of impaired reasoning or lack of thought do not recognize or intend what may be obvious to the reasonable observer. The function of subjective *mens rea* is "to prevent the conviction of the morally innocent — those who do not understand or intend the consequences of their acts."[9]

The Supreme Court has kept clear the distinctions between subjective and objective fault elements, but it has been increasingly willing to see the latter as an appropriate form of fault. In *Wholesale Travel Group*,[10] Cory J. stated:

---

7   *R. v. Buzzanga* (1979), 49 C.C.C. (2d) 369 at 387 (Ont. C.A.) [emphasis added] [*Buzzanga*]. "Where liability is imposed on a subjective basis, what a reasonable man ought to have anticipated is merely evidence from which a conclusion may be drawn that the accused anticipated the same consequences. On the other hand, where the test is objective, what a reasonable man should have anticipated constitutes the basis of liability." *R. v. Tennant* (1975), 23 C.C.C. (2d) 80 at 91 (Ont. C.A.).

8   This formulation also accords with the presumption of innocence. See ch. 1, "Right to be Presumed Innocent."

9   *Théroux*, above note 3 at 458.

10   *R. v. Wholesale Travel Group Inc.* (1991), 67 C.C.C. (3d) 193 (S.C.C.) at 252 [*Wholesale Travel Group*].

It should not be forgotten that *mens rea* and negligence are both fault elements. . . . *Mens rea* focuses on the mental state of the accused and requires proof of a positive state of mind such as intent, recklessness or wilful blindness. Negligence, on the other hand, measures the conduct of the accused on the basis of an objective standard, irrespective of the accused's subjective mental state. Where negligence is the basis of liability, the question is not what the accused intended but rather whether the accused exercised reasonable care.

The above statement was made in the context of regulatory offences outside of the *Criminal Code*. Allowing "simple negligence" to suffice for the purposes of criminal liability is more problematic. In the context of *Criminal Code* offences, the Supreme Court has indicated that there generally must be "a marked departure from the standard of care that a reasonable person would observe in the accused's situation."[11]

The exact differences between subjective and objective fault elements will depend on what level of subjective *mens rea* is required, and how the objective standard of negligence is applied.

3) Common Law Presumptions of *Mens Rea*

It is important to keep distinct the issues of what is required under section 7 of the *Charter* to prevent the conviction of the morally innocent and what the courts will presume as a matter of judge-made common law in the absence of a clear legislative intent or design to the contrary. The Supreme Court has been reluctant to constitutionalize *mens rea* for all but the most serious crimes, but they have long relied on common law presumptions in favour of subjective *mens rea* in relation to all aspects of the *actus reus*.[12]

---

11   *R. v. Hundal* (1993), 79 C.C.C. (3d) 97 at 108 (S.C.C.) [*Hundal*]; *Creighton*, above note 3 at 361 (Lamer C.J.), and 383 (McLachlin J.). In *R. v. Tutton* (1989), 48 C.C.C. (3d) 129 at 140 (S.C.C.) [*Tutton*], McIntyre J. (L' Heureux-Dubé concurring) stated in relation to criminal negligence: "The test is that of reasonableness, and proof of conduct which reveals a marked and significant departure from the standard which could be expected of a reasonably prudent person in the circumstances will justify a conviction of criminal negligence." Other means of adapting negligence as a principle of criminal liability will be discussed below.

12   As will be examined in the next chapter, the Court has also relied on a common law presumption in *R. v. Sault Ste. Marie (City)* (1978), 40 C.C.C. (2d) 353 (S.C.C.) [*Sault Ste. Marie*] that regulatory offences will be crimes of strict as opposed to absolute liability.

Long before the enactment of the *Charter*, the Supreme Court presumed that criminal offences would require subjective *mens rea*.[13] Thus, an offence of possession of narcotics was interpreted in 1957 to require proof that the accused had knowledge of the substance that in law constituted the illegal drugs even though Parliament did not specifically require that the offence be the "knowing" possession of drugs. The Court recognized that "[i]t would, of course, be within the power of Parliament to enact that a person who, without any guilty knowledge, had in his physical possession a package which he honestly believed to contain a harmless substance such as baking soda but which in fact contained heroin, must on proof of such facts be convicted of a crime and sentenced to at least 6 months' imprisonment." Nevertheless, the Court would not adopt an interpretation with the "monstrous consequences" of allowing the conviction of the morally innocent unless "the words of the statute were clear and admitted of no other interpretation."[14] Similarly, when interpreting an offence of knowingly or wilfully contributing to the delinquency of a child, the Court concluded that the fault element should be established with regards to all the elements of the *actus reus*, including whether the accused had subjective knowledge that the girl he had sexual intercourse with was actually under eighteen years of age. It was always open for Parliament to provide that the accused's belief about the age of the child was not relevant, but in this case Parliament had not made such a clear statement. Hence a requirement of subjective knowledge would be presumed in relation to all aspects of the *actus reus*.

The leading statement of the common law presumption of *mens rea* is contained in *Sault Ste. Marie*[15] In that case, Dickson J. stated:

> Where the offence is criminal, the Crown must establish a mental element, namely, that the accused who committed the prohibited act did so intentionally or recklessly, with knowledge of the facts constituting the offence, or with wilful blindness toward them. Mere negligence is excluded from the concept of the mental element required for conviction. Within the context of a criminal prosecution a person who fails to make such inquiries as a reasonable and prudent person would make, or who fails to know facts he should have known, is innocent in the eyes of the law.

13 *R. v. Watts* (1953), 105 C.C.C. 193 (S.C.C.); *R. v. Rees* (1956), 115 C.C.C. 1 (S.C.C.) [*Rees*]; *R. v. Beaver* (1957), 118 C.C.C. 129 (S.C.C.) [*Beaver*]; *R. v. Prue* (1979), 46 C.C.C. (2d) 257 (S.C.C.).

14 *Beaver, ibid.* at 141.

15 *Sault Ste. Marie*, above note 12 at 362.

This means that the courts should presume that criminal offences require some form of subjective *mens rea* — intent, knowledge, recklessness, or wilful blindness — in relation to all aspects of the *actus reus* unless Parliament clearly indicates otherwise.

Common law presumptions concerning *mens rea* remain valid. A reluctance to impose criminal liability on the basis of negligence explains why recklessness in Canadian law requires proof that the accused subjectively was aware of the prohibited risk.[16] Common law presumptions remain quite important given the frequency with which Parliament enacts criminal offences without specifying any fault element. Common law presumptions will, however, be overcome once Parliament has clearly indicated, through either the words or design of the offence, that it has intended some other result. Common law presumptions require Parliament to clearly state when it does not desire subjective *mens rea* when enacting a criminal offence.[17]

4) Constitutional Requirements of *Mens Rea*

A constitutional requirement of subjective *mens rea* under section 7 of the *Charter* leaves Parliament far fewer options than a common law presumption. Violations of section 7 of the *Charter* are almost never upheld under section 1 of the *Charter* and the substitution of elements for essential elements are also almost never accepted under section 11(d) of the *Charter*. The remaining legislative option would be the rather draconian use of the section 33 override to allow the legislation to operate for at least five years notwithstanding the legal rights in the *Charter*. The finality of constitutional requirements of *mens rea* may help explain the Supreme Court's caution about constitutionalizing subjective *mens rea* under section 7 of the *Charter*.

In *R. v. Vaillancourt*,[18] Lamer J. expressed preference for a general constitutional principle of subjective *mens rea* in relation to all aspects of the prohibited act, while recognizing that many crimes were based on objective fault. He stated:

---

16   *R. v. Sansregret* (1985), 18 C.C.C [*Sansregret*]. (3d) 223 (S.C.C.). In some parts of English law, however, recklessness can be an objective form of liability that only requires the accused's failure to advert to an obvious risk. *Metropolitan Police Commissioner v. Caldwell* (1981), *Caldwell*, [1982] A.C. 341 (H.L.).

17   As examined in the next chapter, the common law presumption in *Sault Ste. Marie*, above note 12, that regulatory offences will be strict liability, requires legislatures to clearly state if they desire a regulatory offence to be an absolute liability offence.

18   (1987), 39 C.C.C. (3d) 118 (S.C.C.).

It may well be that, as a general rule, the principles of fundamental justice require proof of a subjective *mens rea* with respect to the prohibited act, in order to avoid punishing the "morally innocent." . . . There are many provisions in the *Code* requiring only objective foreseeability of the result or even only a causal link between the act and the result. As I would prefer not to cast doubt on the validity of such provisions *in this case*, I will assume, but only for the purposes of this appeal, that something less than subjective foresight of the result may, sometimes, suffice for the imposition of criminal liability for causing that result through intentional criminal conduct.[19]

Subsequent cases have made it clear that subjective foresight of the prohibited consequences is not required for all crimes. Indeed, subjective *mens rea* so far has only been required under section 7 of the *Charter* for murder,[20] attempted murder,[21] and war crimes.[22] The Supreme Court has ruled that it is not required for many other crimes, including unlawfully causing bodily harm,[23] dangerous driving,[24] unlawful act manslaughter,[25] careless use of a firearm,[26] and failing to provide the necessities of life.[27] As will be discussed in chapter 5, the *Charter* also does not require proof of subjective *mens rea* for regulatory offences found outside of the *Criminal Code* in various provincial and federal statutes.[28]

In *Creighton*,[29] Justice McLachlin indicated that the following considerations were relevant in determining constitutional requirements of *mens rea*:

1. the stigma attached to the offence, and the available penalties requiring a *mens rea* reflecting the particular nature of the crime;
2. whether the punishment is proportionate to the moral blameworthiness of the offender; and
3. the idea that those causing harm intentionally must be punished more severely than those causing harm unintentionally.

---

19 *Ibid.* at 133–34.
20 *Martineau*, above note 6.
21 *R. v. Logan* (1990), 58 C.C.C. (3d) 391 (S.C.C.).
22 *R. v. Finta* (1994), 88 C.C.C. (3d) 417 (S.C.C.) [*Finta*].
23 *DeSousa*, above note 5.
24 *Hundal*, above note 11.
25 *Creighton*, above note 3.
26 *R. v. Finlay* (1993), 83 C.C.C. (3d) 513 (S.C.C.) [*Finlay*]; *R. v. Gosset* (1993), 83 C.C.C. (3d) 494 (S.C.C.) [*Gosset*].
27 *R. v. Naglik* (1993), 83 C.C.C. (3d) 526 (S.C.C.) [*Naglik*].
28 *Hundal*, above note 11.
29 *Creighton*, above note 3 at 374.

This articulates constitutional requirements of *mens rea* at a greater level of generality than often circular conclusions about whether the stigma, penalty, or moral blameworthiness of particular crimes demand a greater degree of *mens rea*.

The first *Creighton* proposition builds on a line of cases culminating in *Martineau* and *Logan* that indicated that murder and attempted murder because of their nature and labelling effects will require a subjective *mens rea* in relation to the *actus reus* of the crime. One open question is whether new crimes of terrorism will be added to the select list of crimes that require subjective fault in relation to the prohibited act because of the extra stigma and punishment contemplated by the offence. An analogy can be made to war crimes where the Supreme Court concluded, albeit in a 4–3 decision, that the prosecutor must establish not only the fault of the underlying offence but also subjective fault, including wilful blindness, of the circumstances which elevated the crime from an ordinary crime into a war crime.[30] Although most of the new terrorism offences created at the end of 2001 require subjective knowledge of terrorist activities and a subjective purpose to assist terrorists, the requirements of subjective fault are diluted with respect to some terrorism offences. In particular, the offence under section 83.19 of the *Code* requires knowing facilitation of a terrorist activity but then provides that it is not necessary to establish that "any particular terrorist activity was foreseen or planned at the time it was facilitated." This provision may be vulnerable under section 7 of the *Charter* should terrorism be found to be one of the few stigma offences that requires a subjective *mens rea* that reflects the particular nature of the crime. Nevertheless, the first *Creighton* proposition will only be relevant with respect to a small number of crimes with a special stigma.

The second *Creighton* proposition relates to proportionality between the moral blameworthiness of the offender and the punishment. This principle might be thought to relate to section 12 of the *Charter*, which has been interpreted to prohibit grossly disproportionate punishment as cruel and unusual punishment.[31] Nevertheless, the Court has recognized that a law that was grossly disproportionate to a state interest could also violate section 7 of the *Charter*.[32] If the punishment of a crime is severe or potentially severe, then it may not be pro-

---

30   *Finta*, above note 22.

31   *R. v. Smith* (1987), 34 C.C.C.(3d) 97 (S.C.C.); *R. v. Latimer* (2001), 150 C.C.C.(3d) 129 (S.C.C.).

32   *R. v. Malmo-Levine* (2003), 179 C.C.C. (3d) 417 (S.C.C.).

portionate to the offender's moral blameworthiness unless his or her *mens rea* reflects the particular nature of the crime. For example, a mandatory sentence of imprisonment for a minor crime of negligence might be held to be disproportionate under either sections 7 or 12 of the *Charter*. The relation between *mens rea* or moral blameworthiness and punishment will not often be tight because the courts have generally been reluctant to find that sentences are grossly disproportionate. For example, in *Creighton*, the Court held that the stigma and penalty inherent in a manslaughter conviction did not demand proof of even objective foreseeability of death. If the serious crime of manslaughter which can be punished by up to life imprisonment does not require subjective fault or even objective fault in relation to the *actus reus* of death, then there will be very few crimes that constitutionally require either subjective fault or fault that relates to all aspects of the *actus reus*.

The idea expressed in the third *Creighton* proposition that the intentional causing of harm should be punished more severely than the unintentional causing of harm was easily satisfied because of the important distinction between murder and manslaughter. Nevertheless, this principle creates the possibility that section 7 might be violated by some broadly defined crimes such as sexual assault, which combine objective and subjective fault elements. This approach, however, would require courts to scrutinize the policy reasons that Parliament may have for broadly defining crimes to include a range of culpable conduct. Courts may very well retreat to the notion, firmly established in the cases, that the stigma, penalty, and blameworthiness of only a few crimes demand a *mens rea* that reflects the particular nature of the crime. Thus, courts may well conclude that the stigma and penalty that accompanies a sexual assault conviction does not require proof of subjective fault for every element of the offence or the creation of a separate less serious offence of negligent sexual assault. In addition, the third *Creighton* proposition may discount that sometimes it may be quite appropriate for Parliament to combine subjective and objective fault elements and that this may not result in disproportionate punishment that punishes those who cause harm unintentionally more than those who cause harm intentionally. Rather the result may be to punish those who had elements of both subjective and objective fault.

Constitutional requirements concerning fault elements will be less easily overcome than common law presumptions. The Supreme Court has concluded that because of the stigma and penalty of a murder conviction, section 7 of the *Charter* requires proof that the accused knew that the victim was likely to die. Thus, subjective knowledge of the *actus reus* is a constitutional requirement for the offence of murder.

It is theoretically possible to substitute another fault element for the fault element required under section 7 of the *Charter*. As examined in chapter 1, however, the Court has been quite stringent and held that another element could only be substituted for a required element if proof of the substituted element would lead inexorably, or prove beyond a reasonable doubt, that the required element was present.[33] In *Martineau*,[34] the Supreme Court held that proof that the accused means to cause bodily harm for the purpose of facilitating a serious offence — the *mens rea* required for constructive murder under section 230(a) — could not be substituted for proof of the essential element of murder required for a murder conviction under section 7 of the *Charter* — namely proof of subjective knowledge that the victim was likely to die. Similarly, proof under section 230(c) that the accused wilfully stops the breath of a human being for the purpose of facilitating a serious offence could not be substituted for the essential element under section 7 of the *Charter* of knowledge of death. Proof of the substituted element in section 230 did not lead inexorably to a conclusion that the state had proven beyond a reasonable doubt the existence of the essential element required under section 7 of the *Charter*.[35]

Another possibility would be to justify the violation of section 7 caused by providing some other fault element as a reasonable limit under section 1 of the *Charter*. The Supreme Court has, however, been extremely reluctant to hold that violations of section 7 of the *Charter* are justified under section 1 of the *Charter*. In both *Vaillancourt* and *Martineau*, the Court held that it was not necessary or proportionate for the Court to use a lesser fault element than knowledge of death in order to advance the important objective of deterring the use of weapons and violence in the commission of serious offences. The Court noted that Parliament could and does punish the use of weapons in the commission of offences and that the accused could always receive a stiff sentence for manslaughter. In other cases, the Court seems even more categorical, even suggesting that a section 7 violation could only be justified under section 1 in exceptional circumstances such as war and other emergencies.[36] A final means to overcome a constitutional

---

33 *R. v. Whyte* (1988) 42 C.C.C. (3d) 97 (S.C.C.) as discussed in ch.1, "Right to be Presumed Innocent."

34 *Martineau*, above note 6.

35 *R. v. Sit* (1991), 61 C.C.C.(3d) 449 (S.C.C.).

36 *Re B.C. Motor Vehicles*, [1985] 1 S.C.R. 486 at 518; *R. v. Heywood*, [1994] 3 S.C.R. 761 at 802; *New Brunswick v. G.(J.)*, [1999] 3 S.C.R. 46 at para. 99; *R. v. Ruzic* 2001 SCC 24 at para. 92.

requirement of fault would be for Parliament to re-enact an offence, such as the constructive murder offence, notwithstanding section 7 of the *Charter*. This section 33 override would be politically unpopular and would have to be re-enacted by Parliament after a five-year period.

A constitutional requirement of *mens rea* under section 7 of the *Charter* is much more difficult for Parliament to overcome than a common law presumption. All Parliament need do in response to a common law presumption of subjective *mens rea* is to indicate clearly that the common law presumptions are not desired. A constitutional requirement of *mens rea* can only be overcome by satisfying the rigorous and almost impossible standards for substituting elements under section 11(d) of the *Charter* or the equally difficult burden of justifying a violation of section 7 of the *Charter* under section 1. This may help explain why the Supreme Court has been relatively cautious in constitutionalizing subjective *mens rea* under section 7 of the *Charter* while it did not hesitate before the *Charter* to apply robust common law presumptions of subjective *mens rea*. It should be remembered that constitutional requirements are a bare minimum. As the content of constitutional requirements become more minimal, the common law presumptions will become more important.

5) Fault Elements in Relation to the Defences of Mistake of Fact and Intoxication

Understanding fault elements is sometimes confused by reference to the "defences" of mistake of fact and intoxication. The availability of both defences depends on the fault element of the specific offence being absent. In other words, both defences operate to raise a reasonable doubt as to whether the accused had the requisite fault element rather than the existence of some other factor, such as self-defence, which may excuse or justify the commission of a crime that is committed with the required fault.

Both mistake of fact and intoxication defences are primarily derived from the fault element of the particular offence. As will be discussed in depth in chapter 6, evidence that the accused was intoxicated may raise a reasonable doubt whether the accused had the required mental element for a specific intent offence such as murder or robbery. The Supreme Court has made clear that the issue is the accused's actual intent, not his or her capacity for the intent.[37] The relation of the

---

37   *R. v. Robinson* (1996), 105 C.C.C. (3d) 97 (S.C.C.).

intoxication defence to the fault element is less clear for offences that are classified as general intent offences. General intent offences such as assault are thought to involve less complex mental processes. Only extreme intoxication may negate such mental elements.[38] It might also be thought that intoxication may never be relevant to offences that only require an objective fault element because the reasonable person would not be intoxicated. Nevertheless, extreme intoxication may raise a reasonable doubt as to whether the accused had voluntarily committed the *actus reus*.[39]

The derivative nature of the mistake of fact defence is revealed by comparing the availability of the defence for crimes with various and no fault elements. Mistake of fact will not be an issue for an absolute liability offence because the only issue is whether the accused has committed the *actus reus*. What the particular accused thought or even what a reasonable person in the accused's position would have perceived is not relevant. If objective negligence is the fault element, a mistake of fact will only prevent a conviction if it is one that a reasonable person would have made. In other words, a mistake of fact would have to be honest and reasonable. If the offence requires a subjective fault element, this opens up the possibility that an honest but not necessarily reasonable mistake of fact will suffice. The issue is what the actual accused perceived, not what a reasonable person perceived. The more unreasonable the accused's mistake, the less likely the jury will be to accept it as genuine and honest, but the ultimate issue is the perceptions of the particular accused. As will be seen later in this chapter, it is possible to combine subjective and objective fault elements and require that a mistake of fact be based on reasonable behaviour given the accused's actual subjective knowledge of the circumstances.

B. THE DEGREES OF SUBJECTIVE *MENS REA*

There are important practical differences between the various forms of subjective *mens rea*. A person who might not be guilty of acting with the purpose or intent to commit a crime might, nevertheless, have acted with subjective knowledge that the prohibited result would occur. Similarly, a person who cannot be said to have acted with subjective knowledge that the prohibited result would occur may, nevertheless, have

---

38   *R. v. Daviault* (1994), 93 C.C.C. (3d) 21 (S.C.C.) [*Daviault*].

39   See ch. 2, "Voluntariness of the Act," and ch. 6, "Extreme Intoxication," for more discussion of this proposition.

acted with subjective recklessness in adverting to or being conscious of a risk that the prohibited result would occur or the prohibited circumstances were present. Such a person could also be wilfully blind by not inquiring into the prohibited risk, when he or she knows there is need for further inquiry. References to "subjective *mens rea*" are unhelpful, and the exact degree of subjective fault must be specified.

1) Intent, Purpose, or Wilfulness

The highest level of subjective *mens rea* is that which requires the accused to act with the intent or purpose to achieve the prohibited result, or to wilfully pursue such a result. An example would be section 229(a)(i), which prohibits murder where the accused "means to cause . . . death." This high level of *mens rea* is used relatively infrequently. Common law presumptions and even constitutional requirements of subjective *mens rea* do not require proof of intent and are satisfied by lower forms of *mens rea* such as knowledge and even recklessness. Where Parliament has specifically used the words "with intent," this will generally exclude lower forms of subjective *mens rea* such as recklessness.[40]

Proof of purpose is required under the various parties provisions in the *Criminal Code*. As examined in the last chapter, these provisions can make a person guilty of an offence even though he or she did not actually commit the offence and thus it makes sense to require a fairly high level of *mens rea*. Section 21(1)(b) requires a party to do or omit "to do anything for the purpose of aiding any person" to commit an offence, and section 21(2) requires the formation of an "unlawful purpose." Similarly, attempts require "an intent to commit the offence," and an accessory after the fact must act for the purpose of enabling a known criminal to escape. The more peripheral the accused's involvement to the completed crime, the more sense it makes to require a higher form of subjective *mens rea*.

The potential difference between guilty intent and guilty knowledge can be illustrated in cases where the accused knowingly engages in prohibited conduct, but does so for another purpose such as avoiding harm. In *R. v. Steane*, the accused was charged with assisting the enemy with the "intent to assist the enemy" after he made wartime propaganda broadcasts. The Court of Appeal held that, given the intent required for the offence, it was wrong for the trial judge to have left the

---

40   *R. v. Chartrand* (1994), 91 C.C.C. (3d) 396 (S.C.C.) [*Chartrand*].

jury with the impression that "a man must be taken to intend the natural consequences of his acts." It was possible that Steane acted not with the intent to assist the enemy, but rather with "the innocent intent of a desire to save his wife and children from a concentration camp."[41] In *R. v. Paquette*,[42] the Supreme Court similarly indicated:

> A person whose actions have been dictated by fear of death or of grievous bodily injury cannot be said to have formed a genuine common intent to carry out an unlawful purpose with the person who has threatened him with those consequences if he fails to co-operate.

In that case, the accused was held not to have formed a common intent under section 21(2) to rob a store when he drove the robbers to the store after being threatened at gunpoint. In both cases, the accused certainly acted with the knowledge that his actions would contribute to the prohibited result. The difficult issue is whether the accused acted with the intent or purpose to achieve the prohibited result.

The Supreme Court in *R. v. Hibbert*,[43] has overruled *Paquette* on the basis that it confused intent and purpose with motive and desire. Lamer C.J. stated that a person, like Paquette, who participates in a robbery because of threats to his life nevertheless forms an "unlawful purpose" under section 21(2) to commit the robbery. His desire or motive of saving his own life does not prevent the formation of the unlawful purpose of intentionally committing the robbery. Similarly, Paquette would act with the purpose of assisting the robbery required under section 21(1)(b) if he intended to drive the getaway car and by doing so assist the robbery. It would not matter to the question of *mens rea* that Paquette's desire or motive was to save his own life. The Supreme Court has rejected the idea that intent or purpose under section 21 should be equated with the accused's desires and motivations. Some caution is in order before applying this ruling to all forms of subjective *mens rea*. The Court made clear it only reached these conclusions for section 21 in large part because an accused who responded to threats could still claim a common law defence of duress.[44] Depending on how the offence was structured, the fact that a person acted as a result of threats could in some instances be relevant to the question of whether he or she possessed the *mens rea* necessary to commit the offence. Thus, a person in Steane's position could perhaps still argue

41   [1947] K.B. 997 at 1006 (C.A.).
42   (1976), 30 C.C.C. (2d) 417 at 423 (S.C.C.) [*Paquette*].
43   *R. v. Hibbert* (1995), 99 C.C.C. (3d) 193 (S.C.C.) [*Hibbert*].
44   See ch. 8, "Duress."

that he did not wilfully act with an intent or purpose to assist the enemy even though he surely knew that his actions would have that effect.

Knowledge that something is very certain to occur, however, may be equated with an intent or a purpose to achieve the prohibited result. In *Buzzanga*,[45] Martin J.A. stated that "as a general rule, a person who foresees that a consequence is certain or substantially certain to result from an act which he does to achieve some other purpose, intends that consequence." Consistent with the presumption of innocence, however, an accused should be allowed to raise a reasonable doubt as to whether he or she intended the consequence, if that is the required mental element.

A requirement that the accused wilfully achieve a prohibited result, such as purpose or intent, imposes a high degree of subjective *mens rea*. In *Buzzanga*,[46] the Ontario Court of Appeal interpreted a prohibition against wilfully promoting hatred against an identifiable group as requiring proof that the accused's "conscious purpose in distributing the document was to promote hatred against that group," or knowledge that the promotion of hatred "was certain or morally certain" to result from their actions. In *R. v. Docherty*,[47] the Supreme Court stated that the word "wilfully" "stresses intention in relation to the achievement of a purpose. It can be contrasted with lesser forms of guilty knowledge, such as 'negligently' or even 'recklessly.' In short, the use of the word 'wilfully' denotes a legislative concern for a relatively high level of *mens rea*." In that case, the accused was held not to have wilfully breached his probation order because he believed that what he was doing, sitting in the driver's seat of a motionless car while drunk, was not a crime that would place him in breach of probation. Parliament subsequently deleted the requirement that the prosecutor prove that the accused "wilfully" breached parole. Instead there is a simple prohibition against breaching parole without a reasonable excuse.[48]

In *R. v. Carker (No. 2)*,[49] a prisoner was convicted of wilfully damaging public property when he smashed plumbing fixtures in his cell

---

45   *Buzzanga*, above note 7 at 384–85, approved in *Chartrand*, above note 40 at 415.
46   *Buzzanga*, above note 7 at 385. This analysis has been approved with reference to a "with intent" requirement. *Chartrand, ibid.*
47   (1989), 51 C.C.C. (3d) 1 at 7 (S.C.C.).
48   *Code*, above note 2, s. 733.1. Applying the common law presumption of subjective *mens rea* discussed above, this new offence would only require proof that accused recklessly breached probation by being aware of the risk that their actions would breach probation.
49   (1966), [1967] 2 C.C.C. 190 (S.C.C.).

during a prison riot, even though he only performed the act after fellow prisoners had threatened to injure him if he did not. On the basis of *Steane* and *Paquette*, it could be argued that Carker did not truly intend to damage public property because he was acting for the purpose of self-preservation. Carker was, however, found to have the necessary *mens rea*, because wilful was defined for the purpose of the offence as including knowledge or recklessness that the prohibited result would occur.[50] Carker knew he was damaging public property, even though his ultimate purpose or intent may have been to save his life. Given the Supreme Court's overruling of *Paquette*, however, it is possible that a court might dismiss Carker's desire to protect his own life as a matter of motive or desire not relevant to the determination of his intent.[51] More fundamentally, it can no longer be maintained with great confidence that a *mens rea* requirement of intent, purpose, or wilfulness will be sharply differentiated from a requirement of knowledge.

2) Intent, Purpose, or Wilfulness Distinguished from Motive

The criminal law does not require proof of a motive for a crime, and an argument that the accused had no motive or some innocent motivation will not exonerate one who has otherwise committed the crime with the necessary guilty intent. As Dickson J. has stated:

> In ordinary parlance, the words "intent" and "motive" are frequently used interchangeably, but in the criminal law they are distinct. In most criminal trials, the mental element, the *mens rea* with which the Court is concerned, relates to "intent," *i.e.*, the exercise of a free will to use particular means to produce a particular result, rather than with "motive," *i.e.*, that which precedes and induces the exercise of the will. The mental element of a crime ordinarily involves no reference to motive.[52]

The Crown does not have to prove motive, but evidence relating to motive can be relevant in a criminal trial and can assist the Crown and sometimes the accused. In *Buzzanga*, the fact that the accused may

---

50   *Code*, above note 2, s. 429(1).
51   Even if Carker had the required fault element, he could argue that he had a defence of duress. As will be seen, however, s. 17 of the *Code*, *ibid.*, as interpreted in this case placed severe restrictions on the availability of this defence.
52   *R. v. Lewis* (1979), 47 C.C.C. (2d) 24 at 33 (S.C.C.).

have intended to counter apathy among francophones when they circulated an anti-French document was relevant in determining whether they were wilfully promoting hatred against that group. On the other hand, Martin J.A. indicated that if the accused were indeed intentionally promoting hatred against francophones, they would be guilty even if their motive was to produce a reaction that would help establish a French language school.

Motive can be difficult to distinguish from intent, and cases on this issue have not always been consistent. In a 1936 case, the Supreme Court held that a person who assisted in a robbery had formed a common intent to commit the crime. The fact that his motivation may have been to avoid threats of death from his accomplices was irrelevant to the issue of *mens rea*.[53] In 1976, however, the Court indicated that a person who assisted in a robbery in response to threats of death could not have formed a genuine intent to carry out the unlawful purpose.[54] In 1995, however, the Supreme Court reverted to its former approach when it overruled the 1976 case on the basis that a person could act with the purpose of assisting a crime under section 21(1)(b) or form a common intent to carry out an unlawful purpose to engage in a crime under section 21(2), even though his or her motives and desires were to avoid threats from accomplices.[55] The Court indicated that in most cases, the motive of avoiding harm to self or others would not negate the issue of intent.

The Supreme Court has continued to draw a broad distinction between motive and intent. Cory and Iacobucci JJ. have stated that "[i]t does not matter to society, in its efforts to secure social peace and order, what an accused's motive was, but only what the accused intended to do. It is no consolation to one whose car has been stolen that the thief stole the car intending to sell it to purchase food for a food bank."[56] Good motive is no defence to intentional crimes. It may, however, be relevant to the exercise of prosecutorial or sentencing discretion.

One exception to the principle that motive is not an essential element of offences are the terrorism offences created by Parliament at the end of 2001. The prosecutor must not only prove various forms of intent beyond a reasonable doubt but also that the act was "committed in whole or in part for a political, religious, or ideological purpose,

---

53 *Dunbar v. R.* (1936), 67 C.C.C. 20 (S.C.C.).
54 *Paquette*, above note 42.
55 *Hibbert*, above note 43.
56 *U.S. v. Dynar* (1997), 115 C.C.C. (3d) 481 at 509 (S.C.C.) [*Dynar*].

objective or cause."[57] In other words, a political or religious motive is an essential element of crimes involving the commission of a terrorist activity. The motive requirement was defended as necessary to distinguish terrorism from ordinary crime. This seems unlikely given that the activities also have to be committed with the intent to intimidate the public or compel governments or persons to act. Concerns were raised that the motive requirement would require the police to investigate the politics and religion of terrorist suspects and that these matters would be front and centre in any terrorist trial. In response, Parliament enacted section 83.01(1.1), which provides that "the expression of a political, religious, or ideological thought, belief or opinion" would not fall under the definition of terrorist activity unless the other intent requirements were satisfied.

3) Knowledge

Knowledge is a slightly lower form of subjective *mens rea* than intent or purpose. Section 229(c) of the *Criminal Code* states that a person is guilty of murder if he "knows" that he "is likely to cause death to a human being, notwithstanding that he desires to effect his object without causing death or bodily harm to any human being."[58] Similarly, section 229(a)(ii) also emphasizes the requirement of guilty knowledge by providing that a person who intentionally causes bodily harm is guilty of murder if he or she knows that the harm is likely to result in death. This requirement of guilty knowledge of the likelihood of death has been held to be sufficient under section 7 of the *Charter* to sustain a murder conviction.[59] A person may have guilty knowledge that their victim will die without necessarily desiring or having the motive of causing death or even intending or meaning to cause death under section 229(a)(i).

Knowledge is a common form of *mens rea* for possession-based offences. In *Beaver*,[60] the Supreme Court held that a person in physical possession of a substance could not be said to possess that substance

---

57   *Code*, above note 2, s. 83.01(1)(b)(I)(A).

58   The reference in that section to objective foreseeability that occurs when the accused ought to know that his or her actions would cause death is unconstitutional because s. 7 of the *Canadian Charter of Rights and Freedoms*, Part I of the *Constitution Act, 1982*, being Schedule B to the *Canada Act 1982* (U.K.), 1982, c. 11 [*Charter*] has been interpreted as requiring a minimal *mens rea* for murder of knowledge that death is likely to occur. *Martineau*, above note 6.

59   *Martineau, ibid.*, discussed in ch. 1, "Fault Requirements."

60   *Beaver*, above note 13.

unless he or she knew the nature of the substance. Cartwright J. explained that a person with an honest belief that a substance was baking soda would not have the *mens rea* for possession even if the substance turned out to be heroin. "The essence of the crime is the possession of the forbidden substance and in a criminal case there is in law no possession without knowledge of the character of the forbidden substance."[61] As discussed in chapter 2, however, a person who makes a mistake about whether a particular drug is illegal would not have a defence because ignorance of the law is no excuse.

In *Lucas*,[62] the Supreme Court interpreted the requirement that the prosecutor prove that an accused who has been charged with defamatory libel know that the statements were false as requiring proof of the accused's subjective knowledge. The Court then qualified this correct statement by indicating that the accused's

> subjective understanding of the statements . . . should not be determinative if this position was adopted, it would always be open to an accused to argue that the "real" meaning which they believed to be true was quite different from the meaning which would be objectively attributed to it by any reasonable reader. Rather the question should be whether the appellants knew that the message, as it would be understood by a reasonable person, was false.

This formulation runs the risk of confusing subjective and objective standards of liability and diluting the relatively high level of subjective *mens rea* required by proof of guilty knowledge. Knowledge is a subjective form of *mens rea* and a person who claims to ignore what a reasonable person would know runs the real risk of being found guilty. Nevertheless, the ultimate issue is the particular accused's knowledge, not what a reasonable person would know.

In *Dynar*,[63] the Supreme Court observed that knowledge has "two components — truth and belief" and that only belief is relevant to the determination of a subjective *mens rea*. The truth of the matter is an objective fact that is required to establish the *actus reus* not the *mens rea*. Thus, an accused who stabbed a manikin believing it to be human would have the subjective *mens rea* of murder. Because the manikin was not in truth a human being, however, there would be no *actus reus* for murder. Even though the accused had the *mens rea* required for murder, he or she could only be charged with attempted murder.

---

61   *Ibid.* at 140.
62   (1998), 123 C.C.C. (3d) 97 at 131 (S.C.C.).
63   *Dynar*, above note 56 at 506.

4) Recklessness

Recklessness is a lower form of *mens rea* than intent, purpose, wilfulness, or knowledge, but in Canada it is still a form of subjective *mens rea*. In Canadian criminal law, a person acts recklessly if he or she has adverted to or become aware of the risk of the prohibited conduct. In *Sansregret*,[64] the Supreme Court stressed the importance of distinguishing recklessness from negligence:

> In accordance with well-established principles for the determination of criminal liability, recklessness, to form a part of the criminal *mens rea*, must have an element of the subjective. It is found in the attitude of one who, aware that there is danger that his conduct could bring about the result prohibited by the criminal law, nevertheless persists, despite the risk. It is, in other words, the conduct of one who sees the risk and who takes the chance.

Recklessness requires subjective advertence to the prohibited risk and can be distinguished from negligence, which requires only that a reasonable person in the accused's circumstances would have recognized the risk.[65] A person recklessly commits sexual assault if he recognizes the risk that the woman is not consenting, while a person would negligently commit sexual assault if a reasonable person in his circumstances would have known there was a risk that the woman does not consent. As will be seen, the actual fault element for sexual assault falls somewhere in between recklessness and negligence.

Recklessness is a common form of subjective *mens rea*. Martin J.A. has stated that "the general *mens rea* which is required and which suffices for most crimes where no mental element is mentioned in the definition of the crime, is either the intentional or reckless bringing about of the result which the law, in creating the offence, seeks to prevent."[66] Similarly, the common law presumption in *Sault Ste. Marie*[67] that a criminal offence have subjective *mens rea* includes recklessness. Recklessness requires only subjective awareness of the risk of the prohibited act, as opposed to knowledge of the likelihood of the prohibited act.

---

64   *Sansregret*, above note 16 at 233.
65   *O'Grady v. Sparling* (1960), 128 C.C.C. 1 at 13 (S.C.C.).
66   *Buzzanga*, above note 7 at 381.
67   *Sault Ste. Marie*, above note 12 at 362.

5) Wilful Blindness

A more recent and controversial form of subjective *mens rea* is wilful blindness. There is no consensus about its definition, but the Supreme Court has stated:

> Wilful blindness is distinct from recklessness because, while recklessness involves knowledge of a danger or a risk and persistence in a course of conduct which creates a risk that the prohibited result will occur, wilful blindness arises when a person who has become aware of the need for some inquiry declines to make the inquiry because he does not wish to know the truth. He would prefer to remain ignorant. The culpability in recklessness is justified by consciousness of the risk and by proceeding in the face of it, while in wilful blindness it is justified by the accused's fault in deliberately failing to inquire when he knows there is reason for inquiry.[68]

On the facts of the case, the trial judge had acquitted the accused of rape on the basis that while the risk that the complainant had not consented would have been obvious to anyone "in his right mind," it was not to the accused, who "saw what he wanted to see, heard what he wanted to hear, believed what he wanted to believe." The Supreme Court reversed and entered a conviction on the basis that the accused was wilfully blind to the lack of consent because he "was aware of the likelihood of the complainant's reaction to his threats." To proceed in the circumstances was "self-deception to the point of wilful blindness. . . . Where the accused is deliberately ignorant as a result of blinding himself to reality the law presumes knowledge, in this case knowledge of the nature of the consent."[69]

Some commentators have argued that if the accused in *Sansregret* genuinely believed that the complainant consented, there was no reason for him to make the inquiry, and the Court was actually imposing liability on the basis of negligence. This interpretation seems strained, given the facts of the case, which included a break-in and violence, as well as a similar encounter less than a month earlier in which the same complainant had reported that she had been raped by the accused. The Supreme Court seems to suggest that given these facts, the accused knew there was a likelihood that the complainant was not consenting, but he deliberately blinded himself to that possibility. On the other hand, if the accused was actually aware of any risk that the com-

---

68   *Sansregret*, above note 16 at 235.
69   *Ibid.*

plainant was not consenting, the courts could have presumably found him to be reckless with regard to the prohibited conduct.

The exact definition of wilful blindness remains illusive. The Quebec Court of Appeal has stressed the subjective nature of wilful blindness by stating that the issue was not whether the accused "'*should*' have known or should '*normally*' have known from the suspicious circumstances that her husband was probably involved in a conspiracy to import cocaine. The question was whether the circumstances were such that she, herself, was, in fact, suspicious that this was the case, but deliberately refrained from making inquiries so that she could remain in ignorance as to the truth."[70] In a subsequent case, the Supreme Court defined wilful blindness in similar terms, stressing that it constitutes shutting one's eye and "deliberately choosing not to know" when the accused strongly suspects that such an inquiry would fix them with guilty knowledge.[71] On the other hand, McLachlin J. has defined wilful blindness in the context of sexual assault to place some affirmative duties on the accused to address his mind to the issue of consent. She has stated that "[t]he person who is not wilfully blind is the person who is appropriately aware, not only of the need to obtain consent (which he is presumed to know), but of what the conduct and circumstances reveal to one who looks to see whether that consent was being given or withheld."[72] The former approach is closer to recklessness while the latter is closer to negligence.

6) Transferred Subjective *Mens Rea*

Section 229(b) codifies the common law doctrine of transferred intent. The *mens rea* of intentionally or knowingly causing death to one person is transferred to the killing of the victim, even though the accused "does not mean to cause death or bodily harm" to the victim and does so "by accident or mistake." This provision was applied in *R. v. Droste (No. 2)*[73] to convict an accused who, in a deliberate attempt to kill his wife, set fire to a car, causing two children buckled in the back seat to die of asphyxiation. The Court concluded that because the attempted murder of the accused's wife was planned and deliberate, the intent of planning and deliberation, as well as the guilty knowledge that death

---

70   *R. v. Comtois Barbeau* (1996), 110 C.C.C. (3d) 69 at 95 (Que. C.A.).

71   *R. v. Jorgensen* (1995), 102 C.C.C. (3d) 97 at 135 (S.C.C.).

72   *R. v. Esau* (1997), 116 C.C.C. (3d) 289 at 310–11 (in dissent but not on this point) (S.C.C.) [*Esau*].

73   (1984), 10 C.C.C. (3d) 404 (S.C.C.).

would result, could be transferred to the children's deaths. The Manitoba Court of Appeal has decided that section 229(b) should not be applied when the accused intends to kill himself but ends up killing another person. The Court of Appeal held that a person who intends to kill himself does not have the same moral blameworthiness as a person who intends to kill another person, but then kills yet another person by accident or mistake.[74]

The courts may transfer intent in other contexts. An accused has been convicted of assault causing bodily harm when, in an attempt to strike another person, he caused bodily harm to a bystander.[75] Statutory and common law doctrines of transferred intent allow *mens rea* directed towards one person to be transferred to an *actus reus* that occurs in relation to another person.

C. THE DEGREES OF OBJECTIVE *MENS REA*

The Supreme Court has indicated that objective, as opposed to subjective, fault is constitutionally sufficient for unlawful act manslaughter and several other criminal offences less serious than murder, attempted murder, and war crimes. Despite increasing acceptance of objective fault as a form of *mens rea*, there has been some uncertainty about how such a standard should be applied in a criminal prosecution. This topic raises some of the same dilemmas encountered when the courts apply objective standards to defences such as self-defence and provocation.[76] The central issue is how to adjust the objective standard so that it does not apply to those who cannot reasonably be held responsible for satisfying that standard, while not collapsing objective standards into subjective ones.

1) Who Is the Reasonable Person?

Some judges have been attracted to the idea of making the reasonable person resemble the accused, but this has yet to win majority support in the Supreme Court. In *Tutton*,[77] Lamer J. would have applied an

---

74   R. v. *Fontaine* (2002), 162 C.C.C.(3d) 360 at paras. 40–45 (Man. C.A.) rejecting R. v. *Brown* (1983) 4 C.C.C. (3d) 571 (Ont. H.C.) holding that an intent to commit suicide could be transferred under s. 229(b) of the *Code*.

75   R. v. *Deakin* (1974), 16 C.C.C. (2d) 1 (Man. C.A.).

76   See ch. 8, "Provocation, Self-Defence, Necessity, and Duress."

77   *Tutton*, above note 11 at 140.

objective standard to determine criminal negligence, but he would have modified it by making "'a generous allowance' for factors which are particular to the accused, such as youth, mental development, education." He noted that if this was done, "the adoption of a subjective or an objective test will, in practice, nearly if not always produce the same result."[78] In *Creighton*,[79] Lamer C.J. elaborated his views and held that the reasonable person used to determine objective liability should be invested with "any human frailties which might have rendered the accused incapable of having foreseen what the reasonable person would have foreseen," as well as any "enhanced foresight" derived from the accused's special knowledge or skill. Human frailties were defined as "personal characteristics habitually affecting an accused's awareness of the circumstances which create risk."[80] They had to be characteristics that the accused could not control or manage in the circumstances. On the one hand, Lamer C.J. would have factored in the inexperience, youth, and lack of education of a mother who did not provide the necessities of life to her child,[81] while on the other hand, he would have considered the enhanced foresight of risk that an experienced drug or gun user would have when dealing with those dangerous objects.[82] Making the reasonable person more like the accused could make it more difficult to convict an accused who habitually was unaware of prohibited risks, while it could also make it easier to convict an accused who was more sensitive to the prohibited risk than the reasonable person.

The Lamer approach to individualizing the reasonable person has not been accepted by a majority of the Supreme Court.[83] In *Creighton*,[84] McLachlin J. for a 5 to 4 majority rejected the Lamer approach on the basis that it "personalizes the objective test to the point where it devolves into a subjective test, thus eroding the minimum standard of care which Parliament has laid down by the enactment of offenses of

---

78   *Ibid.* at 143.

79   *Creighton*, above note 3 at 359–60.

80   *Ibid.* at 362–63.

81   *Naglik*, above note 27.

82   *Creighton*, above note 3; *Gosset*, above note 26.

83   In *Hundal*, above note 11 at 104, there was some recognition that "[t]he potential harshness of the objective standard may be lessened by the consideration of certain personal factors." These were, however, held inapplicable to the offence of dangerous driving because licensing requirements ensure "that all who drive have a reasonable standard of physical health and capability, mental health and a knowledge of the reasonable standard required of all licensed drivers." *Ibid.* at 108.

84   *Creighton*, above note 3 at 381–82.

manslaughter and penal negligence." The only personal characteristics of the accused that are relevant in the majority's approach would be those that establish incapacity to appreciate the nature and quality of the prohibited conduct and consequences. Justice McLachlin elaborated:

> Mental disabilities short of incapacity generally do not suffice to negative criminal liability for criminal negligence. The explanations for why a person fails to advert to the risk inherent in the activity he or she is undertaking are legion. They range from simple absent-mindedness to attributes related to age, education and culture. To permit such a subjective assessment would be "co-extensive with the judgment of each individual, which would be as variable as the length of the foot of each individual" leaving "so vague a line as to afford no rule at all, the degree of judgment belonging to each individual being infinitely various." . . . Provided the capacity to appreciate the risk is present, lack of education and psychological predispositions serve as no excuse for criminal conduct, although they may be important factors to consider in sentencing.[85]

In short, the reasonable person will not be invested with the personal characteristics of the accused unless the characteristics are so extreme as to create an incapacity to appreciate the prohibited risk or the quality of the prohibited conduct. An example given by McLachlin J. of a relevant personal characteristic when applying objective standards would be the accused's illiteracy if he or she was charged with a crime stemming from the mishandling of a marked container containing a dangerous substance. The accused's age and level of education, however, would not normally be considered when applying the reasonable person standard.

Chief Justice Lamer subsequently accepted this un-modified objective approach and justified it on the basis that it applied to those who make a voluntary decision to perform conduct that is subject to punishment for negligence.[86] As will be seen in chapter 8, however, Chief Justice Lamer's modified objective approach of endowing the reasonable person with similar characteristics, frailties and experiences as the accused has won the day with respect to defences in which the accused is held up to standards of reasonable conduct. The justification for the different approaches would appear to be that an accused who commits a crime with a valid defence such as provocation, self-defence, duress, and necessity does not voluntarily commit the crime and that the accused's

---

85   *Ibid.* at 390–91.
86   *Hibbert*, above note 43.

characteristics and experiences must be considered in determining whether he or she had no realistic choice but to commit the crime.

2) Degree of Negligence

Another manner of adapting a negligence standard to the criminal context is to require not only unreasonable conduct or simple negligence, but conduct that amounts to a marked departure from that of the reasonable person. In *Tutton*,[87] McIntyre J. stated that criminal negligence required "proof of conduct which reveals a *marked and significant departure* from the standard which could be expected of a reasonably prudent person in the circumstances," as opposed to simple negligence. In *Hundal*,[88] the Court similarly indicated that although dangerous driving was to be determined on an objective basis, "the trier of fact should be satisfied that the conduct amounted to a *marked departure* from the standard of care that a reasonable person would observe in the accused's situation."

The Supreme Court has required a marked and significant departure from the conduct of a reasonable person even when a criminal offence seems to require simple negligence. In *Finlay*[89] and *Gosset*,[90] the Supreme Court considered manslaughter charges based on the unlawful act of careless use of a firearm. The Court required that a person demonstrate a "marked and substantial departure from the standard of care of a reasonably prudent person in the circumstances," even though the offence seemed only to require careless use of a firearm. A legislated careless or simple negligence standard was essentially read up to require a more severe form of negligence. This is an important development given the Court's recent acceptance of objective standards of *mens rea*.

It seems appropriate that when objective standards of fault are used for criminal offences, that something more than mere negligence be required. A requirement of marked and substantial negligence distinguishes criminal negligence from the simple negligence that is required for conviction of a regulatory offence. At the same time, the courts could be more clear about whether they require this form of negligence under section 7 of the *Charter* or whether they are only invoking a common law presumption that can be displaced by clear legislative

---

87   *Tutton*, above note 11 at 140 [emphasis added].
88   *Hundal*, above note 11 at 108.
89   *Finlay*, above note 26.
90   *Ibid.*

intent. Given the clarity of the legislated standard of careless use of a firearm, the Supreme Court seems to be indicating that a negligence standard when used in the *Criminal Code* will only be constitutional if it requires a marked and substantial departure from the standard of care a reasonable person would have exercised in the circumstances.

3) Objective Foresight, but Subjective Perception, of the Circumstances

Another manner of mitigating the potential harshness of objective standards is to factor in the accused's subjective perception of the surrounding circumstances when determining whether the reasonable person would have been aware of the risk of the prohibited conduct. In the pre-*Charter* case of *R. v. Vasil*,[91] the Supreme Court held that although section 229(c) allowed an accused to be convicted of murder on the basis that he or she ought to have known death was likely to result, this objective standard was to be applied with respect to the circumstances known to the accused at that time. Thus, the jury would be allowed to consider subjective factors, including the accused's intoxication, in determining whether he actually knew that children were sleeping in a house that he set afire.

In *Tutton*,[92] McIntyre J. seemed to indicate that an accused's subjective perception of circumstances could be relevant in determining whether he or she acted with criminal negligence. He warned "the application of an objective test . . . may not be made in a vacuum" because:

> Events occur within the framework of other events and actions and when deciding on the nature of the questioned conduct, surrounding circumstances must be considered. The decision must be made on a consideration of the facts existing at the time and in relation to the accused's perception of those facts. Since the test is objective, the accused's perception of the facts is not to be considered for the purpose of assessing malice or intention on the accused's part but only to form a basis for a conclusion as to whether or not the accused's conduct, *in view of his perception of the facts*, was reasonable.[93]

Although the accused must live up to the standard of a reasonable person, that standard of conduct could be determined on the basis of the accused's own perception of the circumstances.

---

91   (1981), 58 C.C.C. (2d) 97 (S.C.C.).
92   *Tutton*, above note 11.
93   *Ibid.* at 141 [emphasis added].

In a subsequent case dealing with the offence of dangerous driving causing death, Cory J. maintained that objective fault must be determined in the context of the events surrounding the incident. However, Cory J. did not stress, as McIntyre J. had, that the accused's own perception of the facts should be considered. Rather Cory J. stated:

> Although an objective test must be applied to the offence of dangerous driving, it will remain open to the accused to raise a reasonable doubt that a reasonable person would have been aware of the risks in the accused's conduct. . . .
>
> . . . [I]n order to convict, the trier of fact must be satisfied that a reasonable person in similar circumstances ought to have been aware of the risk and danger involved in the conduct manifested by the accused.[94]

These comments suggest that the issue is whether the reasonable person in the same circumstances as the accused would have been aware of the risk of the prohibited act.

At present, it is not entirely clear what role the accused's own perceptions of the facts and circumstances will play in applying objective fault elements. Courts may be willing to consider an accused's mistaken perception of the facts, but probably will be more reluctant to do so the closer the perception of the facts comes to the risk or circumstances that are prohibited in the offence. As with all attempts to adapt the use of objective standards to criminal offences, courts will have to walk the fine line of ensuring fairness to the accused, while not individualizing the objective standard of liability to the point where it is indistinguishable from the lower forms of subjective *mens rea*.

D. MISTAKE OF FACT

Mistake of fact is a controversial defence that conceptually depends on the *mens rea* of the particular offence. If subjective awareness of prohibited circumstances is required, the Crown will not be able to establish the fault element if the accused honestly, but not necessarily reasonably, believes those circumstances do not exist. On the other hand, if the fault element of the offence requires only that a reasonable person would have recognized the prohibited circumstance or risk, then any

---

94   *Hundal*, above note 11 at 106–8.

defence based on mistake must be honest *and* reasonable. Finally, even a reasonable mistake of fact would not be a defence to an absolute liability offence. All that would matter would be whether the accused in fact committed the prohibited act.

Deducing the existence and nature of a mistake of fact defence from the fault element of the offence may, however, be too mechanical. It is possible that a mistake of fact may be based on a combination of subjective and objective factors. For example, section 273 of the *Criminal Code* now provides that the accused's belief that the complainant consented to the sexual activity is not a defence if the accused did not take reasonable steps, in the circumstances known to him at the time, to ascertain that the complainant was consenting. As will be discussed below, this creatively combines objective and subjective fault elements.

1) Early Cases

Mistake of fact defences have frequently been influenced by policy concerns not derived from the fault element of the particular offence. Courts were initially reluctant to accept mistake of fact as a defence. In *R. v. Prince*,[95] an accused was convicted of unlawfully abducting an unmarried girl under sixteen years of age without her parents' permission, even though he had an honest *and* reasonable belief that the girl was eighteen. Bramwell B. concluded: "The legislature has enacted that if anyone does this wrong act, he does it at the risk of her turning out to be under sixteen."[96] He did, however, concede that an accused would have no *mens rea* if he made a subjective mistake about other elements of the offence, such as whether he had received permission from the parents. Only one judge would have acquitted the accused on the basis that:

> a mistake of facts, on reasonable grounds, to the extent that if the facts were as believed the acts of the prisoner would make him guilty of no criminal offence at all, is an excuse, and that such excuse is implied in every criminal charge and every criminal enactment in England.[97]

---

95   (1875), 2 L.R. 2 C.C.R. 154.
96   *Ibid.* at 175.
97   *Ibid.* at 170.

The above passage was adopted in the subsequent case of *Tolson*,[98] so that a mistake of fact was originally recognized as a defence on the basis that it must be both honest *and* reasonable.

2) Mistake Related to the Degree of Fault

With the rise of subjective *mens rea*, courts began to recognize the possibility that an accused could have an honest but not necessarily reasonable belief in a state of circumstances that would make his activity innocent. In *R. v. Rees*,[99] the accused was charged with knowingly contributing to the delinquency of a person under eighteen who he believed to be older. Cartwright J. concluded:

> [T]he essential question is whether the belief entertained by the accused is an honest one and that the existence or non-existence of reasonable grounds for such a belief is merely relevant evidence to be weighed by the tribunal of fact in determining such essential question.

He conceded that the issue might be different if Parliament had not used the word "knowingly," or had specifically excluded a mistake about the girl's age as a possible defence. A year later, Cartwright J. acquitted an accused found in possession of an illegal drug because the accused thought that the substance was harmless. He stressed that the offence required subjective *mens rea*, and that "in a criminal case there is in law no possession without knowledge of the character of the forbidden substance."[100] Two judges dissented, on the basis that Parliament had intended to enact an absolute prohibition of being in possession of the illegal drugs. An absolute liability offence would, of course, allow no defence of mistake of fact.[101] An offence based on negligence would afford a defence of mistake of fact "if the accused *reasonably* believed in a mistaken set of facts which, if true, would render the act or omission innocent."[102] As will be seen in chapter 5, a reasonable mistake of fact is necessary when the accused is charged with a regulatory offence that requires strict liability.

---

98 *Tolson*, above note 1 at 181 and 189. In *D.P.P. v. Morgan* (1975), [1976] A.C. 182 (H.L.) the House of Lords reversed this decision and held in a 3–2 decision that the accused's mistaken belief in a woman's consent must be honest, but not necessarily reasonable, to be a defence to rape.

99 *Rees*, above note 13 at 11.

100 *Beaver*, above note 13.

101 *R. v. Pierce Fisheries Ltd.*, [1970] 5 C.C.C. 193 (S.C.C.).

102 *Sault Ste. Marie*, above note 12 at 374.

3) Mistake of Fact and Drug Offences

As discussed above, an accused would have a defence of mistake of fact if he or she believed that a substance was a harmless substance and not illegal drugs.[103] Courts have, however, been unwilling to apply this strict logic when an accused makes a mistake as to the nature of an illegal drug. In *R. v. Burgess*,[104] an accused was convicted of possession of opium, even though he thought the drug was hashish. This reasoning was extended in *R. v. Kundeus*,[105] when an accused was convicted of trafficking in LSD that he thought was mescaline. Mescaline was a prohibited drug, but not one carrying as serious a penalty as LSD. Laskin C.J.C. dissented on the basis that it was unfair to convict an accused of a more serious offence when he had the *mens rea* only for the commission of the less serious offence. In his view, the accused did not have the *mens rea* required to be convicted of selling LSD because he never thought he was selling LSD.

4) Mistake of Fact and Sexual Assault

Although the contours of a mistake of fact defence can be deduced at a conceptual level from the fault requirement of the specific offence, there may be a case for combining elements of subjective and objective fault for mistake of fact in some contexts. A purely subjective mistake of fact defence may not adequately protect victims of crime and social interests in giving people incentives to avoid unnecessary and harmful mistakes of fact, while a purely objective mistake of fact defence may punish those who, given their failure to correctly perceive circumstances, proceeded in a manner that did not indicate a flagrant disregard for the law.

In *R. v. Pappajohn*,[106] the Supreme Court held that an accused in a rape trial could have a defence of honest but not necessarily reasonable mistake that the complainant consented. Dickson J. derived the defence of mistake of fact from the *mens rea* of the particular offence. He concluded that because the *mens rea* of rape was subjective intent or recklessness relating to all the elements of the offence, it was not necessary that an accused's mistaken belief about consent be reasonable. He stated:

---

103 *Beaver*, above note 13.
104 [1970] 3 C.C.C. 268 (Ont. C.A.).
105 (1975), 24 C.C.C. (2d) 276 (S.C.C.).
106 (1980), 52 C.C.C. (2d) 481 (S.C.C.) [*Pappajohn*].

It is not clear how one can properly relate reasonableness (an element in offences of negligence) to rape (a "true crime" and not an offence of negligence). To do so, one must, I think, take the view that the *mens rea* only goes to the physical act of intercourse and not to non-consent, and acquittal comes only if the mistake is reasonable. This, upon the authorities, is not a correct view, the intent in rape being not merely to have intercourse, but to have it with a non-consenting woman. If the jury finds that mistake, whether reasonable or unreasonable, there should be no conviction. If, upon the entire record, there is evidence of mistake to cast a reasonable doubt upon the existence of a criminal mind, then the prosecution has failed to make its case.[107]

Dickson J. added that although the accused's belief did not have to be reasonable, its reasonableness would be evidence considered by the jury to determine whether the accused actually had an honest belief in consent. The *Criminal Code* was subsequently amended to provide that the judge "shall instruct the jury, when reviewing all the evidence relating to the determination of the honesty of the accused's belief, to consider the presence or absence of reasonable ground for that belief."[108]

a) Establishing an Air of Reality for a Mistake of Fact Defence

Although, the Supreme Court agreed on the conceptual nature of the defence of mistake of fact and its relation to the *mens rea* of the particular offence, it disagreed on its application in particular cases. In *Pappajohn*, Dickson J. was in dissent in concluding that the jury should have been instructed to consider the defence of mistake of fact. McIntyre J. for the majority held that the only realistic issue that could arise on the facts of the case was whether there was consent or no consent, not a third option of a mistaken belief in consent. In his view, there should be something more than the accused's assertion that he believed the complainant consented to justify instructing the jury on the mistaken belief defence. In a subsequent case, however, a majority of the Court indicated that there need not be evidence independent of the accused to support a mistake of fact. It was possible that the defence could arise when the accused alleged consent, and the complainant alleged no consent.[109] At the same time, there must be some plausible evidence to support a claim of mistake of fact, and a bare assertion by

---

107 *Ibid.* at 497.
108 *Code*, above note 2, s. 265(4). This was held to be consistent with ss. 7, 11(d), and 11(f) of the *Charter*, above note 58, in *R. v. Osolin* (1994), 86 C.C.C. (3d) 481 (S.C.C.).
109 *Osolin, ibid.*

the accused of a mistaken belief is not sufficient.[110] In one case, a majority of the Court found there to be an air of reality to the defence of mistaken belief in consent when the accused testified to consent and the complainant testified to absence of memory. Both Justices McLachlin and L'Heureux-Dubé dissented on the basis that there was no plausible evidence of ambiguous conduct that could create the basis for the defence of mistake about consent.[111] The controversy about when the jury should be instructed about the defence of mistaken belief in the complainant's consent continues. As will be seen, however, this debate should be influenced by 1992 changes in the *Criminal Code* that alter the *Pappajohn* defence of mistake of fact.

b) The *Pappajohn* Defence and Rape Shield Evidence

The Supreme Court struck down so called rape shield restrictions on the admission of the complainant's prior sexual conduct as a violation of the accused's *Charter* right to make full answer and defence, in part because the restrictions could deprive the accused of evidence to support the *Pappajohn* defence. McLachlin J. stated that the *Pappajohn* defence:

> rests on the concept that the accused may honestly but mistakenly (and not necessarily reasonably) have believed that the complainant was consenting to the sexual act. If the accused can raise a reasonable doubt as to his intention on the basis that he honestly held such a belief, he is not guilty under our law and is entitled to an acquittal. The basis of the accused's honest belief in the complainant's consent may be sexual acts performed by the complainant at some other time or place.[112]

In dissent, L'Heureux-Dubé J. argued that the complainant's prior sexual activity with a person other than the accused would never provide an air of reality for the jury to consider a defence of mistake of fact, if they were "operating in an intellectual environment that is free of rape myth and stereotype about women."[113]

c) Restrictions under Section 273.2 on the Mistake of Fact Defence

In response to *Seaboyer*, the law of sexual assault was amended in 1992 to restrict the availability of the mistake of fact defence. Section 273.2

---

110 *R. v. Park* (1995), 99 C.C.C. (3d) 1 (S.C.C.).
111 *Esau*, above note 72.
112 *R. v. Seaboyer* (1992), 66 C.C.C. (3d) 321 at 393 (S.C.C.).
113 *Ibid.* at 363.

now states that the accused's belief that the complainant consented is not a defence if it arose from the accused's "self-induced intoxication," his "recklessness or wilful blindness," or if "the accused did not take reasonable steps, in the circumstances known to the accused at the time, to ascertain that the complainant was consenting."

The reference to recklessness contemplates that an accused who adverted to the risk that the complainant did not consent has always had the *mens rea* required for sexual assault. The reference to self-induced intoxication not being relevant represents traditional but constitutionally suspect law that provides that intoxication may never be a defence to crimes classified as general intent.[114]

The reference to wilful blindness would seem to codify *Sansregret* and preclude the defence when an accused is subjectively aware of the need to inquire into consent, but deliberately declines to inquire because he does not wish to know the truth. It will be recalled that in *Sansregret*,[115] the trial judge acquitted the accused on the basis of *Pappajohn*, even though she found that anyone in his right mind, but not the accused, would have been aware of the risk that the complainant was not consenting to the sexual activity. The Supreme Court reversed and entered a conviction on the basis that even if the accused was not subjectively aware that there was no consent, he was wilfully blind to that prohibited risk. The culpability in wilful blindness was the accused's refusal to inquire whether the complainant was consenting, when he was "aware of the need for some inquiry . . . [but declined] to make the inquiry because he . . . [does] not wish to know the truth."[116] *Sansregret* narrowed the *Pappajohn* defence by holding that the accused was presumed to have guilty knowledge of the absence of consent when, knowing the need for inquiry as to consent, he remained ignorant.

The denial in section 273.2(b) of the mistake of fact unless the accused takes reasonable steps in the circumstances known to him at the time to ascertain whether the complainant was consenting to the

---

114 *R. v. Leary* (1977), 33 C.C.C. (2d) 473 (S.C.C.). But for a recognition of a possible defence of extreme intoxication see *Daviault*, above note 38. In addition s. 33.1 of the *Criminal Code*, above note 2, would deem the fault of self-induced intoxication sufficient to form the fault of sexual assault and other general intent offences involving an assault or interference or threat of interference with the bodily integrity of another person. See ch. 6, "Extreme Intoxication," for further discussion.

115 *Sansregret*, above note 16.

116 *Ibid.* at 235. The accused had broken into his ex-girlfriend's apartment and threatened her with a knife. Less than a month earlier, the complainant had reported a rape after a similar incident with the accused.

activity in question combines subjective and objective fault elements in a novel and creative manner. As such it breaks away from the idea in *Pappajohn* that the contours of the mistake of fact can be deduced from the fault element of the offence. On the one hand, section 273.2(b) bases the accused's obligation to take reasonable steps to ascertain consent on the basis of what the accused subjectively knows of the circumstances. The accused's obligation to take reasonable steps is only based on what he subjectively knows at the time. On the other hand, section 273.2(b) requires the accused to act as a reasonable person would in the circumstances by taking reasonable steps to ascertain whether the complainant was consenting. Much will depend on the Courts' view of what reasonable steps are necessary to ascertain consent. Some judges may find that positive steps are required in most, if not all, situations regardless of the accused's subjective perception of the circumstances. Others may only require such steps if the complainant has indicated resistance or lack of consent in some way that is subjectively known to the accused.

It is surprising, but there still is little direct authority on how section 273.2 should be interpreted. In *R. v. Ewanchuk*,[117] the majority of the Court did not directly apply section 273.2 despite the fact pointed out by the dissenters that it applied to the sexual assault in question.[118] Major J. for the majority indicated the traditional *Pappajohn* view that mistake of fact was a denial of *mens rea* and was necessary to protect the morally innocent. In part drawing on the new definition of consent, however, he indicated that:

> In order to cloak the accused's actions in moral innocence, the evidence must show that he believed that the complainant *communicated consent to engage in the sexual activity in question.* A belief by the accused that the complainant, in her own mind, wanted him to touch her, but did not express that desire, is not a defence. The accused's speculation as to what was going on in the complainant's mind provides no defence.[119]

---

117 (1999), 131 C.C.C. (3d) 481 (S.C.C.).

118 L'Heureux-Dubé J. argued that the mistake of fact defence would not arise unless the accused took reasonable steps to ascertain consent. She indicated that moving from a massage to sexual touching without inquiring about consent was not reasonable and that once that complainant had expressed non-consent "the accused has a corresponding escalating obligation to take additional steps to ascertain consent." *Ibid.* at 517.

119 *Ibid.* at 499.

This would seem to restrict the mistake of defence to cases in which the complainant communicated in an ambiguous manner that she consented to sexual activity. The mistake of fact defence was thus influenced more by statutory definitions of consent in section 273.1 as the voluntary agreement to engage in sexual activity than the reasonable steps requirement in section 273.2. *Ewanchuk* suggests that the accused may only have a mistaken belief defence when he mistakenly believes that the victim said yes through her words or actions. The accused may not have a mistaken defence if he only claims not to have heard the victim say no. This would mean that the accused would only have a defence in mistaken belief in consent if 1) he believed the victim communicated consent to the sexual activity in question and 2) he had taken reasonable steps, given the circumstances known to him at the time, to discover whether the victim consented to the sexual activity in question. In any event, the mistake of fact defence was denied in *Ewanchuk* because the complainant said no and "there is nothing on the record to support the accused's claim that he continued to believe her to be consenting, or that he re-established consent before resuming physical contact."[120] In another case, the Ontario Court of Appeal stressed that the complainant's prior rejection of the accused's advances as well as her objections when the accused entered her apartment and tried to kiss her, required the accused to take reasonable steps before he engaged in sexual intercourse: "The legislative scheme replaces the assumptions traditionally — and inappropriately — associated with passivity."[121]

d) The Constitutionality of Section 273.2

The Ontario Court of Appeal upheld the constitutionality of the new provision in *R. v. Darrach*.[122] Although section 273.2(b) introduced an "objective component into the mental element of the offence," it was "personalized according to the subjective awareness of the accused at the time" and did not require the accused to take all reasonable steps to ascertain whether the complainant consented. Morden A.C.J.O. concluded that the subjective *mens rea* requirement "remains largely intact" and that the new provision did not require a mistaken belief to be reasonable. He posited a situation in which an accused who made an unreasonable mistake about consent could be acquitted because he took reasonable steps to ascertain that the complainant was consenting. Although it is true that the provision combines subjective and

---

120 *Ibid.* at 502.
121 *R. v. Cornejo* (2004), 68 O.R.(3d) 117 at para. 21 (C.A.).
122 (1998), 122 C.C.C. (3d) 225 at 252 (Ont. C.A.).

objective fault elements, the likelihood that any mistake that remains after reasonable steps have been taken would still be unreasonable must be very small. The Supreme Court unfortunately did not deal with section 273.2(b) when it dismissed the accused's appeal in this case.[123] Some have warned that section 273(2)(b) is vulnerable under the *Charter* because it does not on its face require a marked departure from reasonable standards and because it does not adequately differentiate the fault of those who commit sexual assault with subjective fault from those who commit sexual assault in a negligent manner.[124] Section 273(2)(b) blends subjective and objective standards in a novel manner that does not fit well into the stark dichotomies between subjective and objective fault drawn in cases such as *Creighton*.

E. MIXED SUBJECTIVE AND OBJECTIVE FAULT ELEMENTS

The classification of fault elements as subjective or objective adds analytical clarity and precision, but it would be a mistake to conclude that a particular offence must necessarily be completely subjective or objective. Some offences contain multiple elements and there is little reason why some of these elements may not require proof of subjective fault while others only require proof of objective fault. Justice L'Heureux-Dubé has stated "that the *mens rea* of a particular offence is composed of the totality of its component fault elements. The mere fact that most criminal offences require some subjective component does not mean that every element of the offence requires such a state of mind."[125] A mixed approach allows the fault requirement to be tailored to the particular element of the offence, but it also requires judges and juries to understand clearly that for some elements of an offence they must consider all the evidence that is relevant to determining the accused's subjective state of mind, whereas for other elements of the same offence, all they need to consider is how the accused's conduct measures up to the reasonable person standard.[126] Justice Dickson in *Pappajohn*[127]

---

123 *R. v. Darrach* (2000), 148 C.C.C. (3d) 97 (S.C.C.).
124 D. Stuart, *Canadian Criminal Law*, 4th ed. (Toronto: Carswell, 2001) at 308–9.
125 *R. v. Hinchey* (1996), 111 C.C.C. (3d) 353 at 385 (S.C.C.).
126 Assuming that the accused is not incapable of perceiving the prohibited risk or circumstances. See *Creighton* discussed above, note 3.
127 *Pappajohn*, above note 106.

argued that it was "unfair to the jury, and to the accused, to speak in terms of two beliefs, one entertained by the accused, the other by the reasonable man." Mixed fault elements require such an approach. Despite the added complexity,[128] both the Supreme Court and Parliament have been attracted in recent years to mixed forms of liability so that some elements of the offence require proof of subjective fault while others require proof of objective fault.

In *R. v. Lohnes*,[129] the Supreme Court interpreted the offence of disturbing the peace as requiring proof of subjective fault as to the underlying act such as fighting or yelling, but objective fault in relation to the actual disturbance of the peace. Similarly, the offence of conspiracy to unduly lessen competition requires a subjective intention among the parties to agree on a course of action and the objective fault that it is reasonably foreseeable that the course of action would unduly lessen competition.[130] In both of these cases, the objective fault elements dominate and the subjective fault only seems to preclude a conviction if the accused unintentionally and almost accidentally engages in an act that disturbs that peace or lessens competition.

A more integrated blending of subjective and objective fault elements is found in section 273.2(b) which provides that the accused's subjective belief that the complainant consented is not a defence to a sexual assault charge if "the accused did not take reasonable steps, in the circumstances known to the accused at the time, to ascertain that the complainant was consenting." The accused's defence of mistake of fact is in part based on the accused's own subjective perception of the circumstances, provided they are not based on self-induced intoxication, recklessness, or wilful blindness.[131] At the same time, the accused's obligation to take reasonable steps is an objective fault element that requires the accused to act as a reasonable person would in situations where consent is not clear. This is a mixed standard of subjective and objective fault and one that may strike the appropriate balance in the circumstances. Those engaged in sexual activity are being required to take reasonable steps to ascertain consent, but they are only required to do what is reasonable given their own subjective perception or knowledge of the circumstances. Another integrated blending of

---

128 The complexity can be overstated given the practical reality that even in determining a subjective *mens rea*, the jury must rely in part on inferences about what is reasonable.

129 (1992), 69 C.C.C. (3d) 289 (S.C.C.).

130 *R. v. Nova Scotia Pharamaceutical Society* (1992), 74 C.C.C. (3d) 289 (S.C.C.).

131 *Code*, above note 2, s. 273.2(a).

subjective and objective fault elements is found in the new section 22.2(c) of the *Code*, which provides for organizational fault on the basis that a senior officer of a corporation subjectively knows that a representative of the organization is or is about to be a party to a subjective intent offence, but fails to take all reasonable measures to stop the representative from being a party to the offence.[132]

CONCLUSION

Many of the uncertainties surrounding the fault element for crimes could be addressed by legislative reform that provides generic definitions of the various levels of fault, that explains their relation to the *actus reus*, and that specifies what level of fault is required should Parliament not specifically address the issue in the drafting of a particular offence. The general rule should be that *mens rea* will relate to all aspects of the *actus reus* and that the lowest form of subjective *mens rea*, namely recklessness, should be the minimum form of fault for offences in the *Criminal Code*.[133] These standards are based on well-established common law presumptions. They are not constitutional standards under section 7 of the *Charter*, and Parliament can clearly depart from them when drafting particular offences.

Although not all levels of fault are the same, the number of fault elements could be reduced. Given the Court's determination to distinguish intent from motive or purpose[134] and its requirement that knowledge of the prohibited act is the constitutionally required fault element for murder,[135] it could be argued that knowledge, as opposed to intent, purpose, or wilfulness should be the highest level of subjective *mens rea*. At the same time, an intent *mens rea* may still be valuable with respect to crimes of peripheral involvement and other crimes, such as wilful promotion of hatred, in which caution should be exercised before employing the criminal sanction. Knowledge should be defined as the accused's certain belief that the prohibited consequences or circumstances exist. Recklessness, the lowest form of subjective *mens rea*, should be defined as an awareness of the risk that the prohibited circumstances or consequences exist. A subjective reading of wilful blindness, which requires some awareness of the risk, should be subsumed

---

132 This provision will be examined in ch. 5, "Section 22.2 of the *Criminal Code*."

133 *Sault Ste Marie*, above note 12 at 362.

134 *Hibbert*, above note 43.

135 *Martineau*, above note 6.

into the above definition of recklessness. An objective reading of wilful blindness as requiring reasonable inquiry into a risk that would be obvious to a reasonable person is better seen as a form of criminal negligence or as part of a blended subjective and objective fault element. Thus, a reformed *Criminal Code* could probably dispense with wilful blindness.

Criminal negligence is a constitutionally sufficient fault element for most criminal offences. It should be defined to require a marked and substantial departure from the standard of care that a reasonable person would have taken in the circumstances. This would clearly distinguish criminal negligence from civil negligence or the negligence that is presumed when a person or corporation charged with a regulatory offence fails to establish a defence of due diligence. In some cases, subjective and objective standards can be blended. An example would be section 273.2(b), which requires the accused to take reasonable steps to ascertain the complainant's consent to sexual activity (that is, act as a reasonable person would have), but only based on the circumstances subjectively known to the accused at the time. Section 22.2(c) similarly requires that a senior officer know that a representative of an organization is committing an offence, but then requires the senior officer to take all reasonable steps to stop the offence from being committed. Blended fault levels may make sense in a particular context, but they may present a challenge to juries and judges who must administer them.

A final issue is whether the reasonable person standard used to determine criminal negligence can be made to account for the frailties and capacities of the particular accused without collapsing the distinction between individual and subjective fault elements. As will be seen in chapter 8, the courts now consider the experience and characteristics of the accused when determining whether he or she acted reasonably for the purposes of most defences. On balance, experiences and characteristics relevant to the accused's capacity to satisfy a reasonable person standard and not within the accused's control should be considered when applying a criminal negligence standard, even though the present law suggests that these characteristics should only be considered if they would render the accused completely incapable of perceiving the prohibited consequences or circumstances.[136] The individuated or modified objective standard would make it more difficult to convict an accused who was habitually and uncontrollably unaware of prohibited risks, but it might make it easier to convict an accused who

---

136 *Creighton*, above note 3.

because of past experience would have a better awareness of the prohibited risks than the reasonable person. Even if this runs some risk of collapsing the distinction between subjective and objective standards, it seems preferable to punishing a person for failing to live up to a standard that he or she cannot, because of personal characteristics, realistically be expected to satisfy.

FURTHER READINGS

ASHWORTH, A., *Principles of Criminal Law*, 4th ed. (Oxford: Clarendon Press, 2003), ch. 5

BRUDNER, A., "Guilt Under the *Charter*: The Lure of Parliamentary Supremacy" (1998) 40 Crim. L.Q. 287

CAIRNS-WAY, R., "The *Charter*, The Supreme Court and the Invisible Politics of Fault" (1992) 12 Windsor Y.B. Access Just. 128

COLVIN, E., *Principles of Criminal Law*, 2d ed. (Toronto: Carswell, 1991), ch. 5

EDWARDS, J. LL.J., "The Criminal Degrees of Knowledge" (1954) 17 Mod. L. Rev. 295

MEWETT, A., & M. MANNING, *Criminal Law*, 3d ed. (Toronto: Butterworths, 1994), ch. 6

PACIOCCO, D., "Subjective and Objective Standards of Fault for Offences and Defences" (1995) 59 Sask. L. Rev. 271

PICKARD, T., "Culpable Mistakes and Rape" (1980) 30 U.T.L.J. 75, 475

SRIBOPOLOUS, J., "The Constitutionalization of 'Fault' in Canada: A Normative Critique" (1999) 41 Crim. L.Q. 227

STEWART, H., *Sexual Offences in Canadian Law* (Aurora, ON: Canada Law Book, 2004)

STUART, D., *Canadian Criminal Law: A Treatise*, 4th ed. (Toronto: Carswell, 2001), chs. 3 and 4

STUART, D., R.J. DELISLE, & A. MANSON, eds., *Towards a Just and Clear Criminal Law: A Criminal Reports Forum* (Toronto: Carswell, 1999)

CHAPTER 5

REGULATORY OFFENCES AND CORPORATE CRIME

Regulatory offences are enacted by the federal, provincial, and municipal governments and they far outnumber offences under the *Criminal Code*. Regulatory or public welfare offences emphasize the protection of the public from the risk of harm and the regulatory interests of the modern state, as opposed to the punishment of inherently wrongful and harmful conduct. A person or a corporation is convicted for performing a regulated activity without a licence or for failing to take specified safety prosecutions not because such non-compliance must be denounced and punished, but because it frustrates the regulatory ambitions of the modern state and creates a danger of harm. Courts have fashioned distinct rules to make it easier for the state to investigate and prosecute regulatory offences.

Traditionally, Canadian courts were faced with the stark choice of interpreting a regulatory offence to require either absolute liability, in which a conviction followed from the commission of the prohibited act, or proof beyond a reasonable doubt of a subjective fault element. The former standard could impose liability without fault, while the latter might frustrate the objectives of the regulatory scheme by requiring the Crown to prove that someone in a large organization had guilty knowledge. A third option, strict liability, has now emerged to dominate the field. Absolute liability offences are now vulnerable under section 7 of the *Charter*, at least when they deprive individuals of life, liberty, or security of the person by imposing terms of imprisonment.

Strict liability offences require fault based on negligence, and for this reason they satisfy the requirement under section 7 of the *Charter* that the morally innocent who act without fault not be punished. They do, however, violate the presumption of innocence under section 11(d) of the *Charter*. After the Crown proves the prohibited act of a strict liability offence beyond a reasonable doubt, negligence is presumed, and the accused must establish that it was not negligent. The accused makes its case by establishing on a balance of probabilities a defence of due diligence or reasonable mistake of fact. This approach violates the presumption of innocence by allowing a conviction even if there is a reasonable doubt about whether the accused was negligent. Nevertheless, it has been held to be justified because of the danger of acquitting an accused who has entered a regulated field and committed an *actus reus* when there is only a reasonable doubt about negligence. An accused who enters a regulated field can be expected to bear the burden of establishing that it was not negligent in allowing a harmful or dangerous act to occur.

Regulatory offences frequently apply to corporations that have engaged in harmful conduct such as pollution, misleading advertising, or violations of health, safety, or licensing requirements. The difficulty of establishing fault in a large organization is one of the reasons why it is the accused who must establish a lack of negligence when charged with a strict liability offence. When a corporation is charged with a criminal offence, however, it is necessary to find someone within the corporation who has the required fault. That individual must have enough responsibility within the corporation so that his or her fault can be attributed to the corporation and the Crown must prove fault beyond a reasonable doubt. This makes it considerably more difficult to convict a corporation of a criminal offence than a regulatory offence.

Until recently, only the fault of a "directing mind" of the corporation could be attributed to the corporation for the purpose of establishing its criminal liability. At the end of 2003, Parliament introduced extensive reforms designed to make it easier to convict and punish corporations and other organizations for criminal offences. The common law concept of a "directing mind," which had previously been restricted to those who had enough power to establish corporate policy, was replaced by a new statutory concept of a corporate "senior officer." This position includes not only those who play an important role in establishing a corporation's policies, including its board of directors, chief executive officer and chief financial officer, but also those who are "responsible for managing an important aspect of the organization's activities."[1] Parliament also specified the fault required by the senior officer in order to convict the corporation of a negligence-based criminal offence[2] and a subjective intent criminal offence.[3] The criminal liability of corporations and other organizations is still based on the attribution of the fault of individuals to the organizations, but Parliament has replaced the common law definition of a corporation's directing mind with a broader concept that allows the fault of its senior officers to be attributed to the organization.

A. ABSOLUTE LIABILITY OFFENCES

An absolute liability offence requires the Crown to prove the commission of the prohibited act beyond a reasonable doubt, but does not require proof of any additional fault element such as guilty knowledge or negligence. For offences of absolute liability "it is not open to the accused to exculpate himself by showing that he was free of fault."[4] This form of liability has been controversial. Supporters of absolute liability argue that its imposition can persuade a person or an organization to take additional measures to prevent the prohibited act. Opponents stress that the imposition of absolute liability can punish the morally innocent, and that one who has not acted with subjective fault or negligence cannot be expected to do anything more to prevent the prohibited act.[5]

Courts have recognized offences as requiring absolute liability when they have been convinced that the legislature did not intend the Crown to prove fault or that such a requirement would frustrate the purpose of the statute. In *R. v. Pierce Fisheries Ltd.,*[6] the Supreme Court

---

1   *Criminal Code of Canada,* R.S.C. 1985, c. C-46, [*Code*], s. 2 (as amended by S.C. 2003 c. 21).

2   *Ibid.,* s. 22.1.

3   *Ibid.,* s.22.2.

4   *R. v. Sault Ste. Marie (City)* (1978), 40 C.C.C. (2d) 353 at 374 (S.C.C.) [*Sault Ste. Marie*].

5   In *R. v. Hess* (1990), 59 C.C.C. (3d) 161 (S.C.C.) [*Hess*], Wilson J. argued for the majority that an absolute liability offence for statutory rape served no useful purpose and was unfair to the accused who believed that the girl was over fourteen years of age. In dissent, McLachlin J. would have upheld the offence under s. 1 of the *Canadian Charter of Rights and Freedoms,* Part I of the *Constitution Act, 1982,* being Schedule B to the *Canada Act 1982* (U.K.), 1982, c. 11 on the basis that it would discourage men from having sex with girls who might be under fourteen years of age.

6   [1970] 5 C.C.C. 193 (S.C.C.) [*Pierce Fisheries*].

held that the possession of undersized lobsters contrary to regulations under the *Fisheries Act* was an absolute liability offence. Ritchie J. refused to apply the Court's previous decision in *R. v. Beaver*[7] that a person could not be held to possess drugs without subjective knowledge. He reasoned:

> I do not think that a new crime was added to our criminal law by making regulations which prohibit persons from having undersized lobsters in their possession, nor do I think that the stigma of having been convicted of a criminal offence would attach to a person found to have been in breach of these regulations.[8]

This approach recognized that regulatory offences did not carry with them the same stigma as criminal offences and that it would be difficult to achieve the objectives of regulatory offences if proof of subjective fault was required. Cartwright J. dissented and, following *Beaver*, would have required proof that the accused knew about the undersized lobsters.

There are problems with both the decisions in *Pierce Fisheries*. Under the minority's approach of requiring subjective *mens rea*, it would be difficult, if not impossible, to establish that individuals who were directing minds of the corporation[9] knew that they were catching undersized lobsters. Under the majority's absolute liability approach, however, the corporation could have been convicted even if it had taken reasonable precautions to ensure that undersized lobsters were not caught by, for example, training its employees properly and using proper equipment. The majority imposed absolute liability that could punish without fault while the minority insisted on proof of subjective fault that would often be very difficult for the state to establish beyond a reasonable doubt in the regulatory context.

1) The Common Law Presumption against Absolute Liability

In *Sault Ste. Marie*,[10] the Supreme Court indicated that it would not interpret public welfare or regulatory offences as absolute liability

---

7   (1957), 118 C.C.C. 129 (S.C.C.).

8   *Pierce Fisheries*, above note 6 at 201.

9   Only the subjective *mens rea* of a person classified as one of the corporation's directing mind could be attributed to the corporation. See ch. 5, "The Common Law DIrecting Mind Approach." Now the fault of senior officers, including important managers, could be attributed to the corporation.

10 *Sault Ste. Marie*, above note 4 at 374.

offences unless "the Legislature has made it clear that guilt would follow proof merely of the proscribed act." The Court, in effect, created a common law or judge-made presumption that regulatory offences would be interpreted as requiring strict liability unless the legislature clearly indicated that the offence was an absolute liability offence that would punish the accused who had acted reasonably and with due diligence.

In the actual case, the Court held that the offence of causing or permitting the discharge of pollution was a strict as opposed to an absolute liability or subjective *mens rea* offence. This meant that the accused had an opportunity to establish that it had acted reasonably or with due diligence to avoid the commission of the *actus reus*. The accused could also establish that it had made a reasonable mistake of fact. The Crown, however, did not have to prove subjective fault. The Supreme Court applied its new common law presumption against absolute liability in another case to hold that a prohibition on hunting within a quarter mile of a baited area was a strict liability offence.[11] The accused would again have an opportunity to demonstrate that it had exercised due diligence to avoid the prohibited act or made a reasonable mistake of fact. Negligence would be inferred as the fault element in these regulatory offences, even though it was not specifically mentioned in these offences. Under the *Charter*, the courts have generally been reluctant to interpret a statute as imposing absolute liability, unless the legislature has clearly indicated that this is its intent.[12] As will be seen, an absolute liability offence when combined with imprisonment may violate the *Charter*.

Offences will, however, be recognized as absolute liability offences if the legislature clearly indicates an intent that they not be interpreted as offences of strict liability. In the *B.C. Motor Vehicle Reference*, the legislature clearly indicated such an intent by stating that the offence of driving with a suspended driver's licence was "an absolute liability offence in which guilt is established by proof of driving, whether or not the defendant knew of the prohibition or suspension."[13] As will be discussed later, the Court ruled that absolute liability offences, when combined with imprisonment, violated section 7 of the *Charter* and could not be justified under section 1 especially as compared with the alternative of a strict liability offence.

---

11   *R. v. Chapin* (1979), 45 C.C.C. (2d) 333 (S.C.C.).

12   *R. v. I.L.W.U., Local 500*, [1994] 1 S.C.R. 150; *R. v. Rube* (1992), 75 C.C.C. (3d) 575 (S.C.C.); *R. v. Nickel City Transport (Sudbury) Ltd.* (1993), 82 C.C.C. (3d) 541 (Ont. C.A.) [*Nickel City Transport*].

13   *Motor Vehicle Act*, R.S.B.C. 1979, c. 288, s. 94(2).

Even after the British Columbia legislature deleted the specific reference to the offence of driving with a suspended driver's licence being an offence of absolute liability, the Supreme Court held in a 5-to-4 decision that the offence remained one of absolute liability.[14] The majority stressed that the offence applied when the accused had his or her licence "automatically and without notice" suspended after conviction of a number of offences. Given that any mistake that the accused made about whether his or her licence was suspended would be classified as a mistake of law and hence prohibited as a defence,[15] the majority concluded that the offence was one of absolute liability. The minority in this case, however, would have interpreted the offence as one of strict liability. Thus, the minority would allow a defence of due diligence in ascertaining whether the accused had been convicted of a driving offence and a defence of reasonable mistake of fact about the existence of such a conviction. It also warned that the majority was making an incursion into the principle that ignorance of the law was not an excuse by holding that the legislation effectively deprived the accused of a due diligence defence.

Pontes[16] suggests that it is possible for an offence that does not clearly state it is one of absolute liability still to be classified as one. It does not, however, displace the common law presumption against absolute liability started by *Sault Ste. Marie*. Courts should only interpret a regulatory offence to be an absolute liability offence if the legislature clearly indicates that it does not intend the offence to be one of strict liability or if it is clear that the accused will effectively be denied any due diligence defence. As will be seen, interpreting a regulatory offence as an absolute liability offence raises constitutional problems that will not occur if the offence is interpreted as a strict liability offence.

2) The *Charter* and Absolute Liability

As discussed in chapter 1, the Supreme Court of Canada held in the *B.C. Motor Vehicle Reference*[17] that absolute liability offences offend the principles of fundamental justice by allowing the conviction of the

---

14   R. v. *Pontes* (1995), 100 C.C.C. (3d) 353 (S.C.C.) [*Pontes*]. As will be examined below, the absolute liability offence was not struck down, but the Court indicated that no one could be imprisoned for its violation.

15   See ch. 2, "Ignorance of the Law," on the principle that ignorance or mistake of law do not constitute an excuse.

16   *Pontes*, above note 14.

17   *Reference re s. 94(2) of the Motor Vehicle Act (British Columbia)* (1985), 23 C.C.C. (3d) 289 at 311 (S.C.C.) [*B.C. Motor Vehicle Reference*].

morally innocent. Justice Lamer observed that "it is because absolute liability offends the principles of fundamental justice that this Court [in *Sault Ste. Marie*] created presumptions against Legislatures having intended to enact offences of a regulatory nature falling within that category." Yet the Court also held that an absolute liability offence would violate section 7 of the *Charter* "only if and to the extent that it has the potential of depriving of life, liberty, and security of the person." Lamer J. suggested that a person's liberty would be broadly construed to include not only the mandatory imprisonment that was at issue in the case, but also probation orders.[18] Other courts have concluded that a fine threatens a person's liberty if there is a possibility of imprisonment if the fine is not paid.[19]

The Supreme Court has refused to strike down an absolute liability offence in *Pontes* on the basis of a general provision in British Columbia's legislation that provided that no one could be imprisoned for violation of an absolute liability offence. Cory J. indicated that "generally speaking, an offence of absolute liability is not likely to offend the Charter unless a prison sanction is provided" and refused to strike down an absolute liability offence on the basis that an individual convicted of driving without a licence "faces no risk of imprisonment and there is, accordingly, no violation of the right to life, liberty and security of the person under s. 7 of the Charter."[20] The Ontario Court of Appeal subsequently refused to strike down an absolute liability offence that provided for the operator of a commercial motor vehicle to be fined at least $2,000 and not more than $50,000 when a wheel becomes detached from a vehicle on a highway. Although an absolute liability offence violates the principles of fundamental justice, there was no section 7 violation because the rights of life, liberty, and security of the person were not affected since the offence provided that no one could be imprisoned or placed on probation for violation of the offence. The Court of Appeal concluded that the offence did not involve state-imposed serious psychological stress on the accused that would trigger section 7 of the *Charter*. "The right to security of the person does not protect the individual operating in the highly regulated context of commercial trucking for profit from the ordinary stresses

---

18   Lamer J. stated: "[o]bviously, imprisonment (including probation orders) deprives persons of their liberty. An offence has that potential as of the moment it is open to the judge to impose imprisonment. There is no need that imprisonment, as in s. 94(2), be made mandatory." *Ibid.* at 311.

19   *R. v. Burt* (1987), 38 C.C.C. (3d) 299 (Sask. C.A.) [*Burt*]; *Nickel City Transport*, above note 12 at 572.

20   *Pontes*, above note 14.

and anxieties that a reasonable person would suffer as a result of government regulation of that industry."[21] In the commercial context at least, significant and mandatory fines, as well as the stigma that may accompany conviction for regulatory offences associated with deaths, appears not to engage the rights to life, liberty, and security of the person under section 7 of the *Charter*.

In the *B.C. Motor Vehicle Reference*, Lamer J. suggested that an absolute liability offence would rarely, if ever, be justified under section 1 of the *Charter*, because only in exceptional cases "such as natural disasters, the outbreak of war, epidemics and the like" should the liberty or security of a person "be sacrificed to administrative expediency."[22] In *Hess*,[23] the Supreme Court held that a statutory rape offence of having sexual intercourse with a girl under fourteen years of age constituted an absolute liability offence because Parliament had specifically provided for the accused's guilt upon proof of the *actus reus* "whether or not he believes that she is fourteen years of age or more." The offence was one of absolute liability because the Crown was not required to establish subjective fault such as knowledge or objective fault such as negligence concerning an essential element of the statutory rape offence. The majority of the Court held that the offence was an unjustified violation of section 7 of the *Charter* when compared to a less restrictive alternative that would allow the accused a limited defence that he took all reasonable steps to ascertain the age of the complainant[24] and would thus require objective fault or negligence. In *R. v. Wholesale Travel Group Inc.*,[25] the Court concluded that provisions that required the prompt correction of misleading advertising, even in cases where it was not reasonable for the accused to know that the advertising was misleading, amounted to absolute liability that could not be justified under section 1.

3) Corporations and the *Charter*

In the *B.C. Motor Vehicle Reference*, Lamer J. recognized that there might be a case for the use of absolute liability offences against corporations "in certain sensitive areas such as the preservation of our vital

---

21   *R. v. 1260448 Ontario Inc.* (2003), 68 O.R. (3d) 51 (C.A.).
22   *B.C. Motor Vehicle Reference*, above note 17 at 311.
23   *Hess*, above note 5.
24   *Code*, above note 1, s.150.1(4).
25   (1991), 67 C.C.C. (3d) 193 at 214–215, 262–263 (S.C.C.) [*Wholesale Travel Group*].

environment and our natural resources." He hinted, however, that such concerns "might well be dispelled were it to be decided, given the proper case, that s. 7 affords protection to human persons only and does not extend to corporations."[26] Subsequently, the Court held that corporations were not protected under section 7 of the *Charter*, on the basis that only human beings can enjoy life, liberty, and security of the person and that it would be "nonsensical to speak of a corporation being put in jail."[27] Despite this conclusion, a corporate accused can, when charged with an offence, bring a *Charter* challenge on the basis that the offence violates the section 7 rights of individuals who might be charged.[28] Legislatures can insulate absolute liability offences from invalidation under section 7 of the *Charter* by enacting offences that apply only to corporations. So far, legislatures have not made extensive use of this option to insulate absolute liability offences from *Charter* review. As will be seen, however, new provisions for organizational liability under the *Criminal Code* may be immune from section 7 review because they do not apply to natural persons who enjoy rights to life, liberty, and security of the person under section 7 of the *Charter*.

4) Corporate Liability for Absolute Liability Offences

Corporations have "automatic primary responsibility"[29] for absolute liability offences. A corporation may be guilty whenever one of its employees or someone under its control commits the prohibited act.[30] In a sense, this is a form of vicarious liability, because it attributes the acts of the employee to the corporation. Courts have not seen this as a problem, however, because it is only the acts of the employees that are attributed to the corporation, and not some fault element. Corporations can also be guilty if they had an ability to control the commission of the *actus reus* by an independent contractor. In *Sault Ste. Marie*,[31] Justice Dickson indicated that although a homeowner who hires a company to collect garbage is probably not responsible for polluting if the company dumps the garbage in a river, a corporation or a municipality may well be.

---

26 *B.C. Motor Vehicle Reference*, above note 17 at 314.

27 *Irwin Toy Ltd. v. Quebec (A.G.)*, [1989] 1 S.C.R. 927 at 1003 [*Irwin*].

28 *Wholesale Travel Group*, above note 25.

29 *Canadian Dredge & Dock Co. v. R.* (1985), 19 C.C.C. (3d) 1 at 8 (S.C.C.) [*Canadian Dredge & Dock*].

30 A corporation will not be guilty if an independent operator on their premises commits a crime. *R. v. F.W. Woolworth Co.* (1974), 18 C.C.C. (2d) 23 (Ont. C.A.).

31 *Sault Ste. Marie*, above note 4.

5) Defences to Absolute Liability Offences

A defence of honest or even reasonable mistake of fact will not be a defence to an absolute liability offence. Thus, an accused's subjective reliance on a faulty speedometer would not be a valid defence even if the reliance was reasonable.[32] The defences of automatism, mental disorder, or extreme intoxication might possibly apply to an absolute liability offence, because they would indicate that the accused acted in an involuntary manner that is inconsistent with proof of the *actus reus*.[33] There is also some authority that the defence of necessity might apply to a person who committed an absolute liability offence such as speeding because of an urgent need to save a life.[34]

B. STRICT LIABILITY OFFENCES

A strict liability[35] offence requires the Crown to prove the prohibited act beyond a reasonable doubt, but then gives the accused an opportunity to prove due diligence or absence of negligence on a balance of probabilities. Strict liability offences are a halfway house between absolute liability offences and full *mens rea* offences. They "seek a middle position, fulfilling the goals of public welfare offences while still not punishing the entirely blameless."[36] In 1978 the Supreme Court indicated that all regulatory offences would be presumed to be strict liability offences, unless there was a clear indication from the legislature that either absolute liability or subjective *mens rea* was intended.

---

32 *R. v. Hickey* (1976), 30 C.C.C. (2d) 416 (Ont. C.A.).

33 In *R. v. Daviault* (1994), 93 C.C.C. (3d) 21 at 25 (S.C.C.), Lamer C.J.C. stated that he preferred to characterize the mental element involved in voluntary and conscious activity "as relating more to the *actus reus* than the *mens rea*, so that the defence clearly be available in strict liability offences." The same logic should apply to absolute liability offences.

34 *R. v. Kennedy* (1972), 7 C.C.C. (2d) 42 (N.S. Co. Ct.); *R. v. Walker* (1979), 48 C.C.C. (2d) 126 (Ont. Co. Ct.).

35 Note that this terminology is distinctly Canadian, so that what other jurisdictions call strict liability would in Canada be classified as absolute liability. Similarly, strict liability in tort law is analogous to absolute liability in Canadian criminal law.

36 *Sault Ste. Marie*, above note 4 at 374.

1) Simple Negligence

The blameworthiness of a strict liability offence is negligence. The Crown does not have to prove this fault element; rather the accused is given an opportunity to establish on a balance of probabilities that it was not negligent.[37] In *Sault Ste. Marie*, Dickson J. contemplated that an accused who took all reasonable care, but still committed the prohibited act, would not be convicted of a strict liability offence. Given that regulatory offences are designed to encourage people and corporations to take appropriate safeguards to avoid harmful results, such as pollution or workplace accidents, courts will not likely require negligence to amount to a marked and substantial departure from the conduct of a reasonable person, as they do when applying negligence in criminal offences.[38] The reasonableness of the accused's conduct also should be determined on the basis of the circumstances that a reasonable person would have seen, not the circumstances that the accused actually perceived. Thus, any mistake of fact would have to be both honest and reasonable. To avoid a conviction for a regulatory offence, the corporation would have to demonstrate that it took reasonable steps to avoid the prohibited act or that it made an honest and reasonable mistake of fact.[39] It is important that the accused be given the opportunity to demonstrate that it was not negligent in order to avoid a strict liability offence becoming an absolute liability offence in which guilt is established simply by the prosecution proving the prohibited act beyond a reasonable doubt.

2) Negligence and the *Charter*

In *Wholesale Travel Group*,[40] the Supreme Court unanimously upheld negligence as a sufficient fault element for an offence of false or misleading advertising. The accused had argued that subjective *mens rea* was required because of the stigma that would accompany a conviction, and it relied upon dicta in *Vaillancourt* which had suggested that proof of subjective *mens rea* might be required because of the stigma attached to theft. Lamer C.J. stated that a conviction for misleading advertising will not "brand the accused as being dishonest," but, in many cases, would indicate that the accused had been careless. Negli-

---

37 *R. v. Timminco Ltd.* (2001), 42 C.R. (5th) 279 (Ont. C.A.).

38 See ch. 4, "Degree of Negligence."

39 *R. v. MacMillan Bloedel Ltd.* 2002 BCCA 510.

40 *Wholesale Travel Group*, above note 25.

gence was sufficient, even if the accused faced imprisonment. Adoption of a higher fault element was a matter of public policy for the legislature. Cory J. similarly concluded that "the demands of s. 7 will be met in the regulatory context where liability is imposed for conduct which breaches the standard of reasonable care required of those operating in the regulated field."[41] It thus appears that negligence will be a constitutionally sufficient fault element for all regulatory offences.

3) The Defence of Due Diligence

Although the fault element for a strict liability offence is negligence, the Crown need not prove negligence beyond a reasonable doubt. Rather, the accused must prove a defence of due diligence or lack of negligence on a balance of probabilities. Once the Crown has proved the wrongful act beyond a reasonable doubt, the fault element of negligence is presumed, unless the accused can demonstrate that it took reasonable care or acted under a reasonable mistake of fact. In *Sault Ste. Marie*,[42] Dickson J. stressed that the burden of establishing due diligence should fall upon the accused, because it "will generally have the means of proof." This is especially true, when as in the case, it was alleged that "a large and complex corporation" caused pollution. He concluded that the burden was not unfair, "as the alternative is absolute liability which denies an accused any defence whatsoever," and the accused need only prove the defence on a balance of probabilities. The burden on the accused is an important component of the halfway house approach of strict liability offences, because it means that the Crown is not required to prove negligence beyond a reasonable doubt and that the accused is not acquitted because there is a reasonable doubt as to negligence.

The courts look to a large range of factors in determining whether the accused has established a defence of due diligence to a regulatory offence. Some factors look to the likelihood and gravity of the risk, including whether it was foreseeable and the effect that it could have on vulnerable people and neighbourhoods. Other factors look to the ability of the accused to control or manage the risk of the prohibited act from occurring. Factors such as alternative solutions, regulatory compliance, industry standards and preventive systems, efforts made to address the problem, and the promptness of the accused's response are

---

41   *Ibid.* at 252. See also *R. v. Eurosport Auto Co.* (2002), 11 C.R. (6th) 327 (B.C.C.A.).
42   *Sault Ste. Marie*, above note 4 at 373.

significant. Other matters such as factors beyond the control of the accused, technological limitations, skill level expected of the accused, complexities involved, and economic considerations, can be relevant in determining whether the accused has taken all reasonable steps to prevent the risk.[43] The accused must be given an opportunity to establish due diligence in order to ensure that a strict liability offence does not become an absolute liability offence in which a conviction follows automatically from the fact that the risk sought to be managed has been realized and the prohibited act occurred.

4) The Defence of Due Diligence and the *Charter*

In *Wholesale Travel Group*, the Supreme Court in a 5-to-4 decision upheld a statutory defence that required those who committed the wrongful act of false or misleading advertising to prove on a balance of probabilities that they exercised due diligence to prevent the occurrence of such error. Seven judges agreed that placing such a burden on the accused violated the presumption of innocence as protected under section 11(d) of the *Charter* because it allowed an accused to be convicted, even though there was a reasonable doubt as to whether it acted in a negligent fashion. Lamer C.J., with three other judges in dissent, found that this restriction on section 11(d) could not be justified under section 1, because the legislature could achieve its objective by means of an evidential as opposed to a persuasive burden. He contemplated a mandatory presumption of negligence following proof of the *actus reus*, but one that could be rebutted by evidence that could raise a reasonable doubt as to whether the accused was negligent. Such a mandatory presumption would violate section 11(d) of the *Charter*, but would constitute a less drastic means of advancing the legislature's objectives.[44]

However, a majority of the Court concluded that imposing the burden on the accused to establish due diligence on a balance of probabilities could be justified. Iacobucci J. stated that an evidential burden "would shift to the accused the burden of simply raising a reasonable doubt as to due diligence and would not thereby allow the effective

---

43   These factors are taken from R. v. *Commander Business Furniture* (1992), 9 C.E.L.R.(N.S.). 185 (Ont. Ct. of J. Prov. Div.). They are discussed at greater length in Archibald, Jull, and Roach, *Regulatory and Corporate Liability: From Due Diligence to Risk Management* (Aurora, ON: Canada Law Book, forthcoming), ch. 4, where it is suggested that the due diligence defence may require reasonable risk management.

44   R. v. *Downey* (1992), 72 C.C.C. (3d) 1 (S.C.C.); R. v. *Laba* (1994), 94 C.C.C. (3d) 385 (S.C.C.) discussed in ch. 1, "Right to be Presumed Innocent."

pursuit of the regulatory objective."[45] He argued that the accused, as participants in regulated activities, "are in the best position to prove due diligence, since they possess in most cases the required information" to prove that they were not negligent. Cory J. also stressed that the accused would be in the best position to prove whether it exercised reasonable care, and concluded, "in the regulatory context, there is nothing unfair about imposing that onus; indeed, it is essential for the protection of our vulnerable society."[46] He feared that with only an evidential burden, the accused would always be able to point to some evidence of measures it had taken to prevent the prohibited act, and the Crown would then have the difficult task of proving beyond a reasonable doubt that the accused was negligent.

The majority's judgment in *Wholesale Travel Group* endorses the functional justifications given in *Sault Ste. Marie* for requiring the accused to prove the defence of due diligence or lack of negligence. Although it is technically necessary to justify each reverse burden under section 1, the Court has applied the section 1 analysis used in *Wholesale Travel Group* to other regulatory offences in different contexts.[47]

5) Corporate Liability for Strict Liability Offences

The same considerations apply when holding corporations accountable for strict liability offences as apply for absolute liability offences. In *Canadian Dredge & Dock*,[48] Estey J. stated:

> As in the case of an absolute liability offence, it matters not whether the accused is corporate or unincorporated, because the liability is primary. . . . It is not dependent upon the attribution to the accused of the misconduct of others. . . . [T]he corporation and the natural defendant are in the same position. In both cases liability is not vicarious but primary.

As with absolute liability offences, this approach suggests that the corporation will have committed the *actus reus* when one of its employees or another person subject to its control has committed the prohibited act. In *Sault Ste. Marie*, the accused could be liable, even though it had contracted out the pollution-causing activity to another company.

---

45   *Wholesale Travel Group*, above note 25 at 267.
46   *Ibid.* at 256–57.
47   *R. v. Ellis-Don Ltd.* (1992), 71 C.C.C. (3d) 63 (S.C.C.); *R. v. Martin* (1992), 71 C.C.C. (3d) 572 (S.C.C.).
48   *Canadian Dredge & Dock*, above note 29 at 9.

The primary liability of a corporation for a strict liability offence suggests the corollary that the corporation must establish a defence of due diligence for the organization. In *Sault Ste. Marie*,[49] however, Dickson J. suggested that "the availability of a defence to a corporation will depend on whether such due diligence was taken by those who are the directing mind and will of the corporation, whose acts are therefore in law the acts of the corporation itself." As will be seen, this standard is no longer used for attributing subjective fault to a corporation and has been replaced by a broader concept of a senior officer who exercises policy-making or important managerial functions within the organizations. There may be cases in large organizations where the directing mind or even the senior officers act with due diligence, but the corporation as a complex organization does not. An example of this would occur when no one informed a directing mind or senior officer about certain problems or warning signs that the *actus reus* was likely to occur. In that case, it is possible that the directing mind or senior officer will be found not to be negligent (unless he or she should have made inquiries) even though the corporation as an organization might be negligent. It would be more consistent with the logic of strict liability offences to require the corporation as an organization to prove a due diligence defence.

C. VICARIOUS LIABILITY

Vicarious liability occurs when the acts and fault of another person are attributed to the accused for the purpose of determining liability. It is used in tort law as a means of ensuring that employers are not allowed to profit from civil wrongs committed by their employees. Even before the *Charter*, courts resisted this doctrine on the basis that "criminal law regards a person as responsible for his own crimes only."[50] A judge-made or common law presumption against holding a person responsible for the acts and faults of another could, however, be displaced by clear legislative intent.[51] As will be seen in relation to corporate liability for *mens rea* offences, Canadian courts struggled to avoid holding corporations vicariously liable for crimes committed by their employees.

---

49   *Sault Ste. Marie*, above note 4 at 377–78.
50   *Tesco Supermarkets Ltd. v. Nattrass* (1971), [1972] A.C. 153 at 199 (H.L.); *R. v. Stevanovich* (1983), 7 C.C.C. (3d) 307 at 311 (Ont. C.A.).
51   *R. v. Budget Car Rentals (Toronto) Ltd.* (1981), 57 C.C.C. (2d) 201 (Ont. C.A.).

1) Vicarious Liability and the *Charter*

In *Bhatnager v. Canada (Minister of Employment & Immigration)*,[52] the Supreme Court suggested that it might violate section 7 to hold ministers of the government vicariously liable for acts of criminal contempt committed by their officials without their knowledge. Several *Charter* cases have considered statutes that make the owners of automobiles vicariously liable for violations committed by any person driving their cars. In *Burt*,[53] the Saskatchewan Court of Appeal concluded:

> The principles of fundamental justice simply do not recognize the ascribing to one person of another's state of mind. Accordingly, where a statute purports to make one person vicariously liable for another's *mens rea* offence the statute may be said to offend . . . the principles of fundamental justice.

An offence that bases the accused's liability on the acts and faults of another may be found to be an absolute liability offence that punishes the accused without fault. At a minimum, a person could not be imprisoned for such an offence.[54] Many motor vehicle offences that impose vicarious liability on the owner of a vehicle for offences committed with the vehicle contain a limited defence allowing the owner to establish that the vehicle was taken without his or her consent. Courts of Appeal are divided on whether this limited defence make a vicarious liability offence one of absolute or strict liability.[55] The statutory defence does allow the owner a limited opportunity to show that he or she was not at fault. At the same time, however, it does not exhaust the range of due diligence defences that an accused would ordinarily have to a strict liability offence. Thus, the better view is that even with this limited defence, the offence remains one of absolute liability because it can convict an accused who was not at fault. The accused may still be convicted but not imprisoned for the violation of a vicarious liability offence that imposes absolute liability.

---

52 [1990] 2 S.C.R. 217.

53 *Burt*, above note 19 at 311. See also *R. v. Pellerin* (1989), 47 C.C.C. (3d) 35 (Ont. C.A.).

54 *R. v. Gray* (1988), 44 C.C.C. (3d) 222 (Man. C.A.); *R. v. Smith* (1989), 14 M.V.R. (2d) 166 (Y.C.A.); *R. v. Free* (1990), 110 A.R. 241 (Q.B.).

55 The British Columbia Court of Appeal has held that such a vicarious liability offence remains one of absolute liability while the Nova Scotia Court of Appeal has held that it makes the offence one of strict liability. *R. v. Geraghty* (1990), 55 C.C.C. (3d) 460 (B.C.C.A.); *R. v. Sutherland* (1990), 55 C.C.C. (3d) 265 (N.S.C.A.).

D. CORPORATIONS AND *MENS REA* OFFENCES

1) The Common Law Directing Mind Approach

Canadian courts resisted holding corporations vicariously liable for the *mens rea* offences of their employees. Instead, they identified the corporation with a senior official who acts as the corporation's directing mind, and attributed the fault or mental element of that person to the corporation for the purpose of determining the corporation's liability for a criminal offence. In doing so, they followed English authorities that suggest that a corporation is liable only for what is done by "the directing mind and will of the corporation, the very ego and centre of the personality of the corporation."[56] Under this identification or alter ego theory, the wrongful action of the directing mind is attributed to the corporation so that the corporation has primary, not vicarious, liability for the acts and mind of an official who is a directing mind of the corporation.

A corporation could not insulate itself from the crimes committed by a directing mind by claiming ignorance or issuing instructions that the crime not be committed. Thus, the Supreme Court has stated: "Acts of the ego of a corporation taken within the assigned managerial area may give rise to the corporate criminal responsibility, whether or not there be formal delegation; whether or not there be awareness of the activity in the board of directors or the officers of the company, and . . . whether or not there be express prohibition."[57] One relatively narrow exception was that a corporation would not be held liable if the directing mind acted wholly in fraud and against the interest of the corporation. In that case, the corporation would be the victim of the crime, not responsible for it. The Court has restricted this principle so that the corporation remains liable if the directing mind's activities were "by design or result partly for the benefit of the company."[58] Thus, a corporation may be guilty of fraud if it receives kickbacks, even though the directing mind fraudulently keeps some of the kickbacks from the corporation.

---

56   *Lennard's Carrying Co. Ltd. v. Asiatic Petroleum Co. Ltd.*, [1915] A.C. 705 at 713 (H.L.). Note that s. 2 of the *Code*, above note 1, defines "everyone" to include corporations and fines are generally available to punish corporations.

57   *Canadian Dredge & Dock*, above note 29 at 17.

58   *Ibid.* at 38.

Canadian courts defined the directing mind of the corporation somewhat more broadly than English courts, in part because of the decentralized nature of much corporate activity in Canada. In the leading case of *Canadian Dredge & Dock*, the Supreme Court made clear that there could be more than one directing mind of a corporation. Directing minds could include "the board of directors, the managing director, the superintendent, the manager or anyone else delegated . . . the governing executive authority of the corporation." In *R. v. Waterloo Mercury Sales Ltd.*,[59] the manager of a used car lot was held to be the corporation's directing mind for the purpose of determining whether it had committed fraud by rolling back odometers, even though the president of the corporation had no knowledge of the acts and had circulated written instructions not to roll back odometers. The manager was acting as the corporation's directing mind within the field of operation assigned to him. An employee with lesser responsibility, such as a salesperson or a mechanic, would not be a directing mind.

In the 1990s, Canadian courts placed limits on who might be classified as a corporation's directing mind. A directing mind must be an officer or manager of a corporation, acting in the scope of his or her responsibility. A directing mind must also have "an express or implied delegation of executive authority to design and supervise the implementation of corporate policy rather than simply to carry out such policy."[60] Under this test, both a tug captain who exercised considerable discretion[61] and a truck driver who was a corporation's sole representative in an area[62] were held not to be directing minds of their corporations. The courts reasoned that these employees did not have the power to design or supervise the implementation of corporate policy and that their fault could not be attributed to the corporation. This trend made it difficult to hold corporations criminally accountable for crimes committed in Canada. Not infrequently, those with the degree of responsibility required of a directing mind would be sheltered within the corporate hierarchy and not have the required fault, while those with the required fault would not have enough policy-making power within the corporation to be classified as the corporation's directing mind. The designers and even the supervisors of corporate policies in

---

59 (1974), 18 C.C.C. (2d) 248 (Alta. Dist. Ct.).
60 *"Rhone"(The) v. "Peter A.B. Widener" (The)*, [1993] 1 S.C.R. 497 at 521 [*Rhone*].
61 *Ibid.*
62 *R. v. Safety Kleen Canada Inc.* (1997), 114 C.C.C. (3d) 214 (Ont. C.A.) [*Safety Kleen*].

a large and economically dependent country such as Canada often were so far away from any criminal acts that took place that they did not have the *mens rea* required for the particular crime. Those closer to the ground who would have the required fault, were not classified as directing minds because they did not design or supervise the implementation of corporate policy and even though they exercised an important managerial role in the corporation.

2) Bill C-45: New Statutory Provisions for Corporate Criminal Liability

There were many calls to abandon the identification, alter ego or directing mind approach in favour of less restrictive approaches. One option would be to hold corporations vicariously responsible for the actions of all their employees and agents. This would run against the criminal law's reluctance to impose vicarious liability based on the fault of another. Such vicarious liability likely offends the principles of fundamental justice, but it may not violate section 7 of the *Charter* because corporations have no rights to life, liberty, and security of the person. In any event, vicarious liability would still only attribute the fault of individuals to corporations. Another option would have been to to impose liability on corporations based on their organizational fault or "corporate culture," as is done in some Australian jurisdictions.[63] The focus under such proposals would not be on the fault of individuals within the corporation, but the fault of the corporation as a whole.

In late 2003, Parliament enacted Bill C-45 that amended the *Criminal Code* to provide a new regime to determine when corporations and other organizations were guilty of criminal offences and its provisions took effect at the end of March 2004. The Bill also provided a new punishment regime to allow courts not simply to fine corporations, but also to place them on probation in an attempt to ensure that the offences were not repeated. This new regime is a fundamental change to corporate criminal liability in response to corporate misconduct that led to the death of twenty-six miners in the Westray Mine disaster, as well as events such as the Enron scandal. The new regime replaces the common law concept of a directing mind with a new and broader statutory concept of a senior officer, which now includes those who are

---

63   D. Stuart, "A Case for a General Part" in D. Stuart, R.J. Delisle, & A. Manson, eds., *Towards a Clear and Just Criminal Law: A Criminal Reports Forum* (Toronto: Carswell, 1999) 135–38.

responsible for managing an important aspect of the corporation's activities. At the same time, the new regime retains the idea that a senior officer of the corporation must be at fault before that person's fault can be attributed to the corporation for either a negligence or subjective fault offence under the *Criminal Code*. The new provisions do, however, allow organizations to be found criminally liable for crimes of negligence because of the aggregate actions of more than one of its representatives and the aggregate or collective fault of more than one of its senior officers. It does not go as far as vicarious liability for the fault of all employees or fault that inheres in "corporate culture" as opposed to the senior officers of the corporation.

The new regime also lends some structure to the *Criminal Code* by providing a separate provision for determining organizational liability for criminal offences of negligence and for criminal offences of subjective fault. It also builds on the parties provisions of the *Criminal Code* by tying organizational liability to individuals in the organization being a party to the specific offence. This underlines the reality that in many cases both individuals within the organization and the organization itself may face criminal charges. Nevertheless, it does make the new sections complex and can in some circumstances result in the corporation being found guilty for a subjective intent offence because its senior officers ought to have known that the offence would be committed.

a)   Organizational Liability

The new provisions apply not only to corporations, but any "public body, body corporate, society, company, firm, partnership, trade union or municipality."[64] This makes sense because municipalities have long been held liable for regulatory offences and there is no reason in principle why other public bodies and alternatives to formal corporations should not be held responsible under the *Criminal Code*. All of these entities are united in not being natural persons who enjoy a right to life, liberty, and security of the person under section 7 of the *Charter*.[65]

The new provisions also apply to less formal associations that are "created for a common purpose, has an operational structure and holds itself out to the public as an association of persons."[66] This suggests that the formal legal status of the organization will not be determinative with respect to the applicability of the new principles. It also raises the novel possibility that prosecutors could charge associations like criminal

---

64   *Code*, above note 1, s. 2.
65   *Irwin*, above note 27.
66   *Code*, above note 1, s. 2.

gangs with a criminal offence as a means of fining the organization or placing the organization itself on probation as opposed to relying solely on prosecutions of individuals within the informal association.

b)   Representatives of an Organization

The prohibited act or *actus reus* must be committed by one or more of the organization's "representatives." Representatives are defined broadly in section 2 of the *Criminal Code* as including not only the directors, partners, employees, and members of the organization, but also its agents and contractors. A public body or a corporation that contracts out work to non-employees can still be held liable for prohibited acts performed by the contractor or agent.

c)   Senior Officers of an Organization

In general, the required fault element or *mens rea* for the offence must be found in a senior officer of the organization. The definition of a senior officer in section 2 of the *Criminal Code* is perhaps the most crucial feature of the new regime because the new statutory concept of a senior officer replaces the old common law concept of the corporation's directing mind. Senior officer is defined as a:

> [r]epresentative who plays an important role in the establishment of the organization's policies or is responsible for managing an important aspect of the organization's activities and, in the case of a body corporate, includes a director, its chief executive officer and its chief financial officer.[67]

This definition follows the common law concept of directing mind to the extent that it provides that 1) directors, chief executive, and chief financial officers and 2) those who play an important role in the establishment of policies are senior enough in the organization that their fault can fairly be attributed to the corporation. The most important difference between the old directing mind concept and the new senior officer concept is that the latter also covers 3) those responsible for managing an important part of the organization's activities. This last aspect of the definition of a senior officer overrules previous cases that suggested that those who exercised important managerial functions in an organization were not high enough in the corporate hierarchy to represent the corporation for the purpose of determining fault. Thus, it is likely the tugboat captain in *The Rhone*[68] and the truck driver who

---

67   *Ibid.*
68   *Rhone*, above note 60.

represented a waste disposal corporation in *Safety Kleen*[69] would now be found to be senior officers whose fault could be attributed to the corporation. Even though such persons were held not to be directing minds because they did not play an important role in establishing corporate policy, they did manage an important aspect of the corporation's activities and on that basis would satisfy the expanded definition of senior officer in section 2 of the *Criminal Code*. At the same time, the new concept of a senior officer is limited to managers and not mere employees and the manager must be responsible for managing an important aspect of the organization's activities.

d) Section 22.1 of the *Criminal Code* and Organizational Fault for Negligence Offences

As mentioned above, the new regime differentiates between organizational fault for criminal offences based on negligence and subjective intent. This helpfully differentiates between the two main varieties of criminal fault. As will be seen, the new legislation also incorporates the idea that negligence in the criminal context requires more than unreasonable conduct or simple negligence. Following cases such as *Creighton*, discussed in chapter 4, a marked departure from a standard of reasonable care is required. Section 22.1 provides:

> In respect of an offence that requires the prosecution to prove negligence, an organization is a party to the offence if:
> a) acting within the scope of their authority
> > i) one of its representatives is a party to the offence, or
> > ii) two or more of its representatives engage in conduct, whether by act or omission, such that, if it had been the conduct of only one representative, that representative would have been a party to the offence; and
> b) the senior officer who is responsible for the aspect of the organization's activities that is relevant to the offence departs — or the senior officers, collectively, depart — markedly from the standard of care that, in the circumstances, could reasonably be expected to prevent a representative of the organization from being a party to the offence.

Section 22.1(a) defines how the representative(s) of the organization can commit the prohibited act or *actus reus* of the offence whereas section 22.1(b) defines how the senior officer(s) of the organization

---

69 *Safety Kleen*, above note 62.

will have the required fault element for a negligence-based criminal offence. Such offences could include causing death or causing bodily harm by criminal negligence.[70]

i) The Commission of the Prohibited Act by the Organization's Representative(s)

Section 22.1(a) requires that the representative(s) of the organization commit the prohibited act. The first requirement is that the representative(s) be acting in the scope of their authority. A corporation thus will not be liable for something done by employees, agents, or contractors outside the scope of their authority. For example, a corporation would not be guilty of criminal negligence causing death should an employee be involved in a fatal accident after he or she had stolen the company's truck.

In many cases, one representative of an organization acting within the scope of his or her authority will commit the prohibited act. Section 22.1(a)(ii), however, provides that multiple representatives of the organization may culmulatively be held responsible for commission of the prohibited act. This provision recognizes the corporate misconduct can often be the aggregate of the behaviour of separate individuals, each of whom taken by themselves may not have committed the prohibited act. A mining disaster, for example, may be caused by the combination of two or more individuals failing to take safety precautions. The failure of each may not have caused death, but the combined actions of the individuals may be sufficient to cause death.

ii) Marked Departure from Reasonable Standards by the Organization's Senior Officer(s)

Section 22.1(b) requires that senior officer(s) of the organization have the fault of departing markedly from the standard of care that could reasonably be expected to prevent a representative from being a party to the offence. The fault element does not require that a senior officer necessarily know that a representative of the organization was committing the offence. Nevertheless, it does require more than simple negligence or a lack of due diligence by the senior officer. The fault element

---

70 *Code*, above note 1, ss. 220 and 221. Criminal negligence under s. 219(b) can also be found on the basis of omissions. Section 217.1 of the *Code* now provides that "every one who undertakes, or has the authority, to direct how another person does work or performs a task is under a legal duty to take reasonable steps to prevent bodily harm to that person, or any other person, arising from that work or task."

that is required is criminal negligence in the sense that the departure from reasonable conduct must be a marked departure. This follows from the Supreme Court's repeated statements that negligence in the criminal context must be "marked."[71]

The relevant standard is the standard of care that in the circumstances could reasonably be expected to prevent a representative of the organization from being a party to the offence. This suggests that all organizations should establish systems designed to prevent their representatives from committing offences based on negligence, such as causing death or bodily injury by criminal negligence. The exact contours of this standard of care will depend on the particular circumstances and may be informed by some of the factors discussed above in relation to the due diligence defence.

In general, the requisite degree of negligence will be found in the conduct of the senior officer "who is responsible for the aspect of the organization's activities that is relevant to the offence." For example, the senior officer responsible for mine safety would generally be the relevant person in determining whether the mining company had acted with criminal negligence in the causing of death or bodily harm. It will be recalled that this senior officer need not establish corporate policy; it is sufficient under the definition of senior officer in section 2 of the *Criminal Code* that he or she be responsible for managing an important part of the organization's activities. This could include a mine manager in Canada even though corporate policy is established in head office in some other country.

Section 22.1(b) also provides for an innovative form of aggregate fault by multiple senior officers. In a sense this mirrors the concept of the aggregate commission of the prohibited act by multiple representatives of the organization in section 22.1(a). Section 22.1(b) contemplates a conviction of an organization if "the senior officers, collectively, depart markedly from the standard of care that, in the circumstances, could reasonably be expected to prevent a representative of the organization from being a party to the offence." Even if the required criminal negligence cannot be located in one senior officer, it may be found in the collective fault of the senior officers, including the board of directors, the chief executive, and those who play an important role in establishing corporate policies or managing an important aspect of the organization's activities. Thus, in a case where no one at a mine is responsible for

---

71   See *R. v. Creighton* (1993) 83 C.C.C. (3d) 346 at 382–83 (S.C.C.); *R. v. Hundal*, [1993] 1 S.C.R. 867; *R. v. Finlay*, [1993] 3 S.C.R. 103 discussed in ch. 4, "The Degree of Negligence."

safety, the required level of criminal negligence might be found in the collective conduct of the senior officers of the mining company.

Corporate liability for criminal offences of negligence may in practise blur with corporate liability for strict liability regulatory offences as discussed above. Both are offences based on negligence in allowing a prohibited act to occur. The differences, however, are that criminal offences under section 22.1 of the *Criminal Code* must be based on 1) a marked departure from the standard of care and 2) the Crown must prove beyond a reasonable doubt that senior officer(s) had this fault whereas it is the accused corporation who must demonstrate that it took all reasonable steps to prevent the prohibited act from occurring when the offence is a regulatory offence of strict liability or simple negligence.

e) Section 22.2 of the *Criminal Code* and Organizational Fault for Subjective Intent Offences

Section 22.2 applies to organizational liability for all criminal offences other than those based on negligence. In other words, it applies when the organization is charged with a subjective intent offence such as fraud, obscenity, or facilitating terrorism. Section 22.2 provides:

> In respect of an offence that requires the prosecution to prove fault — other than negligence — an organization is a party to the offence if, with the intent at least in part to benefit the organization, one of its senior officers
>
> a) acting within the scope of their authority, is a party to the offence;
>
> b) having the mental state required to be a party to the offence and acting within the scope of their authority, directs the work of other representatives of the organization so that they do the act or make the omission specified in the offence; or
>
> c) knowing that a representative of the organization is or is about to be a party to the offence, does not take all reasonable measures to stop them from being a party to the offence.

Section 22.2 contemplates subjective intent offence being committed by 1) senior officers acting on their own within the scope of their authority; 2) senior officers directing representatives so that they commit the offence; or 3) senior officers knowing that representatives are or will commit offences but failing to take all reasonable measures to stop them from doing so. Unlike section 22.1, it does not contemplate fault based on the collective or aggregate fault of multiple senior officers. In other words, one responsible senior officer must have the fault under section 22.2, which is then attributed to the organization.

i)   Senior Officers Being a Party to the Offence

The simplest form of organizational liability for a subjective intent offence is when the senior officer commits the offence. The only restrictions under section 22.2(a) are that 1) the senior officer must be acting in the scope of his or her authority and 2) have the intent at least in part to benefit the organization. The latter requirement codifies the holding in *Canadian Dredge and Dock*[72] that a corporation will not be held responsible if the senior officer acts totally in fraud of the corporation. Nevertheless, corporations can be held criminally responsible when they receive some benefits from the senior officer's activities, even though the senior officer is also defrauding the corporation.

Under section 22.2(a) the senior officer does not necessarily have to the person who actually commits the offence. All that is required is that the senior officer be a party to the offence which as discussed in chapter three includes aiding and abetting under section 21(b) and (c), common unlawful intent under section 21(2) and counselling the commission of an offence under section 22. Thus the corporation could be liable for a subjective intent offence under section 22.2(a) on the basis that its senior officer intentionally assisted or counselled a representative of the corporation to commit the offence. Indeed, sections 21(2) and 22(2) suggest that in some circumstances a senior officer may be a party to a subjective intent offence on the basis that he or she ought to have known that the offence would be committed as a result of the carrying out of an unlawful purpose or as a result of intentionally counselling the commission of another offence.

ii)   Senior Officers Directing Representatives to Commit the Offence

Section 22.2(b) is a complex provision that makes the corporation liable when a senior officer directs other representatives of the corporation so that they commit an offence. As under section 22.2(a), the senior officer must be acting in the scope of his or her authority. The senior officer must also be "directing the work of other representatives of the organization so that they do the act or make the omission specified in the offence." This requires not only that the senior officer directs the work of representatives, but also directs them in such a manner that they commit the prohibited act or omission. The wording of this provision, as well as the requirement that the senior officer must also have "the mental state required to be party to an offence," suggests that the reference to directing the work of representatives so that they

---

72   *Canadian Dredge & Dock*, above note 29.

commit the *actus reus* of the offence is a broader concept than counselling the commission of the offence. Indeed, a senior officer who intentionally and successfully counselled the commission of the offence under section 22 would be a party to the offence counselled and would already be covered by section 22.2(a) discussed above.

In addition to the direction requirement, the senior officer must "have the mental state required to be a party to the offence." As with section 22.2(a) discussed above, this incorporates the party provisions of sections 21 and 22 of the *Criminal Code* into the new corporate criminal liability provisions. Section 21(1)(b) and (c) make a senior officer liable if he or she intentionally and knowingly assists in the commision of a crime. The fact that the senior officer may have been motivated by a desire to save his or her job will not negate this fault element. Section 21(2) extends liability to offences that the senior officer either knew or ought to have known would be a probable consequence of carrying out a common unlawful purpose that was intentionally formed with at least one other person. Thus, if a senior officer intentionally forms an unlawful purpose to commit a fraud with another person, the corporation will also be liable for other offences that the senior officer either knew or ought to have known would be committed in carrying out that unlawful purpose. A senior officer would have the mental state required under section 22(1) if he or she counselled another person to commit an offence that is then in fact committed. Section 22(2) extends liability to include every offence that the senior officer would have known or ought to have known would have been carried out as a likely consequence of the counselling. Both sections 21(2) and 22(2) could be applied to make an organization liable for an subjective intent criminal offence even though its senior officer only had objective fault in relation to that particular offence. In other words, the corporation could be liable if its senior officer, having formed a common unlawful purpose or having counselled the commission of an offence, ought to have known that some further offence would be committed. Any illogic or unfairness in this state of affairs is the fault of the party provisions incorporated as an important part of the new organizational liability provision of section 22.2 and have only been partially mitigated by cases such as *Logan*[73] that hold that the objective arm of section 21(2) should not be applied for offences such as murder and attempted murder that constitutionally require subjective fault.

---

73   *R. v. Logan* (1990), 58 C.C.C. (3d) 391 (S.C.C.). See ch. 3, "Common Intention to Commit an Unlawful Purpose and Section 21(2)."

iii) Senior Officers Failing to Prevent Representatives from Committing the Offence

The organization's liability for subjective intent offence is further extended by section 22.2(c) that applies when a senior officer knows that a representative of the organization is or is about to be a party to the offence but fails "to take all reasonable measures" to stop the representative[74] from being a party to the offence. This section requires subjective fault in the form of guilty knowledge by the senior officer about the commission of an offence. As discussed in chapter 4, knowledge is a fairly high form of subjective knowledge and does not encompass recklessness or wilful blindness.

Section 22.2(c) also requires objective fault by the senior officer in the form of a failure to take all reasonable steps to stop the commission of the offence. The requirement of liability for a failure to take all reasonable steps is one usually associated with regulatory offences as opposed to criminal offences of subjective fault.[75] Indeed, this requirement is quite close to the due diligence requirement for strict liability offences and courts may well look to the multiple factors that are relevant in determining to due diligence in order to determine whether a senior officer took all reasonable steps to prevent a representative from committing or continuing to commit the offence.

There are still some differences between section 22.2(c) as it applies to organizations charged with a criminal offence of subjective intent and the due diligence available to corporations charged with a regulatory offence. One difference is that an organization will not be liable under section 22.2(c) unless its senior officer also had guilty knowledge that a representative of the organization was committing or was about to commit the offence. A second difference is that the failure of the senior officer to take all reasonable steps must be proven beyond a reasonable doubt. Organizations are made liable under this section through a combination of subjective and objective fault elements,[76] both of which must be proven beyond a reasonable doubt.

---

74 The section at first refers to "a representative" but later uses the plural "them" in reference to the representative. This is confusing but fails to clearly introduce the novel concept of aggregate liability found in s. 22.1, which applies to criminal offences of negligence.

75 But see s. 150.1(4) requiring an accused to have taken "all reasonable steps" to ascertain the age of a complainant under the age of 14 for the purpose of various sexual offences.

76 See the discussion of s. 273.2(2(b) in ch. 4, "Mistake of Fact and Sexual Assault," for a somewhat similar combination of subjective and objective fault that requires a person arguing mistaken belief in consent to take "reasonable steps,

CONCLUSION

Although the Supreme Court has disapproved of absolute liability offences since its decision in *Sault Ste. Marie*[77] and declared them contrary to the principles of fundamental justice in the *B.C. Motor Vehicle Reference*,[78] it appears that such offences are constitutionally permissible so long as no imprisonment is imposed.[79] Absolute liability offences would also be permissible if only applied to corporations who do not enjoy the rights to life, liberty, and security of the person protected under section 7 of the *Charter*.

Strict liability offences have also narrowly survived *Charter* challenge. The courts have not disapproved of the fault element of simple negligence, but they have noted that the mandatory presumption that the accused is negligent unless it establishes a defence of due diligence on a balance of probabilities does violate the presumption of innocence under section 11(d) of the *Charter*. The Court in *Wholesale Travel Group* did not accept that the less drastic alternative of an evidential as opposed to a persuasive burden would adequately advance the objectives of regulatory offences. It expressed concerns that regulatory objectives could be frustrated if accused were acquitted simply because there was a reasonable doubt whether they were negligent in allowing an *actus reus* to occur.

When a corporation is charged with a criminal offence, the required fault must now under new statutory provisions designed to facilitate the prosecution of corporations be attributed to senior officer(s) who either play an important role in establishing policy or who are responsible for managing an important aspect of its activities. If the criminal offence is based on negligence, the prohibited act under section 22.1 of the *Criminal Code* must be committed by representative(s) of the corporation (not only employees but also agents and contractors) acting in their scope of authority. No one individual need be responsible for the prohibited act which can be committed in aggregate by multiple representatives. Either the responsible senior officer or the senior officers collectively must be at fault in the sense of a marked departure from the standard of care that could reasonably be expected

---

in the circumstances known to the accused at the time, to ascertain that the complainant was consenting."

77   *Sault Ste. Marie*, above note 4.
78   *B.C. Motor Vehicle Reference*, above note 17.
79   *Pontes*, above note 14.

to prevent the commission of the offence. If the criminal offence requires subjective fault, a senior officer acting in the scope of his or her authority must be 1) a party to the offence; or 2) direct the work of the organization's representatives so that they commit the offence; or 3) fail to to take all reasonable steps to stop the commission of the offence when he or she knows that representative of the organization is committing an offence. Sections 22.1 and 22.2 of the *Criminal Code* are new and complex provisions designed to facilitate the process of holding organizations responsible for criminal offences in a manner consistent with the requirements of objective and subjective fault found in the criminal law.

FURTHER READINGS

ARCHIBALD, T., K. JULL, & K. ROACH, "The Changed Face of Corporate Criminal Liability" (2004) 48 C.L.Q. 367

ARCHIBALD, T., K. JULL, & K. ROACH, "Corporate and Regulatory Liability: From Due Diligence to Risk Management (Aurora, ON: Canada Law Book, forthcoming)

BRAITHWAITE, J., *Responsive Regulation and Restorative Justice* (Oxford: Oxford University Press, 2002)

COLVIN, E., *Principles of Criminal Law*, 2d ed. (Toronto: Carswell, 1991), ch. 6

"Corporate Crime: Regulating Corporate Behavior Through Criminal Sanctions" (1979) 92 Harv. L. Rev. 1227

EDWARDS, J. LL.J., *Mens Rea in Statutory Offences* (London: Stevens, 1955)

FISSE, B., "Corporate Criminal Responsibility" (1991) 15 Crim. L.J. 166

HANNA, D., "Corporate Criminal Liability" (1989) 31 Crim. L.Q. 452

MEWETT, A., & M. MANNING, *Criminal Law*, 3d ed. (Toronto: Butterworths, 1994), ch. 7

ONTARIO LAW REFORM COMMISSION, *Report on Provincial Offences* (Toronto: Queen's Printer, 1992)

RUBY, C., & K. JULL, "The *Charter* and Regulatory Offences: A Wholesale Revision" (1992) 14 C.R. (4th) 226

STUESSER, L., "Convicting the Innocent Owner: Vicarious Liability under Highway Traffic Legislation" (1989) 67 C.R.(3d) 316

STUART, D., *Canadian Criminal Law: A Treatise*, 4th ed. (Toronto: Carswell, 2001), ch. 9

WELLS, C., *Corporations And Criminal Responsibility*, 2d ed. (Oxford: Oxford University Press, 2001)

INTOXICATION

Intoxication from alcohol or drugs may be a condition that prevents the Crown from proving that the accused had the fault element required for a particular offence (see chapter 4). Some extreme forms of intoxication may even result in involuntary conduct which, as discussed in chapter 2, is increasingly seen as inconsistent with proof of the prohibited act. Nevertheless, the intoxication defence has been influenced by policy considerations beyond those that relate to the fault element or the prohibited act of the particular offence. For these reasons, it will be examined here in a separate chapter.

Intoxication was historically considered an aggravating factor to a crime because it "was occasioned by [the accused's] own act and folly, and he might have avoided it."[1] In the nineteenth century, as greater emphasis was placed on subjective *mens rea*, courts became more concerned about the relevance of intoxication as a possible defence. The object was not to determine whether the accused was intoxicated, but whether intoxication, combined with any other factors, prevented the formation of the fault element required for the particular offence. At the same time, however, courts never completely abandoned the older idea that an intoxicated offender was not morally innocent, and they placed restrictions on the availability of the intoxication defence. Intoxication was admissible and could raise a reasonable doubt to the

---

1   *Reniger v. Fogossa* (1548), 75 E.R. 1 (Ex.).

mental element for specific intent offences, which required an ulterior objective beyond the immediate act. It was not, however, admissible when the accused was charged with general intent offences, which required proof only of an intent to perform the immediate act. In practice, this meant that intoxication could be a defence to more serious crimes such as murder and robbery, but not to less serious offences such as manslaughter and assault.

The distinction between general and specific intent offences has frequently been criticized. As examined in chapter four, there are different levels of *mens rea*, but fault elements are not usually classified as either general or specific intent. At best, the general/specific intent dichotomy serves as a rough and ready distinction between the various degrees of subjective *mens rea* and how they may be affected by the accused's intoxication. The classification of a particular fault element as general or specific intent may be uncertain and will likely be driven by policy concerns about the ultimate disposition of the accused. In any event, the classification of intent as either general or specific remains a relevant factor in the administration of the intoxication defence. Its continued relevance reveals concerns about whether voluntary intoxication by the accused should lead to a complete acquittal. As will be seen in this and the next two chapters, defences are often influenced by concerns about the ultimate disposition of the accused.

A. BEARD'S CASE

The genesis of the modern defence of intoxication is found in the House of Lords' 1920 decision in *D.P.P. v. Beard*.[2] In that case, the Court articulated the following propositions:

1) [T]hat intoxication could be a ground for an insanity defence if it produced a disease of the mind.

2) "That evidence of drunkenness which renders the accused incapable of forming the specific intent essential to constitute the crime should be taken into consideration with the other facts proved in order to determine whether or not he had this intent."

3) "That evidence of drunkenness falling short of a proved incapacity in the accused to form the intent necessary to constitute the crime, and merely establishing that his mind was affected by

---

2   [1920] A.C. 479 (H.L.) [*Beard*].

drink so that he more readily gave way to some violent passion, does not rebut the presumption that a man intends the natural consequences of his acts."[3]

In the actual case, Beard had been drinking when he killed a woman in the course of a rape. Shortly after the killing, he was accepted into a trade union after answering "not unintelligently certain questions which were put to him." The House of Lords confirmed his conviction for constructive murder in the course of a rape by stating: "drunkenness in this case could be no defence unless it could be established that Beard at the time of committing the rape was so drunk that he was incapable of forming the intent to commit it, which was not in fact, and manifestly, having regard to the evidence, could not be contended."[4]

B. THE DISTINCTION BETWEEN GENERAL AND SPECIFIC INTENT OFFENCES

Courts in England and Canada have taken the reference in *Beard* to "forming the specific intent essential to commit the crime" as drawing a distinction between crimes of specific intent and those of general intent. It is arguable, however, that the word "specific" was used in *Beard* only to refer to the particular crime, and not to a distinct category of offences. No reference is made in *Beard* to "general intent" offences as a category of offences distinct from "specific intent" offences. Moreover, the relevance of intoxication to rape was considered even though that offence has subsequently been classified as a general intent offence. Nevertheless, *Beard* has been interpreted in England and Canada as establishing a distinction between crimes of specific and general intent, with intoxication traditionally being a defence only with respect to the former.

---

3   *Ibid.* at 500–2.
4   *Ibid.* at 504–5. Constructive or felony murder bases liability for murder on the commission of a serious underlying offence such as rape, whether or not the accused intended to kill the victim or knew that death was likely. If *Beard's* case arose today in Canada, he could not be charged with constructive murder. See *R. v. Vaillancourt* (1987), 39 C.C.C. (3d) 118 (S.C.C.) and *R. v. Martineau* (1990), 58 C.C.C. (3d) 353 (S.C.C.) discussed in chs. 1 and 4. Evidence of intoxication would be relevant in determining not whether Beard would have the intent for sexual assault, but for murder. In other words, the question would be whether given the evidence of intoxication and any other factors, the prosecutor had established that Beard knew that his victim was likely to die.

In *George*, the Supreme Court held that robbery was a specific intent offence to which drunkenness was relevant, but assault was a general intent offence to which evidence of intoxication was rarely, if ever, relevant. Fauteux J. explained:

> In considering the question of *mens rea*, a distinction is to be made between (i) intention as applied to acts considered in relation to their purposes and (ii) intention as applied to acts apart from their purposes.[5]

Robbery fell into the first category because it required the application of force in order to facilitate the taking of property, while assault fell into the second category because it required only the minimal intent required for the application of force without consent. Ritchie J. similarly distinguished:

> between "intention" as applied to acts done to achieve an immediate end on the one hand and acts done with the specific and ulterior motive and intention of furthering or achieving an illegal object on the other hand. Illegal acts of the former kind are done "intentionally" in the sense that they are not done by accident or through honest mistake, but acts of the latter kind are the product of preconception and deliberate steps taken towards an illegal goal.[6]

In the result, the intoxicated accused was acquitted of robbery, but convicted of the included offence of assault.

In *R. v. Bernard*,[7] McIntyre J. stressed that specific intent offences require the mind to focus on an objective further to the immediate one at hand, while general intent offences require only a conscious doing of the prohibited act. In that case, the majority held that the offence of sexual assault causing bodily harm was a general intent offence. In a companion case, breaking and entering and committing the indictable offence of assault was held to be a general intent offence. It was suggested, however, that the different offence of breaking and entering with the intent to commit an indictable offence was a specific intent offence, because it required proof of an ulterior intent beyond the immediate prohibited acts.[8] In dissent, Dickson C.J. argued that the distinction between general and specific intent offences was an artificial, uncertain, and confusing device to exclude relevant information

---

5   *R. v. George* (1960), 128 C.C.C. 289 at 301 (S.C.C).
6   *Ibid.* at 306.
7   (1988), 45 C.C.C. (3d) 1 at 24–25 (S.C.C.) [*Bernard*].
8   *R. v. Quin* (1988), 44 C.C.C. (3d) 570 (S.C.C.) [*Quin*].

from the jury's consideration. He also argued that the distinction was not necessary to ensure social protection.[9] Juries could be relied on not to accept specious claims that the accused's intoxication deprived him or her of the intent required for the particular crime.

The distinction between general and specific intent has been criticized as illogical and difficult to apply. The Supreme Court has recognized that the distinction is largely driven by policy concerns. In *R. v. Daviault*,[10] Sopinka J. noted that specific intent offences were generally more serious offences requiring some ulterior intent, and that "failure to prove the added element will often result in conviction of a lesser offence for which the added element is not required. One example is the offence of assault to resist or prevent arrest which is a specific intent offence. Absent the intent to resist arrest, the accused would be convicted of assault *simpliciter*, a general intent offence."[11] The distinction between specific and general intent offences has often served the practical purpose of ensuring that even if the accused's voluntary intoxication prevents conviction for the specific intent offence, the accused will normally still be convicted of a less serious general intent offence. A classic example is when evidence of intoxication raises a reasonable doubt about the intent for murder, but the accused is then convicted of the general intent offence of manslaughter.

Murder, theft, robbery, aiding and abetting a crime, and attempted crimes have all been held to be specific intent offences, on the basis that they require proof of an ulterior objective beyond the immediate act. Thus, intoxication is admissible and can raise a reasonable doubt about the mental element for these offences. Manslaughter, assault, sexual assault, assault causing bodily harm, and mischief, however, have all been classified as general intent offences on the basis that they require proof only of intent in relation to the prohibited act. In addition, crimes based on an objective fault element would also seem to preclude considering the accused's intoxication as a defence. Recent developments, however, suggest that extreme intoxication may be a defence to general intent offences. To the extent that extreme intoxication negates the voluntariness of the accused's actions it may also be a defence to crimes that require objective fault and even absolute liability offences.

---

9   *Bernard*, above note 7 at 9–13; *Quin*, above note 8 at 574.
10   (1994), 93 C.C.C. (3d) 21 (S.C.C.) [*Daviault*].
11   *Ibid.* at 41 (in dissent, but not on this issue).

C. LIABILITY FOR THE INTOXICATED COMMISSION OF GENERAL INTENT OFFENCES

In *R. v. Leary*,[12] the Supreme Court followed *R. v. Majewski*[13] and decided that intoxication could not be a defence to a general intent offence. In *Majewski*, Lord Elwyn-Jones relied on the controversial proposition that the accused, by becoming voluntarily intoxicated, had committed the *mens rea* for a general intent offence such as assault causing bodily harm. He stated:

> If a man of his own volition takes a substance which causes him to cast off the restraints of reason and conscience, no wrong is done to him by holding him answerable criminally for any injury he may do while in that condition. His course of conduct in reducing himself by drugs and drink to that condition in my view supplies the evidence of *mens rea*, of guilty mind certainly sufficient for crimes of basic intent. It is a reckless course of conduct and recklessness is enough to constitute the necessary *mens rea* in assault cases.[14]

Under this approach, the recklessness of becoming drunk is deemed to be sufficient to supply the fault element for the commission of the particular general intent offence. This creates an exception to the general proposition, examined in chapter 2, that the fault element should occur at the same time as the *actus reus*. The fault element would be formed not when the assault took place, but before that time while the accused was becoming intoxicated. At the time the assault was committed, the accused would have no fault element. It also creates an exception to the general proposition, examined in chapter 4, that the fault element should be directed towards the *actus reus*. An extremely intoxicated person may not necessarily have formed the intent to commit the general intent offence while he or she was becoming intoxicated.

In a strong dissent in *Leary*,[15] Dickson J. argued that the recklessness in becoming intoxicated was not legally sufficient because "recklessness in a legal sense imports foresight. Recklessness cannot exist in the air; it must have reference to the consequences of a particular act," namely, the crime charged. He argued that the dichotomy between gen-

---

12 (1977), 33 C.C.C. (2d) 473 (S.C.C.) [*Leary*].
13 (1976), 62 Cr. App. Rep. 262 (H.L.).
14 *Ibid.* at 270.
15 *Leary*, above note 12 at 494.

eral and specific intent was irrational and that evidence of drunkenness should be left to the jury regardless of the offence charged. "In the case of an intoxicated or drugged accused, the jury may have little difficulty in drawing an inference of intent or recklessness in the relevant sense, but that remains an issue of fact for the jury to determine in each particular case."[16] New Zealand and Australia follow this approach and allow evidence of intoxication to be considered by the trier of fact in all cases and without regard to the classification of offences as general or specific intent.[17]

D. INVOLUNTARY INTOXICATION

Under the approach taken in *Majewski* and *Leary*, an accused may be convicted of a general intent offence on the basis of the fault or recklessness of voluntarily becoming intoxicated. This raises the question of what should the courts do if the accused becomes involuntarily intoxicated through no fault of his or her own? If the accused is to be held at fault for a general intent offence for voluntarily becoming intoxicated, it is only fair that he or she not be convicted if the intoxication was not the accused's fault.[18]

The Supreme Court has not applied the traditional rule of only allowing intoxication to be a defence to specific intent offences in cases where the accused became involuntarily intoxicated. In other words, it has not attributed the fault of involuntarily becoming intoxicated for the fault that may not be present when the accused commits a general intent offence while severely intoxicated. In *R. v. King*,[19] the Supreme Court indicated that an accused who had been impaired by a drug given to him by his dentist should not be convicted of impaired driving if he "became impaired through no act of his own will and could not reasonably be expected to have known that his ability was impaired or might thereafter become impaired when he undertook to drive and drove his motor vehicle." It is also significant that the 1962 case of *King* seems to acknowledge that there could be a degree of intoxication that is inconsistent with the formation of the *mens rea* of a general intent

---

16   *Ibid.* at 495.

17   *R. v. Kamipeli*, [1975] 2 N.Z.L.R. 610 (C.A.); *R. v. O' Connor* (1980), 54 A.L.J.R. 349 (H.C.).

18   Courts in England have, however, convicted an accused despite his involuntary consumption of drugs. *R. v. Kingston*, [1994] 3 W.L.R. 519 (H.L.).

19   (1962), 133 C.C.C. 1 at 19 (S.C.C.).

offence such as impaired driving. *King* suggests that involuntary intoxication can be a defence that may negate either the *mens rea* or the *actus reus* of a general intent offence. Evidence of either voluntary or involuntary intoxication could also be considered in determining whether the accused had the *mens rea* of a specific intent offence.

King has been applied in a case in which the accused went into an automatic state and assaulted another person after overdosing on prescription pills that contained no specific warnings[20] or was surreptitiously given vodka in his drink.[21] It has been distinguished in cases in which the accused were convicted of impaired driving caused by overdoses of cold medication;[22] by a deliberate overdose of prescription pills in an attempt to commit suicide[23] and in a case in which smoking marijuana had an unexpected effect on the accused.[24]

E. EXTREME INTOXICATION AND GENERAL INTENT OFFENCES

1) The Development of the *Daviault* Defence

The rule in *Leary* that holds that becoming intoxicated could supply the *mens rea* for general intent offences was vulnerable under the *Charter* because 1) it departed from the requirement that the *mens rea* occur at the same time as the *actus reus*; 2) it transferred the general or at-large fault of becoming intoxicated for the fault of the particular general intent offence; and 3) it would allow the conviction of a person who was so severely intoxicated that he or she acted involuntarily or without the intent required for the particular general intent offence.

The Supreme Court first considered the constitutionality of the *Leary* rule in *Bernard*.[25] The Court was deeply divided. Two judges would have upheld the Leary rule in its full vigour so that even if the accused "was so intoxicated as to raise doubts as to the voluntary nature of his conduct," the Crown could demonstrate the necessary *mens rea* from the fact of voluntary self-intoxication. McIntyre J. argued

---

20 R. v. *Vickberg* (1998), 16 C.R. (5th) 164 at 184 (B.S.S.C.) [Vickberg]. As will be seen, s. 33.1 of the *Criminal Code* places restrictions on when "self-induced intoxication" will be a defence.

21 R. v. *Tramble* (1983), 33 C.R. (3d) 264 (Ont. Co. Ct.).

22 R. v. *Rushton* (1963), [1964] 1 C.C.C. 382 (N.S.C.A.).

23 R. v. *Honish* (1991), 68 C.C.C. (3d) 329 (Alta. C.A.).

24 R. v. *Brenton* (1999) 28 C.R. (5th) 308 at 320 (N.W.T.S.C.).

25 *Bernard*, above note 7.

for the traditional position that proof of the accused's "voluntary drunkenness can be proof of his guilty mind"[26] even though this fault would not necessarily be present when the prohibited act was committed, or have been directed at the prohibited act.

At the other end of the spectrum, Chief Justice Dickson, with the concurrence of Justices Lamer and LaForest, not only adhered to his strong dissent in *Leary*, but argued that the *Leary* rule violated sections 7 and 11(d) of the *Charter* by substituting the intent of becoming intoxicated for the intent of the particular general intent offence. He concluded:

> The effect of the majority holding in *Leary* is to impose a form of absolute liability on intoxicated offenders, which is entirely inconsistent with the basic requirement for a blameworthy state of mind as a prerequisite to the imposition of the penalty of imprisonment [under section 7 of the *Charter*]. . . .
>
> The majority holding in *Leary* also runs counter to the s. 11(d) right to be presumed innocent until proven guilty. With respect to crimes of general intent, guilty intent is in effect presumed upon proof of the fact of intoxication. Moreover, the presumption of guilt created by the *Leary* rule is irrebutable.[27]

The exclusion of evidence of intoxication converted general intent offences to absolute liability offences by not considering a potentially crucial factor in determining whether the accused had the required *mens rea*. In addition, the presumption of innocence was violated when the fault of becoming intoxicated was substituted for the fault of the particular general intent offence. Dickson C.J. also concluded that the *Leary* rule could not be justified under section 1 of the *Charter* because it would require people to be convicted for unintended or unforeseen crimes. He argued: "[I]t has not been demonstrated that risk of imprisonment of a few innocent persons is required to attain the goal of protecting the public from drunken offenders."[28] If public protection required special measures to deal with intoxicated offenders, that should be done by Parliament, not the courts. This could be done through the creation of an offence that punished the accused for being drunk and dangerous.

Justice Wilson fashioned a novel compromise position that was later to command support from a majority of the Court in *Daviault*.

---

26   *Ibid.* at 36.
27   *Ibid.* at 16–17.
28   *Ibid.* at 18.

Unlike Dickson C.J., she retained the distinction between general and specific intent offences. In most cases, the minimal intent required for the commission of a general intent offence could be inferred from the commission of the act. In *Bernard*, for example, the accused was guilty of the general intent offence of sexual assault causing bodily harm because it was clear that he engaged in "intentional and voluntary, as opposed to accidental or involuntary, application of force."[29] Wilson J. also disagreed with Dickson C.J. that the *Leary* rule violated section 7 of the *Charter*. An accused who voluntarily became so intoxicated as not to have the minimal awareness required for a general intent offence was not a morally innocent person who should be protected from conviction under section 7 of the *Charter*.[30] However, the "real concern" for Wilson J. arose under section 11(d), because the fault of becoming drunk would under the *Leary* rule be substituted for the fault of the particular offence charged. Wilson J. elaborated:

> While this court has recognized that in some cases proof of an essential element of a criminal offence can be replaced by proof of a different element, it has placed stringent limitations on when this can happen. . . . In my tentative view, it is unlikely that in those cases in which it is necessary to resort to self-induced intoxication as the substituted element for the minimal intent, proof of the substituted element will "inexorably" lead to the conclusion that the essential element of the minimal intent existed at the time the criminal act was committed.[31]

Wilson J. would apply the basic *Leary* rule in a more flexible fashion that would allow "evidence of extreme intoxication involving an absence of awareness akin to a state of insanity or automatism" to go to the trier of fact in "those rare cases in which the intoxication is extreme enough to raise doubts as to the existence of the minimal intent which characterizes conscious and volitional conduct."[32]

---

29   She concluded: "[t]here is no evidence that we are dealing here with extreme intoxication, verging on insanity or automatism, and as such capable of negating the inference that the minimal intent to apply force was present. . . . The evidence of intoxication in this case was simply not capable of raising a reasonable doubt as to the existence of the minimal intent required." *Ibid.* at 39–40.

30   Such persons would nevertheless have rights under ss. 7 and 12 of the *Canadian Charter of Rights and Freedoms*, Part I of the *Constitution Act, 1982*, being Schedule B to the *Canada Act 1982* (U.K.), 1982, c. 11 [*Charter*] "to be protected against punishment that is disproportionate to their crime and degree of culpability." *Ibid.* at 43–44.

31   *Ibid.* at 44.

32   *Ibid.* at 42–43.

Six years later, Justice Wilson's approach, with some variations, commanded support from a majority of the Supreme Court. In *Daviault*,[33] the Supreme Court decided that extreme intoxication could in rare cases be a defence to general intent offences such as assault or sexual assault. In such cases, the minimal intent required for a general intent offence could not be inferred from the commission of the prohibited act because "the very voluntariness or consciousness of that act may be put in question by the extreme intoxication of the accused."[34] Moreover, the application of the *Leary* and *Majewski* rule would violate both sections 7 and 11(d) of the *Charter* by substituting the intent of becoming intoxicated for the intent of the offence. Cory J. concluded:

> The consumption of alcohol simply cannot lead inexorably to the conclusion that the accused possessed the requisite mental element to commit a sexual assault, or any other crime. Rather, the substituted *mens rea* rule has the effect of eliminating the minimal mental element required for sexual assault. Furthermore, *mens rea* for a crime is so well recognized that to eliminate that mental element, an integral part of the crime, would be to deprive an accused of fundamental justice.[35]

Not considering evidence of intoxication in cases of extreme intoxication could lead to conviction without proof that the accused had the *mens rea* required for the general intent offence. Whatever fault element could be inferred from becoming intoxicated did not prove beyond a reasonable doubt that the accused had the fault element for a general intent offence, in this case, sexual assault.

In *Daviault*, the Supreme Court purported to adopt Wilson J.'s position in *Bernard*, but the Court's reasoning differed in two respects. First, the Court held that the *Leary* rule violated not only section 11(d), but also section 7 of the *Charter*. In contrast, Wilson J. suggested in *Bernard* that a person who voluntarily became so intoxicated that he or she did not have the minimal intent necessary to commit a general intent offence was not a morally innocent person protected from punishment under section 7 of the *Charter*.[36] This is not a doctrinal quibble given that the courts have been much more willing to uphold violations of section 11(d) under section 1 than violations of section 7 of the *Charter*.[37]

---

33   *Daviault*, above note 10.
34   *Ibid.* at 58.
35   *Ibid.* at 60.
36   Wilson J., however, contemplated that such a person would be protected from disproportionate punishment under both s. 7 and s. 12 of the *Charter*, above note 30.
37   See ch. 1, "Right to be Presumed Innocent."

Second, the Court in *Daviault* required an accused to prove extreme intoxication as a defence to a general intent crime on a balance of probabilities, whereas Wilson J. would have allowed such evidence to rebut the Crown's usual duty to prove the fault element beyond a reasonable doubt. Cory J. explained that the burden on the accused to prove extreme intoxication violated the presumption of innocence in section 11(d), but was justified because "it is only the accused who can give evidence as to the amount of alcohol consumed and its effect upon him. Expert evidence would be required to confirm that the accused was probably in a state akin to automatism or insanity as a result of his drinking."[38] Because of concerns about social protection, the Supreme Court violated the presumption of innocence in its own development of the common law. As will be seen in chapter 7, an accused wishing to take advantage of the mental disorder or automatism defences must also prove the defence on a balance of probabilities. At the same time, the reversal of the burden can be criticized as unprincipled. In countries such as Australia and New Zealand which have abandoned the specific and general intent distinction, the accused has no burden to establish the defence of intoxication and will be acquitted whenever the evidence of intoxication raises a reasonable doubt about the intent of the offence charged. There is no compelling evidence that social protection has been sacrificed by maintaining the presumption of innocence.

The defence contemplated in *Daviault* applies only if the accused is extremely intoxicated. Cory J. argued:

> those who are a "little" drunk can readily form the requisite mental element to commit the offence. The alcohol-induced relaxation of both inhibitions and socially acceptable behaviour has never been accepted as a factor or excuse in determining whether the accused possessed the requisite *mens rea*. Given the minimal nature of the mental element required for crimes of general intent, even those who are significantly drunk will usually be able to form the requisite *mens rea* and will be found to have acted voluntarily. . . .
>
> It is obvious that it will only be on rare occasions that evidence of such an extreme state of intoxication can be advanced and perhaps only on still rarer occasions is it likely to be successful.[39]

Despite evidence which suggested that Daviault, a chronic alcoholic, had a blood alcohol level that would kill most people, and the trial judge's acquittal, the Court sent the case back for a new trial to require

---

38   *Daviault*, above note 10.
39   *Ibid.* at 67–68.

the accused to establish the defence of extreme intoxication on a balance of probabilities.

Daviault dealt with the crime of sexual assault which, at the time, required subjective *mens rea*.[40] Other general intent offences, notably unlawful act manslaughter, require only proof of an objective fault element. An extremely intoxicated accused could still have objective fault if his or her conduct demonstrated a marked and substantial departure from what a reasonable person would have done in the circumstances. If, however, the extreme intoxication negates the voluntariness required for the *actus reus*, the accused may have a defence because he or she did not consciously and voluntarily commit the criminal act. In *Daviault*, Cory J. indicated that when extreme intoxication produced a state akin to automatism it would "render an accused incapable of either performing a willed act or of forming the minimal intent required for a general intent offence." In their concurrences, both Lamer C.J. and LaForest J. indicated that such extreme intoxication would also raise a reasonable doubt as to the commission of the *actus reus*.[41]

Daviault raises the possibility that extreme intoxication would be a defence not only to general intent offences but to absolute or strict liability offences. The extreme intoxication contemplated under *Daviault* may negate the voluntariness that is increasingly seen as part of the *actus reus*.[42] Cory J. recognized that "the mental aspect involved in

---

40 Subsequent amendments to sexual assault have introduced objective components in relation to the defence of mistake of fact and have affirmed that self-induced intoxication should not be considered in relation to that defence. *Criminal Code of Canada*, R.S.C. 1985, c. C-46, s. 273.2(b) [*Code*]. See ch. 4, "Mistake of Fact and Sexual Assault." In his dissent, Sopinka J. concluded "sexual assault does not fall into the category of offences for which either the stigma or the available penalties demand as a constitutional requirement subjective intent to commit the *actus reus*. . . . I cannot see how the stigma and punishment associated with the offence of sexual assault are disproportionate to the moral blameworthiness of a person like the appellant who commits the offence after voluntarily becoming so intoxicated as to be incapable of knowing what he is doing. The fact that the *Leary* rules permit an individual to be convicted despite the absence of symmetry between the *actus reus* and the mental element of blameworthiness does not violate a principle of fundamental justice." *Daviault*, *ibid.* at 37–38.

41 In Australia, extreme intoxication can be a defence to manslaughter if it indicates that the accused's acts were not voluntary. *R. v. Martin* (1984), 51 A.L.R. 540 (H.C.). Presumably, a similar defence would apply in Canada after *Daviault*, above note 10, albeit one that requires the accused to prove on a balance of probabilities that the unlawful act for the manslaughter was not voluntary because of extreme intoxication.

42 See ch. 2, "Voluntariness of the Act."

willed or voluntary conduct may overlap to some extent in both the concept of *mens rea* and *actus reus*."[43] In their concurrences, both Lamer C.J. and LaForest J. stated that they preferred to characterize the minimal mental element of general intent offences "as relating more to the *actus reus* than the *mens rea*, so that the defence [of extreme intoxication akin to automatism] clearly be available in strict liability offences."[44] In such cases, it would not matter that the accused could not prove a defence of due diligence because of his negligence in becoming drunk, since the *actus reus* necessary for conviction would not be present. The accused would still bear the burden of proving the defence of extreme intoxication on a balance of probabilities even though extreme intoxication might prevent the Crown from proving the commission of the *actus reus* beyond a reasonable doubt.

Daviault did not abolish the much criticized distinction between general and specific intent offences, and it introduced two distinct intoxication defences with different burdens of proof. When an accused is charged with a specific intent offence such as murder, evidence of intoxication will always be relevant, and it has only to raise a reasonable doubt about whether the accused had the required intent. In many cases, however, the accused would still have to face a charge on a general intent offence such as manslaughter or assault. With respect to general intent offences, evidence of intoxication will be relevant only in rare cases supported by expert evidence. The accused must prove on a balance of probabilities that he or she was so extremely intoxicated as to be incapable of having the minimal intent required for a general intent offence. An accused with this defence may, however, not be convicted of any offences, because there are generally no lesser included offences to convict a person acquitted of a general intent offence.[45] For example, while a person acquitted because of intoxication of the specific intent offence of murder will often be convicted of manslaughter, a person acquitted of manslaughter, assault, or sexual

---

43   *Daviault*, above note 10 at 49.

44   *Ibid.* at 25. The Chief Justice's reasoning would also seem to apply to absolute liability offences to the extent that they survive *Charter* scrutiny.

45   One exception may be offences such as impaired driving, which have intoxication as an essential element. See *R. v. Penno* (1990), 59 C.C.C. (3d) 344 (S.C.C.), discussed below at note 48. On the other hand, it could be argued that an accused should still have a *Daviault* defence, because the extreme intoxication prevents the voluntary commission of even the *actus reus* required for intoxication-based offences. This is also suggested by the Court's recognition that involuntary intoxication may be a defence to impaired driving. See *R. v. King* (1962), 133 C.C.C. 1 (S.C.C.) [*King*].

assault because of extreme intoxication will often not be guilty of any lesser crime.

2) The Legislative Response to *Daviault*: Section 33.1

Although the Supreme Court believed the *Daviault* defence would apply only in rare cases, it recognized that Parliament might wish to respond to the social danger of an acquittal of a severely intoxicated accused who committed a general intent offence. The Court indicated that "it is always open to Parliament to fashion a remedy which would make it a crime to commit a prohibited act while drunk."[46] There are many ways that such legislation could be formulated. Parliament could have provided a new offence of being "drunk and dangerous," committing harm while extremely intoxicated, or committing a specific wrongful act while extremely intoxicated. All these options would mean that an extremely intoxicated person who did not have the minimal intent to commit a general intent offence would be acquitted of that offence, but convicted of a new offence that contained intoxication as an essential element. Such offences have long been proposed as a means to ensure public safety should the courts abolish the common law distinction between specific and general intent offences, and allow evidence of intoxication to go to the jury in all cases. An offence that included intoxication as an element would undoubtedly be held consistent with the *Charter*. In *Penno*,[47] the Supreme Court rejected the notion that intoxication could be a defence to a crime of intoxicated driving and it has in several subsequent cases indicated that the denial of a defence that would be at odds with the very mischief that the offence seeks to prohibit would not violate the *Charter*.[48]

Another alternative would be to treat those with a *Daviault* defence in the same manner as a mentally disordered offender. They would then be found not criminally responsible but be subject to further detention and treatment if they are a significant danger to the public. The House of Lords in *Beard* seemed to contemplate that drunkenness could produce a state of insanity, but Canadian courts have indicated

---

46 *Daviault*, above note 10 at 68.

47 Above note 45. Only Lamer C.J. found that the denial of the intoxication defence might violate ss. 7 and 11(d) of the *Charter* because it could convict a person on the basis of an involuntary act, but he held that such violations were justified under s. 1 of the *Charter*. The rest of the judges found no *Charter* violation.

48 *R. v. Finta*, [1994] 1 S.C.R. 701 at 865 [*Finta*]; *R. v. Ruzic* 2001 SCC 24 at para. 23 [*Ruzic*]; *Canadian Foundation for Children v. Canada (A.G.)* 2004 4 SCC 4 [*Canadian Foundation for Children*].

that self-induced intoxication and other transitory states should not qualify for the insanity or mental disorder defence.[49] In his dissent in *Daviault*, Sopinka J. explicitly rejected this option and argued that those who voluntarily become extremely intoxicated "deserve to be punished for their crimes" because their condition was self-induced and avoidable.[50]

In any event, Parliament did not respond to *Daviault* through the creation of a new intoxication-based offence or by creating a treatment disposition. Rather, it amended the *Criminal Code* so that those with a *Daviault* defence will be convicted of the same violent general intent offences that they would have been convicted of before the Court's decision.[51] Section 33.1(1) and (2) of the *Criminal Code* now contemplates that it will not be a defence that the accused "by reason of self-induced intoxication, lacked the general intent or the voluntariness required to commit the offence," because:

> a person departs markedly from the standard of reasonable care generally recognized in Canadian society and is thereby criminally at fault where the person, while in a state of self-induced intoxication that renders the person unaware of, or incapable of consciously controlling, their behaviour, voluntarily or involuntarily interferes or threatens to interfere with the bodily integrity of another person.[52]

This confusing provision seems to deem that a person who has become so drunk as to engage in involuntary violence has departed markedly from an at-large standard of reasonable care "generally recognized in Canadian society." This marked departure from the standard of reasonable care is then substituted for the intent required to commit the particular general intent offence charged whether it be assault or sexual assault. This seems to be a legislative reaffirmation of the controversial proposition in *Majewski* and *Leary* that if an accused charged with a general intent offence does not have the necessary *mens rea* at the time that the offence was committed, his actions and mind in voluntarily becoming so intoxicated can be substituted for the *mens rea* required

---

49   *R. v. Cooper* (1979), 51 C.C.C. (2d) 129 (S.C.C.). See ch. 7, "Mental Disorder or Disease of the Mind."

50   *Daviault*, above note 10 at 45.

51   Section 33.1(3) of the *Code*, above note 40, applies only to offences that include "as an element an assault or any other interference or threat of interference by a person with the bodily integrity of another person." An accused could still raise a *Daviault* defence, and be acquitted of a general intent property crime such as mischief.

52   *Code*, ibid., s. 33.1(2).

for the particular offence. The only extra step is that the *Criminal Code* now deems that becoming so intoxicated is a marked departure from "the standard of reasonable care generally recognized in Canadian society." In a sense, what Dickson J. originally criticized in *Leary* as "recklessness at large" has been codified for general intent offences which involve assaults or other interference or threat of interference with bodily integrity. The following chart demonstrates the similarities between the *Leary* rule and section 33.1.

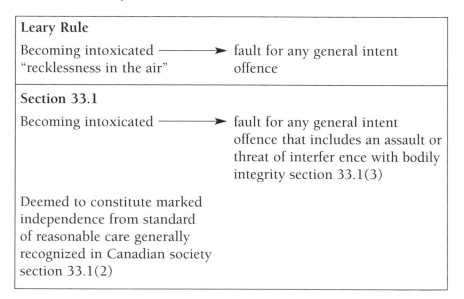

Leary Rule

Becoming intoxicated ──────► fault for any general intent
"recklessness in the air"   offence

Section 33.1

Becoming intoxicated ──────► fault for any general intent
                              offence that includes an assault or
                              threat of interfer ence with bodily
                              integrity section 33.1(3)

Deemed to constitute marked
independence from standard
of reasonable care generally
recognized in Canadian society
section 33.1(2)

3) The Constitutionality of Section 33.1

The Supreme Court's response to this "in your face" reply to *Daviault* is not yet known. It would seem that the fault of becoming extremely intoxicated does not lead inexorably to the intent required for a particular general intent offence. Thus, the provision probably violates section 11(d) of the *Charter* by substituting the fault of becoming intoxicated for the fault of the particular general intent offence. The fact that Parliament has deemed such intoxication as departing from the standard of care generally recognized in Canadian society does not alter the fact that such fault is not the fault that Parliament has required for assault and sexual assault. Unless the Court reverts to Justice Wilson's position in *Daviault* that a person who commits a general intent offence while in an involuntary state produced by self-induced intoxication is not morally innocent, it would also seem that section 33.1 violates section 7 of the *Charter*. Even if a person who become extremely intoxicated is not morally innocent, a person who commits a crime in either a physically or morally involuntary manner would also be protected under section 7 of the *Charter*.[53] Section 33.1 clearly allows a person to be convicted of a crime even though he or she "lacked the general intent or the voluntariness required to commit the offence" and was "incapable of consciously controlling" the behaviour. The Court in both *Daviault* and a number of other non-intoxication cases has confirmed that it would violate the fundamental principles of justice to convict a person for involuntary actions.[54]

When enacting section 33.1, Parliament included a lengthy preamble emphasizing its concern about violence and intoxication. It expressed a particular concern that such "violence has a particularly disadvantaging impact on the equal participation of women and children in society and on the rights of women and children to security of the person and to equal protection and benefit of the law as guaranteed by sections 7, 15, and 28 of the *Canadian Charter of Rights and Freedoms*."[55] Such considerations may be used to urge the Court to view a *Charter* challenge to section 33.1 through a framework of reconciling competing rights, as was done when the Court upheld a law restricting access to the therapeutic records of complainants in sexual assault cases,[56] even though the legislation, like section 33.1, seemed at odds with a previous *Charter* decision of the Court.[57] Such a reconciliation of rights approaches runs the risk of undermining the obligation placed on the state under section 1 of the *Charter* to justify restrictions on rights and of ignoring the extent to which legislation may infringe one of the competing rights including, in this case, the basic principle that a person should not be convicted for involuntary conduct. One judge who has held that section 33.1 was an unjustified violation of sections 7 and 11(d) of the *Charter* has been quite critical of the preamble, concluding that while "victim's rights are, undoubtedly, a component of society's interests but society's interests must also include a system of law, gov-

---

53   *Ruzic*, above note 48.
54   *R. v. Stone*, [1999] 2 S.C.R. 290 at paras. 155–58; *Ruzic, ibid.* at paras. 42–43.
55   The preamble generally speaks more to the importance of the objective rather than to the crucial issue of the proportionality of the means used to advance the objective. It does, however, refer to Parliament sharing with Canadians "the moral view that people who, while in a state of self-induced intoxication, violate the physical integrity of others are blameworthy in relation to their harmful conduct and should be held criminally accountable for it." See *An Act to Amend the Criminal Code (Self-Induced Intoxication)*, S.C. 1995, c. 32 [*Code Amendment*].
56   *R. v. Mills*, [1999] 3 S.C.R. 668.
57   *R. v. O'Connor*, [1995] 4 S.C.R. 1411.

erned by the principles of fundamental justice. . . . The section cannot accurately be said to address victim's section 7 rights; nor does it address any special needs of women or of children; rather, it sets out to protect victims against intoxicated automatons who act violently."[58] Section 33.1 does indeed apply to forms of violence committed by the accused and is not as specifically tailored to the interests of women and children as the legislation restricting access to confidential records in sexual offence cases.

A better approach than attempting to reconcile the rights of the accused and the victim may be to determine whether the infringements of sections 7 and 11(d) of the *Charter* in section 33.1 can be justified under section 1 of the *Charter*. A threshold issue will be whether a violation of section 7 of the *Charter* can ever be saved under section 1 of the *Charter*. The Court has suggested that a violation of section 7 could only be justified in "exceptional circumstances, such as the outbreak of war or a national emergency."[59] Such an approach runs the danger of undermining the structure of the *Charter* that contemplates legislatures being able to place and then justify limits on all *Charter* rights.

The first step in a section 1 analysis would be to determine the objective of section 33.1 and whether it is important enough to justify limitations on the relevant *Charter* rights. Responding to alcohol-induced violence that could result in the complete acquittal of the accused is obviously a compelling objective that could justify the infringement of *Charter* rights. The fundamental question under section 1 of the *Charter* will be whether section 33.1 is a proportionate response to these important objectives.

The Crown will argue that Parliament has adopted a more tailored rule than the previous common law rule. Thus, section 33.1 does not transfer the fault of becoming extremely intoxicated for the *mens rea* or voluntariness of all general intent offences as contemplated under the *Leary* rule, but only for crimes involving violence. Moreover, it will be argued that Parliament's policy decision not to respond to *Daviault* by introducing a new intoxication based crime or treatment disposition deserves more judicial deference than the Court's previous common law rule in *Leary*.[60] It may be assumed that Parliament examined other

---

58   *R. v. Dunn* (1999), 28 C.R. (5th) 295 at 303 (Ont. S.C.J.) [*Dunn*].
59   *Ruzic*, above note 48 at para 92.
60   In *R. v. Swain* (1991), 63 C.C.C. (3d) 481 (S.C.C.), the Supreme Court indicated that "where a common law, judge-made rule is challenged under the *Charter*, there is no room for judicial deference" that can apply when Parliament as an elected body places limits on *Charter* rights.

options such as introducing new intoxication-based crimes, but found them wanting for a variety of reasons including their possible effects on police discretion and plea bargaining and the felt need to label a drunken sexual assaulter or assaulter as a person who nevertheless committed a sexual assault or an assault.[61] Parliament also heard evidence suggesting the alcohol cannot produce involuntary behaviour. This evidence, however, does not relate to other drugs. One judge has dismissed such scientific concerns: "[T]he issue is not whether an accused can scientifically prove [automatism]; the issue is whether it is constitutionally permissible to deny an accused even the opportunity to try to prove it just because his or her intoxication was self-induced. In my opinion, it is not."[62]

The accused will argue that Parliament rejected a number of more proportionate responses when it introduced new legislation that effectively reversed *Daviault* for general intent offences of violence. Section 33.1 follows the minority in *Daviault* and the *Leary* rule by substituting the fault of voluntarily becoming drunk for the fault of the general intent offence. It labels the drunken automaton as guilty of the same crime as the person who consciously committed an assault or sexual assault with the required *mens rea* at the time the offence was committed. It may thus run afoul of the principles that those who cause harm intentionally be punished more severely than those who cause harm unintentionally and that punishment be morally proportionate to the gravity of the offence.[63] There were other ways that Parliament could have advanced its interest in social protection that were more respectful of the accused's rights under sections 7 and 11(d) of the *Charter*. For example, a new intoxication-based crime would recognize that an accused with a *Daviault* defence did not have the voluntariness or *mens rea* required for an assault or a sexual assault even though he committed an act that caused harm and required punishment. It will also be argued that the harm caused by convicting an accused who acted involuntarily and without *mens rea* outweighs the benefits of section 33.1 especially with regard to the dubious proposition of deterring severely intoxicated people from violence and the rarity that an accused will be

---

61   The preamble for example states that Parliament "shares with Canadians the moral view that people who, while in a state of self-induced intoxication, violate the physical integrity of others are blameworthy in relation to their harmful conduct and should be held criminally accountable for it." See *Code Amendment*, above note 55.

62   *R. v. Brenton* (1999), 28 C.R. (5th) 308 at 331 (N.W.T.S.C.) [*Brenton*].

63   *R. v. Creighton* (1993), 83 C.C.C. (3d) 346 (S.C.C.). See ch. 4, "Constitutional Requirements of *Mens Rea*."

so extremely intoxicated as to be able to establish a *Daviault* defence on a balance of probabilities.

The constitutionality of section 33.1 has been considered in a few cases. In *Vickberg*,[64] a trial judge found that section 33.1 violated sections 7 and 11(d) of the *Charter* because it substituted "proof of voluntary intoxication for proof of the intent to commit an offence of general intent, most commonly assault." Nevertheless, these violations were held to be justified under section 1 of the *Charter* as a proportionate means to ensure accountability for violence related with intoxication. In the actual case, however, the trial judge did not apply section 33.1 to convict the accused who committed an assault while in a state of drug-induced automatism. Section 33.1 only substitutes the fault of being intoxicated for the fault of the offence if the intoxication is self-induced. The trial judge found that the accused's intoxication in *Vickberg* (an overdose of drugs prescribed to treat his heroin addiction) constituted involuntary intoxication producing non-mental disorder automatism leading to a verdict of acquittal. This is an interesting finding given that on its face section 33.1 applies to "self-induced intoxication," which arguably could be seen as a broader concept than voluntary intoxication.[65] Although section 33.1 was not struck down as an unconstitutional reversal of *Daviault*, it was also not applied to an accused who committed a general intent offence in a state of drug-induced automatism. Should section 33.1 be held to be constitutional, it will be important that courts, as in *Vickberg*, expand the defence of involuntary intoxication to apply to unanticipated effects of self-induced drugs.[66]

In two subsequent cases, trial judges have found section 33.1 to be unconstitutional. In *Dunn*,[67] the judge stressed the importance of focusing on the objective of limiting the sections 7 and 11(d) rights as articulated in *Daviault*. The judge doubted that the objective of removing the *Daviault* defence for violent general intent offences was important enough to limit the accused's rights, but in any event concluded that the good of convicting such accused did not outweigh the harms of convicting a person who acted in an involuntary manner. "When an

---

64   *Vickberg*, above note 20 at 193.
65   The Court applied *King*, above note 45. As discussed in ch. 7, "Mental Disorder or Disease of the Mind," courts have been reluctant to classify transitory states of intoxication as a mental disorder for the purposes of section 16 of the *Code*.
66   In *Brenton*, above note 62, the court held that unanticipated effects of marijuana consumption did not result in involuntary intoxication. The court, however, found that s. 33.1 was an unjustified violation of the *Charter* and acquitted the accused on the basis of the *Daviault* defence.
67   *Dunn*, above note 58.

accused can be convicted without proof that he intended his actions or without proof that his actions were voluntary, then absolute liability has become a component of Canadian criminal justice, the presumption of innocence is eroded and the principles of fundamental justice are seriously compromised."[68] In *Brenton*,[69] section 33.1 was also struck down with the judge stressing that it "in effect re-enacts as legislation the very same common law rule that was held unconstitutional" in *Daviault*. By eliminating the need to prove either intent or voluntariness at the time the offence was committed, Parliament had created an absolute liability provision and ignored the more proportionate response of enacting a new offence based on the accused's intoxication.

The Supreme Court will ultimately decide the fate of section 33.1. Although it is rare that violations of section 7 of the *Charter* will be held to be justified under section 1 of the *Charter*, it is possible that courts will defer to this strong articulation of legislative will. Section 33.1 is more narrowly tailored than the common law *Leary* rule because it is restricted to general intent crimes of violence. The new legislation deserves a greater margin of deference than the previous judge-made common law rule. The Court may also hold that section 33.1 engages conflicting rights, even though such an approach would overestimate what the section actually accomplishes in convicting the rare accused who will be able to establish intoxicated automatism. The reconciliation of rights approach will also diminish the heavy burden that the Crown should bear in justifying the violation of the accused's sections 7 and 11(d) rights where the result is to convict someone who has acted in an involuntary manner and to base the conviction on the prior and unfocused fault of becoming extremely intoxicated. To uphold section 33.1 would require the Court to back down from its previous and controversial decision in *Daviault*.

F. INTOXICATION AND MISTAKE OF FACT

The relevance of intoxication to claims about mistaken belief in consent in sexual assault cases has been troublesome. In *Leary* and *Bernard*, the Supreme Court affirmed that rape and sexual assault were crimes of general intent for which intoxication would not be relevant. In *R. v. Pappajohn*,[70] the Supreme Court recognized a defence of honest

---

68   *Ibid.* at 307.
69   *Brenton*, above note 62.
70   (1980), 52 C.C.C. (2d) 481 (S.C.C.).

but not necessarily reasonable mistaken belief in consent. In that case, there was evidence that the accused had been drinking and that intoxication may have contributed to his alleged mistake of fact. The relevance of intoxication to the mistake of fact defence was not decided, however, because the majority of the Court held that the jury need not have been instructed about the defence because it lacked an air of reality. Nevertheless, the recognition of a honest but not necessarily reasonable mistake of fact defence based on the subjective perceptions of the accused sits uneasily with the traditional, pre-*Daviault* position that evidence of intoxication would not be relevant when the accused was charged with sexual assault.

In *R. v. Moreau*,[71] the Ontario Court of Appeal dealt with the tensions between *Leary*, which suggested that intoxication was irrelevant to crimes such as rape, and *Pappajohn*, which created the possibility that an accused might have a defence of honest, but not necessarily reasonable, mistake as to whether the woman consented. Martin J.A. held that even though intoxication could contribute to a mistaken belief in consent, for the policy reasons articulated in *Leary*, the trier of fact should be instructed to disregard evidence of intoxication when determining whether the accused had a *Pappajohn* defence of mistake of fact. This position, although criticized as illogical and artificial, has now been reaffirmed by section 273.2(a)(i) of the *Criminal Code*, which provides that an accused's belief in consent to sexual activity is not a defence where it arose from the accused's self-induced intoxication. This provision may qualify section 273.2(b), which provides that the accused's obligation to take reasonable steps to ascertain whether the complainant was consenting is based on the circumstances subjectively known to the accused at the time. The accused may be prevented by statute from arguing that his subjective perceptions of the circumstances were impaired by alcohol. The judge and jury would be required to determine what the accused's perceptions would be had he not been intoxicated. This will be a difficult and artificial task.

It could be argued that this exclusion of intoxication as a basis for a mistake of fact defence violates the accused's right to make full answer and defence and injects objective elements of fault into sexual assault. At the same time, however, section 272(a)(i) follows the traditional law and might be justified if it were permissible to require the accused to satisfy objective elements in the mistake of fact defence. If

---

71   (1986), 26 C.C.C. (3d) 359 (Ont. C.A.). See also *R. v. Murray* (1986), 31 C.C.C. (3d) 323 (N.S. C.A.).

it is permissible to require the accused to take reasonable steps to ascertain consent, it is not a far step to preclude self-induced intoxication as a source for the mistake of fact defence.

G. LIABILITY FOR THE INTOXICATED COMMISSION OF SPECIFIC INTENT OFFENCES

Since *Beard*,[72] it has been possible for an accused to be acquitted of a specific intent offence where evidence of intoxication alone or in combination with other factors produced a reasonable doubt as to whether he or she had the intent required for the offence. The role of the intoxication defence in relation to specific intent offences has not been as controversial as the possibility raised in *Daviault* that extreme intoxication might be a defence to a general intent offence. The practical reason is that an accused acquitted of a specific intent offence because of intoxication will almost always be convicted of a lesser general intent offence. For example, evidence of intoxication could raise a reasonable doubt to the specific intent of murder, but would normally not be considered in determining whether the accused was guilty of the general intent offence of manslaughter. In *George*, the accused was acquitted of the specific intent offence of robbery because of intoxication, but was convicted of assault because his intoxication was not so extreme as to prevent the Crown from proving the minimal intent required for that general intent offence.

Nevertheless, the traditional common law rules allowing the intoxication defence for specific intent offences have not been free from controversy. Like the more controversial *Leary* rule, they have been subject to successful *Charter* challenge.

1) Intent Not Capacity to Commit the Offence

In *Beard*, the House of Lords referred to evidence of intoxication that would render the accused incapable of forming a specific intent. This seems to require the trier of fact to have a reasonable doubt about whether the accused was capable of forming an intent, whereas general *mens rea* principles would suggest that the actual intent, not the capacity for intent, should be the issue. Nevertheless, in a long line of

---

72 *Beard*, above note 2.

cases, Canadian courts followed *Beard* and held that the issue was whether evidence of drunkenness raised a reasonable doubt as to the accused's capacity to form a specific intent.[73]

In *R. v. Robinson*,[74] the Supreme Court held that the *Beard* rules violated sections 7 and 11(d) of the *Charter* because they required the jury to convict even if they had a reasonable doubt about the accused's actual intent. In other words, the Court was concerned that an accused who was not so intoxicated as to lack the capacity to form the intent may nevertheless have not exercised that capacity and formed the specific intent. A conclusion that evidence of intoxication did not raise a reasonable doubt as to the accused's capacity to form the specific intent did not lead inexorably to the conclusion that the Crown had proven beyond a reasonable doubt that the accused had actually exercised that capacity and had the required intent. The *Beard* rule concerning capacity could not be justified under section 1 because social protection could be achieved without casting the net of liability so far as to convict all those who had the capacity to form the requisite intent, but who may nevertheless not have had the intent required for a murder conviction. As in *Daviault*, the Court was less deferential to judge-made common law rules that infringed *Charter* rights than to legislation enacted by Parliament. The Court also noted that the capacity rule was not necessary because the intent rule only reduced the accused's culpability from murder to manslaughter.

After *Robinson*, judges can still instruct the jury to consider the accused's capacity to form the intent if evidence, such as expert evidence, was directed to the issue of capacity. Nevertheless, a judge who instructs on capacity has an onerous obligation to make sure that at the end of the day the jury understands that the ultimate issue is whether evidence of intoxication raised a reasonable doubt as to the accused's actual intent and not his or her capacity to form the intent. A new trial will be ordered if the jury is misled into thinking that the accused's capacity to form that intent was the ultimate issue because this could result in convicting an accused even though there might still be a reasonable doubt as to his or her actual intent.[75]

To make matters even more complex, capacity as opposed to actual intent still seems to be the issue when the accused is charged with a

---

73   *R. v. MacAskill* (1931), 55 C.C.C. 81 at 84 (S.C.C.); *Leary*, above note 12 at 482–84; *Bernard*, above note 7 at 26.

74   (1996), 105 C.C.C. (3d) 97 (S.C.C.) [*Robinson*].

75   See, e.g., *R. v. McMaster* (1996), 105 C.C.C. (3d) 193 (S.C.C.).

general intent offence. In *Daviault*,[76] the Supreme Court stated that "'drunkenness akin to insanity or automatism' describes a person so severely intoxicated that he is *incapable* of forming even the minimal intent required of a general intent offence." The focus in *Daviault* is on the accused's capacity to form the minimal intent required for general intent offences as determined by expert evidence. The Court has yet to address whether its focus on intent in the specific intent case of *Robinson* alters its focus on capacity in the general intent case of *Daviault*. Given the nature of the extreme intoxication defence and the requirement that the accused prove the defence with expert evidence, the courts may accept that capacity is the ultimate issue for general intent offences, whereas intent is the ultimate issue for specific intent offences.

2) Threshold Air of Reality Tests

In cases involving either general or specific intent offences, the accused must establish that there is an air of reality that justifies instructing the trier of fact about the intoxication defence. Threshold air of reality tests are designed to ensure that the jury is not instructed about irrelevant defences. They have not generally be seen as presenting presumption of innocence problems. Nevertheless, they can keep the jury from considering defences such as mistake of fact, intoxication, and necessity and they may play an important role in the criminal trial.

With respect to murder, the threshold test is whether "the evidence of drunkenness was sufficient to permit a reasonable inference that the accused may not in fact have foreseen that his act of firing the gun at the deceased would cause her death."[77] This threshold was not satisfied in the murder case of *Lemky* where an accused with a blood alcohol level slightly above the legal limit for driving was capable before and after the shooting of being aware of the consequences of his actions and who argued at trial that his shooting of the deceased was not done without *mens rea*, but was the result of an accident. With respect to specific intent offences, at least, the evidential threshold is directed to

---

76 *Daviault*, above note 10 at 67 [emphasis added].

77 *R. v. Lemky* (1996), 105 C.C.C. (3d) 137 at 144 (S.C.C.). In *Robinson*, above note 74 at 116, the Court articulated the threshold standard in a seemingly less restrictive manner by stating that the trial judge must instruct the jury concerning intoxication if "the effect of the intoxication was such that its effect *might* have impaired the accused's foresight of consequences sufficient to raise a reasonable doubt" [emphasis in original].

the issue of actual intent and not capacity. With respect to the *Daviault* test of extreme intoxication to a general intent offence, the threshold issue should be the capacity to have the minimal intent associated with general intent offences as opposed to the actual intent. A recent case on automatism suggests that a judge should focus on whether a properly instructed jury could reasonably acquit on the evidence. The judge should not determine the credibility of the evidence or hold the defence from the jury on the basis that the accused may not be able to establish the defence on a balance of probabilities.[78]

CONCLUSION

The Canadian law concerning intoxication is not only intensely controversial, but complex. There are four different ways in which intoxication can operate as a "defence" or more accurately prevent proof of the required fault for various criminal offences. The first and simplest is that evidence of intoxication can raise a reasonable doubt as to whether the accused had the intent required for a specific intent offence such as murder or robbery. The issue is the accused's actual intent, not whether intoxication impaired the accused's capacity to form the required intent.[79] The only difficult issues may be whether a particular offence will be classified as a specific intent offence that requires an intent directed at some purpose beyond the immediate action and whether there is an air of reality to justify instructing the jury about this defence.

The second intoxication defence is the rare defence of involuntary intoxication. It could apply to prevent the conviction of a person charged with a general intent offence who involuntarily becomes intoxicated and commits a criminal act,[80] as well as to a specific intent offence. It seems to be based on the logic that if the fault of becoming voluntarily intoxicated can supply or be substituted for the fault for the particular offence, then a person who becomes intoxicated through no fault of his or her own should not be held culpable. In other words, the substitution of the fault of becoming intoxicated for the fault of the particular offence should not occur if the accused was without fault in becoming intoxicated — for example, if someone spiked his drink or gave him

---

78   See *R. v. Fontaine* 2004 SCC 27 discussed in chs. 1 and 7.

79   *Robinson*, above note 74.

80   *King*, above note 45; *Vickberg*, above note 20.

medication without adequate warnings. Some judges have expanded the defence of involuntary intoxication to encompass totally unanticipated reactions to drugs,[81] but others have been more cautious.[82]

The third intoxication defence is the *Daviault* defence of extreme intoxication to general intent offences that do not include an element of an assault or any other interference or threat of interference with of the bodily integrity of another person.[83] The accused must establish the *Daviault* defence of extreme intoxication to a general intent crime on a balance of probabilities and with expert evidence. The issue seems to be whether the accused was capable of forming the minimal intent required for general intent offences and not whether the accused actually had that intent, as in the case with the first intoxication defence to specific intent offences. The *Daviault* defence only exists unimpeded by legislation when the accused is charged with a general intent offence such as mischief to property that does not involve an assault or threat of violence.[84] If the accused establishes the *Daviault* defence to such a general intent crime on a balance of probabilities, he or she will be acquitted. The *Daviault* defence does not apply to crimes that require intoxication as an element of the offence because such a defence would be inconsistent with the mischief of the offence.[85]

The fourth and most controversial intoxication defence is when the accused raises a *Daviault* defence to a violent general intent offence such as manslaughter, assault, or sexual assault. The Supreme Court's decision in *Daviault* suggests that it would violate the accused's rights under sections 7 and 11(d) of the *Charter* to convict a person who was so extremely intoxicated at the time of the criminal act that he or she acted involuntarily and without the minimal intent required for a general intent offence. Parliament's reply to *Daviault* in section 33.1 of the *Criminal Code*, however, adds legislative support to the traditional rule in *Leary*. Section 33.1 substitutes the fault of becoming extremely intoxicated for the fault of committing the general intent crime of violence, even though the accused may have acted involuntarily at the time the assault occurs. It remains to be seen whether the Supreme Court will find that section 33.1 can be upheld under the *Charter*.

---

81   *Vickberg, ibid.*

82   *Brenton*, above note 62.

83   *Code*, above note 40, s. 33.1(3).

84   *Ibid.*

85   *Penno*, above note 45, *Finta* above note 48, *Ruzic*, above note 48, *Canadian Foundation for Children*, above note 48. But see *King*, above note 45, recognizing involuntary intoxication as a defence to impaired driving.

On the one hand, the substitution of the fault of becoming intoxicated for the fault of committing the general intent offence offends principles that require fault to be related to the *actus reus* and to overlap in time with the *actus reus*. As suggested by Justice Wilson in *Bernard*, this is mainly a substitution problem under section 11(d). In *Daviault*, the Supreme Court also held that basing the fault of sexual assault on the fault of becoming extremely intoxicated also violated section 7 of the *Charter* by punishing an accused who had no *mens rea* at the time of the act. Although courts frequently accept violations of the presumption of innocence under section 11(d) as reasonable limits, they have been reluctant to accept violations of section 7 under section 1 of the *Charter*. The section 1 defence will likely focus on the fact that substitution of the fault of becoming extremely intoxicated for the fault of the particular offence is restricted under section 33.1 to general intent crimes of violence.

The time may have passed for general reforms that would abolish the much criticized distinction between general and specific intent offences and allow intoxication as a defence to all offences that require subjective *mens rea*. Such reform proposals were usually accompanied by proposals for the introduction of separate intoxication-based offences. After *Daviault*, there was reluctance to introduce new intoxication-based offences, in part because of a concern that a person who commits assault or sexual assault while intoxicated should still be labelled as an assaulter or sexual assaulter, and in part because of concerns about the impact of broad intoxication-based offences on the discretion of police and prosecutors in laying and reducing charges. There is no easy solution to the many dilemmas produced by the various intoxication defences and the most important immediate issue is whether section 33.1, restricted as it is to general intent offences of violence, will survive a *Charter* challenge.

FURTHER READINGS

COLVIN, E., *Principles of Criminal Law*, 2d ed. (Toronto: Carswell, 1991), ch. 8

"Criminal Reports Forum on Daviault" (1994) 33 C.R. (4th) 269

GRANT, I., "Second Chances: Bill C-72 and the *Charter*" (1996) 33 Osgoode Hall L.J. 379

HEALY, P., "Intoxication and the Codification of Canadian Criminal Law" (1994) 73 Can. Bar Rev. 515

HEALY, P. "*Beard* Still Not Cut Off" (1996) 46 C.R. (4th) 65

MEWETT, A., & M. MANNING, *Criminal Law*, 3d ed. (Toronto: Butterworths, 1994), ch. 12

QUIGLEY, T., "Reform of the Intoxication Defence" (1987) 33 McGill L.J. 1

SHAFFER, M., "R. v. *Daviault*: A Principled Approach to Drunkenness or a Lapse of Common Sense?" (1996) 3 Rev. Constitutional Studies 311

SMITH, K., "Section 33.1: Denial of the *Daviault* Defence should be held Constitutional" (2000) 28 C.R.(5th) 350.

STUART, D., *Canadian Criminal Law: A Treatise*, 4th ed. (Toronto: Carswell, 2001), ch. 6

MENTAL DISORDER AND AUTOMATISM

Like intoxication, the defences of mental disorder and automatism apply to accused who commit criminal acts, but who cannot be found criminally responsible because their mental processes were impaired. It has long been accepted that an offender who, because of a mental disorder, is incapable of appreciating the nature and quality of a criminal act, or of knowing that it is wrong, should not be convicted. The verdict is not a pure acquittal, but rather a verdict of not criminally responsible on account of mental disorder or what used to be called not guilty by reason of insanity. The accused does not automatically go free and can be subject to detention or release with conditions until he or she is determined no longer to be a significant danger to society. In Canada, the mental disorder defence is set out in section 16 of the *Criminal Code*, and has been revised by both the Supreme Court and Parliament to take into account various *Charter* concerns.

The defence of automatism is more novel, and applies to an accused who has committed a criminal act while in a state of impaired consciousness that results in involuntary behaviour. If that state is caused by a mental disorder, the accused will be held not criminally responsible by reason of mental disorder. If the cause of the automatism is some other factor such as a blow to the head, an extraordinary psychological shock, or a condition such as sleepwalking, the present disposition is to acquit the accused. The defence of non-mental disorder automatism is a common law defence that is not codified.

Section 16(3) of the *Criminal Code* requires that the mental disorder defence be established on a balance of probabilities and the Supreme Court has also required the accused to establish the defences of both drunken and non-mental disorder automatism on a balance of probabilities.[1]

A. PROCEDURAL CONSIDERATIONS IN THE MENTAL DISORDER DEFENCE

1) Unfitness to Stand Trial

The mental disorder defence applies to an accused who, at the time that the criminal act was committed, suffered from a mental disorder that made him or her incapable of appreciating the nature or quality of the act or omission or of knowing that it was wrong. It is possible that a person who suffered from a mental disorder at the time of the crime will continue to suffer from that condition and be found unfit to stand trial. Conversely, a person who was sane when the crime was committed might subsequently suffer a severe mental disorder that would make it unfair to have a trial. Section 672.23(1) allows the court on its own motion, or on an application from the accused or the prosecutor, to determine whether an accused is fit to be tried. A person is unfit to stand trial if he or she is:

> unable on account of mental disorder to conduct a defence at any stage of the proceedings before a verdict is rendered or to instruct counsel to do so, and, in particular, unable on account of mental disorder to
> (a) understand the nature or object of the proceedings,
> (b) understand the possible consequences of the proceedings, or
> (c) communicate with counsel.[2]

The accused is presumed to be fit to stand trial, and unfitness must be proven on a balance of probabilities.[3] It is not necessary that a person

---

1   *R. v. Daviault* (1994), 93 C.C.C. (3d) 21 (S.C.C.); *R. v. Stone* (1999), 134 C.C.C. (3d) 353 (S.C.C.) [*Stone*].

2   *Criminal Code of Canada*, R.S.C. 1985, c. C-46, s. 2 [*Code*].

3   *Code*, above note 2, ss. 672.22 and 672.23. The burden placed on the accused when the accused argues unfitness to stand trial has been held to be justified under the *Charter. R. v. Morrissey* (2002), 8 C.R. (6th) 41 (Ont. S.C.J.). As will be seen, similar burdens on the accused to establish the mental disorder and automatism defences have also been held to be justified under the *Charter*.

be able to act in his or her own best interests or to employ analytical reasoning, but it is necessary that he or she have "limited cognitive capacity to understand the process and to communicate with counsel."[4] A person who satisfies these minimal standards may still be found at trial to have a mental disorder defence.

A person found unfit to stand trial is subject to the same disposition hearing as a person found not criminally responsible because of a mental disorder. The difference, however, is that where an accused is found unfit to stand trial, the Crown may not have proven beyond a reasonable doubt that the accused committed the criminal act. For this reason, judges have the power to postpone the determination of fitness until the Crown has made its case and the accused has been found not to be entitled to an acquittal or a discharge. If the accused is found unfit to stand trial, the Crown is required to establish a *prima facie* case against the accused every two years until the accused is either found fit to be tried or is acquitted because the Crown cannot establish a *prima facie* case.[5] These safeguards are designed to ensure that a factually innocent accused is not subject to detention in the same manner as an accused who committed the criminal act, but was found not guilty by reason of a mental disorder.

2) Who Can Raise the Mental Disorder Defence?

Canadian courts have been more willing than British or American courts to allow the prosecutor to raise the mental disorder defence. The rationale is that society has an interest in not convicting an accused who may not be responsible because of a mental disorder, but who has chosen not to advance the insanity defence. This latitude presents dangers that 1) the Crown could bolster a weak case by presenting evidence of the accused's mental disorder, and 2) an accused could be exposed to indeterminate detention as a person found not guilty on grounds of mental disorder when he or she wishes either to plead guilty or to contest his or her innocence.

In *R. v. Swain*,[6] the Supreme Court found that the common law practice of allowing the Crown to raise the insanity defence violated the accused's right under section 7 of the *Charter* to control his or her own defence. Lamer C.J. stated:

---

4   *R. v. Whittle* (1994), 92 C.C.C. (3d) 11 at 25 (S.C.C.).

5   *Code*, above note 2, s. 672.33. The unavailability of an absolute discharge for a permanently unfit accused who does note pose a significant threat to society violates s.7 of the *Charter. R. v. Demers* 2004 SCC 46.

6   (1991), 63 C.C.C. (3d) 481 (S.C.C.) [*Swain*].

The mere fact that the Crown is able to raise a defence which the accused does not wish to raise, and thereby to trigger a special verdict which the accused does not wish to trigger, means that the accused has lost a degree of control over the conduct of his or her defence.[7]

The Court concluded that the principles of fundamental justice generally would allow the Crown to raise the insanity defence only after the accused had otherwise been found guilty. A permissible exception is that the Crown can raise the insanity defence in rebuttal if the accused has placed his or her capacity for criminal intent in issue. For example, if the accused raised a defence of non-mental disorder automatism, the Crown could then raise the defence of mental disorder and introduce evidence to indicate that section 16 of the *Code* should apply and the verdict should be not criminally responsible on account of mental disorder. An accused who argued that he or she went into a state of automatism because of a severe emotional blow may find the Crown arguing that the cause of the automatism was a mental disorder and that the appropriate disposition is further detention and treatment, not a complete acquittal.[8] It is even possible that the court will determine that there is no air of reality to the non-mental disorder automatism defence and only the mental disorder defence will be left for the jury to consider.[9]

3) Burden of Proof

Sections 16(2) and 16(3) of the *Criminal Code* provide that every person is presumed not to suffer from a mental disorder so as to be exempt from criminal responsibility and that the party who raises this issue must prove it on the balance of probabilities. In *R. v. Chaulk*,[10] the Supreme Court found that the requirement that an accused prove the defence of insanity on a balance of probabilities violated the presumption of innocence under section 11(d) of the *Charter*, because it allowed the conviction of an accused in spite of a reasonable doubt as to a factor essential to guilt, namely sanity. Lamer C.J. reasoned:

> Whether the claim of insanity is characterized as a denial of *mens rea*, an excusing defence or, more generally, as an exemption based on

---

7   *Ibid.* at 506.

8   See, e.g., *R. v. K.* (1970), 3 C.C.C. (3d) 84 (Ont. H.C.J.) [*K.*]; *R. v. Rabey* (1977), 37 C.C.C. (2d) 461 (Ont. C.A.), aff'd (1980), 54 C.C.C. (2d) 1 (S.C.C.) [*Rabey*], discussed below.

9   See, e.g., *Stone*, above note 1, discussed below.

10   (1990), 62 C.C.C. (3d) 193 (S.C.C.) [*Chaulk*].

criminal incapacity, the fact remains that sanity is essential for guilt. [The section] allows a factor which is essential for guilt to be presumed, rather than proven by the Crown beyond a reasonable doubt. Moreover, it requires an accused to disprove sanity (or prove insanity) on a balance of probabilities; it therefore violates the presumption of innocence because it permits a conviction in spite of a reasonable doubt in the mind of the trier of fact as to the guilt of the accused.[11]

The Chief Justice went on, however, to find that the statutory requirement that an accused prove the insanity defence on a balance of probabilities was justified under section 1 of the *Charter* because of the difficulties that the Crown would have proving beyond a reasonable doubt that an accused was sane. Wilson J. dissented and held that, as in some American jurisdictions, once the accused produced some evidence of insanity, the prosecutor should bear the burden of proving beyond a reasonable doubt that the insanity defence did not apply.

The Court did not consider the burden of proof if the prosecutor raises the mental disorder defence. Section 16(3) suggests that the prosecutor, like the accused, would have to prove the defence on a balance of probabilities. Normally, however, the prosecutor must prove its case against the accused beyond a reasonable doubt. Given this general principle and the fact that the prosecutor would only be required to establish a mental disorder defence against an accused who did not wish to rely on such a defence, it would be best if the prosecutor was required to establish a mental disorder defence by proof beyond a reasonable doubt.

4) Disposition of an Accused Acquitted by Reason of Mental Disorder

An accused acquitted on grounds of insanity used to be subject to automatic indeterminate detention at the pleasure of the Lieutenant Governor in Council. In practice, this meant detention until a review board determined that release was in the accused's interests and not contrary to the public interest. In *Swain*,[12] the Supreme Court held that such automatic detention without a hearing and with no criteria to authorize detention violated the accused's rights under sections 7 and 9 of the *Charter*. That case raised the issue because the accused, who did not wish to plead insanity as a defence, was found to have been insane at

---

11   *Ibid.* at 213.
12   *Swain*, above note 6.

the time of the crime, but had successfully been treated with anti-psychotic drugs at the time of sentencing. Lamer C.J. noted, however, that some automatic detention and delay following an acquittal by reason of insanity is a "practical reality," because the evidence of insanity at trial relates to the mental condition of the accused at the time of the offence and not the accused's "present mental condition and dangerousness."[13]

Amendments to the *Criminal Code* in the wake of Swain now instruct the court to hold, if possible, a disposition hearing for the accused when the accused is found unfit to stand trial or not criminally responsible on account of mental disorder.[14] In any event, a review board of a judge and two mental health professionals is required to hold such a hearing "as soon as is practicable but not later than forty-five days after the verdict was rendered."[15] At the disposition hearing, the court or review board is instructed to discharge the accused absolutely if "the accused is not a significant threat to the safety of the public."[16] The Supreme Court has interpreted this provision to require an absolute discharge unless the court or review board finds that release would present a significant risk to the safety of the public by the commission of a crime that presents a real risk of physical or psychological harm that is not merely trivial or annoying.[17]

If an absolute discharge is not warranted, the court or review board is instructed under section 672.54 to make the disposition "that is the least onerous and least restrictive to the accused," considering "the need to protect the public from dangerous persons, the mental condition of the accused, the reintegration of the accused into society and the other needs of the accused."[18] The Supreme Court has stressed that there is no presumption that a person found not criminally responsible by reason of mental disorder is dangerous.Courts or review boards no longer are faced with the draconian disposition of automatic indeterminate detention and should impose the least restrictive conditions compatible with public safety.[19] There is no burden or onus of proof on either the accused or the Crown. The court or review board may consider and seek evidence from a broad range of sources. The Supreme

---

13   *Ibid.* at 539.
14   *Code*, above note 2, s. 672.45.
15   *Ibid.*, s. 672.47(1).
16   *Ibid.*, s. 672.54(a).
17   *Winko v. British Columbia (Forensic Psychiatric Institute)* (1999), 135 C.C.C. (3d) 129 (S.C.C.) [*Winko*].
18   *Code*, above note 2, s. 672.54.
19   *Penetanguishene Mental Health Centre v. Ontario (Attorney General)* 2004 SCC 20.

Court also found that this scheme does not violate sections 7 and 15 of the *Charter* in large part because it avoids stereotypical assumptions about those who suffer a mental disorder and requires individual assessment of each and every person found not criminally responsible by reason of mental disorder and unconditional release if they do not present a significant threat to the safety of the public.[20] Continued detention or conditions placed on those found not criminally responsible by reason of mental disorder are subject to yearly reviews by the review board.[21] There are provisions in the *Criminal Code* not yet proclaimed in force which would cap the ultimate period of time a person could be detained, or could be subject to conditions, based on the seriousness of the offence charged.[22] At the same time, other unproclaimed provisions would also allow the Crown to apply to have a person declared a dangerous mentally disordered accused, subject to a disposition cap of life.[23]

B. THE *M'NAGHTEN* RULES AND THEIR CODIFICATION

The substantive rules governing the insanity or mental disorder defence are derived from the 1843 decision of the House of Lords in *M'Naghten's Case*.[24] In that case, the accused was found by a jury to be not guilty by reason of insanity of murdering the prime minister's secretary. He suffered from delusions of persecution from the government. Subsequent controversy led to a reference to the House of Lords, which affirmed the availability of the insanity defence if it was "clearly proved that, at the time of the committing of the act, the party accused was labouring under such a defect of reason, from disease of the mind, as not to know the nature and quality of the act he was doing, or, if did know it, that he did not know he was doing what was wrong."[25] The House of Lords added that an accused suffering from delusions should have his responsibility determined on the basis that the delusions were real. Thus, an accused who killed another, supposing himself under

---

20 *Winko*, above note 17.
21 *Code*, above note 2, s. 672.81(1).
22 *Ibid.*, s. 672.64.
23 *Ibid.*, s. 672.65.
24 (1843), 8 E.R. 718 (H.L.).
25 *Ibid.* at 722.

deadly attack, may not be responsible, but one imagining only an injury to his character would be guilty of murder.[26]

In 1892 the *M'Naghten* rules were embodied in the *Criminal Code* of Canada with some variations. A person was defined as legally insane if he or she laboured "in a state of natural imbecility or disease of the mind, to such an extent as to render him incapable of appreciating the nature and quality of an act or omission or knowing that an act or omission was wrong." This introduced the idea that an accused would have an insanity defence if he or she did not "appreciate," as opposed to "know," the nature and quality of the act. An error in the 1927 revisions to the *Criminal Code* required the accused to be incapable of both appreciating the nature and quality of the act and of knowing that it was wrong. This was soon corrected as a misreading of the disjunctive *M'Naghten* rules.[27] Thus, either a failure to appreciate the nature and quality of the criminal act or to know that it was wrong will suffice to ground the mental disorder defence.

In 1992 the insanity defence was renamed the mental disorder defence, and the verdict of not guilty by reason of insanity was renamed the verdict of not criminally responsible by reason of mental disorder. The mental disorder defence now provides:

> No person is criminally responsible for an act committed or an omission made while suffering from a mental disorder that rendered the person incapable of appreciating the nature and quality of the act or omission or of knowing that it was wrong.[28]

This provision indicates more clearly that the accused must have committed the act or omission charged, but other changes are more cosmetic. Section 2 of the *Criminal Code* defines mental disorder as a disease of the mind, preserving the old jurisprudence on that issue. Section 16(1) preserves the traditional two-prong test that allows the defence on the basis that 1) a mental disorder "rendered the person incapable of appreciating the nature and quality of the act or omission," or 2) a mental disorder "rendered the person incapable . . . of knowing that it was wrong." The most significant changes in the 1992

---

26   This provision was codified in Canada until its repeal. S.C. 1991, c. 43, s. 2. Delusions would now be considered with reference to whether the accused was able to appreciate the nature and quality of the act or was able to know that it was wrong. See *R. v. Landry* (1991), 62 C.C.C. (3d) 117 (S.C.C.) [*Landry*]; *R. v. Oommen* (1994), 91 C.C.C. (3d) 8 (S.C.C.) [*Oommen*], discussed below for two cases considering mental disorder defences based on the accused's delusions.

27   *R. v. Cracknell* (1931), 56 C.C.C. 190 (Ont. C.A.).

28   *Code*, above note 2, s. 16(1).

amendments related not to the substantive defence, but rather to the abolition of automatic indeterminate detention as discussed above. For example, the 1992 amendments did not embrace American reforms that attempt to broaden the insanity defence so that it applied to crimes that were a product of mental disorder or to offenders whose mental disorder made them unable to obey the law.

C. MENTAL DISORDER OR DISEASE OF THE MIND

In order for the defence to apply, an accused must suffer from a disease of the mind or a mental disorder. A person who is unable to appreciate the nature and quality of an act or is incapable of knowing that the act is wrong, but does not suffer from a mental disorder, will not qualify for the defence.[29] However, holding that a person suffers from a mental disorder is not sufficient. The condition must be severe enough to render the person incapable of appreciating the nature and quality of the act, or incapable of knowing that it was wrong.

1) Policy Considerations

The categories of disease of the mind have expanded since 1843 when the *M'Naghten* rules were first defined. Judicial interpretation of what constitutes a disease of the mind will be influenced by medical developments, but it remains a question of law for the courts to define, and may involve policy considerations not known to the discipline of psychiatry. These policy concerns relate to concerns about how wide the mental disorder defence should be and the need to protect the public "by the control and treatment of persons who have caused serious harms while in a mentally disordered or disturbed state."[30] The Supreme Court in *Stone* has stated that it is open to trial judges to find new policy considerations to influence their interpretation of what constitutes a disease of the mind. "Policy concerns assist trial judges in answering the fundamental question of mixed law and fact which is at the centre of the disease of the mind inquiry: whether society requires protection from the accused and, consequently, whether the accused

---

29   As will be discussed below, they may have the common law defence of non-mental disorder automatism.

30   *Rabey*, above note 8.

should be subject to evaluation under the regime contained in Part XX.1 of the Code."[31] The Court in that case endorsed a "holistic" approach to determining disease of the mind that includes an open-ended list of policy factors, as well as other factors such as whether the accused presents a continuing danger and whether his or her conduct can be explained by an internal as opposed to an external cause.

2) Continuing Danger and Internal Causes

A disease of the mind has often been defined in relation to whether there is a continuing danger to the public,[32] or whether the disturbance is related to an internal cause stemming from the psychological make-up of the accused as opposed to an external factor.[33] LaForest J. has warned against exclusive reliance on either the continuing danger or the internal cause theories, but has noted that they are united in their common concern for recurrence. In his view, however, even "recurrence is but one of a number of factors to be considered in the policy phase of the disease of the mind inquiry," and "the absence of a danger of recurrence will not automatically exclude the possibility of a finding of insanity."[34] Nevertheless, the danger of recurrence does seem to be the most important policy factor in determining whether a particular condition constitutes a disease of the mind. It is related to concerns about both the need to protect public safety and to treat and rehabilitate the accused.

In *Stone*,[35] the Supreme Court confirmed that the existence of a continuing danger or an internal cause are legitimate and non-mutually exclusive factors indicating that the accused may suffer from a mental disorder. The psychiatric history of the accused and the likelihood of the recurrence of violence or the stimulus that triggered violence in the past are important considerations in determining whether the accused is a continuing danger. "The greater the anticipated frequency of the trigger in the accused's life, the greater the risk posed to the public and, consequently, the more likely it is that the condition alleged by the accused is a disease of the mind."[36] Thus, an accused who goes into

---

31   *Stone*, above note 1 at 441.
32   *Bratty v. A.G. for Northern Ireland* (1961), [1963] A.C. 386 (H.L.).
33   *R. v. Quick*, [1973] 3 All E.R. 347 (C.A.) [*Quick*]; *Rabey*, above note 8.
34   *R. v. Parks* (1992), 75 C.C.C. (3d) 287 at 310 (S.C.C.) [*Parks*]; *Stone*, above note 1 at 438. See also *R. v. Sullivan* (1983), [1984] A.G. 156 (H.L.) [*Sullivan*].
35   *Ibid.*
36   *Ibid.* at 440.

an automatic state[37] and assaults or kills another because of ordinary teasing or nagging is more likely to be classified as having a disease of the mind than a person who goes into an automatic state after a rare stimulus such as seeing a loved one assaulted or killed. At the same time, the Court warned that the absence of a continuing danger does not preclude a finding of a mental disorder or a disease of the mind.

The existence of an internal cause will be most relevant in cases of psychological blow automatism discussed later in this chapter. An internal cause may reveal itself when the accused goes into an automatic state when faced with something less than "an extremely shocking trigger"[38] that would send "a normal person" in similar circumstances into an automatic state. Comparing how the accused reacted with how a normal person would have acted in similar circumstances is motivated by concerns about public safety when an accused responds atypically and violently to what may be the ordinary stresses and disappointments of life. There may be cases where a focus on internal causes is not helpful and the accused will be found not to suffer from a mental disorder even though there might be an internal cause to his or her actions. As will be discussed below, sleepwalking may be an internal cause of automatic behaviour, but it may not be classified as a disease of the mind. Conversely, a person might be classified as having a disease of the mind even though there is no apparent internal cause.

The existence of either a continuing danger or an internal cause are simply factors which suggest that the accused may have a mental disorder. The absence of these factors does not mean that for other policy reasons concerning the need to protect the public by potentially indeterminate detention or conditions placed on a person found not criminally responsible by reason of mental disorder that an accused will not be classified as having a disease of the mind. In a fundamental sense, the definition of whether a person has a mental disorder or disease of the mind is driven by policy and public safety concerns about the ultimate disposition of the accused.

---

37 It is assumed that such a state will be definition produce a situation in which the accused is incapable of appreciating the nature and quality of his or her actions or knowing that they are wrong. The crucial issue in determining whether the mental disorder defence applies or not will be determining whether the accused suffers from a mental disorder or disease of the mind.

38 *Stone*, above note 1 at 436.

3) The *Cooper* Definition

In *R. v. Cooper*,[39] Dickson J. defined disease of the mind as:

> any illness, disorder or abnormal condition which impairs the human mind and its functioning, excluding however, self-induced states caused by alcohol or drugs, as well as transitory mental states such as hysteria or concussion.

This is a broad definition of disease of the mind that includes all medically recognized disorders except those in which transitory disturbances are caused by external factors such as drugs. Psychopathic personalities[40] or personality disorders[41] have been recognized as diseases of the mind. Brain damage and severe mental disability may also be considered diseases of the mind.[42] *Delirium tremens*, or deterioration of the brain cells produced by chronic alcoholism, and toxic psychosis produced by extended drug use have also been recognized as diseases of the mind.[43] Thus, alcohol or drug use will generally only fall under the mental disorder defence when it produces a permanent condition as opposed to temporary intoxication.

The Supreme Court has held that sleepwalking is not a disease of the mind, so that a person rendered unconscious by this condition was entitled to a complete acquittal, rather than possible detention as a person found not guilty by reason of insanity.[44] This suggests that even though a condition might fall within the broad contours of an illness or abnormal condition that impairs the human mind, it will not necessarily be classified as a disease of the mind.

4) Disease of the Mind and Transitory States

The House of Lords in *Beard* suggested that "if actual insanity in fact supervenes, as the result of alcoholic excess, it furnishes as complete an

---

39   (1979), 51 C.C.C. (2d) 129 at 144 (S.C.C.) [*Cooper*].

40   *R. v. Simpson* (1977), 35 C.C.C. (2d) 337 (Ont. C.A.) [*Simpson*].

41   *Rabey*, above note 8.

42   *R. v. Revelle* (1979), 48 C.C.C. (2d) 267 (Ont. C.A.) aff'd (1981), 21 C.R. (3d) 225 (S.C.C.) [*Revelle*]; *R. v. R.(M.S.)* (1996), 112 C.C.C. (3d) 406 (Ont. Gen. Div.).

43   *R. v. Malcolm* (1989), 50 C.C.C. (3d) 172 (Man. C.A.); *R. v. Mailloux* (1985), 25 C.C.C. (3d) 171 (Ont. C.A.), aff'd (1988), 45 C.C.C. (3d) 193 (S.C.C.).

44   *Parks*, above note 33. The Court based this decision on the evidence presented in the particular case, and suggested that it could reconsider its decision on different evidence.

answer to a criminal charge as insanity induced by any other cause."[45] On the other hand, the *Cooper* definition excludes self-induced states caused by alcohol and other drugs as a disease of the mind. In his dissent in *Daviault*, Sopinka J. argued that extreme intoxication should not be considered a disease of the mind, because those who voluntarily become intoxicated and commit a crime should be punished, not treated.[46] The majority in that case contemplated a complete acquittal and not a mental disorder defence for an accused who committed a crime while in a state of automatism caused by voluntarily induced intoxication. It thus appears that transitory states of even extreme intoxication will not qualify as a disease of the mind but that chronic conditions produced by drug abuse may qualify as a disease of the mind.[47]

The *Cooper* definition of disease of the mind also excludes "transitory mental states such as hysteria or concussion." Those subject to a one-time mental disturbance because of external factors such as a blow to a head or an extraordinary trauma should probably not be subject to potential indeterminate detention or conditions as a person found not criminally responsible on account of a mental disorder. However, this more intrusive disposition may be appropriate when the accused's inability to appreciate the nature and quality of the acts or to know that they are wrong is caused by a "malfunctioning of the mind arising from some cause that is primarily internal to the accused, having its source in his psychological or emotional make-up, or in some organic pathology, as opposed to a malfunctioning of the mind which is the transient effect produced by some external factor such as, for example, concussion."[48] In *Rabey*, a disassociative state produced by the accused's disappointment at being romantically rejected was found to have been derived from internal factors within the accused that could constitute a disease of the mind. However, if the accused had been subjected to "extraordinary external events" such as being involved in a serious accident, escaping a murderous attack, or seeing a loved one killed, then a disassociative state could perhaps be explained "without reference to the subjective make-up of the person exposed to such experience."[49] In such a case, the disassociation would not be likely to recur, because of the extraordinary nature of the external factor. As such, it would be unduly intrusive to subject the accused to possible detention

---

45   *D.P.P. v. Beard*, [1920] A.C. 479 at 500 (H.L.).
46   *Daviault*, above note 1 at 45–46. The majority did not deal with this issue.
47   *Ibid.*, above note 42.
48   *Rabey*, above note 8 at 477–78.
49   *Ibid.* at 482–83.

and treatment as a person found not criminally responsible on account of mental disorder.

5) Disease of the Mind and Organic Conditions

A focus on factors internal to the accused has led English courts to conclude that various conditions that are not commonly considered mental disorders are nevertheless diseases of the mind for the purpose of the insanity defence. For example, epilepsy has been found to constitute a disease of the mind,[50] as has arteriosclerosis.[51] The focus on internal factors has produced strange results where diabetics are concerned. If the accused takes insulin and does not eat, the resulting disassociative state has been held not to be a disease of the mind, because it was caused "by an external factor and not by a bodily disorder in the nature of a disease which disturbed the working of the mind."[52] If, however, a diabetic goes into a disassociative state because he or she has not taken insulin, then the resulting condition is a disease of the mind because it is caused by the internal factor of the accused's diabetes.[53] In such cases, it would be better not to focus on whether the cause of the state was internal or external, but whether it was likely to recur and to present a continuing danger.

The Supreme Court's holistic approach to categorizing a disease of the mind suggests that a focus on whether the cause was internal can and should be dispensed with in those cases in which it will produce an absurd result not necessary for public safety. In *Parks*,[54] sleepwalking was not classified as a disease of the mind even though it could be seen as an organic or hereditary condition internal to the accused. Canadian courts should not classify organic conditions such as epilepsy or diabetes as diseases of the mind simply because they are internal causes that explain the accused's behaviour. The ultimate issue should be whether the public requires protection through potentially indeterminate conditions or detention imposed on those found not criminally responsible on account of mental disorder. In a case subsequent to *Parks*, however, a trial judge held that sleepwalking should be considered a mental disorder under the holistic *Stone* test because it was a matter internal to the accused, it was not triggered by specific external

---

50   R. v. O'Brien, [1966] 3 C.C.C. 288 (N.B.C.A.) [O'Brien]; Sullivan, above note 34.
51   R. v. Kemp (1956), [1957] 1 Q.B. 399.
52   Quick, above note 33.
53   R. v. Hennessy, [1989] 2 All E.R. 9 (C.A.) [Hennessy].
54   Parks, above note 34.

stimuli and there was a continuing danger to the public from a risk of reoccurence.[55] This case certainly underlines the tension between the Court's decision in *Parks* that sleepwalking was not a mental disorder and its more open-ended and holistic approach to defining a mental disorder in *Stone*.

D. CAPACITY TO APPRECIATE THE NATURE AND QUALITY OF THE ACT

Even if the accused is held to suffer from a mental disorder or disease of the mind, he or she must qualify under one of the two arms of the mental disorder defence. Canadian courts have stressed that section 16 of the *Criminal Code* refers to an inability to *appreciate* the nature and quality of acts, as opposed to the *M'Naghten* rules, which refer to an inability to *know* the nature and quality of the act. The ability to appreciate the nature and quality of an act involves more than knowledge or cognition that the act is being committed. It includes the capacity to measure and foresee the consequences of the conduct. In *Cooper*, Dickson J. stated:

> The requirement, unique to Canada, is that of perception, an ability to perceive the consequences, impact, and results of a physical act. An accused may be aware of the physical character of his action (i.e., in choking) without necessarily having the capacity to appreciate that, in nature and quality, the act will result in the death of a human being.[56]

An accused who is unable to appreciate the physical consequences of his or her actions because of a mental disorder will have a valid section 16 defence. In a murder case, this also mirrors the *mens rea* requirement that the accused subjectively know that his or her actions would cause death. Of course, a successful section 16 defence could result in a disposition far more intrusive than an acquittal in a murder case.

The courts have not expanded the defence to apply to those who, because of mental disorder, were unable emotionally to appreciate the effect of their actions on the victim. In *Simpson*,[57] Martin J.A. stated that the defence did not apply to an accused:

---

55   *Canada v. Campbell* (2000), 35 C.R. (5th) 314 (Ont. S.C.J.).
56   *Cooper*, above note 39 at 147.
57   *Simpson*, above note 40 at 355.

who has the necessary understanding of the nature, character and consequences of the act, but merely lacks appropriate feelings for the victim or lacks feelings of remorse or guilt for what he has done, even though such lack of feeling stems from "disease of the mind." Appreciation of the nature and quality of the act does not import a requirement that the act be accompanied by appropriate feeling about the effect of the act on other people. . . . No doubt the absence of such feelings is a common characteristic of many persons who engage in repeated and serious criminal conduct.

An inability to appreciate that a victim may die can result in a mental disorder defence. An inability to have appropriate emotions about the death of another person, however, does not result in a section 16 defence, even if it is an indication of a mental disorder such as a psychopathic personality.

The courts have also held that an inability to appreciate the penal consequences of an act does not render an accused incapable of appreciating the physical consequences of the act. In *R. v. Abbey*,[58] the accused believed that he was protected by an external force from punishment for importing narcotics. The Supreme Court held that the trial judge had erred in law "in holding that a person who by reason of disease of the mind does not 'appreciate' the penal consequences of his actions is insane."

In *Landry*,[59] the Supreme Court rejected the Quebec Court of Appeal's conclusion that an accused who killed while under the delusion that he was God, and the victim, Satan, did not appreciate the nature and circumstances of the act. Lamer C.J. reasoned that the prior precedents had clearly established that an accused would have an insanity defence only if a mental disorder prevented him from appreciating the physical, as opposed to the moral, consequences of the act. He also added that the Court of Appeal had erred in holding that section 7 of the *Charter* required it "to modify the established interpretation of this statutory provision."[60] As will be seen below, however, the majority of the Supreme Court affirmed the verdict of not guilty by reason of insanity on the alternative basis that the accused's severe psychosis and resulting delusion rendered him incapable of knowing that the killing was wrong. It is important to be sensitive to how the two alternative arms of the mental disorder defence interact.

---

58 (1982), 68 C.C.C. (2d) 394 at 405–6 (S.C.C.) [*Abbey*].
59 *Landry*, above note 26.
60 *Ibid.* at 124.

E. CAPACITY TO KNOW THAT THE ACT IS WRONG

Section 16(1) of the *Criminal Code* provides two alternative arms or formulations of the mental disorder defence. The first, discussed above, applies when a mental disorder renders the accused incapable of appreciating the physical consequences of the act. The second is when the disease of the mind renders the accused incapable of knowing that the act was wrong.

In *R. v. Schwartz*,[61] the Supreme Court divided 5 to 4, with the majority holding that an accused must be unable to know that an act was legally wrong. Martland J. for the majority concluded that the test "is not as to whether the accused, by reason of mental disease, could or could not calmly consider whether or not the crime which he committed was morally wrong. He is not to be considered as insane . . . if he knew what he was doing and also knew that he was committing a criminal act."[62] Dickson J. in his dissent seemed more concerned with giving the insanity defence a generous reading. He noted that Parliament had chosen in section 16 to use the word "wrong," which could refer to either legal or moral wrong. In most cases, there would be no practical difference, but he was concerned about a case in which an accused was capable of knowing that his or her acts were illegal, but was not capable of knowing they were morally wrong. He cited the example of an accused who knew that it was legally wrong to kill, but did so believing that his killing followed a divine order and therefore was not morally wrong. Dickson J. held that the reference to wrong in section 16 should be interpreted to mean morally wrong. In his view, this broader definition would not give the amoral offender a defence, because the incapacity to know that an act was morally wrong must stem from a disease of the mind and indicate a complete loss of the "ability to make moral distinctions."[63]

In *Chaulk*,[64] the Supreme Court reversed *Schwartz* and concluded that accused should have an insanity defence if, because of a disease of the mind, they were incapable of knowing that an act was morally wrong, even if they were capable of knowing that the act was legally wrong. Lamer C.J. argued for the majority that this broader reading of the insanity defence:

---

61 (1977), 29 C.C.C. (2d) 1 (S.C.C.).
62 *Ibid.* at 12.
63 *Ibid.* at 22.
64 *Chaulk*, above note 10.

will not open the floodgates to amoral offenders or to offenders who relieve themselves of all moral considerations. First, the incapacity to make moral judgments must be causally linked to a disease of the mind. . . . Secondly, as was pointed out by Dickson J. in *Schwartz, supra*, "'moral wrong' is not to be judged by the personal standards of the offender but by his awareness that society regards the act as wrong.' " . . . The accused will not benefit from substituting his own moral code for that of society. Instead, he will be protected by s. 16(2) if he is incapable of understanding that the act is wrong according to the ordinary moral standards of reasonable members of society.[65]

This distinction between the accused's own moral code and his or her ability to know society's moral standards may be difficult to draw in some cases. In *Chaulk*, the accused were young boys suffering from a paranoid psychosis that made them believe that they had the power to rule the world and that killing was necessary. It was clear that they did not have a defence under *Schwartz*, because they knew that killing was illegal. Unfortunately, the Supreme Court did not rule on the crucial issue of whether their belief that the law was irrelevant to them constituted an inability to know that what they did was morally wrong in the eyes of society.[66]

A subsequent case suggested that the insanity defence would not apply to a "psychopath or a person following a deviant moral code" if such a person "is capable of knowing that his or her acts are wrong in the eyes of society, and despite such knowledge, chooses to commit them."[67] The insanity defence will also not apply if the act was motivated by a delusion but the accused was still capable of knowing "that the act in the particular circumstances would have been morally condemned by reasonable members of society."[68] It will also not apply if the accused understands society's views about right and wrong but, because of a delusion, choses to do the wrong thing.[69]

The Supreme Court applied the new moral wrong standard in *Landry*,[70] when it concluded that the accused had an insanity defence because his disease of the mind produced a delusion that he was God killing Satan. This condition rendered him "incapable of knowing that the act was morally wrong in the circumstances." The Court was pre-

---

65   *Ibid.* at 232–33.
66   The insanity defence did succeed at their subsequent trial.
67   *Oommen*, above note 26 at 19.
68   *R. v. Ratti* (1991), 62 C.C.C. (3d) 105 at 113 (S.C.C.) [emphasis in original].
69   *R. v. W.(J.M.)* (1998), 123 C.C.C. (3d) 245 (B.C.C.A.).
70   *Landry*, above note 26 at 124.

sumably satisfied that the mental disorder was so severe that the accused was not capable of knowing that society would consider the killing immoral. In *Oommen*,[71] the Supreme Court indicated that an accused, even though he was generally capable of knowing that killing was wrong, could have an insanity defence if his paranoid delusion "at the time of the act deprived him of the capacity for rational perception and hence rational choice about the rightness or wrongness of the act." The focus is on the accused's capacity for rational choice about the particular criminal act at the time the act was committed, not his or her general intellectual ability to know right from wrong.

F. IRRESISTIBLE IMPULSE

Canadian courts have long refused to recognize irresistible impulse as a separate category of the insanity defence. At the same time, however, evidence of an irresistible impulse, like evidence of delusions, may be relevant in determining whether an accused otherwise qualifies for the mental disorder defence.[72]

G. EFFECT OF A MENTAL DISTURBANCE SHORT OF INSANITY ON *MENS REA*

Evidence of a mental disorder may fall short of establishing a mental disorder defence, but may raise a reasonable doubt as to whether the accused had a subjective mental element required for a particular offence. The insanity defence focuses on capacity and has to be proven on a balance of probabilities, whereas the mental element focuses on actual intent and is rebutted by any evidence that raises a reasonable doubt. Thus, it should not be surprising that evidence of mental disturbance, short of establishing a full section 16 defence, could still raise a reasonable doubt about some forms of *mens rea*.

In *R. v. Baltzer*,[73] Macdonald J.A. reasoned that in order to determine what was in the accused's mind, the jury must have evidence of the accused's "whole personality and background including evidence of any mental illness or disorder that he may have suffered from at the

---

71   *Oommen*, above note 26 at 18.
72   *Abbey*, above note 58; *Chaulk*, above note 10.
73   (1974), 27 C.C.C. (2d) 118 at 141 (N.S.C.A.).

material time." It is an error of law for a judge to instruct the jury to disregard evidence of mental disorder if the defence of insanity fails.[74] All the evidence, including that of mental disorder, should be considered in determining whether the accused had the requisite intent. The higher the degree of *mens rea*, the more likely it is that mental disorder may raise a reasonable doubt about the particular intent. For example, evidence of mental disorder short of establishing the insanity defence may raise a reasonable doubt as to whether murder was planned and deliberate.[75]

Some judges have confused the relevance of evidence of mental disturbance to the determination of *mens rea* with the separate issue of Parliament's choice not to create a defence of diminished responsibility to reduce a killing from murder to manslaughter.[76] Although there is no defence of diminished responsibility in Canadian criminal law, the growing consensus is that evidence of mental disturbance or illness should be considered when determining whether the accused had the required *mens rea*. Such evidence may prevent the Crown from proving that the accused had the subjective foresight of death required for a murder conviction. In such a case, an accused could be acquitted of murder, but could still be found to have the *mens rea* necessary for manslaughter. This would occur through ordinary *mens rea* principles and not through the recognition of a separate defence of diminished responsibility.

H. AUTOMATISM

Automatism is a legal term that refers to unconscious or involuntary behaviour. The Supreme Court has defined automatism as "unconscious, involuntary behaviour, the state of a person who, though capable of action, is not conscious of what he is doing. It means an unconscious, involuntary act, where the mind does not go with what is being done."[77] More recently, the Court has noted that an accused acting as an automaton may not necessarily be actually unconscious, but that his or her consciousness must be so impaired that he or she "has

---

74 *R. v. Allard* (1990) 57 C.C.C. (3d) 397 (Que. C.A.); *R. v. Jacquard* (1997), 113 C.C.C. (3d) 1 (S.C.C.) [*Jacquard*].

75 *Jacquard*, ibid. at 14; *R. v. McMartin* (1964), [1965] 1 C.C.C. 142 (S.C.C.); *More v. R.*, [1963] 3 C.C.C. 289 (S.C.C.).

76 This is a defence in England. *Homicide Act*, 1957 (U.K.), c. 11, s. 2.

77 *Rabey*, above note 8 at 6.

no voluntary control over that action."[78] Those who act while sleep-walking or in a dazed condition from a concussion are examples of those who may be acting in an automatic state.

1) Relation to Mental Disorder and Consequences of an Automatism Defence

Automatism is related to the mental disorder defence because both involve conditions in which the accused cannot be held criminally responsible for his or her actions owing to a lack of mental capacity. If an accused leads evidence of automatism, the Crown can counter with evidence that the cause of the automatism was a mental disorder. Because an accused who acts in an automatic state will generally satisfy either arm of the mental disorder defence, the crucial issue in automatism cases is whether the cause of the automatism is a mental disorder or some other factor. If it is established that the cause of the automatism is a disease of the mind, the accused is held not criminally responsible by reason of a mental disorder and is subject to a disposition hearing and potential indeterminate detention or conditions as outlined above in relation to the mental disorder defence.

If the accused's automatism is not caused by a mental disorder, however, then the verdict is a simple acquittal. In *R. v. Bleta*,[79] the Supreme Court affirmed the acquittal of an accused who, while in a dazed condition following a severe blow to his head, killed another person. The Court concluded that "the question of whether or not an accused person was in a state of automatism so as not to be legally responsible at the time when he committed the acts with which he is charged, is a question of fact"[80] for the jury. In *Parks*[81] an accused successfully raised a defence of automatism after he stabbed two people, killing one of them. The cause of his automatism was sleepwalking, and the Supreme Court found this condition, on the evidence presented to it, not to be a disease of the mind. The accused was acquitted and was not subject to a disposition hearing or any form of treatment. Lamer C.J. expressed concerns about setting the accused "free without any consideration of measures to protect the public, or indeed the accused himself, from the possibility of a repetition of such unfortunate

---

78   *Stone*, above note 1 at 417.
79   (1964), [1965] 1 C.C.C. 1 (S.C.C.) [*Bleta*].
80   *Ibid.* at 58.
81   *Parks*, above note 34.

occurrences."[82] The majority of the Court held, however, that in the absence of a verdict of not criminally responsible on account of mental disorder, the courts did not have jurisdiction to make preventive orders. The Supreme Court has also speculated that "anger conceivably could, in extreme circumstances, cause someone to enter a state of automatism in which that person does not know what he or she is doing, thus negating the voluntary component of the *actus reus*."[83] In such a circumstance, the Court noted that the appropriate disposition would be an acquittal. The possiblity that the accused's state of automatism may negate either the voluntary commission of the prohibited act or the required fault element makes it even more anomalous that, as will be discussed below, the accused has the burden of establishing the defence of automatism on a balance of probabilities.[84]

Federal proposals to amend the *Criminal Code*, made in 1993 but not implemented, would have made an accused acquitted on the basis of non-insane automatism subject to the same disposition hearing and possible conditions or detention as a person held not criminally responsible by reason of mental disorder. If enacted, it would have for all practical purposes eliminated the present distinction between a defence of mental disorder or non-mental disorder automatism by eliminating the different dispositions for the two defences. As will be seen, the Supreme Court subsequently in *Stone*[85] narrowed the distance between the two defences by requiring the accused to establish the defence of non-mental disorder automatism on a balance of probabilities and by indicating that automatism will be presumed to be caused by mental disorder unless the accused establishes otherwise. Nevertheless, non-mental disorder automatism still results in an acquittal.

2) Evidential and Persuasive Burdens of Proof

As late as 1992, the Supreme Court held that an accused who raised a defence of non-insane automatism was entitled to an acquittal if the evidence presented at trial raised a reasonable doubt as to whether the accused acted in a voluntary or conscious manner.[86] This was because

---

82   *Ibid.* at 299.
83   *R. v. Parent* (2001), 154 C.C.C.(3d) 1 at para. 10 (S.C.C.).
84   *Stone*, above note 1.
85   *Ibid.*
86   *Parks*, above note 34. The accused would have had an evidential burden to point to some evidence in the case which makes automatism a viable issue, but not a persuasive burden.

such evidence would raise a reasonable doubt as to whether the accused acted with the required fault element (including the capacity to live up to an objective fault element) or, alternatively, whether the accused consciously and voluntarily committed the *actus reus*.

In the 1999 case of *Stone*,[87] however, the Supreme Court held that an accused claiming a non-mental disorder defence of automatism must establish on a balance of probabilities that he or she acted in an involuntary manner. The majority of the Court was concerned that an automatism defence might easily be faked under the traditional law that allowed the defence to go to the jury so long as the accused pointed to some evidence, that if believed, would raise a reasonable doubt about the voluntariness of his or her actions. The Court was also concerned about consistency in allocating burdens of proof given that the accused had the onus to establish on a balance of probabilities the *Daviault* defence of extreme intoxication producing a state akin to automatism and the mental disorder defence under section 16(3) of the *Criminal Code*.

The Court in *Stone* also concluded that the new persuasive burden on the accused to establish the automatism defence on a balance of probabilities also influenced the threshold decision by trial judges about whether there was a sufficient air of reality to justify instructing the jury about the defence. On the facts in *Stone*, the Court held that a trial judge was justified in not instructing the jury on the defence of non-mental disorder automatism because there was no "evidence upon which a properly instructed jury could find that the accused acted involuntarily on a balance of probabilities."[88] The Court indicated that even to satisfy this threshold air of reality burden, the accused will not only have to assert involuntariness, but also produce collaborating psychiatric evidence. Even these two factors will not necessarily suffice. Other relevant factors that should be considered include the severity of the triggering stimulus, the corroborating evidence of bystanders, the corroborating evidence of the accused being in states of automatism at other times, whether there was a motive for the crime, and whether the alleged trigger of automatism was also the victim of the crime. Finally, if the crime could be explained without reference to automatism, this suggested that the automatism defence should not be put to the jury. The Court not only imposed a novel persuasive burden on the accused to establish non-mental disorder automatism, but raised the evidential burden considerably.

---

87   Above note 1.
88   *Ibid.* at 426.

In a strong dissent joined by three other members of the Court, Binnie J. noted the virtues of the traditional law in giving the accused the benefit of a reasonable doubt about the voluntariness of his or her actions. He persuasively argued that the majority's decision on the threshold air of reality test would deprive the accused of having claims of non-insane automatism considered by the jury. *Stone* indeed suggested a stringent test that may significantly reduce the number of claims of non-mental disorder automatism that are considered by the jury especially in cases in which the accused argues that he or she went into an automatic state because of an emotional blow.

In *R. v. Fontaine*,[89] the Supreme Court qualified *Stone* as it relates to the evidential air of reality burden but not the persuasive burden on the accused to establish automatism. Fish J. stated for an unanimous Court that "there is language in *Stone* that may be understood to invite an assessment by the trial judge as to the likely success of the defence. This in turn, may be seen to require the judge to weigh the evidence in order to determine whether it establishes, on a balance of probabilities, that the accused perpetrated the criminal act charged in a state of automatism." The Court, however, held that a trial judge who followed such an approach erred and that the factors set out in *Stone* were better used to guiding the trier of fact in deciding whether the automatism defence had been established on a balance of probabilities. A trial judge should not weigh evidence or judge its credibility in deciding whether there is an air of reality that justifies leaving the defence to the jury. The question should rather be whether there is "in the record any evidence upon which a reasonable trier of fact, properly instructed in law and acting judicially, could conclude that the defence succeeds."[90] The Court

---

89   2004 SCC 27 at para. 63.

90   *Ibid.* at para. 57. Note, however, that other parts of this judgment suggest that the fact that the accused has to establish automatism on a balance of probabilities may still influence the threshold air of reality decision. Fish J. stated: "In the case of 'reverse onus' defences, such as mental disorder automatism, it is the accused who bears both the persuasive and the evidential burdens. Here the persuasive burden is discharged by evidence on the balance of probabilities, a lesser standard than proof beyond a reasonable doubt. Reverse onus defences will therefore go to the jury where there is any evidence upon which a properly instructed jury, acting judicially, could reasonably conclude *that the defence has been established in accordance with this lesser standard.*" *Ibid.* at para. 54 [emphasis added]. The rest of the judgment, however, stresses the need to apply a consistent air of reality test to all defences regardless of whether the accused has a persuasive burden to establish the defence on a balance of probabilities or whether the Crown has to prove beyond a reasonable doubt that the defence does not exist.

stressed that judges should not lightly deny the accused an opportunity to have a jury consider the defence. In this case, the Court determined that the jury should have been instructed about the defence of mental disorder automatism. The accused gave detailed evidence that he acted in an involuntary manner and did not simply assert that the defence existed in law. A psychiatrist also testified that the accused was suffering from a psychotic episode induced by substance abuse and was "seeing things" when he shot the victim. *Fontaine* lowers the evidential burden in *Stone* but leaves intact *Stone*'s assignment of a persuasive burden on the accused to establish the defence of non-mental disorder automatism on a balance of probabilities.

If the accused or the Crown raises a defence of mental disorder automatism, then, under section 16(3) of the *Criminal Code*, that party must prove on a balance of probabilities that the accused suffers from a mental disorder and that this condition rendered the accused incapable of appreciating the physical consequences of his actions or of knowing that they were morally wrong. The jury can be left with a choice between mental disorder and non-mental disorder automatism if, for example, the accused places his or her capacity for the mental element in issue by claiming non-insane automatism, and the Crown argues that the cause of any automatism is a mental disorder.[91] After the Court's decision in *Stone*, however, it will be more difficult for the accused to satisfy the threshold evidentiary burden to have the jury instructed about non-mental disorder automatism. As in *Stone* and in *Fontaine*, the judge may frequently be justified in only leaving the defence of mental disorder automatism to the jury. In such cases, a jury which accepts that the accused committed the crime will only be left with the options of a guilty verdict, or if it finds the crime was committed while the accused was in an automatic state, a verdict of not criminally responsible on account of mental disorder.

3) Automatism and Sleepwalking

An early American case recognized that sleepwalking could produce a defence of non-insane automatism because the "law only punishes for overt acts done by responsible moral agents. If the prisoner was unconscious when he killed the deceased, he cannot be punished for that act." An unconscious accused could not be held guilty for killing a person who tried to rouse him from a deep sleep even if the accused had

---

91 See, e.g., *K.*, above note 8.

committed "a grave breach of social duty in going to sleep in the public room of a hotel with a deadly weapon on his person."[92]

In *Parks*,[93] the Supreme Court upheld the acquittal of a man who drove 23 kilometres to his in-laws' house and attacked them with a knife, fatally wounding one of them. The jury had obviously concluded that the accused was acting in an involuntarily or unconscious manner at the time of the attacks. Lamer C.J. concluded that the trial judge had acted properly in not instructing the jury on the defence of insanity because there was uncontradicted evidence that "sleepwalking is not a neurological, psychiatric, or other illness," but rather a sleep disorder from which "there is no medical treatment as such, apart from good health practices, especially as regards sleep."[94] The Supreme Court's definition of a disease of the mind in *Parks* does not follow English law which somewhat mechanically assesses sleepwalking, like epilepsy, as a disease of the mind because it is a cause that is internal to the accused.[95] The Supreme Court stressed medical issues in *Parks*, not policy issues concerning whether the accused's condition was prone to recur or presented a danger to the public. However, the Court left open the possibility that, on different evidence, sleepwalking could be held to be a disease of the mind. The Court's decision in *Stone* does not overrule *Parks*, but it does encourage judges to use policy concerns about the need to protect the public as a factor in concluding that the accused suffers from a disease of the mind. Indeed, in one case subsequent to *Stone*, the trial judge held that sleepwalking was a mental disorder because it was a factor internal to the accused that was not triggered by specific external factors and because of the risk of reoccurrence and public danger. The trial judge also expressed a greater confidence about holding that sleepwalking is a mental disorder because of reforms to the disposition of those found not criminally responsible because of mental disorder that require the least restrictive conditions be placed on a person found not criminally responsible because of a mental disorder.[96]

---

92   *Fain v. Commonwealth of Kentucky*, 78 Ky. Rptr. 183 at 189 and 193 (C.A. 1879).
93   *Parks*, above note 34.
94   *Ibid.* at 297.
95   *R. v. Burgess*, [1991] 2 Q.B. 92 (C.A.).
96   *Canada v. Campbell* (2000), 35 C.R. (5th) 314 (Ont. S.C.J.).

4) Automatism and Emotional Blows

In *Rabey*,[97] the Supreme Court considered whether an accused who committed a criminal act while in an automatic state caused by an emotional or psychological blow should have a defence of insane or non-insane automatism. The majority, following Martin J.A. in the Ontario Court of Appeal, decided that an accused would only have a defence of non-insane automatism if he or she went into an automatic state because of an "extraordinary event" such as being in a serious accident or seeing a loved one killed. Such an event "might reasonably be presumed to affect the average normal person without reference to the subjective make-up of the person exposed to such experience." The accused, who assaulted a fellow student a day after learning that she was not romantically interested in him, was held not to have a defence of non-insane automatism. The Court determined that the accused was only being exposed to "the ordinary stresses and disappointments of life which are the common lot of mankind."[98] If he had gone into an automatic state, the defence would have to be insane automatism because his "disassociative state must be considered as having its source primarily in the respondent's psychological or emotional make-up."[99]

Dickson J. dissented in *Rabey* on the basis that the medical evidence in the case suggested that the accused did not suffer from psychosis, neurosis, personality disorder, or an organic disease of the brain and that his violence "was an isolated event" and "the prospect of recurrence of disassociation is extremely remote."[100] In its reliance on medical evidence, this dissent bears some resemblance to the Supreme Court's decision in *Parks*. Dickson J. also objected to placing an objective threshold on when an emotional blow should be allowed as a basis for a defence of non-insane automatism. He stressed that "the fact that other people would not have reacted as [Rabey] did should not obscure the reality that the external psychological blow did cause a loss of consciousness."[101] He noted that in the case of a physical as opposed to a psychological blow, the only issue would be whether the particular accused, not a reasonable person, went into a disassociative state.[102]

---

97 *Rabey*, above note 8 at 7.
98 *Ibid.*
99 *Ibid.*
100 *Ibid.* at 27.
101 *Ibid.* at 29.
102 See, e.g., *Bleta*, above note 79.

In *Stone*,[103] the Supreme Court followed *Rabey* in holding that a trial judge did not err by refusing to instruct the jury about the defence of non-mental disorder automatism in a case in which an accused, after being provoked by his wife's verbal insults, felt a "whoosh sensation" and stabbed her forty-seven times before disposing of her body and fleeing to a foreign country. The Court indicated that trial judges should start from the proposition that involuntary and automatic behaviour was caused by a disease of the mind. They should only instruct the jury about non-insane automatism if there was confirming psychiatric evidence that established an air of reality for the defence of non-mental disorder automatism.[104] The Court held that the requirement in *Rabey* that the trigger of the involuntary conduct be an extraordinary event that could send a "normal person" in similar circumstances into an automatic state did not violate sections 7 and 11(d) of the *Charter*. The majority reasoned that the objective standard only affected the classification of the defence as mental disorder or non-mental disorder automatism and not whether the Crown had proven that the accused had voluntarily committed the offence as a matter relating to proof of the *actus reus* or the *mens rea*. This distinction is a fine and somewhat artificial one given that 1) the presumption of innocence applies to defences as well as to elements of the offence, 2) the different dispositions for the two automatism defences, and 3) the Court's novel imposition of a persuasive burden on the accused to establish automatism on a balance of probabilities. In any event, *Stone* reaffirms that the definition of disease of the mind, and the characterization of automatism as insane or non-insane, is driven by policy concerns about the ultimate disposition of the accused. Even if, as in *Rabey* and *Stone*, a psychiatrist would not agree that the accused suffered from a mental disorder, courts are reluctant to hold that an accused who responds violently but perhaps involuntarily to non-extraordinary emotional blows should receive the complete acquittal that follows a verdict of non-mental disorder automatism.

Justice Binnie's dissent in *Stone* followed Justice Dickson's dissent in *Rabey* in stressing that there was no medical evidence before the court that the accused was suffering from a mental disorder and arguing that the accused had a right to have his defence of non-mental disorder automatism considered by the jury. Both judges were confident

---

103 *Stone*, above note 1.

104 As discussed above, the evidential burden on the accused was onerous and reflected a new persuasive burden that the accused must establish a defence of non-mental disorder automatism on a balance of probabilities.

that juries would reject frivolous and untruthful claims of non-insane automatism. Binnie J. also strongly argued against the majority's decision to require the accused to prove the defence of non-mental disorder automatism on a balance of probabilities. He was concerned that the Court's decision would deprive the accused of the traditional right to be acquitted if there was a reasonable doubt as to whether he or she acted in a voluntary manner.

5) Automatism and Organic Conditions

As discussed above, accused suffering from conditions such as epilepsy, diabetes, or sleepwalking have been held by English courts to have a disease of the mind. Even if their condition caused them to act in an automatic state and there was little or no need for possible indeterminate detention, their defence has been limited to insanity.[105] These results have most often been justified with reference to a conclusion that the automatic state was the product of a cause internal to the accused. These English cases should not be followed under the holistic Canadian approach to defining a disease of the mind. The existence of an internal cause that explains why the accused acted in an involuntary or automatic state is, at most, only one factor in determining whether the accused should be classified by the courts as having a mental disorder or disease of the mind.

If courts focus on the likelihood of recurrence, continuing danger, or the efficacy of medical treatment, then there seems to be little reason to subject a diabetic or an epileptic to potentially indeterminate detention or conditions because he or she harmed another while in an automatic state. Significantly, these more functional factors rather than the internal cause theory was stressed in *Parks* in order to conclude that sleepwalking was not a disease of the mind. In *Stone*,[106] the Supreme Court indicated that whether automatic conduct was caused by an internal cause is only one factor in a holistic test to determine whether there is a disease of the mind. A focus on internal causes can and should be discarded when it would not accord with the underlying policy concerns, most importantly the need to protect the public through potentially indeterminate detention or conditions that can be applied following a not criminally responsible by reason of mental disorder verdict. If there were not sufficient reasons to impose such potentially drastic restraints on the sleepwalker in *Parks*, there would seem

---

105 *O'Brien*, above note 50; *Sullivan*, above note 34; *Hennessy*, above note 53.
106 *Stone*, above note 1 at 438.

to be even less of a need to impose such restraints on an epileptic or a diabetic who harms another while in a state of automatism. A finding to the contrary might well be based on a stereotyped presumption of dangerousness that would be inconsistent with the need to provide equal benefit of the law without discrimination on the basis of physical disability.

6) Automatism and Intoxication

Before *Daviault*,[107] courts were reluctant to allow the defence of non-insane automatism to go to the jury when the accused's mental condition was a product of voluntary intoxication. In *Revelle*,[108] the Supreme Court upheld a decision of Martin J.A. that concluded:

> It is well established that if automatism is produced solely by drunkenness only the defence of drunkenness, which is limited to crimes of specific intent, need be left to the jury.

An accused who became voluntarily intoxicated to the state of automatism could use this condition to raise a reasonable doubt to a specific intent offence such as murder, but such self-induced automatism could not be used as a defence to a general intent offence such as manslaughter.

As discussed in chapter 6, the Supreme Court's decision in *Daviault* opened the possibility that a voluntarily intoxicated accused could be acquitted of a general intent offence if he or she established, on a balance of probabilities, that the intoxication was severe enough to produce an unconscious condition similar to automatism or insanity. Long before *Daviault*, the Supreme Court seemed prepared to consider that involuntary intoxication might produce a state of automatism that could be a defence to any criminal offence. In *R. v. King*,[109] an accused drove while still under the influence of a drug given to him by his dentist. In his concurring judgment, Taschereau J. came close to recognizing a defence of non-insane automatism when he stated "there can be no *actus reus* unless it is the result of a willing mind at liberty to make a definite choice or decision, or in other words, there must be a willpower to do an act."[110] An accused who acted in an automatic state because of *involuntary* intoxication would still have a defence that could lead to an acquittal of a general intent offence such as impaired

---

107 *Daviault*, above note 1.
108 *Revelle*, above note 42.
109 (1962), 133 C.C.C. 1 (S.C.C.).
110 *Ibid.* at 3.

driving. Unlike in *King*, however, the accused would now have to establish the automatism defence on a balance of probabilities. The scenario is more complex and less certain for an accused who acted in an automatic state because of *voluntary* intoxication. *Daviault* itself would suggest the defence could be established by the accused on a balance of probabilities, but section 33.1 of the *Criminal Code* may deny the offence when the general intent offence involves an assault or threat of interference with bodily integrity.[111]

CONCLUSION

The classification of diseases of the mind has been the most dynamic and uncertain feature of the law defining the defences of mental disorder and automatism. In *Parks*,[112] the Supreme Court held that sleepwalking was not a disease of the mind and indicated that the proper verdict, if the jury found that the accused had acted in an involuntary state, was an acquittal. This remains the law today with the important exception that the accused would now have the burden of establishing his defence of non-mental disorder automatism on a balance of probabilities. In *Stone*,[113] the Supreme Court not only imposed a burden on the accused of establishing an automatism defence on a balance of probabilities, but also followed *Rabey*[114] by indicating that only extraordinary emotional blows that would cause an average person to go into a disassociative state would produce a defence of non-mental disorder automatism and its consequent verdict of acquittal. In all but the most extraordinary cases, an emotional blow producing an automatic state will result in a verdict of not criminally responsible by reason of mental disorder, even if the accused was not diagnosed by a psychiatrist with a mental disorder. In contrast to its earlier decision in *Parks*, the Court in *Stone* has significantly restricted the defence of non-insane automatism and has made it much less likely that the jury will ever get to consider such a defence. This is unfortunate because there was no evidence that the defence was being abused in the period between *Parks* and *Stone*.

The only virtue of *Stone* is its recognition of a holistic and policy-driven approach to defining a disease of the mind. In this, the Court

---

111 The constitutionality of s. 33.1 is examined in ch. 6, "Intoxication."
112 *Parks*, above note 34.
113 *Stone*, above note 1.
114 *Rabey*, above note 8.

has been consistent with *Parks* and wisely avoided the absurd results that English courts, given their exclusive reliance on internal cause theories, have produced in cases holding that sleepwalkers, epileptics, and diabetics who act while in an automatic state should be forced into the insanity defence. Canadian courts will only use the presence of internal causes as a factor in determining disease of the mind and may, as in *Parks*, depart from reliance on that factor if it does not accord with the overall policy objectives of using the mental disorder defence to protect the public.

The exact contours of the two alternative arms of the section 16 defence are relatively settled. The Court has limited the reference to a mental disorder producing an inability to appreciate the consequences of actions to physical consequences as opposed to emotional or penal consequences. The Court is understandably concerned that the mental disorder defence not be expanded so far as to apply to psychopaths who lack empathy for victims and foresight of penal consequences.

Less clear are the exact contours of the accused being incapable of knowing that his or her acts were morally wrong. In *Chaulk*,[115] the Court indicated that the accused could not benefit by substituting his or her own moral code for that of society. Except in extreme cases such as *Landry*,[116] it is not always easy to distinguish the accused's own moral code from his or her ability to know what society generally regards as wrong. The reference in *Oommen*[117] to the defence applying if the accused did not have a capacity for rational perception and choice about the rightness or wrongness of the act does not clarify matters or respond to the danger of expanding the defence so far as to apply to psychopaths who assert their own moral code over society's. If the psychopath is capable of discerning society's moral code but decides to follow his or her own deviant moral code, the mental disorder defence should not apply.

---

115 *Chaulk*, above note 10.
116 *Landry*, above note 26.
117 *Oommen*, above note 26.

FURTHER READINGS

BRUDNER, A., "Insane Automatism: A Proposal for Reform" (2000) 45 McGill L.J. 67

COLVIN, E., *Principles of Criminal Law*, 2d ed. (Toronto: Carswell, 1991), ch. 8

GRANT, I., D. CHUNN, & C. BOYLE, *The Law of Homicide* (Toronto: Carswell, 1994), ch. 6

HEALY, P. "Automatism Confined" (2000) 45 McGill L.J. 87

HOLLAND, W., "Automatism and Criminal Responsibility" (1982) 25 Crim. L.Q. 95

MARTIN, G.A., "The Insanity Defence" (1989) 10 Criminal Lawyers Association Newsletter 19

MEWETT, A., & M. MANNING, *Criminal Law*, 3d ed. (Toronto: Butterworths, 1994), chs. 13 and 14

O'MARRA, A.J.C., "*Hadfield* to *Swain*: The *Criminal Code* Amendments Dealing with the Mentally Disordered Accused" (1994) 36 Crim. L.Q. 49

STUART, D., *Canadian Criminal Law: A Treatise*, 4th ed. (Toronto: Carswell, 2001), at 111–26 and 370–416

TOLLEFSON, E.A., & B. STARKMAN, *Mental Disorder in Criminal Proceedings* (Toronto: Carswell, 1993)

CHAPTER 8

PROVOCATION, SELF-DEFENCE, NECESSITY, AND DURESS

This chapter will outline a variety of defences that may apply when the accused faces external pressures. Unlike mistake of fact or intoxication, these defences are not derived from the fault element of the particular offence, and they can apply even though the accused committed the *actus reus* in a physically voluntary manner and had the *mens rea* required for the offence. For example, a person who intentionally kills another may nevertheless have a defence of provocation or self-defence. A person who intentionally breaks into a house to save themselves from freezing to death may have a defence of necessity and a person who intentionally assists in a robbery because of death threats may still have a defence of duress.

All the defences examined in this chapter, with the exception of provocation, operate as complete defences that result in the accused's acquittal. Provocation is a partial defence that reduces murder to manslaughter. As discussed above in relation to the defences of intoxication, mental disorder, and automatism, the appropriate disposition for an accused is often an important factor in determining the ambit of a particular defence.

All four defences to some extent require a person to have acted reasonably in response to external pressures. In provocation, these external pressures are sudden acts or insults generally from the victim; in self-defence, violence, or threats from the victim; in duress, threats of serious harm from third parties; and in necessity, dire circumstances of peril. The Supreme Court has observed that self-defence, necessity, and duress "all arise under circumstances where a person is subjected to an external danger, and commits an act that would otherwise be criminal as a way of avoiding the harm the danger presents."[1]

The common requirement that the accused respond to these pressures in a reasonable fashion raises the familiar issue of how objective standards should be applied to ensure fairness towards individual accused. This issue first arose in the context of self-defence claims by women who killed abusive partners. The Court's landmark decision in *R. v. Lavallee*[2] to consider particular experiences and circumstances that the accused faced in determining whether the accused acted reasonably has had implications for all the defences examined in this chapter. The Supreme Court has accepted a modified objective standard that invests the reasonable person with the relevant characteristics and experiences of the accused for all four defences examined in this chapter. This stands in contrast to the Court's decision that a modified objective standard based on an individuated or contextual reasonable person is generally not appropriate in applying the objective fault standards discussed in chapter 4.[3] The modified objective standard used to administer these defences responds to the danger of holding accused to unreasonable standards of restraint, but it also risks blurring the distinction between subjective and objective standards and undermining social interests in requiring people to satisfy general standards of reasonable conduct.

Some of the defences examined in this chapter — provocation, self-defence, and duress (as applied to principal offenders) — are codified, whereas others such as necessity and duress (as applied to secondary parties) are common law defences that the courts have recognized and developed.[4] Overly restrictive statutory or common law defences may violate section 7 of the *Charter* by allowing those who have acted in a morally involuntary manner to be punished and defences should not be subject to any special deference under the *Charter*.[5] The Supreme Court has struck out the requirement in the statutory defence of duress that the threats must be of immediate death or bodily harm and that

---

1   *R. v. Hibbert* (1995), 99 C.C.C. (3d) 193 (S.C.C.) [*Hibbert*].
2   (1990), 55 C.C.C. (3d) 97 (S.C.C.) [*Lavallee*], discussed below.
3   *R. v. Creighton* (1993), 83 C.C.C. (3d) 346 (S.C.C.) [*Creighton*] discussed in ch. 4, "Who is the Reasonable Person"
4   Section 8(3) of the *Criminal Code of Canada*, R.S.C. 1985, c. C-46 [*Code*], has been interpreted as allowing courts to develop and recognize new defences. Entrapment, which was examined in ch. 1, "The *Charter* and the Investigation of Crime," has been developed as a common law defence.
5   *R. v. Ruzic* (2001), 153 C.C.C.(3d) 1 (S.C.C.) [*Ruzic*].

the threat must be from a person who is present at the time that the accused commits the crime under duress.[6] As examined in chapter 6, common law restrictions on the defence of intoxication have also been found to be unconstitutional.[7]

A. CONCEPTUAL CONSIDERATIONS

1) Excuses and Justifications

Criminal law defences are sometimes classified as excuses or justifications. A defence that excuses a crime is one that acknowledges the wrongfulness of the action, but holds that in the circumstances the accused should not be punished for the crime. The Supreme Court has stated that excuses rest:

> on a realistic assessment of human weakness, recognizing that a liberal and humane criminal law cannot hold people to the strict obedience of laws in emergency situations where normal human instincts, whether of self-preservation or altruism, overwhelmingly impel disobedience. . . . Praise is indeed not bestowed, but pardon is, when one does a wrongful act under pressure which . . . "overstrains human nature and no one could withstand. . . . At the heart of [necessity conceptualized as an excuse] is the perceived injustice of punishing violations of the law in circumstances in which the person has no other viable or reasonable choice available; the act was wrong but it is excused because it was unavoidable."[8]

In other words, "excuses absolve the accused of personal accountability by focussing, not on the wrongful act, but on the circumstances of the act and the accused's personal capacity to avoid it." Because the accused has no realistic choice but to commit the crime, "criminal attribution points not to the accused but to the exigent circumstances facing him."[9]

In contrast, a defence that acts as a justification "challenges the wrongfulness of an action which technically constitutes a crime." The accused is not punished because, in the circumstances, "the values of society, indeed of the criminal law itself, are better promoted by dis-

---

6   *Ibid.*
7   *R. v. Daviault* (1994), 93 C.C.C. (3d) 21 (S.C.C.).
8   *Perka v. R.* (1984), 14 C.C.C. (3d) 385 at 398 (S.C.C.) [*Perka*].
9   *Ruzic*, above note 5 at paras. 40 and 46.

obeying a given statute than by observing it."[10] A justification is not conceived as a concession to normal human weakness. Most would classify self-defence as a justification on the basis that people have rights to defend their persons and their property.

As will be seen in the case of necessity and duress, whether a defence is conceptualized as an excuse or a justification can have a practical effect on its availability. Excuses are inherently limited by what is thought necessary for a realistic concession to reasonable human weaknesses whereas justifications are more wide-ranging in holding that certain values are so important that they justify disobeying the law. In addition, the Supreme Court has accepted the idea that a conviction of a person who committed a crime in a morally involuntary manner because the circumstances were so exigent that there was no realistic choice but to commit the crime would offend section 7 of the *Charter*. This acceptance is largely based on the self-defining and self-limiting nature of the juristic category of an excuse.[11] Nevertheless, the classification of a defence as an excuse or a justification does not affect the disposition of the accused. Duress and necessity are commonly seen as excuses, yet they lead to a complete acquittal just as the justification of self-defence does.

2) Relation to Fault Element

The defences examined in this chapter are not conceived as an absence of *mens rea* in the same way as the mistake of fact or intoxication defences examined in previous chapters. At the same time, however, evidence relating to these defences could conceivably be relevant to proof of the mental element of some crimes. Evidence of provocation, self-defence, necessity, or duress, perhaps when combined with other factors, could possibly lead the jury to have a reasonable doubt as to whether the accused had the fault element for a particular crime. This would usually be possible only for offences with a high subjective level of *mens rea*. As discussed in chapter 3, the Supreme Court has indicated that duress will not negate the formation of a common intent under section 21(2) or the intent required under section 21(1)(b) when a party performs an act or omission for the purpose of aiding another person to commit an offence.[12] The Supreme Court has also indicated

10   *Perka*, above note 8 at 396–97.
11   *Ibid*.
12   *Hibbert*, above note 1.

that anger, although it may be part of the provocation defence, is "not a stand-alone defence"[13] that can reduce murder to manslaughter when the defence of provocation does not apply.

3) Subjective and Objective Components

In order to qualify for the defences of provocation, self-defence, necessity, or common law duress, the accused must not only subjectively and honestly perceive the need to respond to the relevant external pressures or threats, but the accused must also act reasonably.[14] The Supreme Court has explained that it is "society's concern that reasonable and non-violent behaviour be encouraged that prompts the law to endorse the objective standard."[15] This restriction makes sense when it is recognized that an accused who qualifies for these defences will nevertheless have committed a crime, frequently one involving violence, with the required fault element.

At the same time, the use of objective standards raises the challenge of ensuring that accused with particular characteristics and experiences can fairly be expected to live up to the objective standard required by the law. The dilemma is to make the objective standard fair, without collapsing it into a subjective standard. This task can be attempted in several ways. As examined in chapter 4 in relation to objective fault elements, one approach is to endow the reasonable person with some of the characteristics of the particular accused, such as the accused's age or sex. The Supreme Court is more willing to factor in characteristics of the accused when applying objective standards to defences than to offences. Thus, the accused's youth and gender have been included in the reasonable person standard when deciding whether an act or insult was sufficient to deprive an ordinary person of self-control for the purposes of the provocation defence.[16] The Court has also recognized that

---

13   R. v. *Parent* (2001), 154 C.C.C. (3d) 1 at para. 10 (S.C.C.) [*Parent*].

14   A reasonable basis for the accused's perceptions is not required under s. 17 of the *Code*, above note 4, which codifies the statutory defence of duress. As will be seen, however, this defence is made restrictive in other more categorical ways, such as excluding a long list of offences and requiring the accused to face threats of immediate death or bodily harm from a person present when the crime is committed. The Supreme Court has severed the requirements of immediate death or bodily harm and that the person who threatens be present when the crime was committed and the viability of the rest of s. 17 of the *Code* is very much in doubt.

15   R. v. *Hill* (1986), 25 C.C.C. (3d) 322 at 330 (S.C.C.) [*Hill*].

16   R. v. *Thibert* (1996), 104 C.C.C. (3d) 1 (S.C.C.) [*Thibert*].

evidence of past battering and expert evidence concerning how battered women respond to cycles of violence is relevant in assessing the reasonableness of claims of self-defence.[17] Such evidence may also be relevant to determining "the reasonableness of a battered woman's actions or perceptions" when provocation, duress, or necessity defences are claimed. It has been suggested that such evidence is a means of ensuring that "the perspectives of women, which have historically been ignored, . . . equally inform the 'objective' standard of the reasonable person in relation to self-defence."[18] At the same time, the idea that the objective standard in the provocation defence should reflect the perspective of the ordinary married man or the ordinary heterosexual male is more problematic if it suggests that men can be excused for reacting violently to the breakup of a relationship or an invitation by a gay man to engage in sexual activities.

A related but somewhat different approach is to consider the accused's particular experiences when they are relevant to placing the external pressure faced by the accused in its proper context. The emphasis is on how the accused's experiences affect context, not the level of self-control that the law expects. The fact that the accused's relationship was breaking up or that the accused had previously been beaten would not speak to the level of self-control expected, but could be considered so that the jury could fully understand the implications of the insult or threats that the accused faced. For example, the fact that a woman had been previously battered by a man she assaults or kills may be relevant in determining whether she had a reasonable basis for believing that she was being assaulted by the man and that the violence she used was necessary to escape the threat. Similarly, the history of the accused and victim's relationship may be relevant in assessing the significance of threats or insults for the purpose of administering the defences of duress or provocation. The accused's characteristics would only be considered to put the relevant external pressure in context and not to adjust the level of self-control that society expects. Of course, considering the full context of the pressures that the accused faced may have the practical result of making it easier to excuse the accused's conduct. The distinction[19] between modifying the objective standard in

17   *Lavallee*, above note 2; *Malott* (1997), 121 C.C.C. (3d) 457 (S.C.C.) [*Malott*].
18   *Malott*, *ibid.* at 470–71, L'Heureux-Dubé J. (McLachlin J. concurring).
19   For an example of an application of this distinction see the dissent of Wilson J. in *R. v. Hill*, above note 15, where she concludes that the fact that the accused was male was relevant to place sexual advances by another male in context, but that gender was not relevant to the degree of self-control expected from the

order to place the events in context and modifying it in a manner that affects the standard of reasonable conduct expected may break down when pushed too far.

4) Burden of Proof

Although the extreme intoxication, mental disorder, and automatism defences examined in the last two chapters must be proven by the accused on a balance of probabilities, the defences examined in this chapter must be disproved by the Crown as part of its burden to prove guilt beyond a reasonable doubt. Thus, if the jury has a reasonable doubt that an accused acted in self-defence, or under duress or necessity, it must acquit. In *R. v. Pétel*,[20] Lamer C.J. stated that in a case of self-defence, "it is the accused's state of mind that must be examined, and it is the accused (and not the victim) who must be given the benefit of a reasonable doubt." A new trial was necessary in *Thibert*[21] because the trial judge failed to explain to the jury that the accused need not prove the defence of provocation, but rather that "it rested upon the Crown to establish beyond a reasonable doubt that there had not been provocation."

5) Air of Reality

The judge does not, however, have to instruct the jury about every defence in every case. The accused has to overcome a threshold evidential burden in every case. In *R. v. Cinous*,[22] the Supreme Court indicated that a standard air of reality test should apply to all defences. The appropriate air of reality test was whether a properly instructed jury acting reasonably could acquit on the basis of the evidence. This requires evidence on each necessary element of the defence and that the evidence be such that a properly instructed jury acting reasonably could acquit on the basis of the evidence. In administering the air of reality test, the judge should assume that evidence is true and leave the determination of its credibilty to the jury.

The air of reality test does not impose a persuasive burden on the accused. Once a judge determined there is an air of reality to any of the

---

accused. In that case, she held that the youth of the sixteen-year-old accused was relevant to the issue of self-control or reasonable conduct expected.

20   (1994), 87 C.C.C. (3d) 97 at 104 (S.C.C.) [*Pétel*].

21   *Thibert*, above note 16 at 5.

22   (2002), 162 C.C.C. (3d) 129 (S.C.C.) [*Cinous*].

defences examined in this chapter, the jury should be instructed to acquit if they have a reasonable doubt about the existence of the defence. The majority of the Court in *Cinous*, however, held that there was no air of reality to the accused's claim that he acted in self-defence when he shot the victim in the back of the head. Thus, the jury should not have even been instructed about self-defence.

The *Cinous* test for determining an air of reality applies to all the defences examined in this chapter, as well as to other defences such as mistake of fact. It may constitute a higher threshold and an increased emphasis on the sufficiency of evidence and the range of reasonable inferences that the jury can draw than some previous formulations that had suggested that defences should be put to the jury if there was some evidence of the existence of all the elements of the defence. Three judges dissented in *Cinous* on the basis that it was the role of the jury to determine the sufficiency and reasonableness of the evidence relating to self-defence.

B. PROVOCATION ⟶ partial, excuse

As a partial defence that reduces murder to manslaughter, provocation does not fit easily into the excuse/justification framework. The Supreme Court has stated that the "provocation . . . neither justifies nor excuses the act of homicide. But the law accounts the act and the violent feelings which prompted it, less blamable because of the passion aroused by the provocation."[23] Provocation could be said to operate as a partial excuse when an accused kills another person while in a rage provoked by a sudden act or insult.

Provocation is a controversial defence. Its origins lay in traditions ORIGINS of mitigating violent responses to marital infidelities and it contains archaic phrases about excusing a person who acts in the heat of passion. Some argue that it should be abolished as a defence because it AGAINST allows deadly rage and violence, often directed against women, to be treated less seriously than other deliberate killings. Others argue that the provocation defence reflects the special significance of murder and FOR the fact that murder, unlike manslaughter, carries a fixed penalty. Still 1) others argue that the defence of provocation should apply to all crimes, 2) not only murder.

---

23   *R. v. Manchuk* (1937), 69 C.C.C. 172 at 173 (S.C.C.) [*Manchuk*].

1) Section 232

The defence of provocation is codified in section 232 of the *Criminal Code*, which states that "culpable homicide that otherwise would be murder may be reduced to manslaughter if the person who committed it did so in the heat of passion caused by sudden provocation." Provocation is then defined in section 232(2) as a "wrongful act or insult that is of such a nature as to be sufficient to deprive an ordinary person of the power of self-control." The proper formulation is whether the ordinary person would rather than could have lost self-control.[24] This definition imposes an objective standard by requiring that the act or insult be severe enough to cause the ordinary person to lose self-control. The provocation defence also contains the subjective requirement that the accused have acted "in the heat of passion"[25] and "on the sudden and before there was time for his passion to cool."[26] Section 232(3) restricts the definition of provocation by providing that "no one shall be deemed to have given provocation to another by doing anything he has a legal right to do,"[27] or by doing anything that the accused incited him to do in order to provide the accused with an excuse for causing death or bodily harm to any human being.

2) Restrictions on What Constitutes Provocation

There are some preliminary legal restrictions on the defence of provocation.[28] The act of alleged provocation must be a sudden act or insult, and the victim who provoked the accused must not be exercising a legal right.

a) Provocation by the Victim

The act or insult that constitutes provocation must generally come from the victim. Provocation cannot be used when the accused knows that the victim was not involved in the act or insult.[29] Provocation may, however, be available when the victim participated with a third person

---

24   *Hill*, above note 15 at 330; *Hibbert*, above note 1 at para. 24; *R. v. Lees* (2001), 156 C.C.C. (3d) 421 at paras. 15–16 (B.C.C.A.).

25   *Code*, above note 4, s. 232(1).

26   *Ibid.*, s. 232(2).

27   Section 232(4) provides that an arrest that exceeds an individual's or a police officer's legal powers is not necessarily provocation, "but the fact that the illegality of the arrest was known to the accused may be evidence of provocation."

28   *R. v. Faid* (1983), 2 C.C.C. (3d) 513 (S.C.C.) [*Faid*].

29   *Manchuk*, above note 23.

in the act or insult, or where the accused makes a reasonable mistake that the victim was involved in the provocation.[30] Cases of transferred intent under section 229(b) of the *Criminal Code* in which the accused intends to kill one person but kills another by accident or mistake may be mitigated by the provocation defence even though the accused was provoked by the person he or she intended to kill and not the person actually killed.[31]

b) Sudden Provocation

The Supreme Court has stated that "'suddenness' must characterize both the insult and the act of retaliation."[32] On this basis, the Court has denied the defence to an accused who had prior knowledge of his wife's unfaithfulness and abortion, but had killed her when she informed him of these previously known facts;[33] to an accused who commenced an argument with his wife and followed her into a room and called her a name;[34] and to an accused who kidnapped the victim, who later provoked the accused by hitting him with a hammer.[35] The act of provocation should be sudden and unexpected; it cannot be a manifestation of a grudge or a foreseeable response to something that the accused has initiated.

The Ontario Court of Appeal has denied the provocation defence to a woman who shot her husband sometime after her husband had argued with her and choked her.[36] The Nova Scotia Court of Appeal denied the provocation defence on the basis that the accused had known for some four hours that his spouse was leaving him.[37] In a series of cases, provincial appellate courts have held that the defence of provocation should not be left to the jury if there was no sudden provocation that would make an unexpected impact on the accused's mind.[38] On the other

---

30 *R. v. Hansford* (1987), 33 C.C.C. (3d) 74 (Alta. C.A.).

31 *R. v. Droste* (1981), 63 C.C.C. (3d) 418 (Ont. C.A.), aff'd on other grounds (*sub nom. R. v. Droste (No. 2)*) (1984), 10 C.C.C. (3d) 404 (S.C.C.).

32 *R. v. Tripodi* (1955), 112 C.C.C. 66 at 68 (S.C.C.).

33 *Ibid.*

34 *Salamon v. R.* (1959), 123 C.C.C. 1 at 12 (S.C.C.) [*Salamon*].

35 *R. v. Louison* (1975), 26 C.C.C. (2d) 266 (Sask. C.A.), aff'd (1978), 51 C.C.C. (2d) 479 (S.C.C.).

36 *R. v. Malott* (1996), 110 C.C.C. (3d) 499 (Ont. C.A.), aff'd on other grounds, above note 17.

37 *R. v. Young* (1993), 78 C.C.C. (3d) 538 (N.S.C.A.), leave denied 81 C.C.C. (3d) vi (S.C.C.).

38 *R. v. Gibson* (2001), 41 C.R. (5th) 213 (B.C.C.A.); *R. v. Merasty* (2000), 30 C.R. (5th) 274 (B.C.C.A.); *R. v. Pawliuk* (2001), 40 C.R. (5th) 28 (B.C.C.A.).

R v Galgay; R v Squire

hand, the Supreme Court in *Thibert*[39] allowed a provocation defence in response to taunts by the deceased to shoot him, even though the accused apparently had known for some time that the deceased was involved in an extramarital affair with the accused's wife, and the accused was pursuing (while armed) an opportunity to speak to his wife alone. This case suggests that sudden provocation can still be found even though the accused has taken the initiative, has produced a confrontation with the victim, and had prior knowledge of the victim's relationship with his wife. At the same time, the deceased's taunts were sudden and were uttered just before the accused shot the victim.

c)   No Provocation When the Accused Incites the Provocation

Section 232(3) states that there is no provocation when the accused has incited the victim to commit the act or insult claimed to be provocation. In *Squire*,[40] an accused who was an aggressor in a fight was held not to have been provoked even if he had been kicked during the fight. The accused should not be allowed to argue provocation when he or she incited the act or insult claimed to be provocation. Provocation was, however, made out in *Thibert*[41] even though the accused, by pursuing an opportunity to speak to his estranged wife while armed, created the opportunity for the deceased to insult him by challenging the accused to shoot.

d)   No Provocation When the Victim Was Exercising a Legal Right

Section 232(3) restricts the act of provocation by providing that there will not be provocation where the person killed was "doing anything he had a legal right to do." In *R. v. Galgay*,[42] the Ontario Court of Appeal held that a trial judge had erred when he informed the jury that the victim's telling the accused that he was no good and she was going to leave him could not be provocation because the victim was only exercising her legal rights. In reversing the trial judge, Kelly J.A. stated that section 232(3) "does not apply to remove from a verbal insult offered by the provoker the provocative quality of the insult." Brooke J.A. added that although the victim had a legal right to leave the accused, she had

---

39   Above note 16 at 17. In his dissent, Major J. argued that the provocation was not sudden because the accused knew of his wife's involvement with the deceased and had seen them together that day. "It cannot be said that . . . [Thibert's] mind was unprepared for the sight of his wife and the deceased such that he was taken by surprise and his passions were set aflame."

40   (1977), 29 C.C.C. (2d) 497 (S.C.C.).

41   *Thibert*, above note 16.

42   (1972), 6 C.C.C. (2d) 539 at 553 (Ont. C.A.).

no legal right to insult him. The absence of a legal remedy for an insult in private does not mean that the victim was exercising a legal right under this section. The approach in *Galgay* limits this exception to cases where the victim was exercising legal rights such as self-defence. It could be rethought if courts consider the domestic violence context in which many provocation defences arise. It could be argued that people have a legal right to leave relationships and even to make disparaging comments about ex-partners. The Court's continued refusal to recognize this broader interpretation of a legal right could deny women the equal protection and benefit of the law.

The restrictive approach in *Galgay* has been adopted by a three-judge plurality of the Supreme Court in *Thibert*.[43] In that case, the deceased was held not to have a legal right to tell the accused to shoot him while holding onto the accused's wife. Cory J. explained: "[i]n the context of the provocation defence, the phrase 'legal right' has been defined as something which is sanctioned by law as distinct from something which a person may do without incurring legal liability." This restricts the meaning of legal right to matters such as self-defence. Even then, the Court took a restrictive approach and held that the deceased's actions in walking towards the accused while the accused was pointing a gun at him "could well be found not to be acts of self-defence."[44] It seems that a deceased will only be held to be exercising a legal right that cannot constitute provocation in the clearest cases of self-defence. This is unfortunate because a broader reading of the deceased's legal rights could respond to many of the concerns that have been expressed about the provocation defence excusing violence in response to rather trivial acts or insults or when women tell men that they are leaving a relationship.

3) Objective Standard of Depriving an Ordinary Person of Self-Control

The most important limitation on what acts and insults can amount to provocation is the requirement in section 232(2) that they be "of such a nature as to deprive an ordinary person of self-control." Dickson C.J. has stated that it is:

> society's concern that reasonable and non-violent behaviour be encouraged that prompts the law to endorse the objective standard. The crim-

---

43   *Thibert*, above note 16 at 14.
44   *Ibid.*

Rational Rit standard inal law is concerned among other things with fixing standards for human behaviour. We seek to encourage conduct that complies with certain societal standards of reasonableness and responsibility. In doing so, the law quite logically employs the objective standard of the reasonable person.[45]

The same could be said about self-defence, necessity, and the common law of duress, which also employ objective standards. A peaceful society does not want to excuse violence solely on the basis of the accused's subjective and perhaps idiosyncratic perceptions and reactions to the ordinary stresses and strains of modern life. The challenge, as is the case with objective standards for *mens rea*, is to ensure that the particular accused can reasonably be required to live up to the objective standard of self-control and reasonable and non-violent behaviour.

a) Who Is the Ordinary Person?

Courts in Canada and England[46] traditionally interpreted the ordinary person without any reference to the accused's circumstances or characteristics. In *R. v. Wright*,[47] the Supreme Court held that the fact that the accused was insulted by his father should not be considered when determining whether an ordinary person would have lost self-control. In *R. v. Parnerkar*,[48] the Saskatchewan Court of Appeal held that the accused's race was not relevant in determining whether an ordinary person would have lost self-control, even though the accused had been told by the victim that she was "not going to marry you because you are a black man." This approach was harsh because it did not allow the Court to consider the relevant context and circumstances behind the act or insult,[49] and could, in the case of a young accused, require "old heads be placed upon young shoulders."[50]

---

45   *Hill*, above note 15 at 330.
46   *Bedder v. D.P.P.*, [1954] 2 All E.R. 801 (H.L.), overruled in *D.P.P. v. Camplin*, [1978] A.C. 705 (H.L.) [*Camplin*].
47   [1969] 3 C.C.C. 258 (S.C.C.).
48   (1972), 5 C.C.C. (2d) 11 (Sask. C.A.), aff'd (1973), 10 C.C.C. (2d) 253 (S.C.C.).
49   Lord Diplock stated that the jury should be able to "take into consideration all those factors which in their opinion would affect the gravity of taunts or insults" when applied to the accused, in part because "[t]o taunt a person because of his race, his physical infirmities or some shameful incident in his past may well be considered by the jury to be more offensive to the person addressed . . . if the facts on which the taunt is founded are true." *Camplin*, above note 46 at 717.
50   *Ibid.*

The Supreme Court has recognized the harshness of applying an objective standard divorced from the relevant characteristics of the accused. In *Hill*,[51] the majority of the Court upheld a murder conviction of a sixteen-year-old boy who killed the victim after he claimed the male victim made sexual advances. The trial judge, following *Wright* and *Parnerkar*, had instructed the jury that, in determining whether the acts and words constituted provocation, "you are not to consider the particular mental make-up of the accused; rather the standard is that of the ordinary person."[52]

For the majority of the Court, Dickson C.J. stated that it would be fair to consider the accused's youth as an "important contextual consideration." He warned, however, that the accused's personal characteristics will not always be relevant. For example, an accused's race would not be relevant if he or she was faced with an insult about a physical disability. The accused's sex would not be relevant if the insult was directed at his or her race. Even with regard to the accused's youth, Dickson C.J. held that the charge to the jury was acceptable and it was not necessary for the judge to instruct the jury to consider whether an ordinary sixteen-year-old would have lost self-control. He explained:

> [T]he "collective good sense" of the jury will naturally lead it to ascribe to the ordinary person any general characteristics relevant to the provocation in question. For example, if the provocation is a racial slur, the jury will think of an ordinary person with the racial background that forms the substance of the insult. To this extent, particular characteristics will be ascribed to the ordinary person.[53]

Although he did not require the jury to be instructed to consider the accused's youth, Dickson C.J. did not seem to believe that considering youth was inconsistent with the purposes of the objective standard in encouraging reasonable and non-violent behaviour. Subsequent cases have considered the accused's youth when determining whether an ordinary person would have lost self-control[54] and it would now be an error of law not to instruct the jury to consider the reactions of an ordinary person of the accused's own age when considering whether an ordinary person would have been deprived of the power of self-control.[55]

---

51 *Hill*, above note 15.
52 *Ibid.* at 327–28. They could consider the accused's emotional and physical conditions and his age when determining if he had acted suddenly, before his passion had cooled.
53 *Ibid.* at 335.
54 *R. v. Jackson* (1991), 68 C.C.C. (3d) 385 at 410 (Ont. C.A.).
55 *Thibert*, above note 16.

Three judges dissented in *Hill* and would have ordered a new trial. Le Dain and Lamer JJ. dissented on the grounds that the trial judge's charge would have left the jury with the impression that they could not consider the accused's age when determining whether an ordinary person would have lost self-control. Wilson J. also dissented and stated that a specific instruction about the accused's youth and sex was necessary in this case. She reasoned that it was appropriate to consider the accused's youth because "the law does not attribute to individuals in the developmental stage of their youth the same degree of responsibility as is attributed to fully adult actors."[56] She cautioned against allowing other factors, including the accused's sex, to determine the amount of self-control expected. In her view, "the underlying principles of equality and individual responsibility cannot be undermined by importing the accused's subjective level of self-control into the 'ordinary person' test."[57] She believed, however, that the accused's sex was relevant as a factor "to put the wrongful act or insult into context for the purposes of assessing its gravity," so that the jury would determine the effect of the act or insult on "the ordinary person similarly situated and similarly insulted" as the accused.[58]

Subsequent cases have affirmed that the jury should be instructed to consider an ordinary person of the same age and sex of the accused. This includes the concerns expressed by the dissenting judges in *Hill* about the relevance of age, but not Justice Wilson's careful distinction between the relevance of gender as a factor that may, depending on the circumstances, place an act or insult in context and as a factor that should not be considered in determining the level of self-control expected by society. This is unfortunate because the Wilson approach addresses real concerns about the provocation defence being used to excuse rage and violence that does occur with males but rarely with females.

b)   The Modified Objective Standard

In *Thibert*,[59] a three-judge plurality of the Court went beyond the relatively cautious approach taken by the majority in *Hill* to relating the accused's characteristics to those of the ordinary person and concluded:

> The "ordinary person" must be of the same age, and sex, and share with the accused such other factors as would give the act or insult in

---

56   *Hill*, above note 15 at 352.
57   *Ibid.*
58   *Ibid.*
59   *Thibert*, above note 16 at 10.

question a special significance and have experienced the same series of acts or insults as those experienced by the accused.

This generously individuated and contextual definition of the ordinary person meant that the accused in the case was held up to the same standard of self-control as would be possessed by a "married man, faced with the breakup of his marriage"[60] who had previously convinced his wife to return to the marriage. The majority concluded that this ordinary man would have lost his powers of self-control when the deceased taunted him to shoot him while holding the accused's wife in front of him. A two-judge minority dissented on the basis that the breakup of a marriage due to an extramarital affair and the deceased's participation in the affair should not be considered as wrongful acts or insults capable of depriving an ordinary person of the power of self-control.

The proper focus should be on the deceased's taunts just before the shooting,[61] but the majority's approach does make the breakup of the marriage and indeed much of the history of the marriage relevant. It also judges the accused's level of self-control on the basis of the standard of the ordinary married man. It is not clear from the majority's decision whether the accused's gender is relevant to place the act or insult in context or to determine the level of self-control or to both. It should be recalled that both Chief Justice Dickson and Justice Wilson in *Hill* expressed more caution about including gender as a factor that may be relevant to the level of self-control expected from the ordinary person. Although Justice Wilson was more explicit, both would have considered the accused's gender to be relevant only when it was necessary to place the wrongful act or insult in context. The Court's decision in *Thibert* to judge conduct by the standard of the married man may too easily excuse male violence towards women simply because of a breakup of a relationship. The decision was only decided by a three-judge plurality and it may be revisited by the Court in the future.

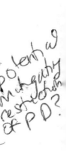

Although *Thibert* is problematic on the gender issue, the other aspects of plurality's judgment are less controversial. The Court clearly indicates that the age of the accused should be factored into the ordinary person test and this is an improvement on *Hill* where there was a danger that the jury may not have considered the fact that the accused

---

60   *Ibid.* at 12.

61   To this end, Cory J. indicated that if the accused had simply brooded over his rejection and gone and shot the deceased, "the history of the deceased's relationship with the wife of the accused could not be used as a basis for a defence of provocation because the necessary final act of provocation was missing." *Ibid.* at 13.

R v Fraser

was only sixteen years old when applying the ordinary person standard. It also seems appropriate that the ordinary person should "share with the accused such other factors as would give the act or insult in question a special significance and have experienced the same series of acts or insults as those experienced by the accused." The accused should be expected to demonstrate reasonable self-control, but it would not be fair to judge the accused's reactions against those of an ordinary person that did have the same factors as give the act or insult special significance. A slur about a person's race or sexuality only takes on full meaning when that person's particular characteristics are considered. In addition, past acts and insults exchanged between the accused and the deceased may be relevant to determining the gravity of the final act or insult.[62] The requirement for sudden provocation should prevent the accused from acting on old grudges.

In summary, *Thibert* defines the ordinary person in a contextual manner which ensures that the ordinary person is endowed with those characteristics and past experiences that are necessary to place the act or insult in context. It also suggests that the ordinary person should be the same age and gender as the accused. This makes clear the idea implicit in *Hill* that youth is relevant to the degree of self-control that can reasonably be expected. At the same time, however, it may make the accused's gender relevant both to placing the act or insult in context and more problematically to the degree of self-control expected from the accused.

Thibert summary

c) Factors Not Relevant to an Ordinary Person

It is clear that factors such as intoxication and temper that may affect an accused's self-control are not relevant in determining whether an ordinary person would have lost self-control. Courts have not been clear about whether and why the accused's sex should be considered when applying the objective test. In *R. v. Fraser*,[63] McDermid J.A. argued in dissent that a reasonable person would not respond with violence to homosexual advances, given contemporary attitudes towards sexuality. This argument is appealing in principle,[64] but must be recon-

---

62   *Ibid.*

63   (1980), 55 C.C.C. (2d) 503 (Alta. C.A.).

64   Especially given that sexual orientation has been included by courts as a prohibited ground for denying gays and lesbians the equal protection and benefit of the law under s. 15 of the *Canadian Charter of Rights and Freedoms*, Part I of the *Constitution Act, 1982*, being Schedule B to the *Canada Act 1982* (U.K.), 1982, c. 11 [*Charter*].

ciled with Dickson C.J.'s implicit and Wilson J.'s explicit indications that the accused's sex in *Hill* was a consideration that was relevant to placing the male deceased's sexual advances towards the sixteen-year-old male accused in context. In any event, the Court's more recent decision in *Thibert*[65] suggests that the ordinary person should always share the same gender as the accused and does not clearly differentiate when gender is relevant to placing an act or insult in context and when gender is relevant to the degree of self-control expected.

In *R. v. Ly*,[66] an accused born and raised in Vietnam argued that his cultural background should be considered when determining whether an ordinary person would have lost self-control when his wife returned home early in the morning and told him that where she had been was none of his business. Macfarlane J.A. concluded:

> I think it was proper for the jury in this case at bar to be told to consider the effect of the words ascribed to the deceased on the ordinary married man who, because of a history of the relationship between the spouses, had a belief that his wife was not being faithful to him. The fact that the husband was Vietnamese and came from a certain cultural background might have been relevant . . . if a racial slur had been involved, but that is not the case.[67]

Under this approach, an accused's cultural background can only be considered if necessary to determine the gravity of the insult. It should not be used to determine the degree of self-control expected from the ordinary person. This approach is appealing in principle, but it must be reconciled with the fact that the Supreme Court has not rigorously or consistently made the same distinction in the context of gender.

Under the generous contextual approach taken by the plurality in *Thibert*,[68] it could be argued that the accused's cultural background in *Ly* should have been considered and was necessary to place the deceased's words in context. At the least, the *Thibert* approach suggests that the accused's past relationship with the victim was relevant and this can include cultural components of the relationship. From this, it is not a far step to also consider the accused's cultural background. At the same time, it should not readily be assumed that minority cultures condone

---

65 *Thibert*, above note 16.
66 (1987), 33 C.C.C. (3d) 31 (B.C.C.A.).
67 *Ibid.* at 38.
68 *Thibert*, above note 16. Recall that in that case, an "ordinary married man" person was applied by the majority.

violence against women. Including cultural background into the ordinary person standard runs the risk of stereotyping.

The Court's contextual approach to defining the ordinary person is
in some tension to its reluctance to consider matters such as gender,
age, or cultural background when applying objective fault elements.[69]
It also raises serious questions whether the social goal of promoting
reasonable behaviour is being watered down by reading in understand-
ings of masculinity or culture that may too easily accept violence, and
particularly, violence against women. If this is being done, it is difficult
to accept majoritarian double standards that embrace as part of the
ordinary person, a culture of masculinity that is possessive, short-tem-
pered, and violent while excluding the cultures of various minorities.
The answer seems to be to stick to the difficult task of considering the
accused's characteristics when required to place an act or insult in context, but not to allow those characteristics to affect the degree of self-
control that society expects from every person in Canada.

d) Proportionality Not Required

The courts in England stress proportionality when they state the issue
is "not merely whether such person would in like circumstances be
provoked to lose his self-control but would also react to the provocation as the accused did."[70] Proportionality also figures in the Canadian
law applying to self-defence, necessity, and common law duress. Nevertheless, under the section 232 provocation defence, Canadian courts
have focused only on whether an ordinary person in the circumstances
would have lost self-control, not whether he or she would have done
what the accused did.[71] This approach seems to eliminate any requirement that the accused's acts be even roughly proportionate to the act or
insult. It also discounts the real possibility that a particularly cutting
insult may cause an ordinary person to lose self-control, but perhaps
not to engage in a vicious and deliberate killing. At the same time, this
approach follows the wording of section 232, which refers only to
whether an ordinary person would have lost self-control.

e) Provocation and the *Charter*

The requirement that an act or insult be sufficient to deprive an ordinary person of self-control has been challenged as inconsistent with
section 7 of the *Charter* and, in particular, the constitutional require-

---

69   *Creighton*, above note 3. See ch. 4, "Who is the Reasonable Person."
70   *Camplin*, above note 46 at 686.
71   *R. v. Carpenter* (1993), 83 C.C.C. (3d) 193 at 197 (Ont. C.A.).

ment that there be subjective fault for a murder conviction. In *R. v. Cameron*,[72] Doherty J.A. concluded:

> The argument misconceives the effect of s. 232. The section does not detract from or negative the fault requirement for murder, but serves as a partial excuse for those who commit what would be murder but for the existence of the partial defence created by s. 232. . . .
>
> The statutory defence of provocation does not detract from the *mens rea* required to establish murder. . . .
>
> The objective component of the statutory defence of provocation serves a valid societal purpose . . . and cannot be said to be contrary to the principles of fundamental justice.

An objective standard for the defence of provocation does not relieve the Crown of the burden of proving that the accused subjectively knew that the victim was likely to die.

As recognized in *Hill*, the objective standard in section 232 is designed to encourage reasonable and non-violent behaviour. The courts have accepted objective standards as constitutionally sufficient for many offences[73] and it is likely that they will continue to uphold objective standards in defences. This is especially true given the generously contextual and individuated approach taken in *Thibert* to applying objective standards of self-control.

Serious thought has recently been given to abolishing the defence of provocation. This raises the issue of whether the absence of a provocation defence would violate section 7 of the *Charter*. A person who kills while provoked is not a morally innocent person. He or she will have the minimum *mens rea* of subjective foresight of death which is constitutionally required for murder.[74] Moreover, he or she will likely not be acting in a morally involuntary manner so that it could be said that he or she had no realistic choice but to kill the victim. It thus appears as if the abolition of the provocation defence would not violate section 7 of the *Charter* by allowing the conviction of the morally innocent or a person who acts in a morally involuntary manner.

---

72 (1992), 71 C.C.C. (3d) 272 at 273–74 (Ont. C.A.). A majority of the Supreme Court has relied on this case and its reasoning that objective standards in a defence did not affect the Crown's obligations to prove the voluntary commission of the *actus reus* with the required *mens rea*. *R. v. Stone* (1999), 134 C.C.C. (3d) 353 at 437 (S.C.C.) See ch. 7, "Automatism."

73 See ch. 4, "The Fault Element, or *Mens Rea*."

74 The Ontario Court of Appeal has observed that "the defence of provocation, unlike duress, does not raise an issue of moral blameworthiness because, even if successful, it does not lead to an acquittal." *R. v. Ruzic* (1998), 128 C.C.C (3d) 97 at 122.

R v Malott

The abolition of the provocation defence would mean under the present law that a person who killed while provoked would be subject to mandatory life imprisonment. On the one hand, it could be argued that because that person had the *mens rea* required for murder that such punishment was appropriate. On the other hand, it could be argued that the automatic life imprisonment that follows a murder conviction could be disproportionate in cases where the accused responded to a sudden and extraordinary insult. Life imprisonment may go beyond what is necessary to recognize the gravity of the offence and the person's responsibility for it and may not be necessary to protect the public and ensure that the person does not violate the law again. The *Charter* jurisprudence concerning what constitutes cruel and unusual punishment will be examined in the next chapter, but absent such a finding, it is likely that courts would find that the abolition of the provocation defence would not violate the *Charter*.

4) Subjective Components of Provocation

Even if the act or insult is sufficient to deprive an ordinary person of self-control, it is still necessary that the accused have acted suddenly and "before there was time for his passion to cool." This test "is called subjective because it involves an assessment of what actually occurred in the mind of the accused. . . . [The] task at this point is to ascertain whether the accused was in fact acting as a result of provocation."[75] In determining this subjective component of the provocation defence, all factors particular to the accused can be considered, including intoxication,[76] his or her "mental state and psychological temperament,"[77] and the history of the accused's relationship with the deceased.[78]

In many cases, the objective test for provocation will be the most difficult for the accused. The accused may, however, fail the subjective test if the killing involved an element of deliberation inconsistent with acting on the sudden and in the heat of passion. In *Malott*,[79] the Ontario Court of Appeal held that a battered woman did not qualify for the provocation defence in part because she had deliberately obtained a gun to shoot her husband and her "behaviour following the shooting

---

75   *Hill*, above note 15 at 336.

76   *Salamon*, above note 34.

77   *Hill*, above note 15.

78   *R. v. Sheridan* (1991), 65 C.C.C. (3d) 319 (S.C.C.), rev'g (1990), 55 C.C.C. (3d) 313 at 321 (S.C.C.); *Thibert*, above note 16 at 10–11.

79   *Malott*, above notes 17 and 36.

was characterized by a lack of passion."*At the same time, the accused in *Thibert* was held to have been subjectively provoked by an insult while he was pursuing an opportunity to talk with his wife without the deceased being present. The history of the relationship between the accused and the deceased may be considered so long as there was a sudden act or insult added to the mix such as the deceased goading the accused to shoot him or the throwing of a bottle.[80] In many ways, the requirement that the accused be subjectively provoked complements the requirement that the provocation be sudden.

5) Relation of Provocation to the Fault Element

As noted above, the defence of provocation applies even though the accused has killed with subjective foresight of the likelihood of death.[81] In such a case, the defence of provocation reduces murder to manslaughter. It is possible, however, that evidence of provocation could prevent the Crown from proving the mental element of murder or even other crimes. Martin J.A. recognized this possibility in *R. v. Campbell*,[82] when he stated there may "be cases where the conduct of the victim amounting to provocation produces in the accused a state of excitement, anger or disturbance as a result of which he might not contemplate the consequences of his acts and might not, in fact, intend to bring about those consequences. . . . Provocation in that aspect, however, does not operate as a 'defence' but rather as a relevant item of evidence on the issue of intent." Provocation is more likely to raise a reasonable doubt about the higher levels of *mens rea*. An accused who damages property in a rage at an act or insult, for example, may not act with the intent or purpose to damage property. The accused would, however, probably be aware of the risk that the property would be damaged and, as such, could be said to have recklessly caused the damage.

In *R. v. Parent*,[83] the Supreme Court held that a trial judge had erred when he left the jury with the impression than anger alone could reduce murder to manslaughter even when the defence of provocation did not apply. The Supreme Court unfortunately did not discuss Justice Martin's statement in *Campbell* or other statements by the Ontario Court of Appeal suggesting that evidence relating to provocation, per-

---

80   *Thibert*, above note 16.
81   *R. v. Oickle* (1984) 11 C.C.C. (3d) 180 (N.S.C.A.).
82   (1977), 38 C.C.C. (2d) 6 at 16 (Ont. C.A.).
83   *Parent*, above note 13.

haps combined with other evidence such as evidence relating to intoxication, could be relevant to proof of *mens rea* for murder.[84]

Parent should be restricted to the idea that anger is not in itself "a stand-alone defence."[85] The anger of the accused is relevant to the subjective arm of the provocation defence, but there is also an objective arm of the defence. Anger itself does not automatically reduce murder to manslaughter, but anger should still be considered relevant evidence with respect to subjective fault elements. It may well be that anger will not likely raise a reasonable doubt that a person accused of murder knew that the victim was likely to die, but it should be considered with all other relevant evidence in determining whether the Crown has proved the required level of subjective fault beyond a reasonable doubt. It would be contrary to the principle of subjective fault to exclude consideration of any factor particular to the accused when determining whether the particular accused subjectively had guilty knowledge.

6) Relation of Provocation to Other Defences

Extreme provocation might cause an ordinary person to act in an involuntary manner. If the provocation resulted in automatism that could only be explained with reference to the accused's internal emotional make-up or that required the public to be protected from a continuing danger, then the defence would be mental disorder automatism. If the provocation could be explained on the basis of extraordinary external factors such as seeing a loved one killed or harmed, the defence might be non-mental disorder automatism, leading to a complete acquittal.[86] Either variety of automatism must be established by the accused on a balance of probabilities as opposed to the provocation defence that applies if there is a reasonable doubt about its existence.

Evidence of intoxication and provocation combined might prevent the Crown from proving the intent of murder beyond a reasonable doubt, even though the evidence considered separately would not be capable of producing either an intoxication or a provocation defence.[87] This follows the logic of subjective *mens rea*, which is open to the effects that all the evidence might have on whether the particular accused had the required mental element.

84   *R. v. Nealy* (1986), 30 C.C.C. (3d) 460 (Ont. C.A.).

85   *Parent*, above note 13 at para. 10.

86   *R. v. Rabey* (1980), 54 C.C.C. (2d) 1 (S.C.C.); *R. v. Stone* (1999), 134 C.C.C. (3d) 353 (S.C.C.). See ch. 7, "Automatism."

87   *R. v. Nealy* (1986), 30 C.C.C. (3d) 460 (Ont. C.A.); *R. v. Friesen* (1995), 101 C.C.C. (3d) 167 (Alta. C.A.).

C. SELF-DEFENCE

The statutory provisions in the *Criminal Code* governing self-defence are notoriously complex. They attempt to define the various circumstances in which an accused might act in self-defence. They also draw distinctions on the basis of whether the accused intended to cause death or grievous bodily harm, or had no such intent. These attempts to classify the various situations in which a claim of self-defence might arise are often criticized as artificial and unnecessary.

The basic elements of all self-defence claims are the accused's apprehension of harm and the accused's perception of the force required to avoid the threatened harm. Self-defence, like the defence of provocation, is concerned both with the accused's subjective perceptions and the reasonableness of those perceptions. The latter question, of course, raises the issue of whether and how objective standards should be tailored to the accused's circumstances and characteristics.

1) Section 34(1)

Section 34(1) applies to everyone who is unlawfully assaulted without having intentionally provoked the assault by blows, words, or gestures.[88] Unlawful assaults are defined broadly in section 265 to include not only applications of force, but also attempts or threats to apply force, which cause the person to believe on reasonable grounds that the aggressor has the present ability to realize his purpose. Thus, a person may be unlawfully assaulted, even though he or she has not yet been struck. Section 34(1) thus is available to those who are unlawfully assaulted without provoking the assault.

An accused under section 34(1) is justified in using force provided 1) the force used is not intended to cause death or grievous bodily harm, and 2) it is no more than necessary to enable the accused to defend himself or herself.

The first requirement means that section 34(1) will not be a defence to murder which requires an intent to cause death.[89] Section 34(1) may, however, be a defence to manslaughter when the accused caused death

---

88   Section 36 of the *Code*, above note 2, defines provocation for the purposes of ss. 34 and 35 and courts have required that provocation which deprives the accused of the s. 34(1) defence must be intended by the accused to provoke an assault. *R. v. Nelson* (1992), 71 C.C.C. (3d) 449 (Ont. C.A.) [*Nelson*].
89   *R. v. Bayard* (1989), 70 C.R. (3d) 95 (S.C.C.).

but did not intend to do so.[90] The second requirement that the accused use no more force than necessary does not require the accused to "measure with nicety the degree of force necessary to ward off the attack"[91] or to retreat.[92] In summary, a jury should acquit an accused under section 34(1) if they have at least a reasonable doubt that "(i) the accused was unlawfully assaulted; (ii) the accused did not provoke the assault; (iii) the force used by the accused was not intended to cause death or grievous bodily harm; and (iv) the force used by the accused was no more than necessary to enable him to defend himself."[93]

2) Section 34(2)

Unlike section 34(1), section 34(2) can apply in cases where the accused provoked the assault and was the initial aggressor[94] and when the accused intended to cause death or grievous bodily harm. Thus, an accused otherwise guilty of murder might have a defence under section 34(2). Section 34(2) can also apply even though the accused did not have the intent to cause death or grievous bodily harm[95] and thus provide a justification for a manslaughter or assault charge. It is possible that both sections 34(1) and 34(2) will be left with the jury, but section 34(2) is the broader defence applying even in cases in which the accused provoked the assault and intended to cause death or grievous bodily harm. Section 34(2) does not, as section 34(1) does, require the accused to use no more harm than is necessary, but rather requires the accused to believe on reasonable grounds that he or she could not otherwise be preserved from death or grievous bodily harm. It also does not require that the force used be proportionate to the assault that the accused defends against.[96]

---

90 R. v. Kandola (1993), 80 C.C.C. (3d) 481 (B.C.C.A.).

91 R. v. Cadwallader, [1966] 1 C.C.C. 380 at 387 (Sask. Q.B.); R. v. Baxter (1975), 27 C.C.C. (2d) 86 at 111 (Ont. C.A.) [Baxter]; R. v. Hebert (1996), 107 C.C.C. (3d) 42 at 50 (S.C.C.) [Hebert].

92 R. v. Antley, [1964] 2 C.C.C. 142 at 147 (Ont. C.A.) [Antley]; R. v. Deegan (1979), 49 C.C.C. (2d) 417 at 440–41 (Alta. C.A.) [Deegan], quoting Justice Holmes that "detached reflection cannot be demanded in the presence of an uplifted knife."

93 Hebert, above note 91 at 51–52.

94 R. v. McIntosh (1995), 95 C.C.C. (3d) 481 (S.C.C.) [McIntosh].

95 R. v. Pintar (1996), 110 C.C.C. (3d) 402 (Ont. C.A) [Pintar]; R. v. Kindt (1998), 124 C.C.C. (3d) 20 (B.C.C.A.); R. v. Trombley (1998), 126 C.C.C. (3d) 495 (Ont. C.A.).

96 Hebert, above note 91 at 50.

There are three elements of self-defence under section 34(2): 1) the existence of an unlawful assault; 2) a reasonable apprehension of a risk of death or grievous bodily harm; and 3) a reasonable belief that it is not possible to preserve oneself from harm except by harming one's adversary.[97] The accused must have a subjective belief as to all three elements and a reasonable basis for such a belief. The test is thus a blend of subjective and objective factors.

In *R. v. Reilly*,[98] Ritchie J. explained the requirements for subjective beliefs and a reasonable basis for those beliefs:

> Section 34(2) places in issue the accused's state of mind at the time he caused death. The subsection can only afford protection to the accused if he apprehended death or grievous bodily harm from the assault he was repelling and if he believed he could not preserve himself from death or grievous bodily harm otherwise than by the force he used. None the less, his apprehension must be a *reasonable* one and his belief must be *based upon reasonable and probable grounds*.

The jury is to be guided by the accused's subjective beliefs "so long as there exists an objectively verifiable basis for his perception." A mistake by the accused as to the existence of the assault, the harm threatened or the force needed is not fatal to a self-defence claim, but the mistake must be reasonable.

a)   Reasonable Apprehension of an Unlawful Assault

In *Pétel*, the Supreme Court held that a person can qualify for a self-defence claim even though he or she was in fact not being unlawfully assaulted. The case arose when a woman who had been threatened by one of two men shot both of them after one of them had given her his gun. She claimed that she reasonably, but perhaps mistakenly, believed she was being unlawfully assaulted by both men. Lamer C.J. stated:

> An honest but reasonable mistake as to the existence of an assault is . . . permitted. . . . The existence of an assault must not be made a kind of prerequisite for the exercise of self-defence to be assessed without regard to the perception of the accused. This would amount in a sense to trying the victim before the accused.[99]

The question for the jury is not "'was the accused unlawfully assaulted?' but rather 'did the accused reasonably believe, in the circum-

97   *Pétel*, above note 20; *Malott*, above note 17.
98   *R. v. Reilly* (1984), 15 C.C.C. (3d) 1 at 7 (S.C.C.) [*Reilly*].
99   *Pétel*, above note 20 at 104.

stances, that she was being unlawfully assaulted?'"[100] In determining the reasonableness of the belief, the jury could consider prior threats and violence received by the accused from the victim[101] and expert evidence concerning battered woman's syndrome.[102]

b) Reasonable Apprehension of Death or Grievous Bodily Harm

In *Lavallee*,[103] the Supreme Court held that there was no legal requirement that the accused wait until she faced an imminent attack from the deceased. In doing so, the Court upheld the acquittal of a woman who had shot her abusive partner in the back of the head after he had threatened that she would be harmed after guests had left their house. Wilson J. stated that expert testimony about the effects of battering on women can cast doubt on the view expressed in a previous case that it was "inherently unreasonable to apprehend death or grievous bodily harm unless and until the physical assault is actually in progress."[104] Expert evidence may suggest "it may in fact be possible for a battered spouse to accurately predict the onset of violence before the first blow is struck, even if an outsider to the relationship cannot." She stressed:

> [t]he issue is not, however, what an outsider would have reasonably perceived but what the accused reasonably perceived, given her situation and her experience. . . .
>
> . . . I do not think it is an unwarranted generalization to say that due to their size, strength, socialization and lack of training, women are typically no match for men in hand-to-hand combat. The requirement . . . that a battered woman wait until the physical assault is "underway" before her apprehensions can be validated in law would . . . be tantamount to sentencing her to "murder by installment."[105]

In the context of spousal battering, "the definition of what is reasonable must be adapted to circumstances which are, by and large, foreign to the world inhabited by the hypothetical 'reasonable man.'"[106] In subsequent cases, the Supreme Court affirmed that evidence of prior threats and beatings would be relevant to the determination of whether the accused could perceive danger from an abuser and had a reasonable

---

100 *Malott*, above note 17 at 464.
101 *Pétel*, above note 20.
102 *Malott*, above note 17.
103 *Lavallee*, above note 2.
104 *Ibid.* at 116, citing *R. v. Whynot* (1983), 9 C.C.C. (3d) 449 (N.S. C.A.) [*Whynot*].
105 *Ibid.* at 120.
106 *Ibid.* at 114.

apprehension of death or grievous bodily harm.[107] The accused's knowledge of the complainant's propensity for violence is also relevant.[108] Although there is no legal requirement of an immiment attack, the presence or absence of imminiency is a factor that can be considered in determining whether the accused had a reasonable apprehension of death or grievous bodily harm.[109]

The jury should not, however, be instructed about section 34(2) if there is no air of reality to the accused's claim that he had a reasonable apprehension of death or grievous bodily harm. An adult son, for example, could not claim to have reasonably apprehended that his frail, asthmatic seventy-five-year-old father presented such a realistic danger of inflicting death or grievous bodily harm.[110]

c) Reasonable Belief in Lack of Alternatives to Prevent Death or Grievous Bodily Harm

In *Lavallee*, the Supreme Court held that evidence of battering and expert evidence on the effects of battering were also relevant in determining whether the accused had a reasonable belief in the lack of alternative means to preserve oneself from death or grievous bodily harm. Such evidence would be particularly relevant in explaining why a woman did not leave an abusive relationship sooner. Wilson J. stressed that the jury should consider the accused's situation and experience when determining whether she had a reasonable belief that she could not save herself except by using deadly force. She explained:

> I think the question the jury must ask itself is whether, given the history, circumstances and perceptions of the [accused], her belief that she could not preserve herself from being killed by [the deceased] that night except by killing him first was reasonable.[111]

In *Pétel*, the Supreme Court affirmed that the prior assaults suffered by the accused and her daughter would be relevant to determining the reasonableness of her "belief that she could not extricate herself otherwise than by killing the attacker."[112] In *Malott*,[113] the Court again affirmed that evidence with respect to past battering may be relevant to determining

---

107 *Pétel*, above note 20; *Malott*, above note 17.
108 *Pintar*, above note 95 at 435.
109 *Cinous*, above note 22.
110 *Hebert*, above note 91.
111 *Ibid.* at 125.
112 *Pétel*, above note 20 at 104.
113 *Malott*, above note 17.

whether the accused believed on reasonable grounds that she could not otherwise preserve herself from death or grievous bodily harm.

The Supreme Court in *Lavallee* affirmed that there is no requirement that the accused retreat in order to qualify for the section 34(2) defence.[114] The origins of this concept are in the old common law notion that "a man's home is his castle."[115] Wilson J. argued that a "man's home may be his castle but it is also the woman's home even if it seems to her more like a prison in the circumstances."[116] This would suggest that courts should not consider retreat as a reasonable alternative to the accused's use of force.

The jury should not, however, be instructed about section 34(2) if there is no air of reality to the accused's claim that he reasonably believed he had no alternative but to act in self-defence. In *R. v. Cinous*,[117] the Supreme Court held that there was no air of reality to put self-defence to the jury in a case in which a man shot another man in the back of the head while they were stopped at a service station en route to steal computers together. The accused feared that the deceased and a companion were planning to kill him because they had put on latex gloves. The accused also testified that he believed he had no alternatives. He had tried to avoid the deceased and he did not think of calling the police to help because he had spent his whole life running from the police. McLachlin C.J. and Bastarache J. for the majority of the Court held that while the jury may reasonably have reached a conclusion that the accused reasonably apprehended an assault and death or grievous bodily harm, it could not have reasonably concluded that the accused reasonably believed he had no alternatives but killing the person. Unlike in *Lavallee*, there was no evidence supporting why the accused may have reasonably believed that there were no other alternatives. The fact that the accused may have reasonably believed that the police could not protect him was not enough. He could still have fled the scene: "Section 34(2) does not require than an accused rule out a few courses of action other than killing. The requirement is that the accused have believed on reasonable grounds that there was *no alternative course of action* open to him. . . . This defence is intended to cover situations of last resort."[118]

---

114 A statutory duty to retreat is imposed by *Code*, above note 2, s. 35(c) on those accused who committed the initial assault or provoked it.

115 *Semayne's Case* (1604), 77 E.R. 194 (K.B.). See also *Antley*, above note 92; *Deegan*, above note 92, affirming the concept in the context of intruders on the accused's property.

116 *Lavallee*, above note 2 at 124.

117 *Cinous*, above note 22.

118 *Ibid*. at paras. 123–24.

Cinous demonstrates a reluctance to extend *Lavallee* beyond the context of expert evidence about battered women.[119]

3) Self-Defence and the Modified Objective Standard

Lavallee was a landmark case because it was the Supreme Court's first decision embracing a modified objective approach that considered the accused's situation and experience when determining whether there was a reasonable basis for his or her beliefs. *Lavallee* does not, however, make the accused's subjective belief or the fact that she has been previously battered determinative of her self-defence claim.[120] Wilson J. warned:

> the fact that the accused was a battered woman does not entitle her to an acquittal. Battered women may well kill their partners other than in self-defence. The focus is not on who the woman is, but on what she did. . . .
>
> Ultimately, it is up to the jury to decide whether, in fact, the accused's perceptions and actions were reasonable.[121]

The modified objective approach of *Lavallee* has been very influential and is now taken not only with respect to self-defence, but also with respect to provocation, necessity and the common law defence of duress.[122]

In *Nelson*,[123] the Ontario Court of Appeal held that an accused's diminished intelligence should be considered in determining whether he had a self-defence claim under section 34(2). The Court of Appeal stated that an accused with an intellectual impairment relating to his or her ability to perceive and react to an assault "may be in a position similar to that of the accused in *Lavallee* in that his or her apprehension and belief could not be fairly measured against the perceptions of

---

119 See also *R. v. Charlebois* (2000), 148 C.C.C. (3d) 449 at para. 16 (S.C.C.).

120 For a subjective approach to self-defence, see *Beckford v. R.* (1987), [1988] A.C. 130 (P.C.). In *People v. Goetz*, 497 N.E. 2d 41 at 50 (1986), the New York Court of Appeals stated that to base self-defence solely on the accused's subjective beliefs "would allow citizens to set their own standards for the permissible use of force" and risk acquitting individuals who use violence "no matter how aberrational or bizarre his thought patterns."

121 *Lavallee*, above note 2 at 126.

122 The modified objective approach has been used with respect to objective standards used in defences but not offences. Compare *Thibert*, above note 16 and *Hibbert*, above note 1, and *R v. Latimer* (2001), 150 C.C.C. (3d) 129 (S.C.C.) with *Creighton*, above note 3.

123 *Nelson*, above note 88 at 467.

an 'ordinary man.'" The jury should be instructed to consider a reasonable person with any of the characteristics and experiences that are relevant to the accused's ability to perceive harm and the accused's ability to respond to the harm. The accused's age, gender, strength, and past experience with the person who presents a threat may be relevant to his or her perception of the harm and response to threatened harm. At the same time, there must still be a reasonable basis for the accused's perceptions.

One characteristic of the particular accused that will not be considered is his or her intoxication. In *Reilly*,[124] the Supreme Court held that the accused's intoxication could not be considered in determining whether he reasonably apprehended harm. The Court concluded:

> The perspective of the reasonable man which the language of s. 34(2) places in issue here is the objective standard the law commonly adopts to measure a man's conduct. A reasonable man is a man in full possession of his faculties. In contrast, a drunken man is one whose ability to reason and to perceive are diminished by the alcohol he has consumed.

The Court left open the possibility that an intoxicated accused could have a valid self-defence claim provided that he or she still had reasonable grounds for his or her beliefs.

4) Section 35

Section 35 is a complicated section that attempts to restrict self-defence for those accused who, without justification, assault another or provoke an assault by words, blows, or gestures. Similar to section 34(2), the section requires a reasonable apprehension of death or bodily harm and a reasonable belief that the force was necessary to preserve the accused from death or grievous bodily harm. In addition, it requires that the accused not have the intent to cause death or grievous bodily harm before the necessity of self-preservation arose, and that the accused retreat as far as feasible before the necessity of self-preservation arose. The section seems designed to deprive an accused who initiates or provokes a fight with the intent to cause death or grievous bodily harm of the defence. An absence of evidence with respect to any of its multiple requirements including the requirement to retreat before

---

124 *Reilly*, above note 98 at 8.

the necessity of self-preservation arises may justify withholding the defence from the jury.[125]

Given that an accused who was the initial aggressor, who provoked the assault and who intentionally causes death or bodily harm, can qualify under the less restrictive section 34(2),[126] section 35 may be something of a dead letter. Somewhat absurdly, its restrictions will apply only in those cases where the accused is the initial aggressor and does not, as required under section 34(2), cause death or grievous bodily harm. Thus, an accused who initiates and provokes a fight, but does not cause death or grievous bodily harm, will have to qualify for the more restrictive section 35 defence. He or she must have retreated and not have formed the intent to cause death or grevious bodily harm before the necessity of self-preservation arose.

5) Section 37

Section 37 extends the ambit of self-defence by stating that "everyone is justified in using force to defend himself or any one under his protection from assault, if he uses no more force than is necessary to prevent the assault or the repetition of it." Thus, a parent could be justified under section 37 for using force to protect his or her child. As with other self-defence provisions, section 37 requires that the accused perceive a threat and respond reasonably to that threat.

Unlike sections 34(2) and 35, section 37 does not require a reasonable apprehension of death or grievous bodily harm, or a reasonable belief that the force used was necessary to prevent death or grievous bodily harm. Rather, the section simply refers to the use of necessary force to defend oneself or anyone under one's protection. In *Whynot*,[127] it was held that the section 37 defence should be withheld from the jury when the deceased was killed when he was asleep, even though he had beaten the accused and her children in the past and threatened to do so again. This holding is overruled by *Lavallee*, which suggests that, in the appropriate case, it may be reasonable for an accused who has been battered in the past to anticipate an assault and believe there is no alternative but self-defence.

Section 37, like section 34(1), requires that the force be no more than necessary. Although this requires some form of proportionality,

---

125 *Pintar*, above note 95 at 423.
126 *McIntosh*, above note 94.
127 *Whynot*, above note 104.

courts have generally not insisted that proportionality be measured with nicety or that proportionality requires a duty to retreat.[128] Section 37 does not explicitly require the accused to have any particular intent or duty to retreat: "Rather, s. 37 affords justification to persons who use force to ward off or prevent an assault against themselves or those under their protection so long as the force used is no more than necessary to prevent the assault or its repetition."[129] Section 37 is, however, broader than section 34(1) and it could avail an accused who uses force to protect another person and who intends to cause death or grievous bodily harm provided that the force was necessary and not excessive.[130]

6) Excessive Self-Defence

Canadian courts have not recognized a partial defence for accused who engage in excessive and unreasonable self-defence, which in some other jurisdictions reduces murder to manslaughter. Dickson J. has concluded in the context of an unsuccessful self-defence claim under section 34(2):

> Where a killing has resulted from the excessive use of force in self-defence the accused loses the justification provided under s. 34. There is no partial justification open under the section. Once the jury reaches the conclusion that excessive force has been used, the defence of self-defence has failed.[131]

This decision is also supported by section 26 of the *Criminal Code* which provides that everyone authorized by law to use force is criminally responsible for any excess of force. The result can make self-defence, especially when the accused has the intent required for murder, an all or nothing proposition. The options are either to acquit on the basis of self-defence or to convict the accused of the most serious offence with its mandatory penalty of life imprisonment. Concern about the ultimate disposition of an accused in cases such as *Lavallee* and *Pétel* may have influenced the development of the law of self-defence. It also places significant pressure on the accused to accept a plea bargain to manslaughter should one be offered.

---

128 *Antley*, above note 92.
129 *Pintar*, above note 95 at 424.
130 *R. v. Grandin* (2001), 154 C.C.C. (3d) 408 (B.C.C.A.).
131 *Faid*, above note 28 at 518.

7) Defence of Property

There are numerous *Criminal Code* provisions dealing with the defence of property. They are complicated by unnecessary distinctions between the defence of personal property as opposed to dwelling houses and real property. Section 38(1) appears to allow those in peaceable possession of personal property and those lawfully assisting them to prevent a person from taking it provided they do not "strike or cause bodily harm to the trespasser." Nevertheless, if the trespasser persists in taking the property, he or she is deemed under section 38(2) to have committed an assault without justification or provocation. In such circumstances, "the amount of force that may be used to prevent or defend against any assault actually committed by the wrongdoer depends upon the ordinary principles of self-defence as set out in section 34 of the Code."[132]

The same approach is used in section 41(1), which allows those in peaceable possession of a dwelling house or real property and those lawfully assisting them to use no more force than necessary to prevent or remove a trespasser. A trespasser who resists being removed or who resists being denied entry in the first place is deemed under section 41(2) to have committed as assault without justification or provocation. In order to claim these justifications, the accused must have been in peaceable possession of the property by not seriously being challenged by others in the possession. The defence has been denied to Aboriginal protesters who have occupied land on the basis that they were not in peaceable possession of the land that could not be seriously challenged by others.[133] Any mistake as to the element of the defence would have to be both honest and reasonable, but a modified objective standard should be applied in determining the latter requirement.

Section 40 provides that everyone in peaceable possession of a dwelling house can use as much force as necessary to prevent any person from forcibly breaking and entering the dwelling house without lawful authority.[134] The courts have, however, been reluctant to contemplate the use of deadly force to defend property. In *R. v. Gee*,[135] Dickson J. quoted with approval an authority that stated it "cannot be

---

132 *Baxter*, above note 91 at 115.
133 *R. v. George* (2000), 145 C.C.C. (3d) 405 (Ont. C.A.); *R. v. Born With A Tooth* (1992), 76 C.C.C. (3d) 169 (Alta. C.A.).
134 *Code*, above note 2, ss. 40 and 41. A police officer must announce his or her lawful authority. *R. v. Colet* (1981), 57 C.C.C. (2d) 105 (S.C.C.).
135 (1982), 68 C.C.C. (2d) 516 at 528 (S.C.C.). See also *R. v. Clark* (1983), 5 C.C.C. (3d) 264 at 271 (Alta. C.A.).

reasonable to kill another merely to prevent a crime which is directed only against property." This would not preclude a person whose house was being broken into from arguing self-defence under sections 34 or 37 of the *Code*.

Section 42(1) allows peaceable entry by day into a dwelling or real property to take lawful possession of it. If a person in peaceable possession or with a claim of right to the property resists such an entry, then under section 41(3) that person's actions are deemed to have been provoked by the person entering. Hence the defender's claim to self-defence would fall under section 34. A person without such a claim to the property, is deemed under section 42(2) to be assaulting the person entering without justification and with provocation. Hence, that defender's claims to be acting in self-defence may be limited by section 35.

8) Related Defences

There are a number of other provisions that allow justifications for the use of force in specific situations. Section 43 justifies the use of force by way of correction by schoolteachers and parents towards children under their care, provided the force does not exceed what is reasonable under the circumstances. The Supreme Court has narrowly interpreted this controversial defence because it restricts the protection of the law afforded to people from unconsented invasions of their physical security and dignity. It has held that section 43 does not apply to the discipline of mentally disabled adults and only applies when used with the intent and for the benefit of correction and education.[136]

In *Canadian Foundation for Children v. Canada*,[137] the Supreme Court upheld section 43 as not violating sections 7, 12, or 15 of the *Charter*. Although section 43 adversely affects children's security of the person, it was consistent with the principles of fundamental justice. The requirement that the force be reasonable in the circumstances was not unduly vague under section 7 of the *Charter*. The Court indicated that the force must be used for corrective purposes and not include corporal punishment for those under two or over twelve years of age, corporal punishment using objects, such as rulers or belts, or slaps or blows to the head.[138] The result of the decision was to place new restrictions on the section 43 defence. These restrictions are expressed in clear and categorical terms. The majority of the Court justified this

---

136 R. v. *Ogg-Moss* (1984), 14 C.C.C. (3d) 116 (S.C.C.).
137 2004 SCC 4.
138 *Ibid.* at paras. 37 and 40.

approach as a proper interpretation of the defence in light of expert evidence and Canada's international obligations while a minority argued that it was an impermissible reading down of a vague and overbroad defence that should have been struck down.

Section 45 justifies the performance of a surgical operation for a person's benefit if the operation was reasonable in the circumstances and performed with reasonable care. A doctor's actions in stopping respiratory support of a patient at the patient's request that nature be allowed to take its course has been held to be justified under this provision on the basis that the doctor's actions were reasonable.[139]

Sections 25 to 33 provide various justifications for the use of force to prevent criminal offences and to assist in enforcing the law. It is possible for an accused claiming to have been enforcing the law to rely on illegal orders as long as they are not manifestly illegal and the official still could voluntarily choose to disobey such orders.[140] Peace officers may use force intended to cause death or grievous bodily harm to stop a fleeing suspect in certain circumstances outlined in section 25(4) and (5). They can act, not only to protect themselves but others, from imminent or future death or grievous bodily harm. A previous provision that authorized the shooting of fleeing felons without regard to whether or not they were dangerous was held to be an unjustified violation of section 7 of the *Charter* by threatening people's lives and security of the person in a disproportionate manner.[141]

D. NECESSITY

Courts were historically reluctant to recognize necessity caused by dire circumstances of peril as either an excuse or a justification. In R. v. *Dudley*,[142] men who killed a boy and resorted to cannibalism when lost at sea were convicted of murder. Noting that it was "the weakest, the youngest, the most unresisting" who was chosen to die, the court declared that any defence of necessity "appeared to us to be at once dangerous, immoral, and opposed to all legal principle and analogy." The Court conceded that the accused were subject to great suffering, but concluded:

---

139 B.(N.) v. *Hôtel-Dieu de Québec* (1992), 69 C.C.C. (3d) 450 (Que. S.C.).

140 R. v. *Finta* (1994), 88 C.C.C. (3d) 417 (S.C.C.); R. v. *Devereaux* (1996), 112 C.C.C. (3d) 243 (Nfld. C.A.).

141 R. v. *Lines*, [1993] O.J. No. 3248 (Gen. Div.).

142 (1884), 14 Q.B.D. 273 at 287 (C.C.R.).

> We are often compelled to set up standards we cannot reach ourselves. . . . [A] man has no right to declare temptation to be an excuse, though he might himself have yielded to it, nor allow compassion for the criminal to change or weaken in any matter the legal definition of the crime.[143]

If the boy killed had not been defenceless, but had provoked the accused or attacked them, they might have had a partial excuse of provocation or a justification of self-defence. If one of the accused had threatened another to kill the boy, the person threatened might have had a defence of duress. As things stood, however, the accused did not have a defence of necessity and they were convicted of murder. They were sentenced to death, but their sentences were commuted to six months' imprisonment in an exercise of royal mercy by the Queen.

In the 1970s, necessity was pleaded as a defence to the crime of performing an abortion without the approval of an abortion committee. Dickson J. stated for the Supreme Court that the defence of necessity was "ill-defined and elusive," and concluded that if it did exist in Canadian law, "it can go no further than to justify non-compliance in urgent situations of clear and imminent peril when compliance with the law is demonstrably impossible." He added that "no system of positive law can recognize any principle which would entitle a person to violate the law because on his view the law conflicted with some higher social value."[144] Laskin C.J. dissented and would have left the defence with the jury, allowing them to decide whether there was an immediate danger to the woman's life or health and whether it was certain that a legal and committee-approved abortion could be obtained to prevent that danger.

The Supreme Court finally recognized necessity as a common law defence in *Perka*,[145] which involved drug smugglers who were forced to come ashore in Canada because of dangerous seas. Dickson C.J. was careful to restrict necessity to "circumstances of imminent risk where the action was taken to avoid a direct and immediate peril"; where the act was "morally involuntary" as "measured on the basis of society's expectation of appropriate and normal resistance to pressure"; and where it was clear that there was no reasonable legal alternative to avoid the peril. The Court recognized necessity as an excuse for morally involuntary conduct but not as a justification.

---

143 *Ibid.* at 288.
144 *R. v. Morgentaler (No. 5)* (1975), 20 C.C.C. (2d) 449 at 497 (S.C.C.).
145 *Perka*, above note 8.

1) Necessity an Excuse and Not a Justification

Dickson C.J. stressed in *Perka* that necessity could only operate as an excuse in the face of immediate and urgent circumstances, and that it should not be based on "the comparative social utility of breaking the law against importing as compared to obeying the law."[146] In her concurring opinion, Wilson J. would have left open the possibility that necessity could operate as a justification. In such a scenario, an accused could have the defence, even though he or she did not act in a morally involuntary manner in the face of an emergency. Rather, the accused could deliberate and decide that the "fulfillment of the legal duty to save persons entrusted to one's care is preferred over the lesser offences of trespass or petty theft."[147] The English Court of Appeal has recognized necessity as a justification to a deliberate and intentional killing in a case of the conjoined twins where it was certain that they would both eventually die if they were not separated.[148] Whether necessity could be a justification as well as an excuse could have had a practical effect in the abortion context, where those who did not comply with the law had often made a deliberate decision to violate the law.

In *R. v. Morgentaler*,[149] the Ontario Court of Appeal held that the defence of necessity should not have been left to the jury when doctors were charged with violating a *Criminal Code* provision that required the approval of a hospital committee before an abortion was performed. The Court stated that the doctors' deliberate and planned decision to violate the law was inconsistent with the morally involuntary response to an immediate peril to life or health that was required for a necessity defence. The Supreme Court[150] did not deal with this issue because it decided that the law requiring approval of an abortion by a hospital committee was an unjustified violation of the rights of women under section 7 of the *Charter*.

The conceptualization of necessity as an excuse may preclude premeditated and deliberate decisions to violate the law. At the same time, it also precludes a "clean hands" argument that would deny the necessity defence to those who were engaged in illegal activity when they

---

146 *Ibid.* at 402. Thus, a moral belief that abortion was or was not moral could not be the basis for a necessity defence. *R. v. Bridges* (1990), 62 C.C.C. (3d) 455 (B.C.C.A.).

147 *Perka*, above note 8 at 420.

148 *A (Children) (Conjoined Twins: Surgical Separation)*, [2000] 4 All E.R. 961 (C.A.).

149 (1985), 22 C.C.C. (3d) 353 (Ont. C.A.).

150 *R. v. Morgentaler (No. 2)* (1988), 37 C.C.C. (3d) 449 (S.C.C.), discussed in ch. 1, "Principles of Fundamental Justice."

were faced with circumstances of urgent and compelling necessity. In *Perka*, the Court rejected the argument that an accused who is engaged in illegal conduct should be disentitled to the necessity defence. This decision meant that the jury could consider the defence, even though the accused had been engaged in drug smuggling when a storm forced them to land on Canadian territory. This followed from the Court's conceptualization of the defence as an excuse that in no way justifies the conduct and the Court's focus on whether the accused had any realistic choice but to commit the crime. Nevertheless, Dickson C.J. indicated that the defence of necessity would not apply "if the necessitous situation was clearly foreseeable to the reasonable observer, if the actor contemplated or ought to have contemplated that his actions would likely give rise to an emergency requiring the breaking of the law."[151] In such circumstances, the defence would be denied, not because the accused was acting illegally, but because his or her conduct was not morally involuntary.

Necessity and duress are recognized in Canada only as excuses. Excuses have a self-defining feature because they are based on what is required by a realistic concession to human weaknesses and do not normally involve a calculation of the respective harms that are avoided and harms that are inflicted.[152] Dickson C.J. elaborated that necessity conceptualized as an excuse "rests on a realistic assessment of human weakness, recognizing that a liberal and humane criminal law cannot hold people to the strict obedience of laws in emergency situations where normal human instincts, whether of self-preservation or of altruism, overwhelmingly impel disobedience."[153] The Court's rejection of necessity as a justification could cause injustice especially if the courts take a narrow and restrictive approach to the question of the iminence of peril.

The Supreme Court in *R. v. Latimer*[154] articulated three elements of necessity: 1) the requirement of imminent peril or danger; 2) the requirement of no reasonable legal alternative; and 3) the requirement of proportionality between the harm inflicted and the harm avoided. As will be discussed below, the first two requirements are evaluated according to the "modified objective standard . . . that takes into account the

---

151   *Ibid.* at 403.
152   As will be seen, however, a proportionality requirement was imposed in *Perka*, above note 8, out of an abundance of caution.
153   *Ibid.* at 398.
154   *R. v. Latimer* (2001), 150 C.C.C. (3d) 129 (S.C.C.) [*Latimer*].

situation of the particular accused person"[155] while the third proportionality standard is assessed on a purely objective standard.

Before the jury is instructed to consider the necessity defence, the judge must determine that there is an air of reality to the defence. This means that there must be evidence relating to each of the three parts of the test and that the evidence must be such that a properly instructed jury acting reasonably could acquit the accused. In *Perka*, the Court indicated that there was an air of reality to the necessity defence in a case where the accused put into shore with thirty-three tons of marijuana because they faced imminent peril on the ocean. In *R. v. Latimer*,[156] however, the Court unanimously held that there was no air of reality with respect to any of the elements of necessity when a father killed his daughter in order to prevent her from suffering severe pain that would be caused by a medically required operation.

2) Imminent Peril and Danger

Dickson C.J. indicated in *Perka* that necessity as an excuse only applied when the accused had no realistic choice but to violate the law. He suggested that "at minimum, the situation must be so emergent and the peril must be so pressing that normal human instincts cry out for action and make a counsel of patience unreasonable."[157] The requirement in *Perka* of an imminent peril might be in tension to the recognition six years later in *Lavallee* that some accused, because of their experience and situation, should not be required to wait until harm was just about to occur. Similarly, what may be a reasonable legal alternative for some accused may not be for others.[158]

In addition, the requirement in *Perka* that the peril be imminent might violate section 7 of the *Charter* if the accused responded in a morally involuntary fashion to a serious and unavoidable threat of future harm. In *Ruzic*,[159] a statutory requirement that the duress defence be limited to threats of immediate death or bodily harm was held to violate section 7 of the *Charter* because it could punish those who acted in a morally involuntary fashion.

---

155 *Ibid.* at para. 32.

156 *Ibid.*

157 *Perka*, above note 8 at 399.

158 In *R. v. Lalonde* (1995), 37 C.R. (4th) 97 at 109 (Ont. Gen. Div.) [*Lalonde*], *R. v. Lavallee* (above note 2) was applied to expand the common law defence of necessity.

159 *Ruzic*, above note 5.

Following *Ruzic*, the requirement of imminence in the related defence of necessity should not be restricted to immediate threats. It is difficult to distinguish between an accused who breaks into a cabin for food before he or she has reached a level of starvation or exposure that is life-threatening and one who waits until the peril is immediate. Similarly, it would be difficult to distinguish between a person who leaves a secluded location by driving while impaired to escape a serious attack that has not yet commenced and one who waits until the attack is actually underway. Both accused in these scenarios would have no safe avenue of escape and no realistic choice but to violate the law. A restrictive approach to the imminence requirement is particularly undesirable given the Court's categorical rejection of necessity as a justification that could apply to deliberate and well-thought-out decisions to break the law.

In *R. v. Latimer*,[160] the Supreme Court affirmed the requirement that "disaster must be imminent, or harm unavoidable and near. It is not enough that the peril is foreseeable or likely; it must be on the verge of transpiring and virtually certain to occur." This restrictive formulation of the imminence requirement creates a risk that the peril may not be held to be imminent until the accused faces an immediate threat. As discussed above, a requirement of an immediate threat would be at odds with developments in self-defence and duress. At the same time, the Court was on firmer ground when it indicated that "where the situation of peril clearly should have been foreseen and avoided, an accused person cannot reasonably claim any immediate peril."[161] On the facts of the case, the Court held there was no imminent peril because Tracy Latimer's "ongoing pain did not constitute an emergency in this case" but was rather "'an obstinate and long-standing state of affairs'"and that the proposed surgery "did not pose an imminent threat to her life, nor did her medical condition."[162]

The accused's subjective belief that there is an imminent peril is not determinative. There must be a reasonable basis for that belief. Reasonableness will be determined on a modified objective standard. In *Latimer*, the Court held that there was no reasonable basis for Latimer's belief in imminence in part because "there was no evidence of a legitimate psychological condition that rendered him unable to perceive that there was no imminent peril."[163] Here an analogy to evidence of the

---

160 *Latimer*, above note 154 at para. 29.
161 *Ibid.* at para. 29.
162 *Ibid.* at para. 38.
163 *Ibid.* at para. 38.

ability of battered women to predict when another round of battering was imminent might be made. In the absence of such psychological evidence, however, the Court rejected Latimer's subjective belief in the imminence of the peril as unreasonable.

3) No Legal Way Out or Safe Avenue of Escape

In *Perka*,[164] the Court suggested that "if there is a reasonable legal alternative to disobeying the law, then the decision to disobey becomes a voluntary one, imperilled by some consideration beyond the dictates of 'necessity' and human instincts." In that case, there was no legal way out because the accused faced disaster and drowning at sea if they did not put ashore with their large cargo of drugs. In the two *Morgentaler* cases,[165] there were legal ways out because a legal abortion could have been approved by a therapeutic abortion committee as then required under the *Criminal Code*. In *Latimer*,[166] the Court affirmed that "if there was a reasonable legal alternative to breaking the law, there is no necessity." It indicated that legal alternatives must be pursued even though they may be "demanding," "sad," and "unappealing."[167] In this case, the Court indicated that allowing Tracy Latimer to go through the required operation and inserting a feeding tube to assist with pain management were reasonable legal alternatives that the accused should have pursued. The determination of no reasonable legal alternative should be determined on a modified objective standard so that any past experiences that the accused had with the victim's pain, pain management, and surgeries in the past should have been relevant in determining the reasonableness of legal alternatives.

There is some overlap in the determination of the imminence of the peril and the existence of reasonable legal alternatives. In both cases, courts should be careful before demanding that the accused wait until the peril is immediate. The defence of necessity has been denied in a case in which an accused engaged in impaired driving to flee a possible attack because there were other safe avenues of escape.[168] This makes sense because the accused had a reasonable legal way out. It would not, however, make sense to deny the defence to a person with

---

164 Above note 8.
165 *R. v. Morgentaler* (1975), 20 C.C.C .(2d) 449 (S.C.C); *R. v. Morgentaler* (1985), 22 C.C.C. (3d) 353 (Ont. C.A.).
166 *Latimer*, above note 154 at para. 30.
167 *Ibid.* at para. 38.
168 *R. v. Berriman* (1987), 45 M.V.R. 165 (Nfld. C.A.).

no safe avenue of escape on the basis that she did not wait until the attack was underway to drive away while in an impaired state. It would also be inconsistent with *Lavallee* to deny the necessity defence until the attack was underway. As with the imminence requirement discussed above, the concept of safe avenue of escape found in the related defence of duress can be helpful in determining whether the peril is imminent and whether there was a reasonable legal alternative.

4) Proportionality Required Between Harm Inflicted and Harm Avoided

Even though he conceptualized necessity as an excuse and not a justification, Dickson C.J. required that, as is the case with self-defence, there be proportionality between the harm sought to be avoided and the harm committed by the accused. He stated:

> Even if the requirements for urgency and "no legal way out" are met, there is clearly a further consideration. There must be some way of assuring proportionality. No rational criminal justice system, no matter how humane or liberal, could excuse the infliction of a greater harm to allow the actor to avert a lesser evil.[169]

In *Latimer*,[170] the Court affirmed the importance of the proportionality requirement and held that killing a person was "completely disproportionate" to "non-life-threatening suffering" should Tracy Latimer have had the proposed operation. This suggests that the Court saw the case as one "where proportionality can quickly be dismissed" so that it might not even be necessary to examine whether the above two requirements of the necessity defence can be applied. On the other hand, the Court recognized that "most situations fall into a grey area that requires a difficult balancing of harms" and warned that it was not necessary that the harm avoided "clearly outweigh" the harm inflicted, but only that the two harms be "of a comparable gravity."[171] In this vein, the Court declined to create an absolute rule that murder would be categorically excluded from the necessity defence as a disproportionate response to all possible perils. At the same time, the case stands for the proposition that killing is disproportionate to relieving non–life-threatening suffering.

---

169 *Perka*, above note 8 at 400–1.
170 *Latimer*, above note 154 at para. 41.
171 *Ibid.* at para. 31.

5) Modified Objective Standard for Imminence and No Legal Way Out but Not Proportionality

As in the other defences in this chapter, the reasonable person will generally be tailored to reflect the past experiences and frailties of the particular accused. In *Hibbert*,[172] Chief Justice Lamer observed that:

> The defences of self-defence, duress and necessity are essentially similar, so much so that consistency demands that each defence's "reasonableness" requirement be assessed on the same basis . . . [namely an objective standard] that takes into account the particular circumstances and frailties of the accused. . . . [I]t is appropriate to employ an objective standard that takes into account the particular circumstances of the accused, including his or her ability to perceive the existence of alternative courses of actions.

In *R. v. Latimer*, the Court confirmed that a modified objective standard that takes into account the situation and characteristics of the accused should be used for determining 1) whether there was an imminent peril and 2) whether there was a reasonable legal alternative. It cautioned that the modified objective standard must be distinguished from the subjective standard. Thus, the fact that an accused like Robert Latimer subjectively believed that there was imminent peril and no reasonable legal alternative was not enough because his beliefs must also be "reasonable given his circumstances and attributes."[173] In the absence of psychological evidence relating to him as a caregiver for a child who lived in much pain, the use of the modified objective standard made little difference in *Latimer*.

The Court in *Latimer* concluded that a modified objective standard should not be used when determining whether there was proportionality between the harm inflicted and the harm avoided. Proportionality was to be determined on a purely objective standard that is not modified by the characteristics and experiences of the accused or the victim. The Court was concerned that a modified objective standard would give too little weight to harms suffered by the victim who was severely disabled. Proportionality is a matter of the moral standards of the community and these standards are "infused with constitutional considerations (such as, in this case, the s.15(1) equality rights of the disabled)."[174]

---

172 *Hibbert*, above note 1 at 227.
173 *Latimer*, above note 154 at para. 33.
174 *Ibid.* at para. 34.

E. DURESS

Like necessity, duress occurs when an accused commits a crime in response to external pressure. In the case of duress, the pressure is threats of harm by some other person. The classic case is the person who commits a crime or assists in the commission of a crime with a gun to his or her head.

The defence of duress in Canada is very complex, in large part because section 17 of the *Criminal Code* contains a very restrictive defence that requires threats of immediate death or bodily harm from a person present when the offence was committed, and excludes a long list of offences ranging from murder to arson. Even before the *Charter*, the courts minimized the harsh impact of this restrictive defence by applying it only to principal offenders, and not parties to crime. Instead, the courts applied the more flexible common law defence to parties to a crime on the grounds that they were not covered by section 17 that applies only to "a person who commits an offence." The Supreme Court has performed some major surgery on section 17 by holding that its requirement that threats must be of immediate death or bodily harm and made by a person who is present when the crime was committed violate section 7 of the *Charter* by denying the defence to those who have no realistic choice but to commit the offence and thus acts in a morally involuntary manner.[175] Section 17 as reformulated by the Court remains valid, albeit perhaps on life support. The Supreme Court has yet to rule whether the surviving parts of section 17 violate section 7 of the *Charter* because they categorically exclude from the defence those who commit offences such as murder, attempted murder, robbery, unlawfully causing bodily harm, and arson. It may well be that the categorical exclusion of such a long list of crimes will eventually be held to violate section 7 of the *Charter*. In such an eventuality, the common law defence of duress would apply not only to parties to a crime but to all offenders. The result would be to make the law considerably less complex and fairer to the accused.

The common law defence is less restrictive and more flexible than section 17 of the *Code*. The common law defence of duress applies when an accused commits a crime in a morally involuntary response to threats where there is no safe avenue of escape. The common law defence of duress, like the other defences examined in this chapter, is applied on the basis of a modified objective standard that makes allowance for the

---

175 *Ruzic*, above note 5.

particular characteristics and attributes of the accused. It does not require the threats to be of immediate death or bodily harm or from a person who is present when the offence is committed. The courts have stressed that duress as a common law defence is similar to necessity and this suggests that, as with necessity, there is some requirement for proportionality between the harm threatened and the harm committed by the accused Finally, circumstances of duress may prevent the Crown from proving some particularly high levels of subjective *mens rea* for a few crimes. In short, duress can refer to 1) the statutory defence available under section 17 of the *Criminal Code* to the principal offender who commits the offence and as modified by section 7 of the *Charter*; 2) the common law defence available to parties to an offence and would be available in all cases should section 17 be found in its entirety to violate section 7 of the *Charter*; and 3) a factor that may in rare cases prevent the Crown from proving the mental element for some crimes.

1) Section 17

Section 17 of the *Criminal Code* provides that the defence of duress is available only when an accused "commits an offence under compulsion by threats of immediate death or bodily harm from a person who is present when the offence is committed." The courts interpreted the requirement of a threat of immediate death or bodily harm quite literally. In *R. v. Carker (No. 2)*,[176] an accused charged with wilfully damaging public property argued that he acted under duress because he was threatened with death and serious bodily harm by fellow prisoners during a prison riot. The Supreme Court held that the defence of duress was not available because the accused and the prisoners issuing the threats were locked in their respective cells. Although the accused acted under compulsion of threats of death and grievous bodily harm that were operative at the time the offence was committed, "they were not threats of 'immediate death' or 'immediate bodily harm' and none of the persons who delivered them was present in the cell with the [accused] when the offence was committed."[177] Likewise, in *R. v. Hébert*,[178] a witness did not face threats of immediate death or bodily harm when he gave false testimony in court, because he could have sought official protection from

---

176 [1967] 2 C.C.C. 190 (S.C.C.) [*Carker*].
177 *Ibid.*
178 (1989), 49 C.C.C. (3d) 59 (S.C.C.).

anonymous phone threats. The Supreme Court has observed that "the plain meaning of section 17 is quite restrictive in scope. Indeed, the section seems tailor-made for the situation in which a person is compelled to commit an offence at gun point."[179]

a) Threats of Immediate Death or Bodily Harm from a Person Who Is Present

Section 17 required that the threats be of immediate death or bodily harm from a person who was present when the crime was committed. As will be discussed more fully below, the Supreme Court held in *R. v. Ruzic* that the requirements of immediacy and presence violated section 7 of the *Charter* because they could result in the punishment of a person who committed a crime in a morally involuntary manner. The Court's remedy in *Ruzic* was to sever these requirements from section 17 so that the statutory defence of duress no longer requires that the threats be of immediate death or bodily harm or that the person issuing the threats be present when the crime was committed.

b) Threats Can Be Directed Against the Accused or a Third Party

The Supreme Court in *R. v. Ruzic* clarified that threats of death or bodily harm against third parties such as the accused's family may be considered under section 17 of the *Criminal Code*.[180] This seems appropriate as threats to one's family or loved ones may be just as compelling as threats to oneself and Parliament has not clearly excluded threats to third parties from section 17.

c) Subjective Belief That Threats of Death or Bodily Harm Will Be Carried Out

Unlike provocation, self-defence, necessity or, as will be seen, common law duress, section 17 of the *Code* requires only that the accused subjectively believe that the threats will be carried out, and does not require a reasonable basis for such a belief. Under the other defences, the reasonableness of the belief is determined on a modified objective standard that takes into account the accused's characteristics and experiences. The subjective approach of section 17 means that even an unreasonable belief by the accused about threats of death and bodily harm may be a sufficient basis for the statutory defence of duress. This

---

179 *Ruzic*, above note 5 at para. 50.
180 *Ibid.* at para. 54.

raises the risk of people committing crimes on the basis of idiosyncratic and flawed perceptions of threats. The danger to social protection was lessened by the requirements that the threats be of immediate death or bodily harm from a person who is present, but, as will be discussed more fully below, these requirements have now been found unconstitutional and severed from section 17. In addition, the section 17 defence, unlike the common law defence, does not explicitly require either that the accused have no safe avenue of escape or that there be proportionality between the harm threatened and the harm caused by the accused. The main remaining restrictions in the section 17 defence are the list of offences that are categorically excluded from the statutory defence of duress.

d) Excluded Offences

Section 17 is not available if the accused is charged with a long list of offences including murder, attempted murder, sexual assault, forcible abduction, assault with a weapon or causing bodily harm, aggravated assault, unlawfully causing bodily harm, robbery, arson, and abduction of a young person. The question that arises in light of the *Ruzic* decision is whether such categorical restrictions on the duress defence can be justified if the accused is truly placed in a position in which he or she has no realistic choice but to commit one of the excluded offences. As will be seen, the excluded offences in section 17 will have to be measured against the constitutional principle that it violates the principles of fundamental justice to convict a person who commits a crime in a morally involuntary manner. Although it can be argued that an accused should not be able to commit a crime such as murder that is clearly disproportionate to a threat of bodily harm, it is also doubtful that the exclusion of offences such as arson can be justified under section 7 of the *Charter* when the accused or a third party has been threatened with death. Subsequent to *Ruzic*, one court has held that the exclusion of robbery in section 17 of the *Code* violated the principle that no one should be convicted for a morally involuntary crime.[181] As will be discussed below, it is not clear that even the exlusion of the most serious crimes such as murder and attempted murder from the section 17 defence can be justified in cases where the accused is threatened with death and commits the crime in a morally involuntary manner. The categorical exclusion of offences from the defence is a blunt

---

181 *R. v. Fraser* (2002), 6 C.R. (5th) 308 (N.S. Prov. Ct.).

and potentially overbroad means of ensuring social protection compared to the more proportionate approach of requiring true moral involuntariness before a defence of duress is recognized for the commission of any crime.

e) No Defence If Accused Is Party to a Conspiracy or Criminal Association

An accused claiming a section 17 defence of duress must not be "a party to a conspiracy or association whereby the person is subject to compulsion." The use of the word "association" suggests that the accused may be deprived of the offence because of prior contact with those who issue the threats, even though he or she had not entered into an agreement to commit a crime. This is a more restrictive exclusion than that contemplated under the common law defence of necessity, where involvement in criminal activity does not disentitle the actor to the excuse of necessity.[182] The Ontario Court of Appeal has held that those who voluntarily associate with a criminal organization should be denied the common law defence of duress.[183] This reasoning would presumably also apply to section 17, but the Court of Appeal did not deal with the Supreme Court's statement in *Perka* that the accused's involvement in illegal activities did not preclude the related defence of necessity in circumstances of true moral involuntariness. The broad exclusion from the section 17 defence of those who conspire or associate with those who subsequently threaten them may, like the excluded categories of offences, be found to violate section 7 of the *Charter* when applied to those who commit a crime under circumstances of true moral involuntariness. The focus should be on whether the accused had any realistic choice but to commit the offence at the time it was committed and not on the prior acts or associations of the accused.

f) Section 17 and the *Charter*

The restrictive defence of duress under section 17 of the *Criminal Code* has been successfully challenged as depriving the accused of liberty contrary to the principles of fundamental justice as protected under section 7 of the *Charter*. In *Langlois*,[184] the accused was charged with drug offences when he smuggled drugs for a prison inmate after receiving anonymous phone calls informing him that his family would be in dan-

---

182 *Perka*, above note 8 at 403.
183 *R. v. Li* (2002), 162 C.C.C. (3d) 360 (Ont. C.A.).
184 (1993), 80 C.C.C. (3d) 28 (Que. C.A.).

ger if he did not deliver the drugs. The threats in this case would not qualify under section 17 because they were not threats of immediate death or injury from a person present when the offence was committed. The Court of Appeal nevertheless concluded that the denial of the defence in these circumstances violated section 7 of the *Charter* by allowing the conviction of a morally blameless person who acted in a "normatively involuntary" manner as contemplated in *Perka*. Fish J.A. stressed that section 17 would allow the conviction of an accused who acted in response to "forceful and paralysing threats . . . of grave injury to a member of his or her family from a person who, though absent when the crime is committed, remains none the less positioned to actualize the threats soon if not immediately."[185] The government had not justified under section 1 of the *Charter* the requirements that the threats be of immediate death or bodily harm from a person present at the time the offence was committed, and the section was declared invalid.

In *Ruzic*,[186] the accused was charged with importing heroin after a person had threatened to kill her mother who lived in a foreign country, if she did not import the drugs. The accused also was threatened, burned with a lighter, and injected with heroin by those who threatened her. As in *Langlois*, section 17 would not apply because the threats faced by the accused were not threats of immediate death or bodily harm from a person who was present when the accused actually imported heroin into Canada. Justice LeBel for an unanimous Supreme Court held that a defence that punished morally involuntary behaviour would violate section 7 of the *Charter*. He reasoned:

> It is a principle of fundamental justice that only voluntary conduct-behaviour that is the product of a free will and controlled body, unhindered by external constraints — should attract the penalty and stigma of criminal liability. Depriving a person of liberty and branding her with the stigma of criminal liability would infringe the principles of fundamental justice if the accused did not have any realistic choice. The ensuing deprivation of liberty and stigma would have been imposed in violation of the tenets of fundamental justice and would thus infringe section 7 of the *Charter*.[187]

An accused could act in a morally involuntary even though he or she was not blameless or morally innocent and committed the *actus reus* of

---

185 *Ibid.* at 33. See also *R. v. Parris* (1992), 11 C.R.R. (2d) 376 (Ont. Gen. Div.).
186 *Ruzic*, above note 5.
187 *Ibid.* at para. 47.

the crime in a physically voluntary manner and did so with the required *mens rea* or fault element.

Applying the principle that people should not be convicted for morally involuntary crimes, the Court in *Ruzic* found that the requirement in section 17 that the threats must be of immediate death or bodily harm from a person who is present violated section 7 of the *Charter*. In order to support its conclusions, the Court observed that the common law of duress in Canada and elsewhere did not have the restrictive requirements of a threat of immediate death or harm from a person present when the crime was committed. Rather, the focus under the common law was on whether there was "any safe avenue of escape in the eyes of a reasonable person, similarly situated."[188] The Court concluded that the requirements of immediacy and presence would prevent a person such as a battered woman or a hostage who acted in a morally involuntary manner from claiming the defence. The violations of section 7 of the *Charter* were not justified under section 1 in part because of the unwillingness of the Court to hold that any violation of section 7 was justified under section 1 and in part because of the less restrictive alternative of the common law defence.

The Supreme Court did not, however, strike section 17 down in its entirety. Instead, it struck down only the immediacy and presence requirements. Although the situation is not crystal clear, it would appear that section 17 remains in force and will be applied to those who commit offences. The reformulated section 17 defence thus applies to those who commit an offence "under compulsion by threats of death or bodily harm . . . if the person believes that the threats will be carried out and if the person is not party to a conspiracy or association whereby the person is subject to compulsion." The reformulated section 17 defence will still not apply to the long list of excluded offences and it still will not apply if the accused was a party to a conspiracy or association whereby the accused was subject to compulsion. The result is the retention of the complex mixture of statutory and common law defences of duress. This approach has preserved Parliament's intent to exclude duress as a defence to many serious crimes and to exclude those who associate or conspire with those who threaten them. At the same time, it is likely that such categorical exclusions may themselves violate section 7 of the *Charter* by requiring the conviction of a person who acted in a morally involuntary manner and had no

---

188 *Ibid.* at para. 62.

realistic choice but to commit the crime. If this is indeed true, it would have been preferable to have simply struck down section 17 in total and apply the common law defence of duress to all accused.

2) The Common Law Defence of Duress

Even before the *Charter*, the Supreme Court revived the common law defence of duress by concluding that "s. 17 is limited to cases in which the person seeking to rely upon it has himself committed an offence."[189] Section 17 was thus read down only to apply to principal offenders, and the common law defence of duress was held to apply to those who aided, abetted, or formed a common unlawful purpose to commit an offence.[190] It is not, however, always clear who was the principal offender and who only acted as a party or accomplice. Thus, juries sometimes have to be instructed about both the section 17 defence and the common law defence. The common law defence of duress continues to apply to all accused who act as accomplices to crimes under section 21(1)(b) and (c) and 21(2). In addition, it would apply to all accused should section 17 be held to be unconstitutional in its entirety.

The common law defence of duress is characterized by the general requirement that the accused respond reasonably and in a morally involuntary manner to threats and by the absence of the categorical exclusions placed on the section 17 duress defence. The Supreme Court has indicated that the common law defence of duress has the same juridical basis as the common law excuse of necessity.[191] The two defences can be expected to be developed in tandem.

a) Imminent Threat of Death or Bodily Harm

In *Ruzic*,[192] the Supreme Court indicated that threats need not be of immediate death or bodily harm or from a person who is present under the common law defence of duress in Canada. Indeed, such restrictive requirements in section 17 of the *Code* violated the principle under section 7 of the *Charter* that no one should be convicted for morally involuntary behaviour. The Court noted that the common law defence of

---

189 The section uses the specific words "a person who commits an offence." It does not use the words "a person who is a party to an offence." *R. v. Paquette* (1976), 30 C.C.C. (2d) 417 at 421 (S.C.C.) [*Paquette*].

190 *Code*, above note 2, ss. 21(1)(b)(c) and 21(2). See ch. 3, "Unfulfilled Crimes and Participation in Crimes" for an explanation of these terms.

191 *Hibbert*, above note 1.

192 *Ruzic*, above note 5 at para. 96.

duress in Canada and other countries, unlike section 17, had not traditionally required the threats to be immediate.

The Court in *Ruzic* did place some restrictions on the common law
defence of duress by indicating that there was a "need for a close temporal connection between the threat and the harm threatened." This
requirement serves a similar purpose as the requirement under the
necessity defence that the peril be imminent. At the same time, the
facts of *Ruzic* suggest that the Court will interpret the imminence
requirement in a flexible manner and there is no magic in any particular time between receiving the threat and committing the crime. Ruzic
was threatened over two months before she committed the crime of
importing narcotics. It took her four days from receiving the heroin
and a false passport to travel from Belgrade to Toronto via Budapest and
Athens. The people who threatened her did not accompany Ruzic but
they remained in Belgrade where threats to Ruzic's mother could have
been carried out. As under section 17 of the *Code*, threats to third parties can be the basis for the common law defence of duress.

The requirement for a temporal connection between the threat and
the harm threatened will interact with the second and primary requirement of the common law defence of duress: the requirement that the
accused have no safe or realistic avenue of escape. As the Court in
Ruzic indicated, a threat that was "far removed in time, would cast
doubt on the seriousness of the threat and, more particularly, on claims
of an absence of a safe avenue of escape."[193]

b) No Safe Avenue of Escape and No Legal Way Out

In *Hibbert*,[194] the Supreme Court concluded that the common law
defence of duress will not apply to parties who had a safe avenue of
escape and could have safely extricated themselves from the situation
of duress. Lamer C.J. reasoned that the common law defence of duress,
like necessity, applied only if the accused had no realistic choice when
deciding whether or not to commit the crime. The lack of alternatives
is not determined solely on the basis of the accused's subjective perception of the available choices, but on the basis of what a reasonable person in the accused's circumstances would have perceived as a safe
avenue of escape and a legal way out. The accused will be obliged to
seek a realistic and safe avenue of escape.

In another case, the common law defence of duress was kept from
the jury even though the accused honestly believed he had no safe

---

193 *Ruzic*, above note 5 at para. 65.
194 *Hibbert*, above note 1.

avenue of escape when he picked drugs up from an airport some four months after he was threatened. The Alberta Court of Appeal stated: "[t]he question is whether a reasonable person, with similar history, personal circumstances, abilities, capacities, and human frailties as the accused, would, in the particular circumstances, reasonably believe there was no safe avenue of escape and that he had no choice but to yield to the coercion," after having taken reasonable steps such as contacting the police, to discover his full range of options.[195]

c) Proportionality and the Question of Excluded Offences

In *Ruzic*,[196] the Supreme Court hinted that there may be a requirement of proportionality in the common law of duress. LeBel J. stated: "the law includes a requirement of proportionality between the threat and the criminal act to be executed, measured on the objective-subjective standard of the reasonable person similarly situated." The requirement of proportionality was not a live issue in *Ruzic* because the crime committed — importing drugs — was clearly not disproportionate to the threatened harm of physical violence.

As discussed above, the Supreme Court has stressed the similarities between necessity and duress and the third requirement of the necessity defence is that there be proportionality between the harm avoided and the harm caused by the accused. In *Latimer*, the Court also indicated that proportionality should be determined on a purely objective standard. *Ruzic* and *Latimer* are unfortunately inconsistent as the former suggests that a modified objective standard should be applied to the proportionality requirement while the latter suggests that a purely objective standard should be applied. The *Latimer* holding that a purely objective standard should apply is the more considered opinion of the two and arguably makes conceptual sense. Proportionality is based on the shared values of the community and should not be influenced by the subjective experiences and characteristics of either the accused or the victim.

At the same time, the courts should be cautious about applying a proportionality requirement to the defence of duress. A strict application of a purely objective test of proportionality could cast doubt on cases such as *Paquette*[197] and *Hibbert*[198] that hold that the common law defence of duress could be a defence to very serious crimes such as mur-

---

195 *R. v. Keller* (1999), 131 C.C.C. (3d) 59 at 68 (Alta. C.A.).
196 *Ruzic*, above note 5 at para. 62.
197 *Paquette*, above note 189.
198 *Hibbert*, above note 1.

der and attempted murder. In *Latimer*, the Court refused to rule out killing as always a disproportionate response. A murder could be a proportionate response to a threat that the accused or a third party would die if the accused did not kill. Those who assist in a killing, or perhaps even those who kill, under agonizing conditions produced by threats that even the reasonable person could not withstand and from which there was no safe avenue of escape should not be branded with the special stigma and penalty reserved for murderers or for those who attempt murders.[199] On the other hand, a murder would be a disproportionate response to a threat of the infliction of non-life threatening pain.

d) The Modified Objective Standard

As with the other defences examined in this chapter, courts will be confronted with the issue of how the objective standard for duress should be tailored to the circumstances of particular individuals or groups. Following *Lavallee*,[200] the reasonable person standard in the common law defence of duress will be tailored to the past experiences and physical capabilities of the accused in order to ensure that the objective standard is administered fairly given the particular accused's capacities and abilities. In *Hibbert*,[201] the Supreme Court stated:

> The defences of self-defence, duress and necessity are essentially similar, so much so that consistency demands that each defence's 'reasonableness' requirement be assessed on the same basis . . . while the question of whether a 'safe avenue of escape' was open to an accused who pleads duress should be assessed on an objective basis, the appropriate objective standard to be employed is one that takes into account the particular circumstances and human frailties of the accused. . . . When considering the perceptions of a 'reasonable person'. . . the personal circumstances of the accused are relevant and important, and should be taken into account.

The Court distinguished the way that it individualizes objective standards in defences to the way it applied objective standards in negligence-based offences on the basis that the experiences and characteristics of the particular accused could be relevant in determining whether that person's only realistic choice was to commit a crime whereas all accused make a voluntary decision to undertake risky

---

199 *R. v. Martineau* (1990), 58 C.C.C. (3d) 353 (S.C.C.); *R. v. Logan* (1990), 58 C.C.C. (3d) 391 (S.C.C.).
200 *Lavallee*, above note 2.
201 *Hibbert*, above note 1 at 227–28.

actions and that this justifies determining whether their conduct was negligent on the basis of a simple reasonable person or non-modified objective standard.

As in *R. v. Latimer*, the modified objective standard should be applied to both the issues of whether there was a sufficient connection between the threat and the harm threatened and whether there is a safe avenue of escape or legal way out. This approach blends subjective and objective standards and makes the accused's "perceptions of the surrounding facts . . . highly relevant to the determination of whether his or her conduct was reasonable under the circumstances, and thus whether his or her conduct is properly excusable."[202] At the same time, as suggested above, proportionality between the threat and the harm inflicted should, consistent with *Latimer*, be judged on a purely objective standard and even though there is dicta in *Ruzic*[203] that suggests that proportionality should be "measured on the objective-subjective standard of the reasonable person similarly situated." The inconsistency in the law on this issue is surprising given that the cases were decided in the same year and the Court has stressed that the defences of necessity and duress should develop in tandem. Although there are arguments that proportionality should not be required for excuses, the Court does require proportionality. The purpose of a proportionality requirement would be to ensure that excuses are administered in a manner that is consistent with social values and social protection. It is thus appropriate to apply an objective standard to proportionality because a modified objective standard could have the effect of diluting societal standards of reasonable behaviour.

3) Duress and *Mens Rea*

Although the common law defence of duress is on the ascendancy, the relevance of duress to *mens rea* is on a decline. As previously discussed in chapter 3, duress will not negate the *mens rea* required to be a party to an offence. The fate of those who reluctantly assist in crimes will depend on the common law defence of duress. Duress will only be relevant to high levels of *mens rea* and even then it remains to be seen whether courts will allow duress to negate *mens rea*. It is quite plausible that they will conclude that duress only speaks to the motive as opposed to the intent with which the accused commits the crime.

---

202 *Ibid.* at 228.
203 *Ruzic*, above note 5 at para. 62.

The Supreme Court held in *Carker*[204] that the accused did not qualify for the defence of duress under section 17 because he was threatened only with future not immediate death. The Court also rejected the accused's separate argument that the threats deprived him of the *mens rea* of wilfully damaging public property. Ritchie J. stated that while the evidence suggested "that the criminal act was committed to preserve . . . [the accused] from future harm . . . there is no suggestion . . . that the accused did not know that what he was doing would 'probably cause' damage." If the *mens rea* of wilfulness had not been defined in the *Criminal Code* to include the lower subjective mental elements of knowledge or recklessness, there may have been a reasonable doubt about whether Carker wilfully destroyed the public property.[205] It might be possible, however, that a court would have only concluded that Carker's motive was to avoid the threats of his fellow inmates and he still wilfully damaged the property.[206]

In *Hebert*,[207] the Supreme Court held that an accused charged with perjury did not have a section 17 defence of duress because he was not threatened with immediate death or bodily harm. The Court nevertheless gave the accused a new trial so that the effects of the threats could be considered in determining whether he had the *mens rea* required for perjury. The Court stressed that the mental element of perjury requires "more than a deliberate false statement. The statement must also have been made with intent to mislead. While it is true that someone who lies generally does so with the intent of being believed, it is not impossible, though it may be exceptional, for a person to deliberately lie without intending to mislead."[208] In this case, for example, the accused testified that he attempted to tell a deliberate lie so that the judge might be alerted to the fact that he had been threatened. Duress may well be relevant to the particular *mens rea* of perjury and other offences relating to interference with the administration of justice.

In *Hibbert*,[209] the Supreme Court narrowed the instances in which duress could raise a reasonable doubt about *mens rea*. It held that duress could not negate the accused's intent required to form an unlawful pur-

---

204 *Carker*, above note 176 at 195.

205 *Code*, above note 2, s. 429(1). See ch. 4, "The Degrees of Subjective *Mens Rea*," for further discussion of this aspect of the case.

206 On the distinction between motive and intent see ch. 4, "Intent, Purpose, or Wilfulness Distinguished from Motive."

207 *Hebert*, above note 91.

208 *Ibid.* at 64.

209 *Hibbert*, above note 1.

pose under section 21(2) or the intent required for doing something for the purpose of aiding an offence under section 21(1)(b).[210] Given that duress will frequently arise in situations where the accused reluctantly assists in the commission of the crime, this decision suggests that duress will rarely be relevant to determining *mens rea*. The Court overruled its earlier decision in *Paquette*[211] to the extent that it suggested that an accused who participated in a robbery under duress did not have the intent to carry out the unlawful purpose as required under section 21(2) of the *Criminal Code*. The Court suggested that the duress faced by Paquette explained his motives and desires in assisting in the robbery, but could not negate or raise a reasonable doubt about his intent.

3) Summary

As discussed above, duress will rarely be relevant to the proof of fault. In most cases, duress will either be considered as part of the section 17 defence of duress or as part of the common law defence of duress. The former statutory defence applies to those who actually commit an offence while the latter common law defence applies to those who are parties to an offence. Although the Supreme Court has recently refor- mulated the section 17 defence by striking down the requirements of threats of immediate death or bodily harm from a person who is pres- ent, the common law defence in many ways remains superior. The cat- egorical exclusion of many offences from the section 17 defence, as well as the categorical exclusion of those who had previously conspired or associated who those who threatened them, run a serious risk of convicting people for morally involuntary conduct. An eventual find- ing that section 17 should be struck down in its entirety would certain- ly simplify the law. The common law defence would apply to all offenders regardless of whether they actually committed the offence or were parties to the offence. The related common law defences of duress and necessity could also develop in tandem. The Supreme Court has drawn analogies between the common law defence of duress and the defence of necessity. Both are available if the accused acts in a morally involuntary fashion in that he or she had no realistic choice but to vio- late the law and no safe avenue of escape. Unlike under section 17, the accused is required to act reasonably, but the court has made clear that the reasonable person will be invested with the same characteristics

---

210 See also *Dunbar v. R.* (1936), 67 C.C.C. 20 (S.C.C.) to a similar effect. See ch. 4, "The Degrees of Subjective *Mens Rea*" for further discussion of these cases.

211 Above note 189 at 423.

and experiences as the accused. Little would be lost in terms of fairness and much would be gained in simplicity were section 17 struck down in its entirety.

CONCLUSION

Unlike the defences of due diligence (chapter 5), extreme intoxication (chapter 6), mental disorder and automatism (chapter 7), the accused does not have to establish the defences of provocation, self-defence, necessity, and duress on a balance of probabilities. They apply whenever there is a reasonable doubt about their existence. The four defences examined in this chapter do not relate to the fault element of particular offences and they have both subjective and objective requirements. In general, they apply if the accused subjectively and reasonably responds to external pressures such as sudden acts or insults (provocation), threats from other people (self-defence and duress), and circumstances of peril (necessity).

In administering the objective requirements of these defences, the Supreme Court has taken a modified objective approach that not only places the reasonable person in the same circumstances that the accused faced, but also invests the reasonable person with the same characteristics and experiences as the particular accused. This, of course, stands in contrast to their unwillingess to consider such factors when applying objective standards of liability.[212] The landmark decision in individualizing the reasonable person was *Lavallee*,[213] which recognized that a woman's past abuse could be relevant in determining whether she had a valid claim of self-defence against her abuser. Thus, the past experiences and characteristics of the accused are relevant in determining whether she had a reasonable apprehension of an unlawful assault, a reasonable apprehension of death or grievous bodily harm, and a reasonable belief that she could not otherwise preserve herself from death or grievous bodily harm. The issue is not whether the accused can be classified as a battered woman, but whether in light of her experiences and characteristics, her actions and perceptions were reasonable.

---

212 *Creighton*, above note 3.
213 *Lavallee*, above note 2.

The willingness to individualize the reasonable person has not been without controversy. In *Thibert*,[214] the Court held that the ordinary person must be of the same age and sex as the accused and share the characteristics and experiences that give the wrongful act or insult a special significance to the accused. This has led to concerns that standards based on the ordinary married man will diminish reasonable standards of self-control and excuse male violence against women who leave relationships or panic in response to sexual advances from other men. This has fuelled serious discussion of abolishing the provocation defence.

There are reform options short of abolition. More attention should be paid to the existing statutory requirements that provocation be sudden and that an act or insult cannot constitute provocation if the deceased was exercising a legal right. Parliament might want to consider specifying particular behaviour that should not be considered provocation and may want to require, as is done with some forms of self-defence, that the accused's response to the act or insult be roughly proportionate to the act or insult. Another alternative would be to abolish mandatory life imprisonment that follows from a murder conviction. As will be seen in the next chapter on sentencing, violence in the domestic context and violence motivated by hatred are aggravating factors that can increase an accused's sentence even when a mandatory sentence does not apply.

Reform is desperately needed with regard to the self-defence provisions that even the Supreme Court has candidly recognized are "unbelievably confusing."[215] The attempt in section 35 to place more restrictions on accused who act as aggressors and the attempt in section 34(1) to place less restrictions on accused who do not intend to cause death or grievous bodily harm should be abandoned. Section 35 in particular is something of a dead letter given that an accused who acts as an aggressor can qualify for self-defence under section 34(2). There is little reason to distinguish as section 37 does with respect to defence of third parties and self-defence. At the same time, there is a continued need for requiring the accused's perception of a threat and response to the threat to be both honest and reasonable. A totally subjective approach to self-defence would excuse irrational and unnecessary resort to violent self-help. Most of the concerns about objective standards have been addressed by the Court's willingness to invest the reasonable person

---

214 *Thibert*, above note 16.
215 *McIntosh*, above note 94 at 489.

with the same characteristics and experiences as the accused. Distinctions between personal and real property in sections 38 and 41 can be abolished and the same reasonableness standards imposed on the accused's perception of a threat to property and the degree of force required to respond to the threat. At the same time, given the value of life over property, there may be a role for a clear statement that in no circumstances would it be reasonable to intend death or grievous bodily harm if the accused's sole purpose was to protect property.

The similarities between the defence of duress and necessity have been recognized. Both of these defences operate to excuse a person who has acted in a morally involuntary manner in the sense that it was not realistic to expect them to obey the law and they had no safe avenue of escape without violating the law. The broad standard requires the accused to act reasonably. As discussed above, however, the courts will consider the accused's circumstances and experiences when determining whether the accused acted reasonably. The Supreme Court in *Ruzic* struck down the restrictive requirements that there must be threats of immediate death or bodily harm from a person who is present when the crime is committed under the section 17 defence of duress. Section 17 has, however, not yet been struck down in its entirety even though its categorical exclusion of a long list of offences and of those who conspire or associate with those who threaten them could result in the conviction of a person who acted in a morally involuntary manner. Striking down the entire section 17 defence on the basis that it violates section 7 of the *Charter* by allowing the conviction of a person who had no realistic choice but to commit the offence would be welcome. Such a development would simplify the law by allowing the common law defence of duress to be applied to all offenders, and not just parties to an offence. It would also eliminate the need in cases where it is not clear whether the accused actually committed the offence or was a party to the offence to instruct the jury about both the statutory and common law defences of duress.

FURTHER READINGS

COLVIN, E., *Principles of Criminal Law*, 2d ed. (Toronto: Carswell, 1991), ch. 7

"Forum on the *Latimer* Case" (2001) 39 C.R. (5th) 29ff

"Forum on the *Latimer* Case" (2001) 64 Sask. L. Rev. 469ff

GORMAN, W., "Provocation: The Jealous Husband Defence" (1999) 42 Crim. L.Q.

GRANT, I., D. CHUNN, & C. BOYLE, *The Law of Homicide* (Toronto: Carswell, 1994), ch. 6

HEALY, P., "Innocence and Defences" (1994) 19 C.R. (4th) 121

HORDER, J., "Self-Defence, Necessity and Duress: Understanding the Relationship" (1998) 11 Can. J. L. & Jur. 143

MEWETT, A., & M. MANNING, *Criminal* Law, 3d ed. (Toronto: Butterworths, 1994), chs. 15 and 16

ROSENTHAL, P., "Duress in the Criminal Law" (1990) 32 Crim. L.Q. 199

SHAFFER, M., "The Battered Woman's Syndrome Revisited" (1997) 47 U.T.L.J. 1

SHAFFER, M., "Scrutinizing Duress: The Constitutional Validity of s.17 of the Criminal Code" (1998) 40 Crim. L.Q. 444

STUART, D., *Canadian Criminal Law: A Treatise*, 4th ed. (Toronto: Carswell, 2001), ch. 7

QUIGLEY, T., "Deciphering the Defence of Provocation" (1989) 38 U.N.B.L.J. 11

QUIGLEY T., "Battered Women and the Defence of Provocation" (1991) 55 Sask. L. Rev. 223

TROTTER, G. "Provocation, Anger and Intent for Murder" (2002) 47 McGill L.J. 669

TROTTER, G. "Necessity and Death: Lessons from Latimer and the Case of the Conjoined Twins" (2003) 40 Alta. L. Rev. 817

YEO, S., "Defining Duress" (2002) 46 Crim. L.Q. 293

YEO, S., "Challenging Moral Involuntariness as a Principle of Fundamental Justice" (2002) 28 Queen's L.J.

CHAPTER 9

SENTENCING

The Supreme Court has recognized that "sentencing is, in respect of most offenders, the only significant decision the criminal justice system is called upon to make."[1] Sentencing in Canada remains largely a matter of judicial discretion because Parliament frequently defines offences broadly to cover behaviour of varying degrees of culpability, and only sets high and infrequently used maximum penalties to limit the judge's sentencing discretion. In contrast, many American jurisdictions rely more on statutory gradations of crimes and minimum sentences attached to each degree of any particular crime. Such attempts to limit sentencing discretion may transfer discretion from the sentencing judge to the prosecutor, when he or she accepts a guilty plea to a particular charge.

Sentencing is a discretionary process not only because judges have few statutory limits, but also because they can emphasize multiple purposes or justifications for punishment. The basic purposes and principles of sentencing were first outlined in the *Criminal Code* in 1996. The fundamental principle of sentencing, as defined in section 718.1 of the *Code*, is that the sentence "must be proportionate to the gravity of the offence and the degree of responsibility of the offender." This is an important first principle, owing to the wide variety of conduct that may be caught by some crimes. For example, a person who planned and exe-

---

1   *R. v. Gardiner* (1982), 68 C.C.C. (2d) 477 at 514 (S.C.C.) [*Gardiner*].

cuted a robbery should receive a more severe sentence than a person who reluctantly assisted the robbery in some manner. The fundamental principle of proportionality also counters the danger that a judge might punish an offender more than the crime deserves because of concerns about deterrence and future danger. It directs the judge to look backwards at the seriousness of the crime and the offender's role in it.

Nevertheless, the *Criminal Code* recognizes other concerns as legitimate purposes in sentencing. Section 718 provides:

> The fundamental purpose of sentencing is to contribute, along with crime prevention initiatives, to respect for the law and the maintenance of a just, peaceful and safe society by imposing just sanctions that have one or more of the following objectives:
> (a) to denounce unlawful conduct;
> (b) to deter the offender and other persons from committing offences;
> (c) to separate offenders from society, where necessary;
> (d) to assist in rehabilitating offenders;
> (e) to provide reparations for harm done to victims or to the community; and
> (f) to promote a sense of responsibility in offenders, and acknowledgement of the harm done to victims and the community.

This provision allows courts to sentence in order to deter the offender or others from committing crimes in the future; to remove an offender from society where necessary to prevent future crimes; and to tailor the punishment to further the rehabilitation of the offender in the future or the ability of the offender to provide reparations for the harm done to victims and the community. Concerns about rehabilitation and reparation may also suggest the use of alternatives to imprisonment, such as probation, restitution, or fines. Different purposes suggest different sentences. For example, a sentence of imprisonment might be thought necessary to deter the accused and others from committing a crime, but it may well not assist in rehabilitating the offender or providing reparation to the victims of crime. Much will depend on what sentencing purposes a judge believes is most important in any particular case.

In addition to these multiple purposes, Parliament has also codified some other sentencing principles. The principle of parity in section 718.2(b) of the *Criminal Code* requires that a sentence "should be similar to sentences imposed on similar offenders for similar offences committed in similar circumstances." This is a broad principle of parity because it focuses not only on the crime committed, but on the offender and his or her circumstances. Offenders are often found guilty of two or more offences at one time and section 718.2(c) codifies the totality principle by instructing judges that where consecutive sentences are imposed, "the combined sentence should not be unduly long or harsh." Absent specific statutory direction to the contrary,[2] Canadian judges have the discretion to allow offenders to serve separate sentences on a concurrent basis, a matter that has led to controversy in some circles. Section 718.21 sets out specific factors that are to be taken into consideration in the sentencing of corporations and other organizations.

Sections 718.2(d) and (e) codify the principle of restraint in punishment by instructing judges not to deprive the offender of liberty "if less restrictive sanctions may be appropriate in the circumstances" and to consider "all available sanctions other than imprisonment that are reasonable in the circumstances . . . with particular attention to the circumstances of aboriginal offenders." Canada has one of the highest rates of imprisonment of industrialized countries as well as gross overrepresentation of Aboriginal people in prison.[3] These principles, as well as a broad array of community sanctions that may not result in actual imprisonment, encourage judges to use alternatives to imprisonment whenever appropriate. An important new sentence, the conditonal sentence of imprisonment, was added to the *Criminal Code* in the 1996 sentencing reforms.

A. PROCEDURAL CONSIDERATIONS

1) The Guilty Plea

In most cases, the accused pleads guilty to an offence. A guilty plea by the accused means that there will be no formal determination of whether the Crown can prove the accused's guilt beyond a reasonable doubt, and the trial process will move directly to the sentencing stage. An early guilty plea is an important mitigating factor in sentencing, on

---

2   *Criminal Code of Canada*, R.S.C. 1985, c. C–46, s. 718.3 [*Code*].

3   The Supreme Court has observed that "although the United States has by far the highest rate of incarceration among industrialized democracies, at over 600 inmates per 100,000 population, Canada's rate of approximately 130 per 100,000 population places it second or third highest." *R. v. Gladue* (1999) 133 C.C.C. R.S.C. 1985, (3d) 385 at 406 (S.C.C.) [*Gladue*]. It also noted that in 1997, Aboriginal people constituted 12% of federal inmates but only 3% of the total population and that they constituted the majority of prisoners in provincial institutions in Manitoba and Saskatchewan. In 2000–2001, Aboriginal offenders accounted for 19% of

the grounds that it indicates remorse and saves the victim and the state the costs of a trial.[4] Courts have held that an accused who is sentenced after a full trial is not deprived of his or her *Charter* rights by not having the advantage of a guilty plea considered in mitigation of sentence.[5] Sometimes a guilty plea is accompanied by a joint submission by the Crown and the accused concerning sentencing. This submission does not, however, bind the trial judge from exercising his or her sentencing discretion.[6]

Canadian courts have not required trial judges to determine whether there is a factual basis for a guilty plea and whether the guilty plea is truly voluntary and unequivocal. In the disturbing case of *Brosseau v. R.*,[7] the Supreme Court did not allow a young Aboriginal accused to withdraw his plea to non-capital murder, even though the accused claimed that he did not understand the consequences of entering the guilty plea. Cartwright C.J. indicated that a trial judge should usually make inquiries if there is a doubt as to whether the accused understands what he is doing, but concluded: "[I]t cannot be said that where, as in the case at bar, an accused is represented by counsel and tenders a plea of guilty to non-capital murder, the trial Judge before accepting it is bound, as a matter of law, to interrogate the accused."[8] In that case, the accused's lawyer had indicated to the judge after sentencing that he did not pretend to have any understanding of his client's intent, a matter quite relevant to whether the accused was guilty of murder.

In a subsequent case, the Supreme Court affirmed the *laissez-faire* approach of *Brosseau* over a strong dissent by Laskin C.J., who argued that judges should be required by law to ensure that the guilty plea "be made voluntarily and upon a full understanding of the nature of the charge and its consequences and that it be unequivocal."[9] Laskin C.J. would also have required that in cases of doubt, the trial judge should ensure that there was a factual basis for the guilty plea. The Laskin approach, at least with respect to determining whether the guilty plea is voluntary and made in full awareness of the consequences, may be more appropriate under the *Charter*, because a person who pleads guilty is waiving his or her rights under the *Charter* to a fair trial.

---

provincial admissions and 17% of federal admissions to custody. J. Roberts & R. Melchers, "The Incarceration of Aboriginal Offenders" (2003) 45 C.J. of Crim. 211.

4   *R. v. Johnston*, [1970] 4 C.C.C. 64 (Ont. C.A.).
5   *R. v. M.(C.B.)* (1992), 99 Nfld. & P.E.I.R. 280 (P.E.I.C.A.).
6   *R. v. Rubenstein* (1987), 41 C.C.C. (3d) 91 (Ont. C.A.).
7   [1969] 3 C.C.C. 129 (S.C.C.).
8   *Ibid.* at 138–39.
9   *Adgey v. R.* (1975), 13 C.C.C. (2d) 177 at 183 (S.C.C.).

2) The Sentencing Hearing

The sentencing hearing is less formal than the trial because of the greater range of information that is relevant when sentencing an offender. The accused does, however, retain procedural rights, such as the right to call evidence, cross-examine witnesses, and address the court. Judges may accept as proved any information disclosed at trial or at the sentencing hearing or any facts agreed by the prosecutor and the offender. If there is a dispute, the party wishing to rely on the disputed fact must establish it on a balance of probabilities. The prosecutor, however, must establish an aggravating factor or a previous conviction beyond a reasonable doubt.[10] Sentencing judges have a discretion to require the production of evidence and compel the attendance of witnesses at sentencing hearings[11] and they are required to provide reasons for their sentence.[12] Sentencing judges are "bound by the express and implied factual implications" of the verdict. For example, they cannot consider a person's death to be an aggravating factor when the accused was charged with dangerous driving causing death but convicted only of dangerous driving.[13]

Victim impact statements and reports by probation officers may be introduced as evidence in the sentencing hearing. Recent amendments require judges to inquire whether victims have been informed of the availability of victim impact statements and allow victims to give their impact statements orally.[14] Judges in some cases have used sentencing circles, in which offenders, victims, and community and family members are allowed to speak informally as a means to enhance community participation and improve the quality of information when sentencing Aboriginal offenders.[15]

3) Sentencing Appeals

Unless the sentence has been fixed by law, both the accused and the Crown can appeal a sentence. The Court of Appeal has a broad jurisdiction to consider the fitness of the sentence and vary the sentence within the limits prescribed by law.[16] The Supreme Court has, howev-

---

10   *Code*, above note 2, s. 724; *Gardiner*, above note 1.
11   *Ibid*, s. 723.
12   *Ibid.*, s. 726.2.
13   *R. v. Brown* (1991), 66 C.C.C. (3d) 1 at 5 (S.C.C.).
14   *Code*, above note 2, s. 722.
15   *R. v. Moses* (1992), 71 C.C.C. (3d) 347 (Y. Terr. Ct.).
16   *Code*, above note 2, s. 687.

er, counselled deference to the decisions of sentencing judges and held that absent 1) an error in principle, 2) failure to consider a relevant factor, or 3) an overemphasis of the appropriate factor, a Court of Appeal should not normally intervene.[17] Courts of Appeal may also intervene if the sentence is demonstrably unfit and a marked and substantial departure from the sentences imposed for similar offenders committing similar crimes. A departure from a starting point established by the Court of Appeal for a particular offence or type of offence, by itself, is not a sufficient reason to overturn the sentence.[18] Sentencing appeals allow Courts of Appeal to develop legal principles to govern sentencing, but absent an error in principle, deference is accorded the decision of the sentencing judge. In recent years, the Supreme Court has also been much more active in sentencing when hearing appeals that raise questions of law of national importance. This, along with the new sentencing provisions in the *Criminal Code*, may bring a greater degree of national uniformity to sentencing. Nevertheless, much will still depend on the discretion of trial judges.

B. THE PRINCIPLES AND PURPOSES OF SENTENCING

In 1953 the Ontario Court of Appeal referred to "three principles of criminal justice requiring earnest consideration in the determination of punishment, *viz.*, deterrence, reformation and retribution."[19] The first two factors, deterrence and reformation, look to the future, while retribution looks to the past and the severity of the crime committed. Although the terms have changed, these remain the primary purposes of sentencing, with some new concerns being introduced about reparation.

One difficulty with the multiple purposes of sentencing is that much depends on what purpose is stressed. For example, in some cases imprisonment might be thought necessary to achieve retribution for a past wrong and perhaps to deter others from committing a crime in the future while such a sentence may not be necessary and may even be counterproductive in achieving the purposes of rehabilitation or deterring the particular offender or allowing the offender to provide reparation to the victim.

---

17   *R. v. M.(C.A.)* (1996), 105 C.C.C. (3d) 327 (S.C.C.) [*M.(C.A.)*].

18   *Ibid.*; *R. v. Shropshire* (1995), 102 C.C.C. (3d) 193 (S.C.C.); *R. v. M.(T.E.)* (1997), 114 C.C.C. (3d) 436 (S.C.C.).

19   *R. v. Willaert* (1953), 105 C.C.C. 172 at 175 (Ont. C.A.).

1) The Fundamental Principle of Proportionality

Parliament has raised one principle above the others by designating the principle of proportionality as the fundamental principle of sentencing. Section 718.1 provides that "a sentence must be proportionate to the gravity of the offence and the degree of responsibility of the offender." This principle contemplates not only that punishment be proportionate to the crime committed, but also to the responsibility or blameworthiness of the offender. This directs judges to pay attention to the offender's actual conduct. The person who reluctantly acted as a lookout for a robbery does not require the same punishment as the person who planned and executed the robbery even though both may be convicted of the offence of robbery.

Before the enactment of section 718.1, the Supreme Court stated that:

> It is a well-established tenet of our criminal law that the quantum of sentence imposed should be broadly commensurate with the gravity of the offence committed and the moral blameworthiness of the offender . . . the principle of proportionality in punishment is fundamentally connected to the general principle of criminal liability which holds that the criminal sanction may only be imposed on those actors who possess a morally culpable state of mind.[20]

This approach should guide the way courts approach the new fundamental principle of proportionality. Punishment should never exceed that which is required to recognize the blameworthiness of the offender's crime and his conduct.

Proportionality is a retributive concept that focuses on the offender's past conduct as opposed to utilitarian concerns about the future effects of the punishment on the offender or others through deterrence or rehabilitation. Retribution is a legitimate concern in sentencing, but it should not be confused with revenge or vengeance which produces

---

20   M.(C.A.), above note 17 at 348. The Court also quoted with approval Justice Wilson's statement in the *Reference re s. 94(2) of the Motor Vehicle Act (British Columbia)* (1985), 23 C.C.C. (3d) 289 at 325 (S.C.C.): "It is basic to any theory of punishment that the sentence imposed bear some relationship to the offence; it must be a 'fit' sentence proportionate to the seriousness of the offence. Only if this is so can the public be satisfied that the offender 'deserved' the punishment he received and feel a confidence in the fairness and rationality of the system." In that case, she held that a mandatory term of seven days of imprisonment was disproportionate to the absolute liability offence of driving with a suspended licence.

an unrestrained and "uncalibrated act of harm upon another, frequently motivated by emotion and anger." In contrast, retribution is "an objective, reasoned and measured determination of an appropriate punishment which properly reflects the *moral culpability* of the offender." It restrains punishment to ensure "the imposition of a just and appropriate punishment, and *nothing more*."[21] As will be seen, a grossly disproportionate sentence may also be unconstitutional and struck down as cruel and unusual punishment prohibited by section 12 of the *Charter*. Proportionality should restrain punishment by ensuring that offenders do not receive undeserved punishment for their own good or other social objectives. The existence of other sentencing purposes, some of which are utilitarian and forward-looking, however, suggests that retribution or "just deserts" restrains but does not determine punishment.

2) The Fundamental Purpose of Sentencing

Section 718 states that the "fundamental purpose of sentencing is to contribute, along with crime prevention initiatives, to respect for the law and the maintenance of a just, peaceful and safe society by imposing just sanctions." Courts often pass over this vague and inspirational purpose to focus on the enumerated objectives. Nevertheless, it should be given some meaning. It combines concerns about proportionality by its reference to just sanctions with concerns about the future through its concern for promoting a peaceful and safe society. It also recognizes sentencing discretion through its recognition that appropriate and just sanctions may have one or more of the enumerated objectives. The Supreme Court has indicated that retribution alone does not determine punishment and other legitimate purposes such as deterrence, rehabilitation, and the protection of society should be considered. The relevant importance of these multiple factors will vary with the crime, the circumstances of the offender, and the needs of the community.[22]

3) Denouncing Unlawful Conduct

Like proportionality, denunciation is a retributive concept that focuses on the past. Unlike proportionality, however, the emphasis is on expressing society's disapproval of the crime committed as opposed to judging the culpability of the particular offender. The Supreme Court has stated:

---

21 *M.(C.A.)*, *ibid.* at 368–69.
22 *Ibid.*

The objective of denunciation mandates that a sentence should also communicate society's condemnation of that particular offender's conduct. In short, a sentence with a denunciatory element represents a symbolic, collective statement that the offender's conduct should be punished for encroaching on our society's basic code of values as enshrined within our substantive criminal law.[23]

A concern about denunciation, as well as deterrence, has motivated some courts to indicate that a custodial sentence should normally be imposed for domestic violence.[24]

Another way of achieving the aim of denunciation is to enact a mandatory minimum sentence for a crime. For example, the mandatory sentence for murder is life imprisonment. Problems may arise, however, because such mandatory sentences apply to the most sympathetic and least blameworthy person that nevertheless has committed the crime with the required act and fault. As discussed in chapter 2, crimes are often defined quite broadly and capture both the actual perpetrator and those who may have assisted the perpetrator. As discussed in chapter 4, a good motive is also no defence to a crime but may be relevant in determining punishment.

4) Deterring and Incapacitating Offenders

Section 718 draws a distinction between general deterrence, which is concerned with the effect of punishment in deterring others from committing similar offences, and specific deterrence, which is concerned about the effect of punishment on deterring the particular offender from committing subsequent crimes. The latter concern may also embrace concerns about the incapacitation or rehabilitation of the offender, if that is the only way to prevent him or her from committing future crimes. The effectiveness of any strategy designed to deter future conduct is commonly thought to depend on a combination of the certainty, speed, and severity of punishment. Courts at the sentencing stage focus on the severity of punishment, because they have little control over the certainty and speed of punishment.

---

23   *Ibid.* at 369.
24   *R. v. Brown* (1992), 73 C.C.C. (3d) 242 (Alta. C.A.); *R. v. Inwood* (1989), 48 C.C.C. (3d) 173 (Ont. C.A.).

a) General Deterrence

Courts have accepted that the deterrence of others is a legitimate objective of sentencing. In *R. v. Sweeney*,[25] Wood J.A. stated:

> The theory behind the general deterrence goal of sentencing is that the legal sanction imposed on actual offenders will discourage potential offenders. While there is little empirical evidence to support such a theory, common sense tells us that, to some extent, that must be so. Indeed, there can be little doubt that the very existence of a criminal justice system acts as a deterrent which prevents many people from engaging in criminal conduct.

Courts often consider general deterrence as a factor in crimes such as drunk driving, sexual assault, and domestic violence, where there is widespread concern about the prevalence of such crimes and a desire to change human behaviour. Section 718(b) recognizes the desire to deter both the offender and other persons from committing offences as a legitimate objective of the sentencing process. In addition, section 718.2 also indicates a concern with general deterrence, by stating that hate crimes, spousal and child abuse, and crimes based on the abuse of a position of trust or authority should be punished more severely.

b) Specific Deterrence

Specific deterrence refers to the goal of preventing the offender from committing another criminal offence. This requires courts to consider the offender's history and other information that may help predict future dangerousness. One court has stated that if the concern is general deterrence, then judges should focus on "the gravity of the offence, the incidence of the crime in the community, the harm caused by it either to the individual or the community and the public attitude toward it," whereas if specific deterrence is the goal, "greater consideration must be given to the individual, his record and attitude, his motivation and his reformation and rehabilitation."[26] Concerns about specific deterrence can blur into concerns about rehabilitation when the best way to ensure that an offender does not reoffend is to help get that person's life back on track. A more punitive approach to specific deterrence would advocate harsher punishments as a means to prevent future crimes. If it was relatively certain that an offender was bound to reoffend, incapacitation of the offender by imprisonment might be con-

---

25 (1992), 71 C.C.C. (3d) 82 at 98 (B.C.C.A.).

26 *R. v. Morrissette* (1970), 1 C.C.C. (2d) 307 at 310 (Sask. C.A.).

sidered the only way to prevent the commission of an offence during that time. Section 718(c) recognizes this concern by naming the separation of offenders from society "where necessary" as a legitimate objective of sentencing. Separation or incapacitation may be necessary in the case of the most dangerous offenders, but it is an expensive strategy and one that does not necessarily protect fellow prisoners or guards from violence in prison.

Provisions in the *Criminal Code* providing for indeterminate detention of repeat dangerous offenders are largely concerned with the incapacitation of repeat violent offenders.[27] They have been upheld under the *Charter*, with the Supreme Court stressing that concerns about preventing future crimes "play a role in a very significant number of sentences. . . . Indeed, when society incarcerates a robber for, say, 10 years, it is clear that its goal is both to punish the person and prevent the recurrence of such conduct during that period."[28] LaForest J. also stated that it did not offend the principles of fundamental justice to punish people for preventive purposes "which are not entirely reactive or based on a 'just deserts' rationale."[29] In 1997, the dangerous offender provisions were toughened to remove a judicial discretion to impose a determinate sentence on a person found to be a dangerous offender[30] and to delay the first parole hearing to determine if the offender is no longer a danger from three to seven years with subsequent hearings every two years after.[31] This new regime is significantly harsher than that upheld in *Lyons* or the regime for the detention of those found not criminally responsible by reason of mental disorder.[32] The new amendments also allowed long-term sexual offenders who present a substantial risk to reoffend to be sentenced to a minimum of two years and then supervised in the community for up to ten years after their release.[33]

5) Rehabilitating Offenders

Section 718(d) of the *Criminal Code* provides that one of the objectives of sentencing is "to assist in rehabilitating offenders." Sections 718.2(d) and (e) encourage courts not to deprive offenders of their liberty or to

---

27   Part XXIV of the *Code*, above note 2.
28   *R. v. Lyons* (1987), 37 C.C.C. (3d) 1 at 22 (S.C.C.) [*Lyons*].
29   *Ibid.*
30   *Code*, above note 2, s. 753.
31   *Ibid.*, s. 761.
32   See ch. 7, "Mental Disorder and Automatism."
33   *Code*, above note 2, s. 753.1.

imprison them, when less restrictive sanctions are appropriate and reasonable in the circumstances.

Although less popular than in the past, rehabilitation remains a valid consideration in sentencing, especially in cases where there is a prospect of not imprisoning the offender. In *R. v. Preston*,[34] the British Columbia Court of Appeal upheld a suspended sentence, with probation orders, for the possession of heroin on the basis that "the principle of deterrence should yield to any reasonable chance of rehabilitation which may show itself to the court imposing sentence." Wood J.A. stated:

> The notion that rehabilitation is a legitimate goal of the sentencing process is neither new nor experimental. Every Royal Commission, official report and extensive study done on sentencing in this country . . . has stressed the obvious, namely, that the ultimate protection of the public lies in the successful rehabilitation of those who transgress society's laws. Those same authorities have also unanimously concluded that rehabilitation is unlikely to occur while the offender is incarcerated.[35]

Given the fundamental principle of proportionality, a concern for rehabilitation should not be used to deprive the accused of greater liberty than is necessary to punish the offender. The traditional justification for restraint in punishment has been a concern about preserving as much of the offender's liberty as possible. In recent years, concerns about the costs of imprisonment and the disproportionate imprisonment of Aboriginal people have also been raised.

6) Providing Reparations and Promoting a Sense of Responsibility

Section 718(e) provides that one of the purposes of sentencing is to provide reparations for harm done to victims or to the community. The idea that an offender should provide reparation for crime is quite ancient and was prevalent in both Aboriginal societies and England before the monarchy asserted its power. Nevertheless, it is a relatively new concept in modern criminal law and, as will be discussed below, there are limited means by which judges can require offenders to make reparation to victims. Judges may stress the idea of reparation to the community more than reparation to the victim, and this may be used to support retributive and denunciatory sanctions.

---

34 *R. v. Preston* (1990), 79 C.R. (3d) 61 (B.C.C.A.) [*Preston*].
35 *Ibid.* at 78.

Section 718(f) provides that another purpose of sentencing is "to promote a sense of responsibility in offenders, and acknowledgement of the harm done to victims and to the community." This provision could also be used to support punitive measures, but it can be better advanced by sentences designed to achieve restorative justice between offenders, victims, and the community. The Supreme Court in *R. v. Gladue* noted that sections 718(e) and (f) introduce new concerns to sentencing, which along with rehabilitation and the need to examine alternatives to incarceration, promote restorative justice. "Restorative sentencing goals do not usually correlate with the use of prison as a sanction," but generally involve "some form of restitution and re-integration into the community."[36] Justices Cory and Iacobucci have explained:

> In general terms, restorative justice may be described as an approach to remedying crime in which it is understood that all things are inter-related and that crime disrupts the harmony which existed prior to its occurrence, or at least which it is felt should exist. The appropriateness of a particular sanction is largely determined by the needs of the victims, and the community, as well as the offender.[37]

In the subsequent case of *R. v. Proulx*, the Supreme Court affirmed that the 1996 sentencing reforms including sections 718(e) and (f) were designed to reduce reliance on incarceration and advance the restorative principles of sentencing. Lamer C.J. explained:

> Restorative justice is concerned with the restoration of the parties that are affected by the commission of an offence. Crime generally affects at least three parties: the victim, the community, and the offender. A restorative approach seeks to remedy the adverse effects of crime in a manner that addresses the needs of all parties involved. This is accomplished, in part, through the rehabilitation of the offender, reparations to the victim and to the community, and promotion of a sense of responsibility in the offender and acknowledgment of the harm done to victims and the community.[38]

The Supreme Court has indicated that restorative sentencing purposes should be considered for all offenders, but especially for Aboriginal offenders because of their overincarceration and the primary emphasis upon the ideals of restorative justice in Aboriginal traditions.

---

36   *Gladue*, above note 3 at 403.
37   *Ibid.* at 414.
38   *R. v. Proulx* (2000), 140 C.C.C. (3d) 449 at para. 18 [*Proulx*].

7) Sentencing Aboriginal Offenders

Section 718.2(e) instructs judges to consider "all available sanctions other than imprisonment that are reasonable in the circumstances" for all offenders but "with particular attention to the circumstances of Aboriginal offenders." The Supreme Court has held that this provision is designed to remedy the overincarceration of Aboriginal people and requires judges to pay attention to the unique circumstances of Aboriginal offenders, including systemic discrimination that may explain why the offender has been brought to court. It also requires courts to consider the availability of restorative and other approaches that may be appropriate because of the offender's Aboriginal heritage or connection. The Court also stated that "the more violent and serious the offence,"[39] the more likely it will be that Aboriginal offenders will receive the same sentence as non-Aboriginal offenders. In the actual case, the Court did not allow the accused's appeal from a three-year sentence of imprisonment for manslaughter in part because the accused had been granted day parole after six months on conditions that she reside with her father, comply with electronic monitoring, and take alcohol and substance abuse counselling. In a subsequent case, the Court upheld a sentence of imprisonment of an Aboriginal offender convicted of sexual assault.[40]

C. AGGRAVATING AND MITIGATING FACTORS IN SENTENCING

Courts consider a wide range of aggravating and mitigating factors in connection with the particular crime and the offender. They often consider the offender's degree of participation in a crime. This consideration is important because criminal offences are often defined to catch a broad range of conduct and people can be convicted of a crime as parties even though they did not actually commit the crime. Courts also consider planning and deliberation, breach of trust, use of violence and weapons, and harm to victims as aggravating factors. Section 718.2 directs the Court to consider aggravating factors such as whether the crime "was motivated by bias, prejudice or hate" on group characteristics, involved spousal or child abuse, or involved an abuse of a position of trust or authority.

---

39   *Gladue*, above note 3 at 417.
40   *R. v. Wells* (2000), 141 C.C.C. (3d) 368 (S.C.C.),

Prior convictions are usually considered an aggravating factor, while the accused's good character, youth, old age, ill health, remorse, and early guilty plea will generally be considered mitigating factors. Even though it also operates as a partial defence that reduces murder to manslaughter, provocation can be considered a mitigating factor in sentencing for manslaughter[41] and presumably other crimes. In a few cases, sentences have been reduced as a remedy for a *Charter* violation suffered by the accused,[42] but some courts have resisted this particular use of the sentencing process.[43]

The use of alcohol and drugs can either be a mitigating factor or an aggravating factor, depending on the circumstances and the purposes of punishment that are stressed. The same can be said of the accused's social status, which may be related to either prospects for rehabilitation and future danger or to the goals of general deterrence and denunciation. Courts also consider time served in custody, and the combined effect of consecutive sentences.

D. CONSTITUTIONAL CONSIDERATIONS

Punishment is restricted by section 12 of the *Charter*, which prohibits cruel and unusual treatment or punishment.[44] In *R. v. Smith*,[45] the Supreme Court held that a mandatory minimum sentence of seven years for importing narcotics violated section 12 and could not be justified under section 1 of the *Charter* because it could in some cases result in punishment that was grossly disproportionate to both the offence and the offender. Lamer J. noted that the offence covered a wide variety of behaviour, so that it could hypothetically catch a person importing one joint of marijuana. He also noted that it could be applied to a range of offenders, including a young person with no prior convictions. He stated that, in determining whether a sentence was "grossly disproportionate":

> [T]he court must first consider the gravity of the offence, the personal characteristics of the offender and the particular circumstances of the case in order to determine what range of sentences would have

---

41   *R. v. Stone* (1999), 134 C.C.C. (3d) 353 (S.C.C.).

42   *R. v. MacPherson* (1995) 100 C.C.C. (3d) 216 (N.B.C.A.).

43   *R. v. Glykis* (1995), 100 C.C.C. (3d) 97 (Ont. C.A.).

44   See ch. 1, "The Criminal Law and the Constitution."

45   (1987), 34 C.C.C. (3d) 97 (S.C.C.).

been appropriate to punish, rehabilitate or deter this particular offender or to protect the public from this particular offender.[46]

Punishment that is disproportionate for the particular offender, but which may be necessary to deter others, must be justified under section 1 of the *Charter*.

The Supreme Court has subsequently upheld minimum sentences of seven days' imprisonment for driving with a suspended licence on the basis that the Court should only consider how a sentence would affect reasonable hypothetical offenders and not remote or extreme examples.[47] If such a remote example actually arose, the courts would then have to consider whether imposing the mandatory penalty would result in cruel and unusual punishment. The Supreme Court eventually held that because the driving without a licence offence remained one of absolute liability, judges could not constitutionally imprison a person for its violation.[48] The Court also has upheld a mandatory minimum sentence of four years' imprisonment for the crime of criminal negligence causing death when a firearm is used. The Court deferred to Parliament's attempts to deter the use of firearms during the commission of crimes.[49] Deterrence is a social objective, but not one that relates to the proportionality of the sentence in relation to the individual circumstances of the offender

The Supreme Court has held that life imprisonment for first-degree murder, without eligibility of parole for twenty-five years, does not violate section 12 of the *Charter*, because of the seriousness of the crime committed and the possibility that after fifteen years a jury will allow the accused to be considered for early parole, royal mercy, and absences from custody for humanitarian and rehabilitative purposes.[50] Since that time, the availability of controversial faint hope hearings have been restricted and eliminated for multiple murderers. The Supreme Court in *R. v. Latimer* also upheld the mandatory sentence of life imprisonment with ten years' ineligibility for parole for the offence of second-

---

46 *Ibid.* at 139.
47 *R. v. Goltz* (1991), 67 C.C.C. (3d) 481 (S.C.C.).See also *R. v. Brown* (1994), 93 C.C.C. (3d) 97 (S.C.C.) upholding a then minimum one-year sentence for using a gun in a robbery. Most Courts of Appeal have upheld an increased minimum four-year sentence for using a gun in a robbery. *R. v. Wust* (1998), 125 C.C.C. (3d) 43 (B.C.C.A.); *R. v. Lapierre* (1998), 123 C.C.C. (3d) 332 (Que. C.A.); *R. v. McDonald* (1998), 127 C.C.C. (3d) 57 (Ont. C.A.).
48 *R. v. Pontes* (1995), 100 C.C.C. (3d) 353 (S.C.C.).
49 *R. v. Morrisey* (2000), 148 C.C.C. (3d) 1 (S.C.C.).
50 *R. v. Luxton* (1990), 58 C.C.C. (3d) 449 (S.C.C.).

degree murder. It stressed the seriousness of the crime and the constitutional requirements of subjective *mens rea* and rejected arguments that the accused's altruistic motives in killing his daughter to prevent her suffering from a needed operation was relevant to the proportionality of the punishment.[51] The problem with mandatory sentences is that by definition they will apply to the most sympathetic and least blameworthy person who nevertheless committed the criminal act with the required fault. In any event, since the 1987 case of *Smith*, the Supreme Court has deferred to Parliament's decision to employ mandatory sentences.

Legislation providing for the indeterminate detention of repeat violent offenders has been held not to violate the *Charter* because of its relation to society's legitimate interest in punishing, rehabilitating, deterring, and incapacitating repeat violent offenders.[52] At the same time, the Court stressed that regular reviews are necessary to ensure that continued detention was not disproportionate to the legitimate aims of punishment. The Court subsequently authorized, by the writ of *habeas corpus*, the release of an offender who served thirty-seven years for sexual offences and who, in its view, no longer presented a danger to society.[53]

E. THE MEANING OF AN IMPRISONMENT SENTENCE: PAROLE AND REMISSION

The general rule is that an offender will be eligible for full parole after serving a third of the sentence and for statutory release after serving two-thirds of the sentence. Offenders may also be eligible for day parole after serving a sixth of the sentence. Thus, a person sentenced to six years for a robbery would generally be eligible for day parole after one year, full parole after two years, and statutory release after four years.

These rules are, however, subject to several exceptions. The sentencing judge can order that a person convicted of a sexual or violent offence and subject to imprisonment for two years or more shall not be eligible for parole until the lesser of half the sentence or ten years has been served.[54] This power is to be exercised with primary regard to the

51   *R. v. Latimer* (2001), 150 C.C.C. (3d) 129 (S.C.C.).
52   *Lyons*, above note 28.
53   *Steele v. Mountain Institution* (1990), 60 C.C.C. (3d) 1 (S.C.C.).
54   *Code*, above note 2, s. 743.6.

purposes of denunciation and specific and general deterrence, not rehabilitation. Some prisoners can be denied statutory release because of concerns about their danger if released. They can then be held to the expiry of their sentence. Thus, the robber sentenced to six years could by order of the judge not be eligible for parole for three years and could be imprisoned for the full six years. Other offenders because of the absence of a prior record and the nature of their offence may be eligible for accelerated parole review.

It should also not be forgotten that parole boards frequently do not grant parole and the number of offenders granted parole has declined in recent years. Parole boards are primarily concerned about the offender's rehabilitation and reintegration into society and the danger of future crime until the sentence has expired. They can, however, consider the crime committed, victim impact, and the offender's sense of responsibility for the crime.

F. SENTENCES OTHER THAN IMPRISONMENT

1) Alternative Measures

Alternative measures allow an accused who accepts responsibility for a crime to engage in supervised activities in the community, without a formal determination of guilt or innocence at trial. They are contemplated under section 10 of the *Youth Criminal Justice Act* and under section 717 of the *Criminal Code*. There must be sufficient evidence to proceed with the charge; the accused must accept responsibility for the offence charged and voluntarily agree to the alternative measures. There is a great variety of alternative measures. Some may focus on various forms of community service and/or education for the offender while others may be based on restorative justice.

2) Absolute and Conditional Discharges

When the accused is charged with an offence not subject to imprisonment for fourteen years or life and without a minimum sentence, the Court can, instead of convicting the accused, order an absolute or conditional discharge if "it considers it to be in the best interest of the accused and not contrary to the public interest."[55] The best interests of the accused include the accused's good character and the harm that can

---

55   *Code*, above note 2, s. 730.

follow from a conviction. The public interest includes society's interest in the general deterrence of the offence. Absolute or conditional discharges do not apply only to trivial or technical violations of the *Code*, but they should not routinely be applied to any particular offence.[56] If the conditions of a conditional discharge are breached, the offender may be sentenced for the original offence as well as for the crime of breaching the probation order.

3) Probation

After convicting an accused, the Court can suspend sentence and make a probation order, or make a probation order in addition to a fine or sentence of imprisonment of not more than two years. Probation orders may also be entered after absolute or conditional discharges. Courts make probation orders "having regard to the age and character of the offender, the nature of the offence and the circumstances surrounding its commission."[57] Compulsory conditions of a probation order are that the offender keep the peace and be of good behaviour, appear before the court when required and notify the court or probation officer of changes of address or employment. Optional conditions are regular reports to the probation officer, abstaining from the consumption of alcohol or other drugs, abstaining from possessing a gun, supporting dependants, performing up to 240 hours community service and complying with other reasonable conditions designed to protect society and facilitate the offender's successful reintegration into the community.[58] It is an offence not to comply with a probation order without a reasonable excuse.[59] Corporations and other organizations can now be placed on probation under section 732.1 of the *Code*.

In *Preston*,[60] the British Columbia Court of Appeal upheld a suspended sentence for an accused convicted of three counts of possession of heroin. The accused's probation orders required her to attend a drug rehabilitation facility and perform fifty hours of community service. Wood J.A. reasoned that only overcoming the accused's addiction would break her cycle of crime. He presumed that there would be adequate resources to supervise the accused while on probation and that she would be brought back before the court if she breached her probation order.

---

56   *R. v. Fallofield* (1973), 13 C.C.C. (2d) 450 (B.C.C.A.).

57   *Code*, above note 2, s. 731.

58   *Ibid.*, s. 732.1.

59   *Code*, above note 2, s. 733.1.

60   *Preston*, above note 34.

4) Conditional Sentences of Imprisonment

If the court imposes a sentence of imprisonment of less than two years, it may, under section 742.1, order that the sentence be served in the community if the court is satisfied that this would not endanger the safety of the community and would not be inconsistent with the fundamental purpose and principles of sentencing set out in sections 718 to 718.2. In *R. v. Proulx*,[61] the Supreme Court indicated that only offences with a mandatory minimum sentence of imprisonment are categorically excluded from conditional sentences. Conditional sentences should be considered in all cases in which the judge rejects probation or a penitentiary term of imprisonment of two years or more. Conditional sentences should be a more punitive sentence than a probation order and should generally include punitive conditions such as house arrest. In addition, a conditional sentence can be longer than an actual term of imprisonment. The judge must determine that the particular offender will not present a danger to the community, but the conditions imposed on the offender will be considered in determining the risk of reoffending and the gravity of the damage caused by reoffending.[62] A conditional sentence can fulfill both the restorative and punitive purposes of sentencing, but imprisonment may be required for offences where the objectives of denunciation and deterrence are particularly important.

The conditions imposed as part of the conditional sentence of imprisonment are very similar to those imposed by probation orders. Unlike probation orders, however, the offender can be required to take a treatment program and some courts have imposed restrictive conditions such as "house arrest" except for limited purposes such as employment. Breaches of the conditions only have to be proven on a balance of probabilities and can result in the offender serving the duration of the conditional sentence in prison or having the conditions changed.[63]

5) Fines

Fines are commonly used in addition to, or as an alternative to, imprisonment. There are no limits to the amount fined except in respect of summary conviction offences, which are limited to $2000 for individuals[64] or

---

61 *Proulx*, above note 38.
62 *R. v. Knoblauch* (2000), 149 C.C.C. (3d) 1 (S.C.C.).
63 *Code*, above note 2, s. 742.6.
64 *Ibid.*, s. 787.

$25,000 for organizations.[65] If fines are not paid, an offender may be imprisoned. In the past, significant numbers of those serving short imprisonment terms were serving time because of a failure to pay their fines. Provinces may provide fine option programs to allow an offender who cannot pay a fine to work off the fine. Section 734(2) of the *Criminal Code* now provides that a court should order fines only when satisfied that an offender will be able to pay the fine or to work off the fine in a fine option program. In *R. v. Hebb*,[66] Kelly J. stressed the importance of ensuring that an accused is financially able to pay the fine assessed. This precaution is necessary to ensure not only that it is not impossible for a person of limited means to pay a fine, but also that a small fine not become trivial to an accused of greater means. Imprisonment for failure to pay parking tickets has been held to be cruel and unusual punishment contrary to section 12 of the *Charter*.[67] As discussed in chapter 5, a person convicted of an absolute liability offence cannot constitutionally be imprisoned.[68] A more drastic sentence, such as a conditional sentence, should not be used because the offender is unable to pay a fine.[69]

There are victim fine surcharges on fines, but these do not have to be assessed if they would cause hardship to offenders.[70] The provinces can use the proceeds to provide assistance to victims of offences. Part XII.2 of the *Criminal Code* provides an elaborate scheme for the forfeiture to the state of the proceeds of many crimes.

6) Restitution

Section 738 of the *Criminal Code* allows judges to order restitution for property damage, pecuniary damage arising from offences involving bodily harm, and reasonable and readily ascertainable expenses when a spouse and children move from an offender's household in cases involving bodily harm or the threat of bodily harm to the spouse or child. Although the Supreme Court has cautioned that the restitution provisions should not be used as a substitute for the civil process,[71] it has more recently emphasized that "in appropriate cases, compensa-

---

65   *Code*, above note 2, s. 735(1)(b).
66   (1989), 47 C.C.C. (3d) 193 (N.S.T.D.).
67   *R. v. Joe* (1993), 87 C.C.C. (3d) 234 (Man. C.A.).
68   See ch. 5, "Absolute Liability Offences."
69   *R. v. Wu* (2003), 180 C.C.C. (3d) 97 (S.C.C.).
70   *Code*, above note 2, s. 737.
71   *R. v. Zelensky*, [1978] 2 S.C.R. 940.

tion orders provide an extremely useful and effective tool in the sentencing procedure" that can help rehabilitate the accused, provide benefits for victims in a "speedy and inexpensive manner" and benefits for society by reducing the use of imprisonment and providing "for the reintegration of the convicted person as a useful and responsible member of the community at the earliest possible date. The practical efficacy and immediacy of the order will help to preserve the confidence of the community in the legal system."[72]

Restitution orders are generally enforced as civil judgments. This can make them difficult to enforce. Restitution can be better ensured by requiring it as a condition of probation or a conditional sentence. Provinces, however, have the option under section 738(2) of enacting regulations to preclude judges from imposing restitution as a condition of probation or a conditional sentence. Although reparation to victims is now recognized as a purpose of sentencing, judges have limited instruments with which to pursue this purpose.

G. CROWN PARDONS AND REMISSIONS

The Crown may extend the royal mercy to a person imprisoned. It may also remit the payment of a fine or grant free or conditional pardons.[73]

CONCLUSION

Sentencing is the most important and visible aspect of the criminal law. The 1996 amendments to the *Criminal Code* have created a statutory framework for the exercise of sentencing discretion, but much discretion remains. The fundamental principle is that the sentence must be proportionate to the gravity of the offence and the offender's degree of responsibility. Courts will also strike down grossly disproportionate sentences as cruel and unusual punishment, but in recent years they have been more willing to uphold mandatory minimum sentences that by definition apply to the most sympathetic offenders and least blameworthy crimes that are caught under often broad definitions of crime.

---

72   *R. v. Fitzgibbon*, [1990] 1 S.C.R. 1005 at 1013.
73   *Code*, above note 2, ss. 748–49. The National Parole Board decides whether to grant pardons. *Criminal Records Act*, R.S.C. 1985, c. C-47.

The offender's crime and responsibility, however, does not determine punishment, and judges are instructed to be concerned about a wide range of other factors including specific and general deterrence, rehabilitation, reparation, and promoting a sense of responsibility. The last three purposes, combined with other instructions to consider alternatives to imprisonment, suggest that restorative justice is a legitimate and important approach to sentencing, especially, but not exclusively, with respect to Aboriginal offenders. There are a wide variety of alternatives to actual imprisonment including pre-trial diversion, probation, restitution, and conditional sentences that allow offenders to be punished and held accountable while remaining in the community.

FURTHER READINGS

ARCHIBALD, B., "Sentencing and Visible Minorities: Equality and Affirmative Action in the Criminal Justice System" (1989) 12 Dal. L.J. 377

CANADIAN SENTENCING COMMISSION, *Sentencing Reform: A Canadian Approach* (Ottawa: Queen's Printer, 1987)

CAYLEY, D., *The Expanding Prison* (Toronto: Anansi, 1998)

COLE, D., & J. ROBERTS, *Making Sense of Sentencing* (Toronto: University of Toronto Press, 1999)

FITZGERALD, O., *The Guilty Plea and Summary Justice* (Toronto: Carswell, 1990)

HEALY, P., & H. DUMONT, *Dawn or Dusk in Sentencing* (Montreal: Themis, 1998)

MANSON, A. *The Law of Sentencing* (Toronto: Irwin Law, 2001)

ROACH, K. "Changing Punishment at the Turn of the Century: Restorative Justice on the Rise" (2000) 42 Can. J. Crim. 249

ROACH, K., "Searching for *Smith*: The Constitutionality of Mandatory Minimum Sentences" (2001) 39 Osgoode Hall L.J. 367

ROBERTS, J. & R. MELCHERS, "The Incarceration of Aboriginal Offenders: Trends from 1978 to 2001" (2003) 45 Can. J. Crim. 211.

ROBERTS, J., & K. ROACH, "Restorative Justice in Canada: From Sentencing Circles to Sentencing Principles" in *Restorative Justice and Criminal Justice*, ed. Von Hirsch et al. (Oxford: Hart Publishing, 2003)

RUDIN, J., & K. ROACH, "Broken Promises: A Response to Stenning and Roberts' 'Empty Promises'" (2002) 65 Sask. L. Rev. 3

ROBERTS, J., & A. VON HIRSCH, "Sentencing Reform in Canada: Recent Developments" (1992) 23 R.G.D. 319

ROBERTS, J., & A. VON HIRSCH, "Statutory Sentencing Reform: The Purpose and Principles of Sentencing" (1995) 37 Crim. L.Q. 22

RUBY, C., *Sentencing*, 5th ed. (Toronto: Butterworths, 1998)

STENNING, P., & J. ROBERTS, "Empty Promises: Parliament, the Supreme Court and the Sentencing of Aboriginal Offenders" (2001) 64 Sask. L. Rev. 137.

CONCLUSION

The criminal law in Canada has undergone significant changes in the past twenty years. The most visible change has been the enactment of the *Canadian Charter of Rights and Freedoms*. As examined in chapter 1, the *Charter* means that criminal courts are concerned not only with the accused's factual guilt, but also with whether the police and prosecutors complied with the accused's legal rights in the investigative and trial process. Non-compliance with *Charter* rights can lead to the exclusion of relevant evidence. Entrapment that would bring the administration of justice into disrepute can result in a stay of proceedings even though the accused may have committed the crime with the required *mens rea*.

The *Charter* guarantees the presumption of innocence. It has been interpreted to be breached whenever the accused bears the burden of establishing an element of an offence, a defence, or a collateral factor. It can even be breached when the accused must satisfy an evidential burden to overcome a mandatory presumption. It is not breached, however, when a judge makes a preliminary decision about whether there is an air of reality to justify putting a defence to a jury. In addition, the *Charter* has provided new substantive standards of fairness by which to measure criminal and regulatory offences and the availability of defences. Constructive murder has been struck down as inconsistent with the minimum *mens rea* for murder and absolute liability offences have been found to be unconstitutional when they result in imprisonment. The intoxication and duress defences have also been expanded

in response to *Charter* concerns about ensuring that the morally innocent are not convicted.

Although some of the effects of the *Charter* on the criminal law
have been breathtaking and unexpected, the overall effect can be overstated, particularly in relation to substantive criminal law, which has
been the focus of this work. Most cases in which the broad presumption of innocence has been violated have nevertheless been sustained
under section 1 of the *Charter* as reasonable and proportionate limits
on *Charter* rights. The Supreme Court has approved the pre-*Charter*
compromise of strict liability for regulatory offences, including the
requirement that the accused rebut a presumption of negligence by
establishing a defence of due diligence. The Court has even violated the
presumption of innocence itself by requiring the accused to establish
the defences of extreme intoxication and non-mental disorder automatism on a balance of probabilities. It has only required subjective fault
in relation to the prohibited result for murder, attempted murder, and
war crimes and has approved the use of objective fault standards for
many criminal offences. Moreover, there is no constitutional requirement that the reasonable person used to administer objective fault
standards have the same characteristics as the particular offender or
that fault be proven for all aspects of the *actus reus*.

Even when the Supreme Court has ruled in favour of the *Charter*
rights of the accused, Parliament has frequently responded with new
legislation that reaffirms the public interest and the interests of victims
and potential victims of crime. The most dramatic example is section
33.1 of the *Criminal Code* which attempts to overrule the Court's decision in *Daviault*, so that an extremely intoxicated accused who acted in
an involuntary or unconscious manner would still be convicted of
crimes such as assault and sexual assault. In an attempt to ensure that
"no means no," Parliament has in sections 273.1 and 273.2 of the *Code*
defined consent for the purpose of sexual assault not to include specific conduct and has restricted the *Pappajohn* mistake of fact defence to
require the accused to take reasonable steps, given the circumstances
known to him, to ascertain whether a complainant consents to sexual
activity. In its preambles to these new provisions, Parliament has asserted that the *Charter* rights of women and children as potential victims of
sexual and domestic assault should be balanced with the *Charter* rights
of the accused. *Charter* decisions striking down warrantless searches
have led Parliament to create new warrant provisions and to authorize
some warrantless searches. Parliament revived tertiary grounds for the
denial of bail after they were struck down by the Supreme Court. The
Charter has not prevented Parliament from responding to court deci-

sions. Legislative replies may be challenged under the *Charter*, but Parliament may frequently have the last word in its dialogue with the courts over the values of the criminal law.

A. THE *CHARTER* AND THE CRIMINAL LAW

1) The *Charter* and the Due Process Model

In his landmark study of the criminal process, Herbert Packer outlined two contrasting models of the criminal process.[1] In the crime control model, the justice system resembled an assembly line, with the police and prosecutors being able to identify the factually guilty and to secure a guilty plea. In contrast, he saw an emerging due process model that resembled an obstacle course, because it required the state to comply with various legal rights in the investigative and trial process before it could secure a conviction. If the police or prosecutor violated the accused's legal rights, courts were prepared to exclude evidence or terminate the case regardless of whether the accused was factually guilty of the crime charged.

The *Charter*, as interpreted by the Supreme Court of Canada, has injected due process elements into the Canadian criminal process. As discussed in chapter 1, suspects now have constitutional rights against unreasonable searches, arbitrary detentions, and the right to counsel. If the police do not comply with these rights, the evidence they obtain can be excluded under section 24(2) of the *Charter*. An accused also has rights in the criminal trial process not to be denied reasonable bail without just cause, to be tried within a reasonable time, to receive disclosure of relevant evidence in the Crown's possession, and to be presumed innocent. The Court has interpreted the latter right broadly, but governments have been able to justify many limitations on that right under section 1 of the *Charter* as reasonable and necessary means to facilitate the prosecution of various crimes.

The due process model describes some elements of the criminal justice system under the *Charter*. At the same time, however, it appears that most cases continue to end in a guilty plea and that prison populations have increased significantly during the *Charter* era. Moreover, the accused is not the only actor in the criminal process that has claimed *Charter* rights, and a number of cases have been influenced by concerns

---

1   H.L. Packer, *The Limits of the Criminal Sanction* (Stanford, CA: Stanford University Press, 1968), Part II.

about the rights of crime victims and groups such as women, children, and minorities who may be disproportionately subject to some crimes.

2) The *Charter* and the Crime Control Model

The enactment of the *Charter* has not eclipsed the utility of Packer's description of the crime control model. Most criminal cases continue to end with guilty pleas that are not well supervised by judges. An early entry of a guilty plea remains an important mitigating factor in sentencing. Although Packer predicted that the due process model would contribute to scepticism about the use of the criminal sanction, this outcome has not proven to be the case in Canada. With the exception of abortion, there seems to be more enthusiasm about the use of the criminal sanction in the *Charter* era. Since the enactment of the *Charter*, offences against sexual assault, proceeds obtained by crime, war crimes, impaired driving causing death or bodily harm, sexual interference with children, the possession of drug instruments, drug literature, and child pornography and committing a crime for a criminal organization have all been passed. In the wake of September 11, Parliament enacted many new crimes of terrorism. It also expanded the provisions for holding corporations and other organizations criminally liable as a response to the Westray mine disaster. The Supreme Court has recently rejected a *Charter* challenge to the criminal offence of possession of marijuana and the proposed decriminalization of such activity does not seem to be a high priority. New sentencing provisions require crimes motivated by hate against identifiable groups and involving child or spousal abuse, or abuse of positions of trust or authority, to be punished more severely and some new hate-crime provisions were created as part of the *Anti-terrorism Act*. Sections 15 and 28 of the *Charter* have also been invoked by Parliament in support of claims that the criminal sanction is necessary to protect the rights of women, children, and other vulnerable groups.

Judicial interpretation of the *Charter* has not been oblivious to crime control values. As described above, violations of the presumption of innocence protected under section 11(d) of the *Charter* have frequently been upheld to facilitate the prosecution of various crimes such as drunk driving, living off the avails of prostitution, and regulatory offences. The Supreme Court has required proof of subjective foresight of the likelihood of death for murder, but has approved of manslaughter convictions when death was unforeseen by the accused and may have been unforeseeable by the reasonable person. The Court has based this latter ruling on the fact that the accused was acting unlawfully and should accept responsibility for the victim's "thin skull."[2] Except in a few excessive cases, the *Charter* has had relatively little impact on sentencing and punishment.

The *Charter* has changed the way conflicting interests are described and balanced in the criminal justice system, but it has not done away with the need to balance these interests. Parliament still plays a leading role in defining the prohibited act, the fault element, and the punishment available for most criminal offences. Enthusiasm for the use of the criminal sanction has not diminished under the *Charter*, and the criminal law is used as a practical and symbolic response to a wide range of social issues, including drunk driving, domestic violence, hate literature, hate crimes, degrading pornography, terrorism, sexual violence towards women and children, and corporate misconduct.

3) The *Charter* and the Punitive Model of Victims' Rights

In a few cases, the *Charter* has encouraged courts to consider the effects of laws in protecting victims of crime, and in particular women and minorities that may disproportionately be the victims of certain crimes. In *R. v. Keegstra*,[3] the Supreme Court upheld hate propaganda offences that violated freedom of expression and the presumption of innocence in large part because the law attempted to protect vulnerable minorities from being the targets of wilful promotion of hatred. In *R. v. Butler*,[4] the Court reinterpreted obscenity provisions so that they prohibited material that was found to be violent, or degrading, or dehumanizing, particularly in relation to its portrayal of women and children. In the *Prostitution Reference*,[5] the Court upheld a new crime of soliciting in a public place for the purpose of prostitution in part because of concerns for communities and women victimized by prostitution. A concern that disabled people might be coerced into suicide in part motivated the Court's decision in *Rodriguez v. British Columbia (A.G.)*[6] not to strike down the offence of assisting suicide.

Parliament and the provincial legislatures have been more active than the courts in protecting the interests of victims of crimes. They

---

2   *R. v. Creighton* (1993), 83 C.C.C. (3d) 346 (S.C.C.) [*Creighton*].

3   (1990), 61 C.C.C. (3d) 1 (S.C.C.).

4   *R. v. Butler* (1992), 70 C.C.C. (3d) 129 (S.C.C.) [*Butler*].

5   *Reference re ss. 193 & 195.1 (1)(c) of the Criminal Code (Canada)* (1990), 56 C.C.C. (3d) 65 (S.C.C.).

6   *Rodriguez v. British Columbia (A.G.)* (1993), 85 C.C.C. (3d) 15 (S.C.C.) [*Rodriguez*].

have enacted various laws designed to provide compensation for the victims of crime. The new sexual assault provisions enacted in response to R. v. Seaboyer,[7] and the legislative response to R. v. Daviault,[8] both include preambles that state that the laws were designed in part to promote the full protection of rights guaranteed under sections 7 and 15 of the *Charter* and to deal with the prevalence of sexual assault and other violence against women and children.

There are real limits, however, as to how far victim interests will be integrated into the present criminal justice system. The *Charter* provides no explicit rights for crime victims and the interests of victims have to be squeezed into the interests protected under sections 7 and 15. In *Canadian Foundation for Children*,[9] the Supreme Court preemptorily rejected arguments that section 43 of the Code violated procedural and equality rights of children by authorizing the use of reasonable force by way of correction against them. McLachlin C.J. stated "thus far, the jurisprudence has not recognized procedural rights for the alleged victim of an offence" and that assuming that such rights existed, "the child's interests are represented at trial by the Crown. . . . There is no reason to suppose that, as in other offences involving children as victims or witnesses, the Crown will not discharge that duty properly. Nor is there any reason to conclude . . . that providing separation representation for the child is either necessary or useful."[10] This case sets real limits on the extent to which the rights of crime victims will be recognized within the existing criminal justice system.

4) The Non-Punitive Model of Victims' Rights

The R. v. *Gladue*[11] decision has recognized the role of restorative justice in sentencing and its ability to respond to the needs of victims as well as offenders. *Gladue* represents a non-punitive model of victims' rights that places less emphasis on competing claims of rights and the imposition of punishment. Other examples of a non-punitive model would include the use of family conferences and victim offender mediation and a greater emphasis on crime prevention. In R. v. *Proulx*,[12] Lamer

---

7   (1992), 66 C.C.C. (3d) 321 (S.C.C.). See *Criminal Code of Canada*, R.S.C. 1985, c. C-46, ss. 273.1–273.2 and 276.1–276.5 [*Code*].

8   R. v. *Daviault* (1994), 93 C.C.C. (3d) 21 (S.C.C.) [*Daviault*]. See *Code*, above note 7, ss. 33.1–33.3.

9   2004 SCC 4.

10   *Ibid.* at para. 6.

11   R. v. *Gladue* (1999), 133 C.C.C. (3d) 385 (S.C.C.) [*Gladue*].

12 (2000), 140 C.C.C. (3d) 449 (S.C.C.).

C.J. explained that restorative justice was a new objective of sentencing that applies to all offenders and was associated with the rehabilitation of the offender and reparation and acknowledgment of the harm done to the victims and the community. The Chief Justice explained:

> Restorative justice is concerned with the restoration of the parties that are affected by the commission of an offence. Crime generally affects at least three parties: the victim, the community, and the offender. A restorative approach seeks to remedy the adverse effects of crime in a manner that addresses the needs of all parties involved. This is accomplished, in part, through the rehabilitation of the offender, reparations to the victim and to the community, and promotion of a sense of responsibility in the offender and acknowledgment of the harm done to victims and the community.[13]

Crime prevention strategies are another example of a concern about preventing crime victimization that do not rely on the threat or imposition of punishment. Another example is the development of an all-risk strategy to respond not only to the crime of terrorism, but also to other harms that can be caused by natural and man-made disasters. Should the possession of marijuana be decriminalized by Parliament some time in the future, it will be important that the government attempts to educate the populace about the health and safety hazards of the drug, as well as other drugs. A non-punitive approach to victimization would often take a public health approach to minimizing the harms of not only crime, but other threats to human security.

B. TRENDS IN THE CRIMINAL LAW

1) Definition of Crimes

The *Charter* has had a limited effect on the ability of legislatures to define what conduct is illegal. A crime that prohibits some activity protected under the *Charter*, such as freedom of expression, must be justified under section 1 of the *Charter*. No crime should be so vague or overbroad that it fails to provide notice to the accused or limit law enforcement discretion.

The criminal law as enacted by Parliament sets a fairly wide net of criminal liability by defining criminal acts quite broadly. Courts will interpret prohibited acts in a purposive fashion, before resorting to the

---

13   *R. v. Proulx* (2000), 140 C.C.C. (3d) 449 at para. 18.

doctrine of strict construction of the criminal law that gives the accused the benefit of reasonable ambiguities. As examined in chapter 3, people can be held guilty as parties to an offence for a wide range of conduct, including aiding, abetting, or counselling a crime, or forming a common unlawful purpose with either subjective or objective foresight that the crime charged will occur.[14] Separate offences of conspiracy, counselling a crime that is not committed, and being an accessory after the fact also exist. Courts have defined the prohibited act of attempted crimes broadly, so that anything beyond preparation will suffice, even if it is not otherwise illegal or harmful. The accused may be guilty of an attempted crime even though it was impossible to commit the complete crime and his or her actions were quite remote from the complete crime.[15] At the same time, courts have stressed that the Crown must prove that the accused acted with the intent to commit the crime. Another alternative to inchoate crimes is to criminalize activities that are preparatory to the commission of crimes. Parliament has taken this approach with organized crime and terrorism offences that apply to financial transactions and participation in groups that may occur well in advance to the commission of any crime.

Various sexual offences have been defined by Parliament broadly in an attempt to protect the sexual integrity of women and children. Parliament has defined consent for the purpose of sexual assault not to include specific conduct[16] and the Supreme Court has held that consent as a matter of *actus reus* depends solely on the subjective intent of the complainant.[17] In *R. v. Jobidon*,[18] the Supreme Court held that, for the purposes of assault, a person could not consent to the intentional infliction of serious hurt or non-trivial bodily harm. This has effectively expanded the law of assault to include consensual fights that result in injury. In *Rodriguez v. British Columbia (A.G.)*,[19] the Court upheld a *Criminal Code* provision that a person could not consent to his or her death. There has also been some relaxation of the traditional requirement that the prohibited act and the fault element occur at the same time. There seems to be less reluctance to criminalize the omission to

---

14   If the crime is murder or attempted murder, there must be subjective foresight that death will result from the carrying out of the unlawful purpose with an accomplice. *R. v. Logan* (1990), 58 C.C.C. (3d) 391 (S.C.C.) [*Logan*].

15   *R. v. Deutsch* (1986), 27 C.C.C. (3d) 385 (S.C.C.); *U.S. v. Dynar* (1997), 115 C.C.C. (3d) 481 (S.C.C.).

16   *Code*, above note 7, s. 273.1.

17   *R. v. Ewanchuk* (1999), 131 C.C.C. (3d) 481 (S.C.C.) [*Ewanchuk*].

18   *R. v. Jobidon* (1991), 66 C.C.C. (3d) 454 (S.C.C.) [*Jobidon*].

19   *Rodriguez*, above note 6.

perform specific legal duties. In the future it appears likely that Parliament will continue to define many crimes broadly, and the manner in which crimes are defined will be an important policy component of the criminal law.

2) Subjective and Objective Fault Elements

It appears that proof of subjective *mens rea* in relation to the prohibited result of a crime will be a constitutional requirement for only a few offences, such as murder, attempted murder, and war crimes. The Supreme Court has stressed that the penalties and stigma that accompany these offences require proof beyond a reasonable doubt of subjective *mens rea* in relation to the prohibited result. It has struck down the constructive (or felony) murder provisions in section 230 of the *Criminal Code*, because they allowed accused who caused death while committing serious crimes to be convicted of murder even if they did not have subjective foresight that death would occur. Liability for murder based on objective, as opposed to subjective, foresight of death contemplated in sections 229(c) and 21(2) has also been struck down.[20] Terrorism may, like war crimes, be found to be a stigma crime that requires subjective fault in relation to the prohibited act. The courts will then have to decide whether some broadly defined crimes with qualified fault elements such as section 83.19 of the *Criminal Code* violate section 7 of the *Charter*. For most other offences, however, the *Charter* prohibits only imprisonment for absolute liability that follows from the commission of the prohibited act and without regard to either subjective or objective fault.

The Supreme Court has rejected as a constitutional requirement, the principle that the fault element should relate to all aspects of the *actus reus*. Thus, the fault element of manslaughter relates not to the causing of death but the causing of non-trivial bodily harm. Many other crimes are based on the consequences of the accused's actions even though the accused may not have had subjective or objective fault in relation to those consequences. The Court has upheld the constitutionality of objective standards of liability for serious crimes, including unlawful act manslaughter, unlawfully causing bodily harm, and dangerous driving. This trend suggests that crimes such as criminal negligence will be interpreted as requiring objective as opposed to subjective fault. As well, the trend seems to require more than simple negligence,

20   *R. v. Martineau* (1990), 58 C.C.C. (3d) 353 (S.C.C.); *Logan*, above note 14.

but rather a marked departure from the standard of care expected from a reasonable person in the circumstances. The new section 22.1 of the *Criminal Code*, for example, requires that senior officer(s) of a corporation demonstrate a marked departure from the standard of care necessary to prevent representatives of the corporation from committing a criminal offence based on negligence. The marked departure standard, as well as the onus on the Crown to prove fault beyond a reasonable doubt, are important distinctions between criminal and regulatory offences.

In *Creighton*,[21] a 5-to-4 majority of the Court rejected attempts to tailor objective standards to a particular accused by endowing the reasonable person with personal characteristics such as the accused's age and intelligence. The majority did keep open the possibility of considering the characteristics of individual accused but only if they meant that the accused lacked the capacity to appreciate the prohibited risk. In most cases, however, the reasonable person used to administer objective standards will not have the same characteristics as the accused and the Court has expressed concerns about not blurring the distinction between subjective and objective standards of liability. In cases dealing with defences, however, the Court has indicated that courts should consider the particular accused's past experiences, characteristics, and frailties when determining whether perceptions and actions are reasonable.[22] This leads to more generous defences, but some blurring of the distinctions between subjective and objective standards. The different approaches to applying objective standards and defining the reasonable person introduces inconsistency in the law. A possible rationale for the divergent approach is that many accused will make a voluntary choice to undertake activities that are judged on a negligence-based standard, whereas the objective standard in defences must be modified to account for the characteristics and experiences of the particular accused in order to ensure that he or she is not found guilty for morally involuntary conduct. In other words, an accused's characteristics and experiences may be relevant to determining whether the only realistic choice open to them in particular circumstances was to violate the law.

---

21 *Creighton*, above note 2.
22 *R. v. Lavallee* (1990), 55 C.C.C. (3d) 97 (S.C.C.) [*Lavallee*]; *R. v. Pétel* (1994), 87 C.C.C. (3d) 97 (S.C.C.) [*Pétel*]; *R. v . Hibbert* (1995), 99 C.C.C. (3d) 193 (S.C.C.) [*Hibbert*]; *R. v. Thibert* (1996), 104 C.C.C. (3d) 1 (S.C.C.) [*Thibert*] discussed in ch. 8, "Provocation, Self-Defence, Necessity, and Duress."

3) Regulatory Offences and Corporate Crime

Following *R. v. Sault Ste. Marie (City)*,[23] most regulatory offences are interpreted as strict liability offences that require the Crown to prove the prohibited act, but then presume the existence of negligence unless the accused can establish a defence of due diligence on a balance of probabilities. In *R. v. Wholesale Travel Group Inc.*,[24] the Supreme Court held that the fault element of negligence was constitutionally sufficient for a regulatory offence of misleading advertising, and it approved the requirement that the accused demonstrate that it was not negligent by proving a defence of due diligence on a balance of probabilities. Absolute liability in which the Crown must prove only the prohibited act is unconstitutional when there is imprisonment. The Court's decision in *R. v. Pontes*[25] suggests that offences may be interpreted as absolute liability offences if the ignorance of the law is no excuse principle would deprive the accused of his or her only possible defence. The courts may also be inclined to make some minimal intrusions into section 19 by recognizing a defence of officially induced error, but while maintaining the distinction that mistakes about the law will not excuse while mistakes about facts often will.

Sections 22.1 and 22.2 of the *Criminal Code* now have replaced the old common law that only attributed the fault of a corporation's directing mind to the corporation for the purpose of determining criminal liability. Now the fault of senior officers can be attributed to the corporation. Unlike the old directing mind concept, a senior officer may include someone who manages an important aspect of the company's operations even when that person does not set corporate policy. Section 22.1 applies to criminal offences of negligence and requires that senior officer(s) depart markedly from the standard of care that would prevent representatives of the corporation from being a party to the offence. Section 22.2 applies to criminal offences of subjective fault and requires the senior officer to be a party to the offence or direct a representative so that they commit an offence or to fail to take all reasonable steps to prevent a representative from committing an offence when the senior officer knows that an offence is being committed. It remains to be seen whether these new provisions, as well as new sentencing provisions that allow a corporation to be placed on probation, will increase criminal charges and convictions against corporations and other organizations and whether this will effectively deter corporate misconduct.

---

23   (1978), 40 C.C.C. (2d) 353 (S.C.C.).
24   (1991), 67 C.C.C. (3d) 193 (S.C.C.).
25   (1995), 100 C.C.C. (3d) 353 (S.C.C.).

4) Intoxication, Mental Disorder, and Other Defences

Some recent cases have expanded the range of defences open to accused. In *Daviault*,[26] the Supreme Court recognized a defence of extreme intoxication akin to automatism. Such a rare state would deprive an accused of the voluntary and conscious behaviour necessary for general intent offences such as assault and sexual assault. Unlike evidence of intoxication, which can always raise a reasonable doubt about the mental element of specific intent offences such as murder or robbery, the defence of extreme intoxication to a general intent offence must be proved by the accused on a balance of probabilities. Parliament responded with section 33.1 of the *Criminal Code*. It attempts to eliminate the *Daviault* defence with respect to violent offences by deeming that the marked and substantial departure from reasonable conduct involved in becoming extremely intoxicated can be substituted for the voluntary and conscious behaviour and fault required to convict a person of assault, sexual assault, or other violent general intent offences. The constitutionality of this provision has not yet been finally settled, but most courts have found that it violates the presumption of innocence by substituting the fault of becoming extremely intoxicated for the fault of committing the crime and that it violates the principles of fundamental justice by allowing the conviction of a person who commits a crime in an involuntary manner. The Supreme Court has also held that the traditional intoxication defence for specific intent crimes violates the *Charter* by requiring a reasonable doubt about the accused's capacity to form the intent rather than the actual formation of the intent.[27]

The mental disorder defence is also quite broad. It applies to a wide range of mental disorders and whenever the mental disorder renders the accused incapable of appreciating the physical consequences of his or her actions. The Courts have not, however, extended the defence to those incapable of appreciating the emotional or penal consequences of their actions, even if this lack of appreciation was caused by a mental disorder. In 1990, the Court expanded the mental disorder defence by holding that people should not be convicted if a mental disorder rendered them incapable of knowing that their acts were morally and not just legally wrong.[28] The Courts are still working out the exact parameters of this holding and are not likely to apply the defence to psychopaths who, although aware that society would regard their actions

---

26   *Daviault*, above note 8.
27   *R. v. Robinson* (1996), 105 C.C.C. (3d) 97 (S.C.C.).
28   *R. v. Chaulk* (1990), 62 C.C.C. (3d) 193 (S.C.C.).

as wrong, decide to substitute their own moral code for that of society. The accused still bears the burden of establishing the mental disorder defence on a balance of probabilities.

The defence of non-mental disorder automatism is less stable. The Court expanded the defence in *R. v. Parks*[29] by holding that it applied to an accused who killed while sleepwalking. Like the *Daviault* defence, the automatism defence would lead to a complete acquittal. The Court has, however, continued to restrict non-insane automatism produced by emotional blows to extraordinary cases that would cause an ordinary person to go into a disassociative state.[30] Moreover, the Court's decision in *Stone* requires the accused to establish the non-mental disorder automatism defence on a balance of probabilities in part because of scepticism about claims of automatism. It also suggests that more cases of automatism will be classified as caused by mental disorders in an attempt to maximize the protection of the public. Cases such as *Parks* in which the accused receives an outright acquittal will increasingly be rare.

When considering defences that apply even though the accused may have committed a crime with the necessary fault element, the Court has been concerned with the fair administration of standards that require reasonable responses to external pressures. In *Thibert*,[31] the Court indicated that the ordinary person considered for the purpose of the provocation defence should be the same age and sex as the accused and have any other characteristic or experience that would give the act or insult special significance. In *Lavallee*[32] and *Pétel*[33] the Court stressed that when determining whether self-defence was reasonable, the trier of fact should consider the accused's past experience, including the fact that she had been battered by the man she killed. A similar modified objective standard will be used when administering the common law defences of duress and necessity.[34] The courts will tailor objective standards in defences to the experiences and frailties of particular accused. In *Latimer*,[35] the Court affirmed that a modified objective standard would be applied in determining whether the accused faced an imminent harm and had no safe avenue of escape or legal way out. At the same time, however, the Court indicated that the requirement of pro-

---

29   (1992), 75 C.C.C. (3d) 287 (S.C.C.).
30   *R. v. Rabey* (1980), 54 C.C.C. (2d) 1 (S.C.C.); *R. v. Stone* (1999), 134 C.C.C. (3d) 353 (S.C.C.).
31   *Thibert*, above note 22.
32   *Ibid.*
33   *Ibid.*
34   *Hibbert*, above note 22.
35   (2001), 150 C.C.C. (3d) 129 (S.C.C.).

portionality between the harm avoided and the harm inflicted should be determined on a purely objective standard and one that did not devalue the life of a victim who was severely disabled.

In *Lavallee*, the Court rejected the idea that self-defence was only justified in response to an immediate threat of harm. At the same time, the more recent case of *Cinous*[36] suggests that in other contexts self-defence may not even be put to the jury in a case in which an accused has alternatives other than killing the person who he believes threatens him. The requirement in section 17 of the *Code* that an accused only has a duress defence if he or she faced immediate death or bodily harm from a person who is present when the crime is committed has been found to violate section 7 of the *Charter* because it could result in the punishment of a person who responded reasonably and in a morally involuntary fashion to threats from which there was no safe avenue of escape.[37]

C. PERSPECTIVES ON THE CRIMINAL LAW

In recent years, a variety of perspectives has been brought to bear on the criminal law. This diversity reflects the interesting and often controversial nature of much criminal law. These various perspectives are beginning to influence the development of the criminal law. What follows are only brief introductions to a variety of perspectives on the criminal law.

1) Historical Perspectives

Although some accounts may stress the history of criminal law as a story of progressive development, there is support for a more complex view. Ancient and Aboriginal societies tended to see crime as a matter involving the victim and the offender with a focus more on reparation than punishment. Into the nineteenth century there was reliance on private prosecutions. The present victims' rights movement does not promise to displace public prosecutions, but it does resemble earlier times by making the victim's interests and wishes more relevant in the criminal prosecution. The Court's acceptance of a restorative approach to sentencing,[38] which is influenced by the needs of victims, offenders,

---

36   (2002), 162 C.C.C. (3d) 129 (S.C.C.)

37   *R. v. Ruzic* (2001), 153 C.C.C. (3d) 1 (S.C.C.).

38   *Gladue*, above note 11, *Proulx*, above note 12.

and the community and attempts to make amends, harkens back to pre-modern approaches to crime in Aboriginal and non-Aboriginal societies. Sentencing has been influenced by successive waves of concern about rehabilitation, followed by increased concern about punishing and deterring crime. A sentencing approach that is currently out of vogue may come back into fashion.

Some historical accounts suggest that the criminal law matured in the late-nineteenth and twentieth century, as more emphasis was placed on subjective *mens rea*. This is reflected in the development of the defences of mistake of fact and intoxication and the directing mind theory for corporate liability. It does not, however, account for the growing importance of regulatory offences with the rise of the modern interventionist state or the growing acceptance of criminal negligence as a form of criminal fault. Regulatory offences at first relied upon absolute liability, and now in Canada require strict liability, which is a compromise between no fault and subjective fault. Even in the context of criminal offences, objective standards of liability and constructive liability tied to unforeseen and perhaps unforeseeable consequences of illegal activity are still employed. They can be seen as a means of responding to harms and risks even though the accused may not be at fault for causing the harms or taking the risks. Historical perspectives suggest that there is much contingency in criminal law and that its development can rarely be seen as an inevitable progression.

2) Economic Perspectives

Economic perspectives focus on the criminal law as an instrument to control human behaviour. People are thought to adjust their behaviour in response to the certainty, speed, and severity of punishment. Much criminal law and sentencing focuses on the severity of punishment, because it is difficult for the criminal law itself to affect certainty of punishment through apprehension and conviction rates, or speed through the processing of cases. The desire to deter harmful conduct has been particularly influential in some areas such as drunk driving, domestic violence, and sexual assault. The criminal law has tried not only to increase the penalties for these offences but also to facilitate convictions by defining the prohibited act broadly and using standards of liability with objective elements. Restrictions on the defence of intoxication could be seen as a means of deterring intoxication that might lead to the commission of crimes, but this assumes that intoxicated offenders are capable of perceiving and adjusting their behaviour to the threat of punishment. Deterrence-based theories presume there is a rational actor who is able to perceive and calculate the costs and benefits of crime. They may also be applied to the activities of third parties who may facilitate the commission of crimes.

Marxist theories focus on the role of the criminal law in supporting capitalism. On the one hand, this support entails the punishment of disorderly and unproductive conduct and conspiracies to commit political crimes, while, on the other, it entails lenient treatment of corporate misconduct and conspiracies. The requirement that the Crown prove that a higher official had the required *mens rea* may play a role in insulating large organizations from criminal accountability. Some Marxists would argue that the role of the criminal law in supporting capitalism has been obscured in recent years by increased focus on identity politics and the effects that criminal law has on women and various identifiable minorities. Criminal justice controversies can be seen as an example of legalized politics in which elaborate legal concepts dominate political debate and disguise the repression of a system that imprisons a significant segment of the population. They can also be seen as an example of criminalized politics as governments use the criminal justice system to respond in a punitive and relatively cheap fashion to much broader social, economic, and cultural problems.

3) Law and Society Perspectives

Law and society perspectives attempt to determine the actual role and effect of the criminal law in society. Most criminal law doctrine is developed in the context of serious and violent offences subject to several appeals, whereas most criminal prosecutions are for minor property and public order offences and end in guilty pleas or withdrawal of charges by prosecutors. Sociological perspectives are often sceptical about the effect that legal doctrine has on the real world. Distinctions between the use of objective and subjective fault elements may be fundamental to the law in the books, but perhaps have little impact on the law in action as applied by police, prosecutors, judges, and juries. Deterrence is not, as in the economical model, based on an assumption of rational behaviour, but on the actual perceptions and behaviour of the target population. This may entail a great deal of overestimation of the chances of getting caught and may be influenced by informal sanctions against breaking the law.

There is also a recognition that informal practices, such as police and prosecutorial discretion, plea bargaining, and sentencing discretion, alter the intended effects of the criminal law. The focus is also often on the interrelationship of the various phases of the criminal process. For example, an intervention such as mandatory minimum sentences designed to limit the sentencing discretion of judges may only shift that discretion to prosecutors who retain the discretion to charge a crime that does or does not have such a mandatory sentence. Mandatory sentences may also affect the willingness of the accused to plea guilty. Cases that generously interpret the accused's right to a trial in a speedy time and to disclosure[39] may in practice place incentives on prosecutors to offer early plea bargains and may increase rather than decrease the efficiency of the crime control assembly line.

4) Legal Process Perspectives

Legal process approaches are concerned with the interaction of various institutions in the criminal process. Before the *Charter*, courts often adopted presumptions that could be overcome by clear legislation to the contrary. For example, criminal laws would be presumed to require subjective fault, and regulatory offences would be presumed to require strict liability. With the *Charter*, some of these presumptions have been raised to constitutional rules. Even then, however, the courts may not always have the last word. Legislatures retain the option of passing new laws in response to court decisions under the *Charter*. Sections 1 and 33 act as safety valves allowing legislatures to respond to judicial decisions. Legislative responses to the Supreme Court's controversial decisions in *Seaboyer* and *Daviault* demonstrate the dynamic nature of the legal process and the role that the media and interest groups can play in persuading legislatures to respond to judicial decisions. At the same time, other court decisions are accepted by the legislature. These judicial decisions may invalidate or reform obsolete statutes not supported by a current political consensus and they may not be visible because they do not attract attention from the media.

The legal process approach, like the law and society approach, is also concerned with the interrelationship of the various stages of the criminal process. A broad offence enacted by Parliament increases law enforcement discretion. Mandatory penalties transfer discretion from sentencing judges to prosecutors. The practice of parole boards can mitigate the severity of punishment. The legal process approach is also amenable to the study of wrongful convictions that often result from cumulative failure by many institutions and actors in the criminal

---

39   R. v. *Askov* (1990), 59 C.C.C. (3d) 449 (S.C.C.); R. v. *Stinchcombe* (1991), 68 C.C.C. (3d) 1 (S.C.C.).

process including the police, prosecutors, defence lawyers, forensic experts, judges, juries, appeal courts, and correctional officials. A recognition of the inherent fallibility of a complex criminal process that is administered by humans has led the Supreme Court to conclude that it is unsafe to extradict a fugitive without securing assurances that the death penalty will not be applied should the fugitive be found guilty.[40]

5) Philosophical Perspectives

Legal theorists approach the criminal law from a wide variety of perspectives. A few see the criminal sanction as a utilitarian instrument designed to secure various social objectives such as the deterrence of crime. Many others see the criminal law as subordinate to various rights possessed by individuals. The former approach might favour the use of strict liability and objective standards of liability as a means to deter harmful behaviour, while the latter might prefer subjective fault as the basis of liability. At the same time, other theorists reject a descriptive approach to fault based on estimates of an accused's subjective perceptions and argue that objective standards of liability are important determinants of fault. Retributive theories of "just deserts" have recently been quite influential. They attempt to tie punishment to the seriousness of the crime committed and to the accused's responsibility for the crime. Indeed, section 718.1 of the *Criminal Code* proclaims the principle of proportionality between the punishment and the offence as the fundamental principle of sentencing. At the same time, the *Criminal Code* also recognizes the legitimacy of deterrent, rehabilitative, and restorative purposes of sentencing within the broad constraints of proportionality.

Liberal theorists have argued that the criminal law should be used only to respond to harm, but have not always agreed on what constitutes harm. In *Butler*,[41] for example, the Supreme Court held that obscenity should be prohibited because of its potential harm, and adopted some feminist insights into the connection between dehumanizing depictions of women and children and violence towards them. Some liberals did not believe that there was a close enough connection between the obscenity targeted and proven harms. In *Sharpe*,[42] the Court read in some exceptions for some privately held materials depicting lawful sexual activity into the offence of possession of child

---

40   *United States of America v. Burns* (2001), 151 C.C.C. (3d) 283 (S.C.C.).
41   *Butler*, above note 4.
42   (2001), 150 C.C.C. (3d) 321 (S.C.C.).

pornography. Finally, the Court dealt liberal principles a blow by holding in *Malmo-Levine*[43] that it was not a principle of fundamental justice that the criminal sanction only be used to prohibit harmful actions. At the same time, a majority of the Court expressed the view that there was sufficient harm to justify the criminal prohibition of the possession of marijuana.

Conservative theorists have seen the criminal law as playing a symbolic role in expressing common views of morality that are not necessarily tied to tangible harms. In *Rodriguez v. British Columbia (A.G.)*,[44] the Supreme Court upheld prohibitions on assisted suicide, in part because of its belief in the importance of affirming the value of life. Similarly, in *Jobidon*,[45] it held that an assault could occur, even though an individual may have consented to a fist fight, because "of the criminal law's concern that Canadian citizens treat each other humanely and with respect." Similar reasoning has been applied to prohibit consensual but harmful sexual activity.

6) Critical Perspectives

There are a variety of critical perspectives on the criminal law, including feminist perspectives that will be examined below. Some critics argue that the traditional orientation of the criminal law and the *Charter* advance liberal values that pit the state against the individual, when state power is in fact often needed to respond to corporate misconduct and to threats to the security of vulnerable minorities and communities. More conservative critics also believe that the criminal law is excessively liberal and that it favours the rights of the accused over those of the public interest and the interests of victims. Other critics argue that the due process values of much criminal law doctrine do not actually fetter crime control but support crime control, by creating the illusion that most accused receive a full and fair trial. These critics argue that due process is for crime control, because it helps legitimize the imposition of the criminal sanction.

Critical perspectives are beginning to be used to examine the effects of the criminal law on racial minorities, gays and lesbians, disabled people, and Aboriginal people. These studies range from law and society approaches, which examine the disparate impact that facially neutral procedures and crimes may have on certain groups, to more doctrinal

---

43   (2003), 179 C.C.C. (3d) 417 (S.C.C.).
44   *Rodriguez*, above note 6.
45   *Jobidon*, above note 18 at 494.

studies of the role that stereotyping may play in the criminal law. Aboriginal perspectives on crime can challenge the adversarial and punitive orientation of the criminal law in favour of more holistic and communitarian approaches. The criminal law has responded to some of these criticisms by, for example, using sentencing circles, by recognizing restorative justice as a legitimate approach to sentencing and by allowing prospective jurors to be questioned about whether they will be influenced by racial stereotypes. Nevertheless, these critical perspectives have not yet had the impact on the criminal law that feminist perspectives have had. The adoption of any critical or outsider perspective also runs the real risk that the critique will be muted or even co-opted by the attempt to reform the criminal law. At the same time, it may not be desirable or possible to ignore the conditions that led to the critique.

7) Feminist Perspectives

Feminist critiques of the criminal law have been particularly influential in recent years in Canada. Subjective fault elements have been criticized in the context of the defence of mistaken belief in consent in sexual assault trials as allowing sexist and irrational male views about sexuality to determine criminal liability. The criminal law relating to sexual assault was frequently amended in the 1980s and 1990s. The prohibited act was broadened in 1983 from rape to include all sexual touching without consent and to emphasize the violence in sexual assault. The marital rape exception which held that, in law, a man could not rape his wife was also repealed at that time. In 1992 amendments, the accused was required to take reasonable steps in the circumstances known to him to determine whether the complainant consented to the sexual activity. In addition, the *Code* defined consent to exclude certain conduct where a woman's consent may not be voluntary and to emphasize that no means no. The Supreme Court has based lack of consent as a matter of *actus reus* on the subjective views of complainants in sexual assault cases and indicated that the mistake of fact defence is limited to situations in which the complainant affirmatively communicated consent by words or actions.[46] Section 273.2(b) further restricts the mistake of fact defence by requiring the accused to take reasonable steps, in the circumstances known to him, to ascertain whether the complainant was consenting.

Feminist perspectives on the criminal law do not uniformly favour the increased use of the criminal law. The provisions in the *Code* that

---

46   *Ewanchuk*, above note 17.

made it a crime to perform or have an abortion without the approval of a hospital committee were criticized by feminists as a paternalistic limit on the freedom of women to choose whether to continue their pregnancies. The law was struck down as an unjustified violation of section 7 of the *Charter* in *Morgentaler (No. 2)*,[47] on the basis of the procedural difficulties in obtaining the committee approval that would provide a defence to the criminal prohibition on abortion. Wilson J. argued that the law was substantively flawed because it interfered with women's rights to choose according to their conscience. She was also prepared to strike down laws against soliciting and keeping a common bawdy house on the basis that Parliament should not indirectly punish prostitutes when it had chosen not to make prostitution itself illegal. Women prostitutes are more likely to be charged under these laws than their male customers. On this issue, Wilson and L'Heureux-Dubé JJ. were in dissent with the majority holding that the prostitution laws were a justified response to the nuisance of prostitution. In *Lavallee*,[48] the Supreme Court held it was unfair to require a battered woman to wait until harm was imminent before acting in self-defence. This approach suggests that an accused's experience, including those relating to gender, should be considered when applying objective standards, and that traditional requirements of imminence may be based on patterns of violence that are not applicable to domestic violence against women. Some feminists have warned, however, that *Lavallee* may require the accused to fit into a stereotyped and medicalized vision of the battered woman. The *Thibert* case, which allows the objective elements of the provocation defence to be judged by the standard of the average married man, can be criticized for incorporating and excusing violent and possessive masculinity. The defence of provocation is also vulnerable to feminist criticism if courts do not recognize that women have the legal right to leave and insult their partners and that males should not be held to lesser standards of self-control than women.

Feminists do not always agree on the role that criminal law should play in strategies to better protect and empower women. Some would support prostitution-related offences as an attempt to protect women against exploitation, while others would prefer decriminalization. In *Butler*,[49] the Supreme Court adopted some feminist views about the harms of pornography by holding that Parliament could constitutionally prohibit sexual depictions that were violent, or dehumanizing and

---

47   (1988), 37 C.C.C. (3d) 449 (S.C.C.).
48   *Lavallee*, above note 22.
49   *Butler*, above note 4.

degrading, in an attempt to prevent sexual violence against women and children. Many feminists have, however, criticized subsequent administrative applications of *Butler* to target gay and lesbian pornography. The Court has, however, maintained the *Butler* approach and upheld new legislation prohibiting the possession of child pornography.[50] The legislative response to the defence of extreme intoxication to general intent offences such as assault and sexual assault was in part motivated by concerns about the effects of acquittals for drunken violence on women and children. Feminists generally opposed the introduction of a new intoxication-based offence in part because of concerns about its effects on other disadvantaged groups and in part because of concerns that offences be labelled as assault and sexual assault and not pled down to a new intoxication-based offence. Feminist criticisms of criminal law will likely continue to have an important effect on the future development of the criminal law by the legislatures and the courts.

FURTHER READINGS

BOYLE, C., ET AL., *A Feminist Approach to Criminal Law* (1985)

CAIRNS-WAY, R., *Dimensions of Criminal Law*, 3d ed. (Toronto: Emond Montgomery, 2002)

CAMERON, J., *The Charter's Impact on the Criminal Justice System* (Toronto: Carswell, 1996)

ERICSON, R., & P. BARANEK, *The Ordering of Justice: The Study of Accused Persons as Dependants in the Criminal Process* (Toronto: University of Toronto Press, 1982)

FRIEDLAND, M.L., "Criminal Justice in Canada Revisited" (2004) 48 Crim. L.Q.

MANDEL, M., *The Charter of Rights and the Legalization of Politics in Canada*, rev. ed. (Toronto: Wall & Thompson, 1994)

MANITOBA ABORIGINAL JUSTICE INQUIRY, *Report* (Winnipeg: Queen's Printer, 1991)

MARTIN, D., "Retribution Reconsidered: A Reconsideration of Feminist Criminal Law Strategies" (1998) 36 Osgoode Hall L.J. 151

---

50   *Little Sisters Book and Art Emporium v. Canada*, [2000] 2 S.C.R. 1120; *R. v. Sharpe*, [2001] 1 S.C.R. 45.

MORAN, M., *Rethinking the Reasonable Person* (Oxford: Oxford University Press, 2003)

PACIOCCO, D., *Getting Away with Murder* (Toronto: Irwin Law, 1998)

PACKER, H., *The Limits of the Criminal Sanction* (Stanford: Stanford University Press, 1968)

ROACH, K. *Due Process and Victims' Rights: The New Law and Politics of Criminal Justice* (Toronto: University of Toronto Press, 1999)

ROACH, K., *September 11: Consequences for Canada* (Montreal: McGill-Queen's University Press, 2003)

GLOSSARY

Absolute discharge: a disposition in which no conviction is recorded. It is available if there is no minimum penalty, the offence is not punishable by life or fourteen years imprisonment, and the judge determines that it is in the accused's best interests and not contrary to the public interest.

Absolute liability: an offence for which the accused is guilty once it is proven that the prohibited act, or *actus reus*, was committed and regardless of the existence of any fault, including negligence.

Actus reus: the prohibited act in a criminal or regulatory offence. Proof of the *actus reus* may also include the requirement that the prohibited act be voluntarily and consciously committed by the accused.

Aiding or abetting: intentionally assisting or encouraging a crime and, by doing so, becoming a party to the crime.

Appellate court: a court that reviews the accused's conviction or acquittal at trial. In summary conviction matters, appeals are usually heard by superior courts, while in indictable matters, appeals are heard by the provincial courts of appeal. Courts, such as the Supreme Court of Canada, which hear subsequent appeals are also called appellate courts.

Attempt: an attempted crime occurs when the accused does something beyond mere preparation for the purpose of committing a crime. It is a separate crime of attempting the specific offence, and is usually subject to less punishment than the completed crime.

Attorney General: the elected official ultimately accountable for prosecutions. For *Criminal Code* offences, this is normally the Attorney General of the province, while for other federal offences it is the Minister of Justice for Canada.

Automatism: a state in which the accused acts in an involuntary manner. It is known as mental disorder automatism if it is caused by a mental disorder, and non-mental disorder automatism if it is caused by some other factor such as a blow to the head.

Bail: also known as judicial interim release. It refers to the release of an accused person pending trial on the grounds that he or she is likely to appear for trial, not likely to commit offences in the meantime, and release will not undermine public confidence in the administration of justice.

Causation: an issue in determining whether the accused has committed the *actus reus* or prohibited act by causing the prohibited consequences, usually death.

Common law: judge-made law as opposed to legislation passed by the legislature.

Conditional discharge: a disposition in which no conviction is recorded so long as the accused successfully satisfies prescribed conditions. This disposition is available only if there is no minimum penalty and the offence is not subject to life or fourteen years' imprisonment.

Conditional sentence: a disposition in which the accused is found guilty and sentenced to imprisonment, but serves the sentence in the community so long as he or she successfully fulfils conditions.

Counselling: procuring, soliciting, or inciting a person to commit a crime. A person who does this counselling can become guilty as a party to an offence that is committed by the person counselled, or can be convicted of a separate crime of counselling if the offence is not committed.

Disease of the mind: a condition necessary for an accused to be found not criminally responsible on account of mental disorder. Diseases of the mind are now defined as mental disorders. They can include any mental disorder but not transitory or self-induced states.

Division of powers: the constitutional allocation of authority between the federal and provincial governments to enact legislation.

Due diligence: a defence available in strict liability offences that allows the accused to prove on a balance of probabilities that it was not negligent.

Duress: a defence available to those who commit crimes because they are threatened with serious harm. A codified defence of duress is found in section 17 of the *Criminal Code* and applies to principal offenders. The requirements of immediacy and presence in section 17 of the *Code* have been severed from the defence as unconstitutional. A common law defence of duress applies to parties to offences. In some rare circumstances, duress may also be relevant to the proof of the fault element.

Entrapment: objectionable police conduct such as offering a suspect an opportunity to commit a crime without a reasonable suspicion that he or she is involved with crime or when the police are not pursuing a *bona fide* inquiry in a high crime area. It also includes disreputable police conduct that goes beyond providing a suspect an opportunity to commit a crime and actually induces the commission of the crime. The remedy for entrapment is a stay of proceedings.

Exclusion of evidence: the situation when evidence that would otherwise be relevant to determining the accused's guilt or innocence is kept out of a criminal trial because it was obtained in a manner that violated the *Charter* and its admission would bring the administration of justice into disrepute. Unconstitutionally obtained evidence is excluded if its admission would affect the fairness of the trial or if the seriousness of the *Charter* violation outweighes the harmful effects of excluding the evidence.

Fault element: the culpable state of mind that must be proven by the state. Fault elements can require proof of a subjective state of mind of the accused such as wilfulness, knowledge or recklessness or can be based on objective fault such as negligence.

General intent: an offence in which the fault element relates only to the performance of the act in question, with no further ulterior intent or purpose. Intoxication has traditionally not been a defence to general as opposed to specific intent offences. Subject to section 33.1 of the *Criminal Code*, extreme intoxication producing involuntary behaviour may be a defence to a general intent offence.

Indictable offences: the most serious category of criminal offences. In most cases, the accused has the option to be tried before a provincial court without a preliminary inquiry or a jury, or tried in a superior court with a preliminary inquiry and/or a jury.

Intoxication: evidence of intoxication by alcohol or drugs that prevents the Crown from proving beyond a reasonable doubt that the accused had the *mens rea*, or fault element, required for the particular crime.

Judicial interim release: *see* bail.

Mens rea: the prohibited mental or fault element for the commission of a criminal offence. May include intent, purpose, wilfulness, knowledge, recklessness, wilful blindness, criminal negligence, or negligence.

Mental disorder: *see* disease of the mind.

Mental disorder or insanity defence: a defence when a person commits a crime while suffering from a mental disorder that renders him or her incapable of appreciating the nature and quality of the act or knowing that it is wrong. An accused found not criminally responsible by reason of mental disorder will be released unless a court or review board concludes that he or she is a significant threat to the public.

Mental element: *see mens rea*.

Moral innocence: The quality of a person who commits a prohibited act with no fault such as negligence or subjective *mens rea*. A morally innocent person cannot be imprisoned under section 7 of the *Charter*.

Moral voluntariness: The quality of a person who commits a crime but who because of emergency circumstances has no realistic choice but to commit the crime. A person who commits a crime in a morally involuntary manner cannot be convicted under section 7 of the *Charter*.

Necessity: a common law defence available as an excuse when an accused acts in response to an urgent and immediate peril that cannot be avoided by obeying the law.

Omission: the *actus reus* when a person is found guilty for failing to perform a specific legal duty, such as providing the necessities of life to a child.

Parole: discretionary release of an accused serving a term of imprisonment granted by a parole board.

Preliminary inquiry: a hearing to determine whether the prosecution has introduced enough evidence that, if believed at trial, would support a conviction.

Presumption of innocence: requirement in section 11(d) of the *Charter* that the Crown prove the accused's guilt beyond a reasonable doubt. The Crown must prove not only the elements of the offence but all matters essential for conviction, including the non-availability of relevant defences.

Probation: a court order that allows an accused to be supervised in the community. The breach of a probation order is a crime.

Provincial courts: the court where most criminal cases are resolved. The judges are appointed by the provincial government and cannot sit with a jury.

Provocation: a partial defence that reduces murder to manslaughter. Available when the accused is faced with a sudden act or insult that would make an ordinary person lose self-control, and which caused the accused to act suddenly and before his or her passions had cooled.

Public welfare offences: *see* regulatory offences.

Regulatory offences: offences enacted by federal, provincial, or municipal governments that are used primarily to regulate risky behaviour that may cause harm. They are presumed to require strict liability.

Search and seizure: any state activity that invades a reasonable expectation of privacy.

Self-defence: a justification to a crime generally available when a person reasonably apprehends a threat and responds in a reasonable manner.

Specific intent: an offence that requires the Crown to prove not only a fault or mental element that relates to the performance of the act in question, but some ulterior intent or purpose. Evidence of intoxication is always relevant when the accused is charged with a specific intent offence, and operates as a defence if it raises a reasonable doubt about the existence of the mental element.

Stay of proceedings: a disposition where the court does not allow a prosecution to proceed because of objectionable police or prosecutorial conduct and/or a violation of the accused's rights. This remedy is not the moral equivalent of an acquittal because it does not reach the merits, but has the same practical effects.

Strict liability: an offence for which the Crown must prove the commission of the prohibited act beyond a reasonable doubt. The existence of negligence is then presumed unless the accused establishes a defence of due diligence on a balance of probabilities.

Summary conviction offences: the least serious offences in the *Criminal Code*. They are subject to a maximum penalty of six months and/or a fine of not more than $2000.

Superior courts: the highest level of trial court in a criminal case that hears all jury trials and the first level of appeal in summary conviction offences.

Suspended sentence: a disposition after conviction where the judge suspends passing sentence, while imposing conditions on the accused's release by means of probation orders. If the conditions are breached, the court may sentence the accused for the original offence.

Unfit to stand a trial: a determination that an accused, on account of a mental disorder, cannot be tried because he or she cannot understand the nature or possible consequences of the proceedings or communicate with counsel.

TABLE OF CASES

INDEX

ABOUT THE AUTHOR

Kent Roach is a Professor of Law and Criminology at the University of Toronto. He formerly served as Law Clerk to Madam Justice Bertha Wilson of the Supreme Court. He has been the editor-in-chief of the *Criminal Law Quarterly* since 1998 and is a co-editor (with Patrick Healy and Gary Trotter) of *Cases and Materials on Criminal Law and Procedure* 9th ed (2004). He has written extensively on criminal justice and anti-terrorism law in both Canada and abroad including a chapter on the criminal process in the *Oxford Handbook of Legal Studies* (2003). He is the author of *Constitutional Remedies in Canada* (1994) which was awarded the 1997 Owen Prize as the best legal text in Canada and (with Robert J. Sharpe) of *Brian Dickson: A Judge's Journey* (2003) which was awarded the 2004 Defoe Prize for best contribution to the understanding of Canada. Other books include *Due Process and Victims' Rights: The New Law and Politics of Criminal Justice in Canada* (1999) and *The Supreme Court on Trial: Judicial Activism or Democratic Dialogue* (2001) which were both short-listed for the Donner Prize for best public policy book and *September 11: Consequences for Canada* (2003). Professor Roach has appeared as counsel for Aboriginal Legal Services of Toronto and the Canadian Civil Liberties Association in cases in the Supreme Court of Canada including *Stillman, Williams, Gladue,* and *Latimer.* He also acted as counsel for the Association in Aid of the Wrongfully Convicted in the systemic issues phase of the Kaufman inquiry into the wrongful conviction of Guy Paul Morin and is presently serving as a member of the research advisory committee to both the Arar and Ipperwash inquiries.